PROPHET MUHAMMAD

The first Sufi of Islam

Farzana Moon

farzanamoon.blogspot.co.uk

Prophet Muhammad
The first Sufi of Islam

Published by
Garnet Publishing Limited
8 Southern Court
South Street
Reading
RG1 4QS
UK

www.garnetpublishing.co.uk
www.twitter.com/Garnetpub
www.facebook.com/Garnetpub
blog.garnetpublishing.co.uk

First Edition

ISBN: 9781859642948

British Library Cataloguing-in-Publication Data
A catalogue record for this book is available from the British Library

Typeset by Samantha Barden
Jacket design by Haleh Darabi

Printed and bound in Lebanon by International Press:
interpress@int-press.com

For Floyd
My handsome son-in-law

Chapter 1

The Holy Bridegroom
Year 595 AD

I cast the garment of love over thee from Me. And this in order that thou mayest be reared under Mine Eye. (Quran 20:39)

A subtle scent of rose and jasmine hung in the air, emanating from Muhammad's very soul as he lay sleeping on a mattress of feathers covered with white sheets. The room in which he was sleeping was in the home of his uncle Abu Talib. It was his home too: he had lived there practically all his life. This small house in the town of Mecca in Hijaz was his haven and sanctuary, ever since he had been orphaned at an early age.

His dreams were dousing his twenty-five years in the baptismal waters of mystery and longing. He had had no intention of taking a siesta; he had been wishing the day to melt into the evening so that he could claim Khadija as his wife. But after indulging himself in the luxury of a cool bath, he had drifted into the bowers of sleep, inhaling the familiar fragrance of rose and jasmine, a scent which never failed to remind him of the first time he'd noticed it, as if it flowed out of his breath. He was a child then, visiting Medina with his mother, and this perfume had become a part of him, shortly before his mother had died on their journey back to Mecca.

In the tapestry of Muhammad's dreams, his childhood was unfolding as a tableau of loss and loneliness. He was still in his mother's womb; his father was far away on a trading trip in the city of Gaza close to Syria, falling ill during his journey back, dying in Medina. Muhammad's dream-vision afforded him the sight to witness his own birth in Mecca, then it carried him to the House of Nabgha, a graveyard in Medina where his father lay buried. A newborn babe again, he could see himself suckled by Thuwaibiyah for two whole days before he was entrusted to the care of Halima from the tribe of Banu Saad. His senses cherished the smell of camel's milk, and the taste of dates and barley cakes on his tongue. The desert birds flew overhead, and a sudden storm of locusts swept past. He was eating locusts, then going home to Halima, and welcoming the aroma of mutton and roasted gazelle.

The scene shifted, lifting him onto the rungs of six happy years as Muhammad Mustafa. He was playing with his foster-brothers. Two men in white were floating towards him, swords of light gleaming in their hands. They were pinning him down and slitting his breast open. He could see them washing his heart with snow, then replacing it within his little breast, and sealing his skin with a wand of light. Suddenly, they had vanished, and so had his foster-brothers. Halima was racing towards him, terror shining in her eyes. She was clasping him to her breast, weeping and praying.

It was a dream made of quicksilver; now it abandoned him into the arms of his mother Amina. He was on the road to Medina with her. This dream too was short-lived; now he was journeying back to Mecca with his mother and an Ethiopian slave by the name of Baraka. His mother was ill, and he as a six-year-old boy was watching her die in the village of Abwa, left alone with Baraka.

Another time, another dream! The face of his grandfather Abu Muttalib was coming alive. But this dear face too was snatched by death, and so he was entrusted into the care of his uncle, Abu Talib.

Muhammad's dreams grew dark; he was startled into waking.

Muhammad, the deep-hearted son of wilderness with his beaming black eyes and deep soul brimming with love, was up on his feet. He looked out of the window at the shimmering plains spruced with grey houses. His gaze shifted to his ivory comb, his little object of luxury, and then lingered over the drinking goblet with silver trimmings. The copper wash bowl was demanding his attention too, but his senses were surrendering to the sweetness of music from downstairs.

The sprightful tunes were goading Muhammad to get dressed into his bridegroom's fineries, but the dreams which he had dreamed were hovering over his awareness. They were not just dreams, they were the mists of daydreams, and more of them were visiting him; his trips to Syria and Yemen with his uncle, Abu Talib, trading silver bars and precious stones for oil, rice, sugar and perfumes. A familiar ache, which had become a part of his soul, was stirring inside him, attaining the voice of a distant thunder.

Why? Why this ache and longing? On this blessed, blessed day of my marriage to Khadija? The eve of desire and blessing, is it not? The dance of joy in my heart – where did it go? Where?

Muhammad began to dress with the precision of an artist.

The holy bridegroom had commenced the ritual of dressing, straightening each crease in his tunic before donning it, and gathering it around his waist with a red sash. The wedding songs accompanied by music were rippling forth afresh from downstairs. His joy was so clear and his perception so keen that he could distinguish the laughter of each of his uncles amidst the rollicking of music and songs. Hamza's mirth was loud in contrast to Al Abbas's, low and trilling. Abu Talib's laughter could not be missed, so clear and bubbling, while Abu Lahab's lifted above them all, booming and uncontrollable. He was claiming the staff of reveries. Khadija was with him. Muhammad's heart ached to hold her in one eternal embrace.

His very thoughts were carrying her into the Cave of Mount Hira, murmuring endearments.

Mount Hira! Muhammad chuckled to himself at his own incredible wish. *She would die of fright.* A boyish smile lit his features to a sunny glow. Mount Hira, a few miles outside Mecca, cradled a great cave in its bosom which had become Muhammad's second home, where he was wont to retire quite often when overwhelmed by the ache and longing inside him to find his own self. Once inside the cave, he would sit there for hours seeking the will of al-Llah, who ruled over the Arab pantheon of idols.

Muhammad's own heart at this precise moment was brimming with love and peace, for the word *Al-Amin* penetrated his awareness, sailing up to him from the lips of his uncles and aunts amidst their symphony of jubilations. Al-Amin, meaning literally *honest,* fetched a broad smile upon Muhammad's lips.

I have never lied! Have remained kind and chaste in this desert of cruelty and corruption! Muhammad's heart was trembling.

Summoning the vision of Khadija before him, Muhammad began draping the length of linen around his head, chanting his fiancée's praises in his thoughts.

Like him, Khadija had been orphaned at an early age, and like him her lineage could be traced back to the family of Quraysh, the same as Muhammad's. Her immediate patrimony was linked to the clan of Makhzum, while Muhammad's filtered down further to the clan of Banu Hashim. The common link between their families was their knowledge that they were the descendants of Ishmael, the son of Abraham. Khadija's father was a noble merchant, and he had bequeathed a rich legacy to her as she was the most favourite of his daughters. As a young woman, she had multiplied her fortunes by striking lucrative deals in selling and trading. While still active in business, she had got married, but she was widowed within a span of a few years. She had married again, becoming the mother of one son and two daughters. Unfortunately, her second husband too was the victim of an untimely death, and for several years after that she was content to be married to her business alone, until she met Muhammad. She had employed Muhammad as her manager, entrusting to him her fleet of caravans to be led to Syria and Yemen for trade and barter. For a long time, Muhammad had no suspicion that she had fallen in love with him, and he would have remained ignorant of her passionate heart, had she not proposed to him herself.

More than two years of his service to Khadija came to Muhammad's mind. His memories of long trips to the towns of Aleppo, Baalbek, Antioch, Palmyra, Beirut and Damascus were vivid and alive. One of Khadija's Ethiopian slaves, by the name of Maisra, had accompanied him on several of those trips. It was during one of those trips that Maisra had confessed her mistress's interest in him.

'How come a man of your good looks and fine family is not married?' Maisra had asked with a sly smile.

'I am poor,' Muhammad had laughed. 'Besides, I am on the road most of the time, dependent upon a gracious lady for salary and commission! How can I ever think of establishing a home?'

'You could marry a wealthy woman?' Maisra had suggested enigmatically.

'A travelling salesman, hoping to marry a woman of wealth!' Muhammad had responded amusedly.

'Suppose a good-looking lady of the best family asked you to marry her?' Maisra had goaded.

'Who could this dream creature be?' Muhammad was thrown into a fit of laughter, but Maisra was quick to mention Khadija's name.

The same evening, when he returned to Mecca, Khadija's close friend Nafisa met him on the road, holding him in the same vice-like grip of inquisition as Maisra. Soon, Khadija's house was in view, and Muhammad's senses were growing numb due to the scene unfolding before his gaze. Khadija was standing on the terrace watching the rocky road, but her eyes were bright as the stars, as if weaving a carpet of welcome under the very feet of the camels.

Muhammad stirred and returned to dressing for his wedding, absent-mindedly claiming his yellow scarf from a low stool. In conformity with Arab custom, he needed to tie the scarf around his forehead to add the final touches to his head-dress. Something inside him was flaring all of a sudden; that familiar ache of longing. The stealth of this ache was so overwhelming that the mists of oblivion were obscuring his senses. He didn't even notice the sudden presence of Baraka.

'Al-Llah will smite you dumb, Muhammad, if you don't hurry, and ride swiftly to the home of your bride!' Baraka scolded, stressing her privilege as a surrogate mother.

'Al-Llah Taala loves me. Didn't you know, Baraka?' Muhammad whirled on his feet, facing her, his gaze a sudden kindling of mischief and laughter.

'Here, let me tie that!' Baraka snatched the scarf from his hands.

'You'll make my head throb like a drum, Baraka! I can't stand your knotting and jabbing!' Muhammad submitted, laughing.

'Laugh as you will, Muhammad, since this is your wedding day.' Baraka pulled the scarf over his forehead with great love and precision. 'Shame on you for laughing at your old nurse! I will get you for that some day. Come now, your uncles are huffing and puffing…' She plodded away without further warnings.

'I am sorry, Baraka, I was laughing at myself.' Muhammad followed her. 'And you are not old. You are as young as my beautiful bride-to-be.'

Downstairs, it seemed the luxuriant home of Abu Talib was hosting the whole Banu Hashim clan. Abu Talib, noticing Muhammad, drifted towards him with open arms, kissing and hugging him amidst a profusion of compliments.

'What impudence, Muhammad! You have stolen the national emblem of Arabia – you are shining like the moon!' Abu Talib imprinted fresh kisses on both his cheeks, commanding, 'Fetch the family ring and the gold staff for the bridegroom!'

Abu Talib's sister, Safiyah, paraded the famous ring on a cushion of velvet, her sister Umaymah twirling a staff encrusted with a gold eagle head. Abu Talib bestowed the gold staff to Muhammad, and he claimed it with devotion.

'This ring once belonged to Manaf bin Qusayy, seventh in line from Fihr, known as Quraysh, and we the Banu Hashim are second in line from that venerable tribe. May it prove lucky for your wedding.' Abu Talib slipped the ring of green agate on Muhammad's finger, kissing him once again.

'Thank you, Uncle. This will be my talisman for a happy marriage.' Muhammad kissed his uncle's hands in return, gratitude shining in his eyes.

'Don't spoil him, Abu Talib! His eloquence will lead us all into a desert of troubles.' Abu Lahab stroked his red beard, as if prophesying.

'The purity of my eloquence comes from the tongue of Banu Saad, Uncle, cultivating only beauty, not discord,' Muhammad sang happily.

'Your ill humour doesn't sit well on the rungs of this auspicious evening, Abu Lahab. Leave Muhammad alone!' Hamza glared at his brother.

'We can't leave the bridegroom alone today! He must ride forth grandly on his Arabian steed, as befits the Banu Hashim clan, accompanied by a mob of his family and friends.' Abu Talib clapped his hands, claiming the attention of his family members. 'We must be on our way before the bride changes her mind!'

The wedding procession was a colourful sea of men, women and children on camels and horseback. The Arabian Desert had claimed Muhammad as its prodigal son. Abu Talib was riding beside him, flushed with pride by this ocean of wealth and opulence, arranged solely by him, donated from his own coffers.

'Are you nervous, Muhammad?' Abu Talib asked suddenly.

'No, Uncle,' Muhammad murmured back. 'Strange as it may seem, I have been thinking more about my parents than about Khadija. I even dreamt about them today. I want to know more about them, my heart wishing – well, seeking – their blessings.'

'Not strange, considering your sensitive nature, Muhammad,' Abu Talib observed aloud. 'Mighty strange though that your father died at the same age as you are now. He married young – he wasn't even seventeen. Your mother belonged to the clan of Banu Jajjir, the descendants of Zuhrah. Her family is in Medina, prosperous and flourishing. You inherited but little from your father's side; a small house, five camels, a few goats, and of course your Ethiopian nurse, Baraka. Your mother's family named you Kothan, but your mother called you Ahmed. And your grandfather named you Muhammad Mustafa. Do you know what your name means?' he asked wistfully.

'My aunt Atika tells me it means 'the Praised One', and my uncles say, 'the Chosen One', though these words are as alien to me as my own self.' Muhammad smiled.

'Talking of strange; come to think of it, your grandfather made a strange comment after naming you Muhammad Mustafa,' Abu Talib began wistfully. 'I can remember our home teeming with guests after your birth. My father, and of course, your grandfather, held you in his arms proudly, calling you Muhammad Mustafa. The guests had never heard that name, so they asked him why he had chosen this strange name for his grandson. He merely laughed and said: "May the Most High glorify in heaven him whom he has created on earth."'

'What was my father like?' Muhammad asked quickly.

'Honest and handsome like you, Muhammad!' Abu Talib declared. 'In Mecca, he was called "the Lamp of the City". You are called Al-Amin; no wonder! But your father, yes, he was the apple of his father's eyes, though he was perceptive and restless like you, concerned about vice and degradation in the land of Arabia.' He paused. 'You, Muhammad, would stop worrying about the conditions of vice and corruption in Mecca, if you knew how they multiplied during the life of your grandfather. Your grandfather was young and only had one son when the tribes in Mecca stirred a violent dispute concerning the gods and the guardianship of the Kaaba. Averse to rifts and disharmony, your grandfather felt alone and helpless, praying to Hubal for the boon of ten sons. He concluded his prayers by making a sacred vow that if he were granted the favour of ten sons, he would sacrifice one to Hubal. His wish was granted in a succession of years, and the youngest one, who later became your father, was named Abdallah. It was time for your grandfather to fulfil his promise to Hubal, so he gathered all his sons and went to the Kaaba. A great trial confronted us ten brothers, as we awaited the will of Hubal by drawing lots amongst us as to who was to be sacrificed. Abdallah's name was drawn by the priest of the Kaaba, followed by laments from our aunts, mothers and sisters. It was decided that lots would be drawn against a certain number of camels as offerings to Hubal, increasing the number in each draw until none of our names appeared on this scale of sons against camels. The first lot was drawn against ten camels, bringing up Abdallah's name as the sacrificial lamb. Nine times, the lots were drawn, Abdallah's name surfacing each time, the number of camels rising to ninety. Finally, the lot fell upon camels alone when the number reached one hundred. Amidst cheers of great relief, our father chose the best camels, offering them to Hubal. They were slaughtered between the hills of As-Safa and Al-Marwa, and the Meccans feasted on their meat for days. This account alone should tell you, Muhammad, how much your grandfather adored your father, and how heartbroken he was when Abdallah died.'

'My memory of my grandfather is vague, but I can still feel the touch of his loving arms, and the laughter in his eyes,'

Muhammad reminisced aloud. 'This is the first time I have heard you talk about grandfather. I wish I knew more about him.'

'Our father – we all remember him as an old man with a clump of grey hair on his head, but then we were told he was born like that!' Abu Talib laughed heartily. 'He loved the Kaaba and the pilgrims who came every year for Hajj. Once someone told him that four centuries before his time one Chief of Mecca by the name of Harith, fearing an invasion, had fled to safety in some other town. But before fleeing, he had filled a well known as Zamzam with earth so the invaders couldn't benefit from its water, known for its healing qualities. After hearing this story, my father's concentration was such that the same night he found the location of Zamzam in his dream. Early in the morning, he led his men to the grave of Hagar and Ishmael, indicating the precise spot where to dig. Lo and behold, before the sun could go down, Zamzam had risen forth like a dream. Since then, Zamzam has been left in the care of Banu Hashim.'

'Had I learnt to read and write, Uncle, I would have studied all the Scriptures ever written,' Muhammad lamented. 'Did my grandfather have any Christian friends?'

'Many, from the towns of Sana and Yemen.' Abu Talib was looking at the grey houses. 'You were not born yet when a Christian Lord of Yemen by the name of Abraha came to the Kaaba to plunder and destroy the Sacred House. He seized two hundred camels of your grandfather's before marching forth to the Kaaba. So your grandfather went to Abraha, demanding his camels back. Abraha was impressed by the dignified appearance of your grandfather, but disappointed that he only wanted his camels and showed no concern for the safety of the Kaaba. "You are talking about your camels and saying nothing about your religion and the religion of your forefathers, Abu Muttalib, which I have come to destroy?" Abraha had asked. To which your grandfather said, "I am the Master of the Camels, and the Kaaba has its own master, who would defend it." And the Master of the Kaaba did defend it, sending birds from the sea, swallows and starlings, carrying stones in their beaks the size of peas and lentils, and attacking the enemy like an army from the heavens. The majority of Abraha's soldiers were killed, and he fled to Yemen with only a handful of his men who had survived.'

'The way you describe it, Uncle, I feel like I have seen the whole thing as it happened, and more.' Muhammad's gaze was lifted to the mysterious stars up above.

'You might have, Muhammad; who knows?' Abu Talib's eyes were shining. 'Remember our trip to Syria when you were twelve? We met a Christian anchorite by the name of Bahirah. He told me that I should take good care of you, for some day you would be the recipient of a divine call. No time to dwell on that though; you are marrying the Princess of Mecca, and you'd better act like a prince yourself.'

'A poor prince!' Muhammad laughed. 'She is also titled Princess of Quraysh, but I prefer the title "Tahira", meaning "the Pure One".'

'The Praised One married to the Pure One!' Abu Talib exclaimed happily. 'Now I can see her wealth tossed to the winds.'

'I don't care about wealth, Uncle, you know that!' Muhammad declared.

'How well do I know!' Abu Talib urged his horse to a full gallop towards the white gate of Khadija's mansion. 'That's why I have added twenty camels to your dowry, so that Khadija doesn't feel that she is marrying a poor orphan.'

'Uncle!' Muhammad's voice was choked. 'How can I ever repay you for that?'

'You don't have to, Muhammad! All that is mine belongs to you,' Abu Talib muttered under his breath, claiming Muhammad's hand.

The high-arched entrance to the mansion was decked with colourful hangings of silks and brocades. The reception room was one great rectangular hall with a gilded ceiling and furnished with a chandelier, housing seven lamps, their wicks feeding on oil. A white carpet adorned the floor, spruced with cushions. The guests were making merry while admiring the bride, under some spell of awe and wonder.

Khadija was seated on a high dais, cradled by velvety cushions at her back. Her fair features had the glow and warmth of sunshine, matching the gold crown on her head studded with pearls. Her black hair, twisted in braids over her shoulders, was arrested in a scarf of gossamer-gold. Muhammad, seated opposite her on the same dais, could barely tear his gaze away from his beloved Khadija. But, always the paragon of courtesy, he was succeeding in forcing his gaze towards the celebrations in the hall.

Men in scarlet tunics were just a few drops of colour in this sea. The colours of the rainbow were woven into the gowns of the ladies, their jewels flashing. Muhammad's thoughts were murmuring disbelief that all the chief members of Meccan families had gathered here this evening in honour of his marriage.

Abu Bakr with his sons, wives and daughters could not escape anyone's notice. Not far from Abu Bakr stood Abu Sofyan, and opposite him his beautiful wife, Hind. Khadija's aunts and uncles were mingling with the guests. The most visible amongst them was Khadija's sister, Hala, her cousin Waraqa, her nephew Khusaima, and her uncle Omar ibn Assad. Muhammad's gaze fell on Hindal, the son of Khadija, and then wandered in search of her daughters. Then he remembered that they were married and settled in Medina.

His gaze shifted to Waraqa, whose voice was soaring above some protests from the lips of Nizam, Khadija's brother, and from Nawfal, her half-brother. It lingered on the old face of Waraqa with a profound interest, and then returned to Khadija, who was now surrounded by her friends Nafisa and Quillah, and by her maids, Khalwa and Maisra. In the background stood

Khadija's Syrian slave, Zaid, dressed in fine linens, his dark face aglow with joy and devotion.

The dreamy look in Muhammad's eyes became tender as he spied his childhood nurse Halima, accompanied by her daughter Shayma. Behind them he could see his uncle Abu Talib weaving his way towards the dais. With a succession of claps, Abu Talib succeeded in gaining everyone's attention.

'There is no one to compare with my nephew, Muhammad Mustafa,' Abu Talib sang with great pride. 'He is the best man in wisdom, intelligence, in distinction of family, in purity of lineage, and in the nobility of his personal life. He has all the markings of a man destined to be great. He is marrying Khadija with a *mehr* of four hundred pieces of gold. I declare Muhammad and Khadija husband and wife. May al-Llah bless them both, and may He be their Protector and Sustainer.'

Amidst cheers of applause and felicitations, Waraqa rose to his feet. He was waiting for the applause to subside. Abu Talib clapped again and a curtain of silence lowered over everyone, reflecting awe and courtesy in honour of this marriage.

'All praise and glory to al-Llah!' Waraqa began with the Meccan invocation. 'We affirm that Banu Hashim is excellent in character and judgement. We cherish the marriage of Khadija to Muhammad Mustafa. Their marriage unites our two houses, and their union is a source of great happiness to us. Oh Lords of Quraysh, I want you as witnesses that I give Khadija in marriage to Muhammad Mustafa with his *mehr* of four hundred gold pieces. May al-Llah grant them happiness together!'

Applause and congratulations soared again, and ceremonial gifts were piled high around the dais. Omar ibn Assad wended his way through the maze of cheers. He was waving his arms and then resorted to clapping, louder than Abu Talib's.

'We invite you to enjoy the wedding feast under the colourful tents at the back of the house.' Omar ibn Assad indicated the direction with a gesture of his arm.

'Make sure you don't wander too far, to where the white tents are pitched. The feast in there is for the poor and the orphans of Mecca to have their fill, and to bless the marriage of Khadija with Muhammad.'

'This eve of festivity doesn't end here,' Abu Talib continued quickly. 'You are all invited to a banquet at my house tomorrow to bless the marriage of my nephew to Khadija. And that banquet will last for three whole days, for the Princess of Mecca deserves to be honoured as befits her status and wealth.'

The rectangular hall was flooded with cheers, followed by laughter. Finally, the bride and the bridegroom were afforded the luxury of solitude to enjoy their own wedding feast. Abu Talib and Omar ibn Assad were the last to leave. An eternity of silence had fallen upon the bridal couple. Khadija was the first one to lower her gaze, unable to hold and behold the dance of ardent stars in the eyes of her husband. And Muhammad sighed with relief at the approach of Zaid, followed by Maisra and Khalwa. They lowered silver trays laden with an Arabian feast. In a flash, they had vanished, leaving the bridal couple in a pool of silence. Both were heaping their plates with the food, a leg of lamb perched high on a mound of thin, flat bread.

'How beautiful you are, Khadija! I was blind all those years not to have noticed,' was Muhammad's anguished confession of love and agony.

'How fortunate to be noticed at last! And by a handsome man like you, Muhammad.' Khadija smiled bashfully.

'We could kill each other with compliments, if not with our silences.' Muhammad laughed suddenly, feeling bold and exhilarated.

'How beautiful, Muhammad, to be united like this, in life or death!' Khadija's own eyes were sparkling with mirth, her heart young and giddy.

'How beautiful your expression is, my beloved Khadija! And I am supposed to be the eloquent one?' Muhammad murmured.

'It is your eloquence, Muhammad, be assured. I borrowed it from you.' Khadija sang, her heart caught in a vortex of bliss that she dared not name or relinquish.

'The privilege of a queen, I am sure.' Muhammad arched his eyebrows. 'I belong to you heart and soul, my Princess of Quraysh.'

'My heart and soul are yours too, Muhammad, but I fear…' Khadija's voice trailed away.

'Fear? What do you fear, Khadija?' Muhammad asked. 'We can spend the wedding night here if you are afraid of the bridal chamber in my uncle's home?'

'No, Muhammad!' Khadija smiled. 'It is nothing; the fear is gone.'

'In that case, let me warn you about that chamber of horror, decorated most lovingly by my uncle and his wife Fatima. Baraka told me all about it. Their daughters Umm Hani and Rahmani added the final touches, and their sons, Jafar, Talib and Aqil kept guard,' Muhammad began eagerly. 'My uncle thinks I don't know, but, thanks to Baraka, all the details are imprinted in my memory. The bed is smothered with silks and velvets, she said, and a canopy of gold cascades down to the floor, revealing a garden of flowers in red and green. All four corners of the room are furnished with jars of incense, and jars studded with the most precious of jewels.'

'Abu Talib is so very sweet and considerate; his family too. I owe them many thanks for their love and generosity.' Khadija's voice quivered with delight.

'You will forget your thanks, my Khadija, when you see how you are to be conducted to my uncle's home at the head of a torchlit procession.' The gleam of love in Muhammad's eyes was holding her prisoner. 'And the she-camel you are to ride, all gaudily decorated and dressed up. My uncle's own chamberlain is instructed to hold a parasol of white silk over your head.'

'I am beginning to feel like a queen after all!' Khadija chimed. 'If I am to be treated like a queen, then I must bestow gifts with the heart of a queen. My wedding gift to you, Muhammad, is my devoted slave, Zaid. He is to be your personal slave.'

'And I will grant him freedom, as I did for Baraka, in honour of our wedding,' Muhammad murmured. 'But though I indulge in freeing the slaves of others, I will remain *your* slave, my love, for life.' He paused, his look gentle and thoughtful. 'I couldn't find any gift worthy of your virtue and beauty, my Khadija. What can a man give to the Princess of Quraysh? A wedding gift, if you would accept, my beloved: I leave all the love in my heart and soul in your sweet possession, while I remain content to be your devoted servant as long as I live, loving you alone, and worshipping the very ground upon which you walk.'

'Such rare and precious gems, Muhammad! Your gift of love alone is priceless. Who could ever buy such a jewel of a gift in the bazaars of Mecca? I would cherish this gift forever,' was Khadija's tremulous response, tears of joy sparkling in her eyes.

'Don't feel cheated, Khadija, when the worth of my gifts is revealed to you,' Muhammad teased. 'You deem them as jewels, but they are pebbles, not worth a straw as compared to your own purity of love. But to safeguard my wedding gift of pebbles, I must urge to you eat, or you will vanish within a week. Look, you haven't even taken a bite!' He laughed.

'You haven't either, Muhammad.' Khadija sucked back her tears. 'Let us pray together, Muhammad, before we eat.' The stars of poetry were dancing in her eyes.

'Beloved, I will kneel and pray to you alone!' Muhammad declared.

'To the gods and goddesses of the Kaaba, Muhammad, who have bestowed great fortunes on us both?' was Khadija's murmured plea. 'Don't you believe in them?'

'I'm not sure, my Khadija.' Muhammad closed his eyes. 'There are so many!'

'Yes, all the deities of the Kaaba, the gods and goddesses of all the Meccans! They are my gods and goddesses too,' Khadija murmured.

'Whatever you believe in, Khadija, is my belief also. Your gods are my gods, and your goddesses my deities, O Princess of Mecca. I will pray if you lead.' Muhammad dared not open his eyes lest he bathe her feet with tears and kisses.

'Al-Llah Taala and al-Allat, bless our marriage and keep us under the guidance of your love and mercy,' Khadija prayed, her eyes closed.

'Amen,' Muhammad chanted under a spell of reverence and confusion.

After this prayer they sat immersed in silence, their eyes closed, not even noticing that Halima had straggled back, looking for her shawl. Noticing the bride and the groom in complete stillness, she stood numb and astonished. She smothered a sigh of relief as Muhammad opened his eyes.

'Have you cast a spell on your bride, Muhammad?' was Halima's dazed enquiry.

'Halima!' Muhammad stumbled to his feet. 'Here, sit with us and bless our marriage. You raised me as a shepherd, not as a sorcerer.'

'Thanks to Hubal and al-Llah for that!' Halima's attention was shifted to Khadija. 'Blessed be your marriage to Muhammad, Princess of Mecca. He brought us a bundle of fortunes while he stayed with us.'

'For blessing our marriage, Halima, and for being a mother to Muhammad, please accept a small gift of forty sheep to add to your fortune,' Khadija offered gratefully.

'Thank you, princess.' Halima could barely murmur.

Before Muhammad could speak, the octagonal hall was filled with songs and music. The dancing girls were floating into the room, carrying lamps, and wafting the scent of flowers and incense. They were followed by a group of family and friends, the foremost amongst them being Abu Talib and Omar ibn Assad.

'Time to exchange the robes of honour amongst our two families!' Omar ibn Assad's eyes were fixed on Khadija. 'You can't leave home, Princess, until you anoint the head of your uncle with oils and perfumes.'

The ritual of leave-taking commenced with a fanfare of drums and tambourines. Friends and family formed a great circle around the bridal couple, singing songs and clapping. Khadija was snatched out of the circle by her friends, who led her towards her uncle. She began anointing her uncle's hair with perfumed oil, sprinkling it with saffron and ambergris. Muhammad was claimed by Abu Talib.

'My nephew must slaughter a camel before he can take his bride home. This will be his offering to the gods of the Kaaba, to seek their blessings.' Abu Talib almost dragged Muhammad towards the door, laughter following at their heels.

The torchlit procession in front of them halted at the courtyard, where a camel stood in the middle. Someone thrust a sword into Muhammad's hand. He obeyed his uncle's command to perform the ritual sacrifice, and in one quick stroke he slit the throat of the camel. Zaid rushed forward to claim the sword, holding out a bowl of rosewater for washing his hands. While Muhammad was absorbed in these age-old rituals of sacrifice, Khadija was being escorted to her camel, followed by the dancing girls with lamps balanced on the palms of their hands.

Muhammad was riding his own Arabian steed, his gaze reaching out to the star-studded heavens, his beloved was gulfs apart on the back of her bridal mount, the she-camel. Something inside him was expanding and exploding. He could barely guide his horse, trying his best as he was to stay in rhythm with the wedding procession.

Khadija! Beloved! My All! Pray for your slave, whose longings exceed the limitations of worldly love and riches. And what those are, he himself doesn't know – but Muhammad's thoughts were snatched away by the heavenly orbs above and beyond.

The stars laughed and the heavens spun in a cosmic dance of love and music. Muhammad was alone and lonely: the bridegroom lost and searching. He could hear the music of silence within himself; the voice of his soul, both near and remote. Music and silence, from within and without. So alive and palpitating was the sound of that roaring silence inside him that he couldn't distinguish between the tunes of the wedding songs and of his inward silence.

Chapter 2

The Cave of White Musk
Year 600 AD

Mount Hira was polished to pewter, gleaming under the glaring sun of the Meccan desert, but inside its great cleft the cave was darkness. Muhammad, squatting on the rocky floor inside, was transported to realms divine and fathomless. His contemplations were suspended between thought and thinking. He was wearing his red cloak Bedouin-style, like a large shawl draped over his shoulders.

Muhammad sat tracing the journey of his breath, his reflections carrying him over the currents of the past five years. After his marriage to Khadija, his heart was filled with so much joy and love that there was no room left in it for anything else. And yet, his soul was tainted with a familiar longing for something greater than life. Khadija was his beloved, and yet he longed for more. He shared his longing with her, and she became his guide and comforter, granting him the luxury of solitude.

Khadija and Muhammad were blessed with a son within the first year of their marriage, but Abul Qasim was barely one year old when he died suddenly. One year after the death of their son, they were blessed with a daughter, named Zainab. He never tired of kissing his daughter; Khadija would laugh and exclaim that he would lick her sweet life away if she was not there to protect her precious daughter.

Zainab, now almost two years old, was appearing at the window of Muhammad's mind as he sat still inside the Cave of Mount Hira. The fountain of love inside him was gurgling all of a sudden, and sprinkling him with the waters of awareness.

Why I am here? What is this longing? Why have I kept returning to this cave, day after day, for the past two weeks? Fasting and praying? The pilgrims will be coming from Basra, Syria, Yemen; from Damascus and Jerusalem; flocking around the Kaaba. The traders and the merchants will be selling their goods, and performing the rites of pilgrimage. Praying to the gods and goddesses. Which ones? How many?

A succession of scenes fluttered into Muhammad's mind. He could see the Arabs converging on the Kaaba. The pilgrims teeming close to the hollow of Muzdalifah, and pleading with the thunder god for winter rains. Pitching their tents around the fringes of Mount Arafat for all-night vigil and prayers, then surging towards Mina in the morning, and hurling pebbles at the three cliffs called the Devil's Pillars. Later, he imagined them retreating into the valley of Mina to offer animal sacrifices.

Where do these gods and goddesses come from?

A sudden stab of anguish cut through Muhammad's pain and silence. He had recognised his longing: it was to meet the Creator face to face. His thoughts scattered like the sandstorms of the Arabian Desert. The god Hubal was rising out of his red granite mould. He hovered over the sea of devotees, while the High God of the Kaaba, al-Llah, watched, invisible to them. The goddess al-Uzzah was resting in the valley of Nakhlah. The shrine of al-Lat at Taif was guarded by the tribe of Thaqif. Al-Manat, the goddess of fate, had her own shrine at Qudayd.

What's a man's goal in life? Where does death take us? Why are there so many blood feuds and murders, when everyone has to die one day anyway? Why are there so many rifts amongst the devotees of all these gods and goddesses? Muhammad could see so many of the different idols.

The idols were speechless, much like Muhammad's thoughts. They were forgotten by the tribes who had collected them from distant lands. Muhammad's thoughts circled around the Kaaba, and then entered its inner sanctuary, looking at the painting of an old man, said to be Abraham. His mind's eye admired the frescoes of Mary and Jesus. The colours were faded, yet the arrows in their hands were painted in bright colours, depicting them as emblems of magic and mystery.

Was the Kaaba not the first House of Worship built by Abraham? Is al-Llah Taala not the God Most High worshipped by Jews and Christians?

Muhammad abandoned his cave and contemplations, his eyes stung by the ocean of sunlight. He stood at the mouth of the cave, in awe. Mecca was calling him, beckoning him to come home, to kiss the hearth of the Kaaba. But his heart longed to be with Khadija, and to fold little Zainab into his arms.

His red cloak wrapped closely around him, and his hair bouncing loose over his shoulders, Muhammad was homeward bound. A three-mile stretch of journey lay before him, but his strides were swift. He could feel his soul dancing the dance of joy, not knowing why it was happy, nor why it bounded up and up towards the heavens.

Soon, we will appear before God in Zion.

Wearing a veil of serendipity across his eyes, Muhammad didn't even know that he had left Mount Hira miles behind, until he became aware of the holy precincts leading towards the Kaaba. His attention was diverted to a procession of Bedouins, chanting prayers and imploring the thunder god for rains.

A horde of Bedouins had fastened dry blades of grass to a cow's tail and set them on fire. The victimised beast was running in circles from the blaze, while the onlookers rolled with laughter. They were praying too, whipped by their belief that the cow's tail looked like a flash of lightning, and that it would surely summon rain to nourish the parched womb of Arabia with fruits and fertility.

This scene of utter barbarity filled Muhammad's heart with such profound sadness that his sense of inner joy disappeared. *Is there nothing on the face of this earth which could help improve the lot of mankind, so blindly steeped into the marshes of cruelty, injustice, and ignorance?* So engrossed was he in contemplating the murky clouds in his head that he almost collided with the famous poet, Imra al-Qais, who was hurling an arrow at an idol in the outer circle of the Kaaba.

'Oh wretch, had it been the murder of your father, you would not have forbidden me to avenge it.' Imra al-Qais sprang to his feet, glowering at the faceless idol.

'I have never seen you in such a fit of rage before, Imra! What's wrong?' Muhammad stood there aghast, his tone gentle and anxious.

'What's wrong, what's wrong?' Imra al-Qais repeated between his grunts of rage and frustration. 'I will tell you, Muhammad, what's wrong. This wretch of an idol, to whom I have been faithful all my life! Today, as usual, I bow before it, pleading for an oracle to avenge the murder of my father. But, no! It forbids me. Look.' He scooped the two arrows into his hands. 'Can you see the one marked with *yes*? And the other with *no*? I have shot these arrows three times, and every time the arrow marked *no* comes back to me!'

'Don't you find it ridiculous, Imra, that most tribes in Arabia have fashioned their own personal gods to satisfy their needs, and nothing stops them making a mockery of the same gods, if the oracles are not in their favour?' Muhammad demurred aloud.

'We can't help but fashion and refashion.' Imra al-Qais waved his arms desperately. 'Jews have their own god, and Christians too. But we have no claim on any god as our own. Even Hubal laughs at us, and the goddesses skip away from our imaginations. Why can't we be blessed with a deity as our own personal god? Maybe a prophet amongst us from our own people?'

'Why? Your arrows of anger and superstition.' Muhammad turned on his heel.

Leaving behind the mad poet, Muhammad continued his journey homewards. He was not making much progress though, watching the pilgrims circling around the Holy House. A crescendo of voices entered his awareness, pouring down a hail of disputes. He knew their cause. For the past few months, he had been watching the men rebuilding the Shrine of the Kaaba, disputing as to who would have the honour of laying the first brick, or of repairing the roof.

He drifted towards the spring of Zamzam, contemplating the statue of Hubal, which peered out at him from its fiery abode of red granite. His heart was fluttering as he lifted his eyes up to the sky, the rude colours of the Arabian sunset glittering. He could not tear his gaze away from the dance of colours in the sky.

Infinity! God is infinite. Infinitely beautiful, beyond the comprehension of us lowly mortals. We, with our puny minds and limited intelligence! How can we fathom the infinite? An arrow of longing pierced Muhammad's thoughts.

The pilgrims were floating past Muhammad, but he was oblivious to them all, listening to the song of love and longing within the silence of his soul. This song had no words, but the fire and the colour of countless sunsets. He was so profoundly absorbed in his solitary contemplations that he couldn't comprehend the cause of a sudden uproar, as he stepped into the courtyard of the Kaaba.

'Here is Al-Amin! Here is Al-Amin!' Loud voices reached him.

Wading quickly through the waters of awareness, Muhammad learnt the cause of the uproar. Before his arrival, a violent dispute had broken out amongst the Arab clans as to who would have the honour of fixing the Black Stone onto the façade of the Kaaba. It was decided by the four major clans of Mecca that they would wait patiently for the first person they saw entering the courtyard of the Kaaba. And whoever he was, they would grant him authority as a decision-maker. So, that's where the matter stood after Muhammad ascertained the facts.

'So, Muhammad, you are chosen as our one and only arbiter!' Ummayad ibn Khalaf declared. 'Tell us, who will have the privilege of laying the Black Stone?'

'The privilege belongs to us all, my friend, to make the matter simple,' Muhammad laughed. 'I will lay my cloak on the ground and we will put the Black Stone in the middle. Then one man each from all the four clans of Mecca can get a firm hold on each edge, carrying the Black Stone to its revered place. None of the clans will be neglected then, and no one will feel slighted. Abu Sofyan from the clan of Banu Shemite is here, and Nawfal from the clan of Banu Humayyah. Abdallah ibn Jash from the clan of Banu Muttalib can do the honours, and if permitted I will represent Banu Hashim.'

'What a genius you are, Muhammad! Saving and protecting us from the necessity of a blood feud!' Abu Jahl's ugly face wrinkled into a smile.

'No wonder his mother named him Ahmed!' Abu Talib announced proudly. 'Without *m*, Ahad means unity. An Arab he is, for sure! But ponder upon this, without *a*, it is "rab", meaning lord!'

'He is no lord, even if he is married to the richest widow in Mecca,' Hind declared. 'You think us all brutal and barbarous, Muhammad, don't you? Though Abu Sofyan is your cousin from the long line of patrimony no one cares to remember.' She lowered her veil which she always wore as a mark of her status and royal birth.

'You misjudge me, Hind,' Muhammad intoned gently. 'More than half the clans in Mecca are far from brutal and barbaric. I find them hospitable and generous.'

'Are Banu Hashim in the scale of the larger half?' Hind challenged.

'Permit me to satisfy your curiosity on that account.' Hamza fixed his fiery gaze on the impudent wife of Abu Sofyan. 'The Banu Hashim clan love their freedom, and they are admired for fidelity to their tribes, and for their manliness.'

'Let's get done with settling this Black Stone in its place, and then go home for feasting and drinking,' Utbah ibn Rabia suggested impatiently.

'Who cares about this Black Stone? It's probably a meteorite from the hellish sky up there!' Mistal, the poet sang in drunken glee.

'I would rather believe in the legend that it was a white hyacinth which grew blacker and blacker due to the sins of men,' was Muhammad's wistful response.

'We have made a mockery of our own religions! Worshipping the gods of stone, and then desecrating the very objects of our worship!' Abu Bakr lamented.

The members of the four clans were holding on to the mantle, bulging with Black Stone, as they carried it to the front wall of the Kaaba. Once there, they were quick to slide it carefully into the crevice reserved for it. Muhammad stood back examining it, but noticing a little chink in the wall, he reached over, sliding the Black Stone to the right until it settled snugly. A great volley of applause broke forth as Muhammad stepped back. He was trying to weave his way out through the teeming crowds, his heart longing for the nearness of Khadija. Barely had he managed to squeeze himself out, when he was confronted by Zaid, his father Ashraf following him.

'Solve this riddle for me, Muhammad, if you would?' Ashraf gouged his way closer, panting with rage. 'You have freed my son, and he still wants to be your slave! I have come to take him home, and he refuses to go!'

'No riddle, Ashraf!' was Muhammad's amused response. 'He likes me and he worships the Princess of Mecca. Besides, he is no slave, but my son.'

'Muhammad!' Zaid gasped, cowering with fright against his father's rage.

'You don't believe me, Ashraf, do you?' Muhammad's eyes were searching the incredulous expression of Zaid's father. 'Come, Zaid, let us prove to your father that you are my son.' He almost dragged him towards the Black Stone. 'Put your hand beside mine, Zaid, and feel the warmth of this Black Stone. Bear testimony, all you who are here, that Zaid is my son. I will be his heir, and he shall be mine.'

Another volley of applause broke forth, while Muhammad made his way out, still holding Zaid's hand, Abu Talib following them. Ashraf was lost in the mêlée of laughter and jesting. Abu Talib was trying to catch up with Muhammad, but a venerable member of the Quraysh by the name of Akram was seeking his attention.

'This stark, windowless cube of a Kaaba, Abu Talib; do you think it will renew some long-forgotten feeling of peace and reverence in our hearts?' Akram flung this query with his usual sense of doubt and curiosity.

'Slow down, Muhammad, and leave Zaid alone. No one is going to steal him away from you.' Abu Talib shot this command before turning to Akram. 'How many lips have kissed this Black Stone, Akram? Don't you think it has been revered much too much, becoming the centre of power, carving rifts through the wrinkled face of time, year after year? Don't start an argument, Akram; go home.' He waved impatiently. 'I want to be with my nephew. I rarely see him these days, and I'm trying to take advantage of this opportunity to have a few words with him on his way home.'

'You know you can talk with me whenever you want to, Uncle. What do you mean, you don't get a chance to see me?' Muhammad laughed.

'You are busy with the Princess and with your daughter, and I with my little son, Ali. Isn't it strange that Ali is only a year younger than Zainab?' Abu Talib remarked. 'Imagine, an old uncle having a son almost the same age as your daughter.'

'You are not old, Uncle; only a few years older than me, being the youngest in the family – well, a few years older than Uncle Hamza.' Muhammad's eyes were a star-dance of mirth. 'Besides, you, as the guardian of the Kaaba, must breed sons to maintain the purity of this Sacred House with holy rites and rituals.'

'We are thirty years apart, Muhammad; don't presume I am still as young as you!' Abu Talib twirled his moustache. 'As to the Kaaba, its holiness never dies, tripling every generation, and no sons are needed to nurture its purity or sanctity. Even Hubal, the High God of Mecca, is not venerated as much as the Holy House of the Kaaba itself.'

'Because the gods are chosen with the dice of greed on the desert sands of Mecca. Isn't that right, Uncle?' Muhammad breathed profoundly. 'Hubal takes precedence over al-Llah, even though more Meccans are inclined to worship al-Llah and His consort, al-Lat, than any other god or goddess?'

'Deities come and go, Muhammad, but the Black Stone reigns supreme, worshipped by the pilgrims more than any High God of the past or present.' Abu Talib stirred his own conflicting thoughts.

'Why?' A cry of agony ripped through Muhammad's soul. 'I have kissed it several times, this Black Stone, and I don't know why! And yet, when I kiss it, it takes my breath away, pouring sweetness into my heart, and then draining all that it has poured till there is nothing left but emptiness.'

'Your words are poetic and strange, Muhammad, considering you have not learnt how to read or write,' was Abu Talib's soft reply. 'You ask why, Muhammad; why the Black Stone is worshipped more? Isn't it sufficient that it is the only supreme mystery lowered to earth from the heavens since the expulsion of Adam? An emblem of the divine covenant between the Creator and the created!'

'I thought Abraham was the first patriarch and he built the Kaaba with its Black Stone, as the centre of worship for one God?' Muhammad asked dreamily.

'Oh, yes, but the Black Stone itself is timeless. It was already there when Abraham came to Mecca. Many tribes before him worshipped it when they came to Mecca to trade goods and wares, but Abraham built the Kaaba as God commanded. Still – it's a mystery that the Kaaba with its Black Stone has attracted more devotion than the God in Whose honour it was built.' Abu Talib was swept up in his own learning.

'Moses and Jesus; were they not sent to proclaim the message of one God as well?' Muhammad murmured, more to himself than to seek an answer.

'And who has been telling you about all this, my wise nephew?' Abu Talib indulged brightly.

'Waraqa, Khadija's cousin, the eldest of all the siblings in her family,' Muhammad confessed softly.

'Isn't he a Christian? Tired of preaching the gospel, I hear; so now he is talking about another Messiah and waiting for him?' Abu Talib laughed.

'He is not waiting, Uncle, but expounding parables from the gospel, which are the very essence of his religion.' Muhammad joined his uncle in his mirth.

'And what is the essence of his religion? He is waiting to die, more likely.' Abu Talib veiled his curiosity in a fresh spurt of laughter.

'Love, peace and unity; that's the essence of his religion, Uncle. He says a Messiah will come as mentioned in the gospel, and he will dissolve all rifts between the Jews and the Christians, and all will live in peace.' Muhammad's look was dreamy again, mirth gone from his eyes and lips.

'And does he hate all the idols at the Kaaba, all three hundred and sixty of them?' Abu Talib's curiosity was on the verge of exploding.

'No, Uncle, he doesn't hate anyone or anything.' Muhammad was quick to defend Khadija's loving cousin. 'He says that the Kaaba represents the four corners of the world. The three hundred and sixty idols around it represent, he says, the symbols of the Sumerian belief in the sanctity of time, comprising the three hundred and sixty days in a year. He thinks of Mecca as it was, a Noble House as it was called, the City of Worship, with the Kaaba as its purest of shrines. The Kaaba in his gospel is the First House at Becca, built for the worship of one God alone, and these stone deities which different tribes have gathered over the years are bound to succumb to the power of Abraham's God, when another Messiah arrives.'

'Becca or Mecca, the Arabs would raise hell more gruesome than the hellfires of the Jews and the Christians if their idols were to be removed, even by the finger of God Most High!' Abu Talib declared fiercely, astonished at his own vehemence.

'They are already suffering the tortures of hellfire, Uncle, don't you think?' Muhammad tossed a gentle challenge. 'The whole of Arabia is a pothole of drinking, gambling, and family feuds, not to mention a bloodbath of greed and hypocrisy!'

'And who would pound sense into the heads of this degenerate race, may I ask? Hubal, al-Llah, al-Lat?' Abu Talib waved his arm desperately.

'Someone, Uncle. We must think and put our thoughts to action before this generation drowns in its own cruelty,' was Muhammad's gentle plea.

A curtain of silence drew over the thoughts of uncle and nephew, as if both were wearied by their inward journeys into a desert of unanswerable questions. Zaid was walking ahead jauntily. Both uncle and nephew were jolted out of their solitary contemplations by an abrupt outpouring of joy from Zaid's lips.

'So good to be home! Princess has been waiting for us, I can tell. All those lamps in every window! When will I get the time to carve that doll for sweet Zainab?' Zaid pushed at the white gates till they swept back, churning sands in half-circles.

'Oh, I took the wrong turn again!' Abu Talib groaned. 'Now I'll have to walk back.'

'You have two choices, Uncle. Either let Zaid walk back with you, or stay and have dinner with us, then I will walk back with you,' Muhammad proposed.

'No, Muhammad. My thoughts will keep me company during my short walk,' Abu Talib murmured. 'Although I am not so sure; they might hurl me back to your doorstep! What is this scent, wafting out of your clothes and filling the air with its fragrance? Is this a musk Khadija bought with her gold?'

'The perfume of love, Uncle!' Muhammad laughed. 'A scent so subtle that only loved ones can catch a whiff of it.'

'I shouldn't have asked. My wife Fatima tells me that the scents which fill our home with the sweetest of smells come from your body; not that you ever use any scents…' Abu Talib kissed him on both cheeks before hurrying back towards the gate.

'We should go inside now, Muhammad. The Princess has been waiting for you and sent me herself to look for you, but then my father…' Zaid sought Muhammad's attention as he stood watching his uncle disappear behind the white gates.

'First I have to settle a score with you, my son.' The sparkling intensity in Muhammad's eyes was now fixed on him. 'Though you are my adopted son, your first duty is to your real father. You should go with him, and don't feel obliged in any way to stay with us.'

'I would rather die under the hot sun of the desert, Muhammad, than go with my father!' was Zaid's anguished protest.

'He is your father, and it is your duty to be obedient,' Muhammad coaxed gently.

'He is cruel! He has thrashed me black and blue so many times.' Zaid's dark face contorted in fear, tears stinging his eyes.

'You mean he has not treated you well? Cruel is a harsh word, Zaid, against one's own father.' Muhammad thought aloud. 'Would you be happy if you got married? Would you marry Baraka?'

'I will do anything you say, Muhammad!' Zaid exclaimed.

'It's not what I say, Zaid. You are the one who has to live with her, if you choose to marry. She is much older than you; almost twenty years.' Muhammad paused, as if realising the disparity in age all of a sudden. 'She has been looking for a husband, that's the only reason I suggested it, but forget what I said.'

'Princess is older than you, if I may say so, Muhammad, and you are so very happy with her,' Zaid chanted, beaming. 'I would be happy, Muhammad; I want to marry Baraka, she is so good to me.' His small eyes were gathering tears of joy.

'That settles it. Now we have to ask Baraka.' Muhammad smiled, hurrying towards the house. 'Now don't go fussing around after me. Make yourself scarce; I want to be alone with the Princess,' he commanded.

Zaid raced past Muhammad. He was exploding with energy, sprinting through the parlour without noticing Khadija and disappearing into the dining hall with the speed of a whirlwind.

When Muhammad entered the parlour and saw Khadija, he was quick to catch her into an eager embrace, his heart aching.

'What's with Zaid?' Khadija murmured, her eyes spilling joy and mirth.

'He is happy, my princess, my all.' Muhammad made her sit with him.

'Not as happy as I am!' Khadija sang. 'Look at you, Muhammad, leaving home without your turban! Though, I love these soft waves over your shoulders.' Her eyes sought the neglected turban on the low table. 'Isn't it customary that you wear your turban when you go out? My only concern is that the sun will lick the sheen out of your hair, and I will have to comb it a thousand times to bring it back.'

'Beloved! I didn't forget. I left it here on purpose as a token of my remembrance,' Muhammad teased, his eyes shining with mirth and tenderness.

'A poet, my husband! A poet and a dreamer, as your uncle Abu Talib says,' Khadija intoned sweetly, her cheeks flushed.

'I have been accused of that several times before by Abu Talib, for sure.' Muhammad laughed. 'Do you know our little Zainab is only a year older than Abu Talib's son Ali? I realised that just today. Oh, my lovely Zainab, where is she?'

'She is sleeping as she is supposed to! She refuses to when you are here. You have spoiled her, Muhammad, and I fear she will be impetuous and demanding when she grows up.' Khadija uttered a mock lament.

'Our sweet Zainab, Khadija? No, it could never be! How could she be, when her mother is endowed with virtues sweeter than honey?' Muhammad protested happily. 'The more I think about Zainab, the more I think about Ali. Don't you find it strange, my Khadija, that my uncle at his age has a son almost as young as our daughter? Actually, he himself finds it strange.'

'Not in the least strange, dear Muhammad,' Khadija intoned, beaming. 'Not strange at all, considering how frequently older men acquire younger brides.'

'You are the only bride for me, my beloved. The one and only, wedded to my mind, heart and soul, and no other woman can invade this altar of love. To even think of such a thing would be faithlessness on my part, if not the desecration of my own pure altar.' Muhammad's eyes were kindling into lamps of worship.

'Not many women are as fortunate as me, dear Muhammad,' Khadija smiled. 'Women are owned by men as a part of their property, if not treated as chattels. Men marry them on their own whims, without even seeking their permission, then divorce them as they please. How convenient for men when all they have to say is *I divorce you* three times, and the marriage is annulled, leaving the woman destitute and grief-stricken. Is there no solution, Muhammad, to stop these evil practices?' She sighed.

'If I had the authority, beloved, I would pound sense into the very folds of men's turbans, hoping that it would reach their brains!' Humour and tenderness held open the compassionate portals of Muhammad's eyes. 'Greed and mendacity have made these men slothful and heartless. They don't even have to repeat that *I divorce you* litany three times; they only have to say *you are my mother,* and the woman is divorced. The absurdity of such customs! Where do they come from, and who carved them into tablets as the sanctified rights of men over women? How does one begin to right the wrongs of stupidity? I have been thinking and thinking, but no answers come my way.'

'The answers might come, Muhammad. *Will* come, some day. Then we will devise ways to bring justice and equality into the land of Mecca, where no child or woman may suffer the indignity of grief and hopelessness, and where no man may lust for blood or vengeance,' Khadija intoned prophetically. 'How could anyone have the heart to bury one's newborn daughter alive?' she murmured.

'If hearts are turned blind and corrupt, Khadija, it is so very hard to find a physician who could cure them.' Muhammad looked deep into her eyes, as if divining the secrets of her soul. 'There may be hope yet, when such men waken from their besotted sleep, realising that if they do not cease the rite of burying their daughters alive, there will be no mothers left to beget sons, either. I am no physician, but I have made friends with young fathers, and told them that they should welcome their daughters into their arms, not abandon them inside cold graves. A few take heed, and some blink ignorance, as if the killing of innocent infants is a holy ritual, not a heinous crime.'

'Is there no help, then, Muhammad?' Khadija pleaded with a sudden vehemence. 'I have this feeling, dear Muhammad, that you, and you alone, could save such men from the pit of ignorance and barbarity.' She paused. 'Forgive me, Muhammad; sometimes I work myself into a passion about issues like these, and then I forget what I am supposed to be doing. You must be hungry. Where is Zaid? He offered to fix us something special this evening. Baraka is cooking a leg of lamb, I know, and mutton roast. But she should at least come and tell us when dinner is going to be ready.'

'I am not that hungry, beloved.' Muhammad's eyes were gathering the stars of mischief. 'I told you Zaid was happy, and you didn't even ask why. But I must tell you, before he babbles it to the whole world and you end up being the last one to know. I suggested that he should marry Baraka. He seemed calm when he agreed, but then joy swept over him like wildfire and he crackled and spluttered. We have to ask Baraka, though. Do you think it's a good match?'

'When did you start in the matchmaking business, Muhammad?' Khadija was drowning in a flood of mirth so spontaneous that she could barely breathe.

So a sea of billowing mirth broke loose, it seemed; Khadija and Muhammad sat laughing, not even noticing Baraka's approach. Baraka had caught Khadija's comment before entering the parlour, and now stood waiting.

'Who is getting married?' Baraka confronted the happy couple.

'You are!' Muhammad's eyes were sparkling, keeping her captive. 'Zaid wants to marry you, Baraka. Would you accept?' he asked.

'If you wish it so, Muhammad?' Baraka stood there, non-committal.

'That's what Zaid said!' Muhammad cried in astonishment. 'You are the one who has to live with him, Baraka, so you decide.'

'Well, I wanted to get married. I still want to get married ... but he is so ugly.' Baraka paused. 'And yet he is twenty years younger than me. So we will be even, I reckon. My age and his ugliness, an even exchange.'

'So, you accept, Baraka!' Khadija clapped her hands with a childlike sincerity. 'We will have a grand wedding, and my personal gift to you will be twenty goats.'

'Thank you, Princess.' Baraka was too overwhelmed to trust her voice.

'You don't see the beauty of Zaid's soul, Baraka?' Muhammad chided.

'Only the poets can look into souls! I didn't teach you that, Muhammad, did I?' Baraka was quick to bounce back from her dudgeon.

'Poets again!' Muhammad eased himself up slowly and thoughtfully.

'Is dinner ready, Baraka?' Khadija lifted herself up gracefully, her look gentle.

'Yes, Princess.' Baraka lowered her gaze. 'Zaid wouldn't let me touch the leg of lamb, even though I cooked it.' She fled as fast as her heavy frame could carry her.

The large dining room, dimly lit by a chandelier, offered Khadija and Muhammad the luxury of privacy as they sat down to share their evening meal. They were seated on low cushions of brocade, the rich carpet under them smooth and comforting. Flat bread, chicken cutlets and mutton roast were just a few of the delicacies amongst many more, and the leg of lamb, of course.

'Will I ever get used to such lavish dinners, my Khadija? Have I not repeated that many times over?' Muhammad murmured, doling her out a big serving of mutton roast.

'If you had your way, dear Muhammad, we would be eating right out of the pots in the kitchen!' Khadija sang merrily, offering him the mutton roast in return.

'Wouldn't it be convenient? Then Khalwa would be saved from the trouble of washing and polishing the silver plates,' Muhammad teased.

'The way our business is going, we might have to beg for alms soon,' Khadija laughed, adding two cutlets to Muhammad's plate.

'Sorry, beloved.' Muhammad's expression was sad and contrite all of a sudden.

'Oh, Muhammad, can't you see I am just joking?' Khadija pleaded earnestly. 'You are free to lose all our worldly wealth, but never your sense of humour.'

'It is true, my Khadija; I have lost interest in business. We are losing money, and the blame rests on me, entirely.' Muhammad chewed on a piece of cutlet thoughtfully.

'I don't want you to worry about business, dear Muhammad. I will handle it myself. You have other weighty things to worry about.' Khadija smiled.

'What weighty things, my Khadija?' Muhammad looked into her eyes, humbled.

'The most important thing, if not a weighty one, is to keep your lamp of peace and harmony kindled in this home of ours. To love Zainab as no other daughter has ever been loved before,' Khadija murmured, as if praying.

'My profoundest of loves for you and Zainab, which I carry inside me, priceless and beautiful, is the only treasure I hoard and cherish. You could never see a treasure like it in the market of greed and ambition. But I digress. You are the light of our home, beloved. My light! My love! Your love for me is a supreme joy, light and precious: I should carry the weight of business with as much pleasure as I carry this weightless bliss of loving.' Muhammad's soul spilled poetry.

'Please, stop worrying about business, dear Muhammad,' Khadija appealed. 'We are saving tons of money by not buying anything for Zainab. Zaid is busy carving all sorts of toys for her, gathering useless pieces of wood; from where, I don't know!'

'Ah, beloved! We will be begging soon, for sure,' Muhammad teased in return, 'the way you dole out money to the orphans, the widows and the mendicants. You even provide dowries for poor brides.'

'Oh no, we won't!' Khadija challenged quickly. 'I have enough to last me a hundred years, if I live that long, and still save something to take with me to my grave.'

'Please don't talk of graves, my Khadija. Before marriage I didn't know I was alive; and now I know I live in the shadow of your love. Without you, I would be lost. Lonesome and inconsolable, forever and ever,' Muhammad murmured intensely.

'Forgive me, dear Muhammad! With a love like that, I can even charm death into submission, so that I can live forever in the shadow of your love.' Khadija smiled. 'Let's talk about you. What do you do inside the Cave of Mount Hira? These are the weighty matters I find difficult to talk about. What do you think during those long stretches? What are you searching for in that solitary place, filled with darkness? God? Is that it?' Her voice was low and pleading.

'Gods, perhaps? Countless – a host of them at the Kaaba!' Muhammad's eyes were lit up by a smile. 'No, beloved, I am not seeking anything, only befriending the pain of my longing; this nameless ache and anguish. And yet most of the time I just sit there, thinking of nothing, just listening to the silence within and without. A sort of white, roaring silence which shatters at times, when thoughts return like little troopers, shooting arrows of protest and argument: "This sorry scheme of the world around us, Muhammad! So much misery and ignorance! Such cruelty and hypocrisy! A sea of corruption and a drunken horde of pilgrims!" I am seeking answers, probably, but my questions are very simple at the level of consciousness. Why are we here in this world? What is the purpose of life? Is our link to peace somehow lost in this whirlwind of chaos called existence?'

'Do you think you will find the answers in that cave, dear Muhammad? Perhaps you will,' Khadija contemplated aloud. 'The world would be a better place, if you could discover a plan to free men from the vices of debauchery and drunkenness, to improve the lot of women, and to save innocent babes from being buried alive. Such a brutal and callous world.'

'Here comes my answer!' Muhammad laughed, noticing Zainab cradled in the arms of Maisra. He held out his arms and Zainab fell into them, squealing with delight.

'Maisra, bring a pot of tea and some sweets,' Khadija murmured, unable to tear her gaze away from the faces of their lovely daughter and her handsome father.

'Yes, Princess.' Maisra obeyed, her eyes brimming with joy and admiration.

'That's what I mean, dear Muhammad, when I say you spoil and coddle her. You haven't finished your dinner. Let me hold her while you eat.'

'Love itself is a feast, beloved!' Muhammad sang happily. 'How can I feel hungry for delicacies like these when I'm offered a feast of pure delight, which even feeds the hungers of my heart and soul?'

'I am carrying another miracle like that one in me, I think,' Khadija announced amidst a spurt of joy and laughter.

'You think, my Khadija? Nay, I am sure you are!' Muhammad pressed her to him, sweet Zainab caught in between on the bridge of love and life. 'Sugar and honey, beloved! I would fill the world with sweetness for you,' he murmured, while Zainab squealed and squirmed.

'This time it will be a son, dear Muhammad,' Khadija sang happily.

'Who wants sons, beloved?' Muhammad sprang to his feet, Zainab still giggling in his arms. 'I want daughters, just like Zainab! Sweetness all! Besides, I have a son. Your son, Hindal, tall and handsome! My very own, for I feel he is a part of my own flesh and blood. And another son I just adopted today; Zaid.' He tossed Zainab into the air, catching her again in his arms. He stood gazing at this miracle of beauty, wide-eyed and adorable.

Chapter 3

Sunsets Painted with Stars
Year 605 AD

The Arabian sunset painted the horizon with rose and glitter as Muhammad rode home. Another five happy years had sailed past on clouds of reveries, and his thoughts were forever soaring past time and space. His adopted son, Zaid, was riding beside him, humming a lovelorn tune. They were returning from a camel race which Muhammad had lost, but nothing could lessen his joy, for this was the eve of the celebration to honour the birth of his fourth daughter, Fatima.

Muhammad inhaled the scent of joy and love from the bouquet of the past five years. A profusion of blessings had fallen his way; his daughters were the eternal blooms. Zainab, the eldest, was now seven years old. Ruqayyah had just turned four, Khultum was on the rungs of two, and Fatima, Muhammad's 'Bird of Paradise' as he called her, was only a month old. His thoughts flew to Khadija, who had invited the whole town of Mecca to celebrate her birth.

The dusk was almost crimson now, shuddering on the verge of death. Muhammad's heart awakened with a sudden pang of anguish; that familiar longing ache. His eyes shone with regret and sadness as he turned his gaze towards the sky, noticing a few stars glinting white loneliness. Unbeknownst to him, his features were awash with pallor and sadness.

'Are you sad, Muhammad, that your camel lost the race?' Zaid asked suddenly.

'No, by al-Llah, no!' Muhammad laughed. 'My Qaswa is a fleet-footed camel, but al-Llah has a right to pull down anything which raises its neck.'

'You looked so happy, and then so sad all of a sudden, Muhammad. I can never tell what you are thinking,' Zaid commented impulsively.

'I was thinking about al-Llah. Or rather, consumed by the beauty of the colours in the sunset. Who could the artist be behind this glorious screen of art and inspiration?' Muhammad thought aloud.

'Next time you go to the Kaaba, Muhammad, ask the deities. Many men claim that they get their answers when they kneel before their idols,' Zaid suggested.

'Those men, Zaid, only plead for riches and good omens. And if they don't get what they want, they mock the very idols they worship,' Muhammad answered. 'I have never asked for riches, yet I am blessed with the fortunes of love and wealth. And yet, my heart groans with the pangs of poverty. It seeks something it cannot name or fathom. Sometimes I think it is searching for a balm to heal the wounds of greed, malice and hatred. I have asked all the gods, my son, but their silence crushes me.' He was watching the women of rank, heavily veiled, pouring out of their grand houses.

'Carry your load of questions to the Cave of Mount Hira then, Muhammad,' Zaid declared simply. 'What do you do when you go there? I am curious.'

'Nothing!' Muhammad laughed again. 'Mostly I just sit, courting silence. At times, my heart is restless, constricting and expanding with a terrible need to pray and kneel, to surrender itself to something higher and divine. It communes with my thoughts and disturbs my peace and silence. It's wild and throbbing and it doesn't rest until it has scattered all its lamenting pebbles. "Why are the Meccans caught in this stagnant pool of depravity? Why are the men sunk knee-deep in a desert of blood feuds? Why are women treated like cheap trinkets to be bartered in the bazaars of lust and cruelty?" You wouldn't understand such laments, my son; and there are many more. The mutilated limbs of our society and the deep-rooted hatred of clan against clan!'

'No, Muhammad, I don't understand; but the little that I do breaks my heart,' Zaid confessed. 'Only a miracle could right all the wrongs in Mecca, I reckon. If not a miracle, then a prophet,' he muttered. 'No man, not even a prophet, can teach these Meccans to stop fighting, or to treat their women with kindness.'

'Do you think so, my son?' Muhammad's look was distant. 'Maybe we need Moses, or Jesus, or Abraham to come back. Somehow, their message got lost. Waraqa tells me they all brought the message of one God, and taught the virtues of love, and peace. They commanded mankind to conduct themselves with justice and to shun hatred.'

'To hear you talk like this, Muhammad, reminds me of a dream Baraka told me about. A dream your mother dreamed before you were born.' Zaid's beady eyes twinkled with excitement. 'Did your mother ever tell you what she dreamed?'

'No. Not that I recall,' Muhammad replied. 'What did Baraka tell you?'

'Baraka told me that one morning your mother woke up all frightened. She was still carrying you, and your father had left for Syria two months before. Baraka was frightened, too, when your mother told her the strange dream she had had late in the night. In her dream, she saw a light coming from her womb, lighting up all the hills and valleys around Mecca,' Zaid recounted, whipping his horse to flight.

'Be gentle with your horse, Zaid! And be grateful that he has carried you all the way from the racing arena to home.' Muhammad's gaze was reaching out to his home. 'As to that dream, it seems Baraka herself dreamt that, for she loves me more than anyone in the world.' He jumped down from Qaswa as she knelt.

'No, she didn't dream it, Muhammad; she remembered the dream as told by your mother!' Zaid shook his head, leaping down from his horse in a fit of impatience.

'Better curb your defiance and impatience, Zaid, before you have sons of your own; for they love to imitate their fathers,' Muhammad murmured over his shoulder. 'You have been married to Baraka for almost four years now.'

A flood of music and singing greeted Muhammad as he entered the parlour. Halima was playing a drum made out of camel skin, all dried and painted, and her daughter Shayma was complementing the rhythm by tapping it with a ladle in the middle. Abu Talib's daughters Umm Hani and Rahmani were trying their luck with the tambourines. Abu Bakr's daughter Asma was entertaining everyone with a song. Encouraged by Khalwa, Zainab was leading her sisters Khultum and Ruqayyah in clapping to the rhythm. Khadija was immersed in her own magical, enchanted world. She was lolling against a round pillow, her black hair braided with glossy pearls.

Zainab was the first to notice her father, flying to him in an explosion of joy, Khultum and Ruqayyah squealing behind her to claim their father's attention. Zainab was on her father's back with the swiftness of a sprite, winding her arms around his neck. Muhammad, laughing, gathered Khultum and Ruqayyah in each arm and hugged them. Khadija heaved herself up. The ladies abandoned their music and singing, greeting Muhammad with a profusion of compliments. Muhammad released his bundles of love on the carpet, while Zainab slid down from his back.

'Stop your compliments and return to your music and songs. They are pure and delightful and they warm my heart, while your praises are bloated with exaggeration and may inflame my ego.' Muhammad turned towards Khadija. 'Besides, grant me the honour of spending a little time with my wife and with Fatima before the guests arrive.'

Once inside the sanctuary of their bedroom, Khadija and Muhammad sought the comfort of the sofa. Fatima's white cot, where she was sleeping, was within their view. They were quiet, and Khadija was the first to break the silence.

'You must have won the race, dear Muhammad, since your eyes are sparkling like the stars, just as your cousins complimented you on,' Khadija murmured, her eyes radiant.

'No, beloved.' Muhammad kissed her hand. 'Qaswa was proud. And even beasts have to pay the price for pride, so she lost. Does she feel humbled, I wonder? If people can't shed their burden of pride, how can beasts?'

'Pride is not the worst of the Meccan people's burdens, dear Muhammad; especially not the men's. Their hearts carry the load of cruelty and injustice. And when they unburden that load, it falls mainly on women. The plight of divorced women is getting worse than the widows'. Have you not noticed, dear Muhammad?'

'I know the despair and the hopelessness of the women well, my Khadija, but don't you notice their pride?' Muhammad teased. 'All veiled, flaunting their rank and nobility?'

'Oh, Muhammad!' was Khadija's hushed exclamation. 'Only the wealthy ones! And they would feed their pride to the flames along with their veils, if they could stop their husbands from gathering more brides – if not concubines.'

'Yes, my scholar and political adviser!' Muhammad smiled. 'Polygamy! Divorce without rhyme or reason, marking the women with despair and destitution! The cruelty of men, burying their daughters alive! Tragedies vast and boundless! Countless fools, and enormous sand-dunes of ignorance!' He closed his eyes. 'Yes, beloved; my prime concern is to improve the lot of women, but the voice of one man cannot reach a pack of fools. The most heated arguments to find audience these days have nothing to do with poverty, injustice or oppression, but with the power of gods. Whose god is more powerful than the others in granting riches, if not safety from the guile of the cut-throats and marauders? Who could guide such men to virtue and honour? Would they heed – anyone?' He opened his eyes.

'They will! Some day. Someone,' Khadija prophesied. 'And to think, dear Muhammad, men have followed in the footsteps of a woman for centuries. They still do, don't they, not even thinking in the frenzy of their pilgrimage? Running seven times back and forth between As-Safa and Al-Marwah, just the way Abraham's wife Hagar did when she searched for water to quench her thirst and the thirst of her son.'

'How do you know, my Khadija? Who taught you all these fables?' Muhammad's gaze was a deep, shimmering ocean of adoration.

'They are not fables, dear Muhammad, but truths from the Holy Scriptures. Waraqa tells me all about Jesus and Mary and about many things from his holy book. He visits me often, but how would you know? You're busy listening to the silence of your heart and soul inside the Cave of Mount Hira,' Khadija teased.

'Silent, my soul mocks me with its lips sealed!' was Muhammad's mock lament. 'Forgive me, beloved, for leaving you alone for days. I don't know what compels me to seek solitude. I do repent, but what's the use when I keep going back? Take solace, though, that the pangs of separation which I suffer in my seclusion are much more terrible than the pain and sweetness of solitude.'

'I don't want you to suffer, dear Muhammad,' Khadija appealed. 'You long for solitude and that's your need. It should bring you joy, not torture. I respect and understand your need. You are searching for answers, and you will find them. You are sensitive to the needs of the poor and the oppressed; you long to free the Meccans from the shackles of their ignorance and corruption. Please don't feel guilty on my account. Why suffer needlessly when you are with me always, even when you are not here? You must never feel that way, and if you do, I will make you stay at home.'

'You don't have to make me, beloved; I am your slave.' Muhammad was moved and humbled. 'You only have to command and I will obey.'

'How fortunate I am, dear Muhammad!' Khadija sighed blissfully. 'An old widow like me blessed with a handsome, loving husband! My heart melts with love and gratitude when I think how other men have several wives, and you don't even think about marrying anyone else. Loving me, nay, even worshipping me as if you have married a virgin, young and beautiful.'

'The virginity of your pure soul and of your beautiful heart, my Khadija. Which thankfully are concealed from the sight of other men.' Muhammad's look was dreamy. 'The light of love in your eyes, and your beautiful, adorable face. How could I ever think of anyone else when you are the soul of my soul? The bread of my existence? The breath of my life? Without you I would be lost. More than that, I'd be forsaken by all the gods of the Kaaba, who tempt me inside the sanctuary of Mount Hira, as if challenging me to explore the secrets of their power and presence? I am the fortunate one to have a soulmate endowed with the sweetness of wisdom. The greatness of the love in your heart nurtures my need in its own throes of poverty and bewilderment.'

'The gold of your modesty and humility is priceless, dear Muhammad. Riches beyond reckoning!' Khadija smiled wistfully. 'The wealth of purity and freshness in you and around you: do others see it as I do? The sweetest scent wafts from you, even though you don't wear perfumes, I know too well. Where does it come from?'

'This perfume comes from being grateful to you, beloved,' Muhammad murmured, distracted by the songs from downstairs, soaring up clear and fresh.

'So, he has shifted from his seat of love to the cushion of gratefulness!' Khadija smothered her laughter so as not to disturb her daughter.

'That seat of love is a mirror bright inside my heart, my poet-scholar, and you are reflected in there as my beloved all!' Muhammad pressed her close. 'You are the perfume in there; the scent of your presence is more sweet than the one emitted from my love and gratitude.' He drifted away towards the cot.

'Such sweetness takes my breath away,' Khadija confessed. 'We should go down, Muhammad. The guests will be arriving soon.'

'All that burden of entertaining on your sweet shoulders, too.' Muhammad stood watching Fatima. 'How good you are to me, my Khadija! My love for you feels like a dewdrop, small and insignificant in the ocean of your great love for me.'

'If you see such an ocean of love and goodness in me, dear Muhammad, then be assured that I have gathered it all from you, and you don't even know it.' Khadija rose to her feet gracefully. 'You don't know the size of your soul either, as it hungers for spiritual food. No rich feasts, not even my love, could satisfy its hunger; only a feast of solitude and contemplation, with just one guest: your own noble wisdom.'

'What little wisdom I have, my Khadija, is commanding me to drown myself in a delicious pool of activity.' Muhammad grasped her hands in his with warm tenderness. 'The body needs nourishment as well as the soul. There is a time for contemplation over the wonder and mystery of creation, and a time for joy and feasting. And now is the time to welcome our guests with all the joy in our hearts.' He laughed.

The rectangular hall in Khadija and Muhammad's home had come alive with laughter as the guests sat talking and feasting. All four of Muhammad's uncles were immersed in argument, Hamza amongst them loud and fiery-eyed, his wife Salma almost invisible in the background. Abu Jahl stood towering over them, claiming their attention with a wild gesture. His wife Umm Hakim joined him, accompanied by her brother Khalid ibn Walid. Abu Sofyan and Hind were seated opposite Abu Bakr and his wife Umm Ruman, their sons Abdullah, Abal Kabah, and their daughter Asma included in the little circle, which gained another member as Abu Bakr's cousin Talha ibn Ubaidullah stumbled into their group. Muhammad's aunts Atika, Safiyah and Umaymah had their own separate niche, graced by the presence of Khadija's family, the most prominent amongst them Hala, Hakim, Nizam, Nawfal, Waraqa and Khusaima. Abu Talib was seeking his wife Fatima, and stumbled upon his daughter Umm Hani and her husband Hudayfah. He stood talking with them, but his gaze was straying towards the merchants, Akram, Huweidib and Ummayad ibn Khalaf.

'Why has the music stopped? Why aren't the girls singing, Muhammad? Tell me, since you're the host.' Umar ibn Khattab swayed.

'Music is your inner voice of silence, Umar. Don't you hear it?' Muhammad teased, with his usual flair for humour and profundity.

'Mysteries of the soul which I don't understand, Muhammad. Are you alluding to those?' Umar ibn Khattab stroked his curly beard. 'I want to hear music; the clapping of hands and the warbling of voices. Silence doesn't offer me the wine of ecstasy.' He glowered at his handmaid Lubainah, who happened to cross his path.

'Silence offers more than that, Umar! How would you know if you have not experienced its delights?' Muhammad's eyes lit up with the stars of spirituality.

'And how do you know, Muhammad?' Umar ibn Khattab challenged, gazing disdainfully at Yasir and his wife Sumayyah, who couldn't boast of riches or status.

'I have tasted the wine of knowledge from the lips of the sages and the mystics who have journeyed far on the path of love to seek union with al-Llah. And I myself have ventured on this road, in silence,' Muhammad expounded wistfully.

'Those sages and mystics would be better off going straight to Hubal if they have to reach somewhere,' Umar ibn Khattab declared in drunken mirth.

'There's no road, nowhere to go, until the fire of love has consumed the seeker of truth,' Muhammad responded profoundly.

'You shouldn't be talking to Muhammad when you are drunk, Umar! Why can't you follow his example of good manners?' Baraka waved a plump fist.

'Muhammad doesn't drink because he doesn't like the taste.' Umar ibn Khattab couldn't control the volume of his drunken mirth.

'No, that's not the reason!' Baraka stood undaunted. 'He doesn't drink because he is good and virtuous. Of noble birth, and pure of heart! Before he was born his mother heard a voice in her dream: "You carry in your womb the lord of this nation. I place him under the protection of the One, safe from the evil of everyone who envies him, and give him the name 'Highly Praised.'" That's why he is named Muhammad!'

'Are you sure you yourself didn't dream that, Baraka?' Muhammad got to his feet, laughing. 'Zaid told me something similar to this—'

'Neither Zaid nor Baraka, and certainly not you, know that your mother confided all her dreams to your grandfather,' Abu Talib interrupted. 'I was there when you were born, and your grandfather carried you in his arms all the way to the Kaaba. He made seven rounds around the Holy Shrine, then held you up proudly for all to see, announcing that he had named his grandson Muhammad Mustafa. Upon hearing this, the crowds broke into joyous applause, singing and clapping.'

'This sounds like a dream; a happy dream,' Muhammad murmured.

'Life's dream, through which we journey, and then wake up suddenly to discover that we are at its end, and have not really lived,' Waraqa muttered, nursing his legs with his bony hands.

'Waraqa!' Muhammad exclaimed. 'I haven't seen you since the day of my marriage. But the memory of that first meeting is still vivid in my mind.'

'We have met twice, not once, Muhammad!' Waraqa stroked his beard. 'The first meeting, though, you wouldn't remember – and I couldn't forget. This old head still holds all the shards of memories. You were only five. Your nurse Halima was bringing you back to your mother, but somehow you managed to get away and wandered into my home. I was greatly pleased by your manners, and impressed by the wealth of your vocabulary. In that short time we struck a chord of friendship; at least, I thought so. Had Halima not come looking for you, I would have kept you all to myself.'

'You would have done a great service to me, indeed, Waraqa!' Abu Talib could not help but exclaim. 'In my old age, I would be at ease if he were kept away from all the poets and politicians of Mecca, who follow him at his heels, hounding him with the daggers of their inquisition as to how he proposes to cure the ills of our society.'

'The ills of our society can only be healed by the hands of a prophet, as prophesied by Jesus,' Waraqa mumbled. 'And I might not live to see such a prophet.'

'What did your Lord Jesus say, Waraqa?' Muhammad asked.

'He told many parables of love, peace and unity, Muhammad. He also told his disciples that a prophet would come to them after he is gone.' Waraqa's voice shook with fervour and devotion. 'When his disciples asked him about his own death, he said, "Nevertheless I tell you the truth; it is expedient for you that I go away; for if I do not go, the Comforter will not come unto you, but if I depart, I will send him unto you."'

'Is that written in your holy book?' Muhammad asked. 'I have this longing for knowledge, to learn everything. Would you share your knowledge with me?'

'I would; but you'd better hurry, Muhammad, for I don't have long to live.' A subtle prophecy trickled from Waraqa's lips.

'You will live long, Waraqa! Yes, you will,' Muhammad breathed fervently.

'My legs are killing me! I must go home and rest.' Waraqa dallied, noticing the approach of Abu Jahl and Abu Sofyan. 'But before I go, let me recite to you another parable about the Comforter. "But the Comforter, which is the Holy Ghost, whom the Father will send in my name, he shall teach you all things."'

'I will assist you, Waraqa.' Nawfal offered him his arm.

'Yes.' Waraqa linked his arm into Nawfal's gratefully, his lips spilling another parable. 'Howbeit, when he, the Spirit of Truth, is come, he will guide you into all truth.'

Muhammad stood there dreamily, watching Waraqa disappear behind the doors.

'Isn't Waraqa a Christian? Apparently he knows everything, and yet I know more about all his prophets and the promise of a new prophet!' Abu Sofyan chuckled. 'Abraham, Ishmael, Moses, Jesus, and a whole horde of them! All parading before our eyes the idea of one God, whom we can't see. How can one God rule over all the unruly people on earth, when all the gods of the Kaaba fail to discipline us, and they're only guiding a few of us?'

'The God of the Kaaba has always been One since the time of Adam. We have forgotten Him. Isn't al-Llah His name?' Muhammad's voice sounded distant.

'Al-Llah died. Hubal is living! And so are all the gods and goddesses whom we can see and worship,' Abu Jahl declared with a sudden vehemence.

'If you are talking about gods, I must retire. For sleep is my goddess and I need her the most, right away.' Khalid ibn Walid staggered away, waving farewell.

'Which gods do you worship, Abu Bakr?' Abu Jahl tossed a challenge.

'Not sure.' Abu Bakr shook his eagle-like head. 'The choices are great and the options fathomless, since we Meccans have the tendency to worship even a sand-hill, if it can serve our needs and our greed for fame and riches.' He stole a glance at his sister Quraybah and his father, Quhafah.

'Let us go to the Kaaba,' Talha ibn Ubaidullah proposed. 'We can decide which god to worship. Each of us can offer a silent prayer to his own patron god, and if those prayers are answered we will have our own personal gods or goddesses.'

'If our wives don't kill us in our sleep before that…' Abu Sofyan chuckled again.

'You'll have to exclude me from this wild venture. I have a houseful of guests,' Muhammad requested, 'and Khadija has worked all day. She won't allow me this night excursion.'

'The guests are leaving, Muhammad.' Abu Jahl indicated the half-empty hall. 'The Princess is kind and generous, the best of wives, everyone knows. Don't expect me to believe that she would deny you a night excursion when she lets you stay at Mount Hira for days and nights.'

'And Mount Hira is not far from the Kaaba,' Muhammad murmured wistfully. 'Worth the temptation!' His gaze reached swiftly out to his wife.

Khadija was the centre of attention amongst her family and friends; everyone was focused on her since she was practising her art of story-telling. Quillah was the most devoted of her audience; seated beside her were Hind and her little daughter Umm Habiba. Muhammad's aunts Atika, Safiyah and Umaymah were there too, as well as Abu Bakr's wife Umm Ruman and his daughter Asma. The wife of Abu Jahl, Umm Hakim, sat whispering to Umar ibn Khattab's wife Zainab, whose little daughter Hafsa was cradled in her lap. Muhammad, unwilling to disrupt, lingered close, not noticing that his uncle Abu

Lahab had stolen up behind him. His wife, Umm Jemil, had followed.

'Don't you think it a lucky coincidence, Muhammad, that my two sons are the same age as Khultum and Ruqayyah? We should seal bonds of marriage between them. What do you say?' Abu Lahab stood beaming.

'Zainab is the eldest, Uncle. We have to think about her marriage first.' Muhammad's voice was low. 'And my daughters have to agree first; before they are married, when they are of age.'

'What in the name of absurdity? No one has ever heard of such a thing. Girls have no say in this matter. They should marry whoever their parents choose!' was Abu Lahab's astonished response, his face flustered.

'If I live to see them married, they will be asked,' Muhammad responded.

'There is no one in the world who could intimidate Muhammad, Abu Lahab, so leave your ranting for your family,' Abu Talib intervened. 'In fact, he wanted to marry Umm Hani before I discovered she was already betrothed to Hudayfah.'

Khadija's eyes turned to Muhammad, her story forgotten. Umm Hani's cheeks were flushed. Her husband Hudayfah materialised from behind her. Asma and Hala, Khadija's sister, were giggling. Umm Habiba's laughter was loud, and it mingled with a chuckle from Hala's youngest son, Abul As. Abu Lahab's wife Umm Jemil was laughing, joined by her younger sister, Maymuna.

'Shame on you, Abu Talib!' was Atika's mild reproof, snatched out of her choking mirth, which dwindled at the approach of her son, Zuhayar ibn Amr.

'We would never have benefited from Khadija's generosity if Muhammad was married to Umm Hani.' Safiyah was watching her son, Zubayr ibn Awwam.

'Truth is, I consider Umm Hani the dearest of friends.' Muhammad was seeking Khadija's sympathy. 'Everyone knows you to be generous, my princess, and I am no exception. So may I be so bold as to ask your permission to go to the Kaaba? This is to be a secret mission, and this time our uncle Abu Talib won't know the secrets in our hearts.'

'Of course, Muhammad, as long as you disclose your secrets to me when you return this time!' Khadija teased, smiling adorably.

'I am coming with you, Muhammad,' Abu Talib challenged. He looked over, seeking Khadija's approval. 'Otherwise he might spend the night inside the Cave at Mount Hira.'

'At least I will know where to find him if he is late coming home in the morning,' Khadija chanted happily.

'I can't be left behind!' called Zaid, cantering after the men, who were already leaving. The Arabian Desert's night air was making all the men light-hearted. Riding close to Muhammad were Ikrimah, the son of Abu Jahl, and Zayd ibn Amr, the uncle of Umar ibn Khattab. Behind them rode the two poets, Mistal, and Imra al-Qais. Suhail ibn Amr and his son Abu Jandal were cantering ahead. Muhammad was so deeply immersed in his own world of contemplations that he didn't even notice the swift emergence of Abdallah ibn Masud from behind him.

'You are honest and truthful, Muhammad, but the great honour which you have gained during these past few years comes from marrying the richest widow in Mecca. All the wealth of the Princess now belongs to you, whether you want it or not,' Abdallah ibn Masud commented gleefully.

'Nothing belongs to us; everything belongs to God,' Muhammad murmured in response. 'And if honour seems to be my fortune, it might be the greatest gift my spiritual poverty could ever earn.'

'The gods are many, but you don't believe in any? No great wonder then that you claim the gift of spiritual poverty,' was Abdallah ibn Masud's puzzled soliloquy.

'I am still seeking the One,' Muhammad murmured again.

'Where?' Abdallah ibn Masud was watching Muhammad's handsome profile.

'Inside the walls of the Kaaba, perhaps?' Muhammad smiled whimsically. 'But I feel the power of a presence everywhere, not contained in anything, yet a part of everything, subtle and pervading. I can feel it even now, inside the very breath of this cool air. Don't you feel it? I have this feeling that if I could silence my thoughts long enough I might even hear it.'

'Just your wild imagination, Muhammad! All I see are the glittering sands, and I feel nothing but exhilaration,' Abdallah ibn Masud chanted. 'The Kaaba is probably the place where one can feel the power of some presence, where all the gods live, and where all the merchants come to fill our coffers with gold and riches. For me, it is enough that all those gods at the Kaaba are there to make us wealthy.'

'To be content with little is riches beyond imagination; more than the mounds of wealth in one's possession, when you are craving for more and more,' Muhammad commented.

'If we wealthy merchants succumbed to such ideas, Muhammad, we would grow poor in no time and become the victims of the warring clans, who would cut our throats without mercy if we didn't die of hunger first!' Abdallah ibn Masud breathed disdain.

'If we could cultivate love in our hearts to love one other, there would be no warring clans left to threaten peace in Arabia. A fountain of love in Arabian sands to quench the thirsts of all greed.' Muhammad was gazing at the bright stars.

'I can sense danger! Robbers and plunderers are not too far away; we might as well turn back,' Utbah ibn Rabia flung out in jest, urging his son Hudayfah not to lag behind.

'Robbed of our senses, there is nothing left to plunder,' Muhammad laughed.

'You told me once, Muhammad, that there is gold buried under these sands. Robbers have a nose for such treasures, and they will come pillaging, won't they?' Utbah ibn Rabia was riding on the currents of hilarity.

'Blinded by greed, they won't be able to see anything, but sandhills!' Muhammad retorted. 'The streets of Mecca would reveal their treasures of gold for all to see, if we could nurture love in our hearts to quench the fires of cruelty.' His eyes were shining. 'You are wise, Utbah; everyone says it, and I believe them, since you know so much about gods, and about the worth of land which appears barren and inhospitable.'

'Gods of stones, and streets paved with gold! Wouldn't that be a glorious dream?' Utbah ibn Rabia sang ecstatically. 'Would you like to hear a real story about an amazing god, Muhammad?' He could see the blue granite of the Kaaba's walls now.

'If you can refrain from mocking the gods you love to worship?' Muhammad's eyes were focused on the luminous moon.

'I mock not gods, but men who have no faith in their gods!' Utbah ibn Rabia declared. 'This story is about one poor man who doesn't even know the difference between mockery and reverence. I watched this man closely one afternoon. He had no idol of his own to worship, so he decided to carve a face on a date. He seemed happy and satisfied after he had done that, praying to his own personal deity and smiling. But when the sun got hot and he felt hungry, he ate his own god! I saw him get up, looking dazed, like he was searching for something else to carve.

'His devotion is worthy of praise!' Muhammad's heart was thundering. 'Worthy of praise, since he is searching for the face of God behind the form of an idol!'

Muhammad dismounted thoughtfully, his friends ahead of him already on their feet, cavorting around the statues of golden gazelles. Muhammad wandered away, his heart constricting with pain for the nearness of some memory dear and nameless. His soul was on fire, surging through the nine gates and eight circuits of the Kaaba. He was inside the sanctuary, suspended in its centre from the wooden beams balanced on the three pillars. His senses were enveloped in darkness. A sliver of light was emanating from some invisible source. The light cut through the darkness, exploding forth into an ocean of such dazzling brightness that Muhammad's very soul was illuminated. He wanted to pray, but no prayers came to his rescue. The ocean of light was swallowed by darkness once again, and he staggered out of the sanctuary, dazed and empty, almost colliding with Umar ibn Khattab.

'Look, Muhammad; my uncle Zayd ibn Amr is kissing the Black Stone!' Umar ibn Khattab stepped back, not noticing Muhammad's dazed expression.

'You are not talking about my son, Zaid?' Muhammad could barely speak.

'O Quraysh, by him in whose hand is the soul of Zayd, not one of you follows the religion of Abraham, but me,' Zayd ibn Amr was lamenting. 'O God, if I knew how you wish to be worshipped, I would so worship you, but I do not know.'

'Come, Muhammad, my uncle has gone mad, but a good night's rest will restore him to his senses.' Umar ibn Khattab sought Muhammad's attention.

'I'd say he's wise.' Muhammad's eyes were brilliant as the stars, and his face livid as the moon. 'A seeker after *truth*! The most loved by al-Llah!'

'Come, Muhammad, everyone is leaving.' Abu Talib came upon the scene before Umar ibn Khattab could respond. 'Did you pray?'

'No, Uncle, I couldn't,' Muhammad confessed, his voice low and distant. 'Please, I want to stay. You leave with the others. I want to be alone, and pray.'

'I won't leave without you, Muhammad. You might decide to spend the night in the Cave of Mount Hira,' Abu Talib persisted. 'I must take you back to Khadija.'

'I have no intention of going to Mount Hira, Uncle, be assured.' Muhammad's eyes were bright. 'Please, Uncle, I want to stay here, just a little longer. I will join you on your way home. If I don't, then you may come after me.' He noticed Zaid, who had stolen up behind Abu Talib.

'I will stay with Muhammad,' Zaid declared with his usual burst of energy.

'No, you won't, Zaid.' Muhammad's very gaze was commanding.

'Come, Zaid, Muhammad wants to be alone,' Abu Talib said.

'Go, my son,' Muhammad appealed, as Zaid stayed still.

'I won't, Muhammad.' Only Zaid's lips moved.

'Why not?' Muhammad's eyes flashed disbelief and astonishment.

'Because your eyes are sparkling like the stars, and your face is brighter than the moon,' was Zaid's spellbound response. 'I am afraid, Muhammad.'

'You will have cause to fear, Zaid, if you do not obey,' Muhammad commanded him. 'The poetry in your soul will keep you company while you look after the horses. I will be there soon. Now, go.'

Zaid obeyed, plodding back under a spell of fever and exaltation. His heart thundered as it had never thundered before. Muhammad's heart, in contrast, was blissful in its silence. One lone murmur of longing trembled on the lips of his soul, singing some sweet, inexpressible song.

Peace and silence were Muhammad's companions as he sank down to his knees in a white puddle, facing the Black Stone. Muhammad's eyes were closing. A star-dance of memories unveiled an astonishing scene from the vaults of his youth. He was only twelve, on a trading trip with his uncle Abu Talib. They were in the town of Bostra. A young monk was telling his uncle that his nephew Muhammad would be the chief of the messengers. His uncle was befuddled, wanting to know what the monk meant. The monk was weeping and laughing, his hands raised in supplication towards the mountains. 'Did you not see that the stones and the trees lay prostrate before Muhammad when he rode down those slopes?'

The monk and his uncle vanished behind a sheet of rain, and music rippled forth on the harp of the wind. The Black Stone hosted a choir of angels in its diamond-soul, and their voices floated above the tides of prophets. Muhammad was cradled inside the ripples of dazzling light, yet his heart was murmuring that he himself was the light, and he himself was the cradle. He was entirely consumed, and yet something inside him was holding on to a grain of nothingness. It was suffused with the light of a memory. Memory was love, and love was God. Love had reduced him to nothingness. But even in his nothingness he was coming alive, commanded by the light of love. Commanded to seek the altar of the Beloved on the wings of love! A Beloved who would grant the gift of unity and love to all!

Zaid was urging Muhammad to wake up, but Muhammad was aware only of the sweet music emanating from the great soul of the world. *Love, Love, Love!*

His eyes were conveying the same song of love as he opened them. Their radiance almost blinded Zaid, who fell into a heap at his feet, more awed than stunned.

Chapter 4

The Music of the Divine Call
Year 610 AD

Khadija, dressed in pale silks, lay resting on a sofa in her spacious parlour. She had been floating in the mists of her own thoughts since morning, her moods shifting from a sense of bliss to one of euphoria. Her loving disposition sensed something vast that she could neither name, nor fathom. This nameless feeling was with her even now; she could feel her soul expanding, as if it was embarking on a journey to gather the earth and the heavens in one wild embrace.

She opened her eyes, more to touch the fabric of reality than to discover if her soul had really left her body for otherworldly realms. Through the rectangular window she could see Ali and Fatima playing in the courtyard. An abrupt pang of love and loneliness tore at her heart and she closed her eyes. Immediately, peace and presence were her companions. She imagined that Muhammad was with her, snuffing out the flame of her loneliness. He had gone to Mount Hira three days ago, and had not returned. She could picture him sitting there alone, seeking guidance from a curtain of darkness.

A different curtain of darkness tore open in Khadija's thoughts, unveiling the tides of the past five years. Three years ago, a son had been born to her, and Muhammad had named him Abdullah, but he had died in infancy. The scene of Zainab's wedding rose, fresh in her memory. The memory was only six months old; sweet Zainab had married Abul As, the son of Khadija's sister, Hala. Ruqayyah was engaged to Utbah, the son of Abu Lahab, and Khultum to Utbah's younger brother, Utabaibah. Halima had died recently and for days Muhammad had been inconsolable.

Suddenly all the memories in Khadija's head were swept asunder by a great tide of dreams. Muhammad was with her, his features waxy and luminescent. She was gazing into the eye of her dream, not even knowing that what she was dreaming was the naked vision most true, embracing Muhammad with all its bounty of love and grace.

Muhammad, indeed, was sitting inside the Cave of Mount Hira, oblivious to his body and his surroundings. The curtain of darkness that enveloped him within and without, which he had seen and touched for the past three days, while praying and meditating, was torn open all of a sudden. It was devoured by a mountain of light, but he himself was not yet aware of the white blaze enveloping the very core of his oblivion. His mind, body and soul had dissolved into such a state of absolute surrender that there was nothing left in him, only the ether of awareness. He was leaning against the rough wall of the cave, his feet tucked under him, his turban abandoned beside him like a white seashell. His pale, gaunt features reflected the glow of dawn. The dark stubble on his chin and cheeks lent him a boyish look, as if he was only a youth of twenty, not a man of forty. An abrupt shudder shook his strong frame.

Muhammad was torn out of the void of his peace and silence. His eyes shot open and were almost blinded by the blaze of light, brilliant and piercing. Stunned, if not dazzled, his heart was crushed under the weight of a presence so awesome and seething that he could neither breathe nor scream. His soul was on fire, lit by an agony of longing and fluttering on the wings of joy, painful and devastating. A voice from the pure radiant mists called out to him, repeating his name twice and scorching his senses with a brand made of light and terror. The pure, naked blades of light upon light were fashioning a beautiful form, robed in light, both earthly and divine. The Man of Light was holding a scroll in his hands, its letters shimmering with gold and sunshine. His eyes were brighter than the stars as he held Muhammad captive in his gaze, unrolling the scroll before him, his very fingers brilliant like bolts of lightning.

'Read, O Muhammad!' the Man of Light commanded.

'I cannot read.' Muhammad's heart was thundering.

'Read, O Muhammad.' The Man of Light repeated his command, floating closer and holding Muhammad in a wonderful embrace.

'I can't read.' Muhammad's breath was sucked into the furnace of terror.

'Read, O Muhammad!' Another lightning-bolt of a command escaped the lips of the Man of Light. His embrace was fiercer than before, on the verge of strangling him.

'What should I read?' A desperate plea tore out from the shuddering depths in Muhammad's soul.

The Man of Light released Muhammad, a beatific smile curling upon his lips of light.

Read in the name of thy Lord who creates –
Creates man from a clot.
Read and thy Lord is most generous,
Who taught by the pen,
Taught man what he knew not. (96:1–5)

Muhammad recited under a dazed spell of awe.

'O Muhammad, truly thou art the Messenger of Allah – the one and the only God of the universe – and I am His angel Gabriel,' the Man of Light sang, dissolving into light and leaving behind chill and darkness.

Muhammad stumbled to his feet in the dark, his terror replaced by shock and bewilderment. He straggled out of the cave as if stung by the fires of love sublime and agony supreme. The tongues of the flaming words recited by Gabriel were a living reality inside him, inscribed upon the scroll of his heart with a pen of light. His heart was a furnace of pain and exaltation as he emerged into the white glare of the early morning. The first streaks of dawn, flashing pure gold and crimson, poured awe and fear into his heart. He stood there in perfect immobility, etched alive on the golden mountain, his gaze transfixed on the scene in his memory, where Gabriel stood haloed by light. Muhammad tried to avoid the vision, but no matter which direction he turned his gaze in, there was Gabriel, radiant and smiling.

'O Muhammad, truly thou art the Messenger of Allah, and I am His angel Gabriel.' Gabriel held Muhammad captive in his gaze.

A sudden eruption of energy, much more volcanic than the clouds of disbelief in his eyes, goaded Muhammad to flee, and he was running down the jagged cliffs as if his feet felt no hurdles but the smooth sands of the desert. Something inside him bubbled and shattered, like a fountain of ice and fire. His soul was kindled by some supreme torment, lofty and ineffable, teasing its own harp of love, and intoxicated by the sound of divine music. So utterly consumed was he by his reveries that the three-mile stretch from Mount Hira to his home melted away like a cloud. The tall, grey houses were left behind, and his feet carried him towards the high-arched entrance of his own home under a spell of fever and exhilaration.

Muhammad found himself in the parlour, not even realising that his eyes, kindled by the light of joy and agony, were pleading with Khadija for solace and comfort. Khadija was lying on the sofa where she had fallen asleep the night before, but she was awake now, her expression dreamy and searching. Muhammad was seized by a sudden fit of trembling so violent that his knees buckled under him. He barely made it to the sofa, where he threw his head into the lap of his beloved Khadija.

'Cover me, beloved, cover me!' Muhammad pleaded feverishly, his body racked with sobs, tears streaming from his eyes.

'Muhammad!' Khadija cried, stroking his hair and murmuring endearments.

She started out of her shock, covered him with a blanket, and urged him to rest. Seated at the edge of the sofa, she massaged his legs, soothing him with tender words till his trembling subsided and his body felt warm and relaxed. She sat beside him patiently, asking no questions, just lending him the comfort of her presence and understanding. The warmth of her love and patience poured strength into Muhammad's heart, and he began to speak, sharing with her the awesome, astonishing experience which had branded his soul with a fire of agony and exaltation.

'Allah, as stressed by Gabriel, is the God of the Kaaba and of all peoples, dear Muhammad, and has been since time immemorial,' Khadija consoled. 'So rejoice and be of good cheer. He in whose hands stands my life is my witness that you will be the Messenger of His people. Have you not been loving to your kinsfolk; kind to your neighbour; charitable to the poor? You have always been hospitable to strangers, faithful to your word, and a defender of truth.'

'But I am afraid, my Khadija,' Muhammad lamented. 'I am not sure of this vision in the cave. Was it real, or merely an hallucination? Have I gone mad like one of those diviners at the Kaaba? Have I lost my mind? Why would Allah choose me, a lowly orphan, to be His Messenger? Wouldn't it be presumptuous of me to believe that Allah has really chosen me as His Messenger? If I did, would I not become an instrument of grief to my own self and to you, my beloved?'

'How could it be possible, dear Muhammad, that one possessed of so many virtues should ever come to grief?' Khadija asked. 'You are always honest and truthful, kind and generous; you help orphans and widows wherever you find them. No wonder Allah is gracious to you. You are the one seeking answers for all the ills in Mecca, and you will be the one to find them, by the grace of Allah, I am sure.'

'This is your love speaking, my Khadija, not your reason,' Muhammad breathed tenderly, with a soothing look. 'Now tell me honestly, have I gone mad?'

'No, my dear Muhammad, no!' Khadija's eyes were brimming with love. 'Allah guides me too, if I may say so. I beheld a glimpse of your vision in my dream. Probably at the same time as Gabriel was visiting you,' she confessed. 'My cousin Waraqa knows much about visions like these. He tells me that Allah is the God of the Hebrews and of the Christians. He reads to me from his Holy Scriptures, and he sometimes quotes a passage where the promise of a new messenger is mentioned. A messenger to come. And no doubt is left in my mind, that you will be the one!'

'This cannot be, my Khadija; I am not worthy of such a great task,' Muhammad murmured, under a spell of despair and sadness.

'You are tired, dear Muhammad.' Khadija pressed his brow. 'You need a few hours of rest, and while you do that, I will go and talk to Waraqa. I will bring him back with me so that you can talk to him concerning your vision. But right now, you stay comfortable in the bedroom,' she urged, taking his hands to assist him to his feet. 'I will tell Khalwa to keep the girls quiet, especially Fatima.'

'Fatima is allowed to disturb me any time of the day or night, if she wants.' Muhammad smiled, feeling like a child, safe and comforted.

Khadija, after making sure that Muhammad had drifted into the comfort of sleep, dressed hurriedly to visit Waraqa. She reached him quickly. Her urgency was thwarted though; she found him sound asleep. But she managed to wake him, and told him about Muhammad's vision and revelation. Waraqa listened intently, convinced that Muhammad, with the grace of his vision, was the new Messenger as promised by God in the Torah and the Bible. Both Waraqa and Khadija were so deeply immersed in their spiritual world that they did not notice the march of time towards midday.

Khadija returned home all flustered. Leaving Waraqa in the care of Zaid and Baraka, she hastened upstairs to see if Muhammad was still sleeping. She watched Muhammad as he lay in slumber, his blanket tossed to one side, but his black mantle still wrapped around his shoulders. She stood, willing her heart to cease its thundering, as the violence of it was invading her ears; but then her senses awakened to other sounds. Muhammad groaned in his sleep, his forehead bathed in beads of sweat. Automatically, she drifted towards the bed, her hands reaching out to wipe the sweat off his brow. Barely had she touched his forehead, when Muhammad's eyes shot open, though he didn't seem to see her. Muhammad recited,

> *O thou enwrapped in thy mantle! Arise and warn, and magnify thy Lord! Purify thy raiment and depart from all uncleanliness.* (74:1–5)

'Muhammad!' Khadija held him close to her thundering bosom.

'I have gone mad, my Khadija. I am insane. Help me, help me!' Muhammad was sobbing, like a child into the arms of his mother.

'You are not insane, dear Muhammad, but the Chosen One of Allah!' Khadija propped a pillow behind his back. 'Do you remember what you just recited?'

'How can I forget? It is engraved on the tablet of my heart! My heart, bleeding with shame for being favoured by the grace of Allah!' Muhammad murmured.

'Your second revelation, Muhammad! I believe in the message from Allah, and I believe in you.' Khadija kissed his forehead, tears welling in her eyes.

'Beloved! My heart is singing that you will be the Mother of all Believers.' Muhammad folded her into his arms in an eager embrace. 'You are so good to me. I don't deserve your love. It is the treasure of your love that gives me the gift of sanity, and drives away the doubt that I am mad. Strange that you could believe in me without a doubt, yet I myself doubt my own sanity.'

'Allah has blessed you – and me! And to doubt His Grace would be faithlessness on our part,' Khadija sang happily. 'It's time to wash up. Khalwa will lay out clean clothes for you.' She got to her feet laughingly. 'Waraqa is waiting downstairs.'

'I thought I had found my beloved, and now I truly have! Allah! Won't you be jealous, my Khadija?' Muhammad teased with a sudden burst of joy.

'We will have the same Beloved then, won't we, dear Muhammad? And you will be the one getting jealous!' Khadija fled, laughter trilling over her shoulders.

The afternoon sun flooding the parlour was gilding the furniture in its own golden colour as Waraqa and Khadija sat talking, or rather whispering. With the help of Zaid and Baraka, a great feast was laid out, along with a jug of milk, Muhammad's favourite drink for lunch. The aroma of bread and mutton wafted from the steaming platters, but neither Waraqa nor Khadija seemed aware of the culinary delights.

Upstairs, Muhammad had bathed. His heart was light and purged of all its doubts and torments. Reflected in his mind was the lamp of love, throbbing with the radiance of truth and wisdom through which his thoughts could catch only a glimpse of the mission and message yet to come. In a flash, he was foundering deep in the baptismal waters of knowledge, tasting the sweetness of Divine Names and Divine Revelations.

Everything was a part of him, yet he was not a part of anything. What was revealed to him was also hidden from him, but he could see everything through the eye of a needle dipped into the honeycomb of compassion and understanding.

'Allah! My All! My Most Gracious! My Ever and Forever! Beloved!' Muhammad aimed straight for the staircase leading down to the parlour.

'What do I hear, Muhammad? You are blessed, you are blessed! Revelations from Allah? Allah has chosen you!' Waraqa lumbered to his feet, embracing Muhammad. 'I swear by Him in whose hands Waraqa's life is, Allah has chosen you to be the Prophet of His people.' He kissed Muhammad's cheeks. 'They will call you a liar, they will persecute you, they will banish you, they will fight against you. Oh, that I could live to see those days; I would surely protect and defend you.'

'Now, Waraqa! You will live to see our grandchildren.' Muhammad snatched Waraqa's hands into his own. 'I am not even sure if I am the one, as you say.'

'The great Confidant of Allah has come to you, Muhammad.' Waraqa's lips were trembling, as if fearing a hurricane of prophetic spells.

'Come, Waraqa, let's eat,' Khadija half pleaded, half requested. 'I have drained your energy with all that talk, and I woke you up early too.'

Waraqa yielded himself to the assistance of Khadija and Muhammad, as they made him comfortable on the carpet, piling cushions behind his back. Maisra brought fresh bread and chicken curry, Waraqa's favourite. Muhammad ate sparsely as was his wont, and then sat nibbling on grapes. A sort of haze and fever alit in Waraqa's gaze as he sat sipping his milk.

'I am old and half blind.' The abrupt lament escaped Waraqa's lips. 'I will not live long enough to witness the advent of one last Holy Scripture, or of your prophethood, Muhammad.' He balanced one grape on the palm of his hand, as if reading an oracle.

'How do you know, Waraqa, that I will be a prophet?' Muhammad laughed suddenly. 'So far, I have received only two revelations, and they could be the figments of my own imagination. Does Allah really talk to sinful men like me, who founder forever in a quagmire of doubt and bewilderment?'

'I see the prophecy of your prophethood in your eyes, Muhammad.' Waraqa's eyes beheld the soul of Muhammad, it seemed. 'The Torah and the Bible are both contained within you, with the promise of another Holy Scripture that will unite all truths in one.' A piercing prophecy scorched his lips. 'I was a polytheist, worshipping all the gods of the Kaaba. Then the light of Moses pierced my heart, and I embraced God in conformity with Jewish law. From that same light flooded forth my love for Jesus, and I was consumed by its brightness. Now the same light of Allah, the one and only God of Abraham, Moses, Jesus, is lowering the Lamp of Grace before my eyes, commanding me to heed the Prophet of all the world. And you, Muhammad, are that Prophet of all ages, the Promised Messiah mentioned in the Torah and the Bible.'

'And I can't even read!' Muhammad murmured, a desperate appeal shining in his eyes. 'I don't know what the Scriptures say.'

'You two figure it out, while I rest.' Khadija heaved herself up thoughtfully, flashing a smile before seeking the comfort of the sofa.

'Those Scriptures are in you, Muhammad, I can tell,' Waraqa prophesied again, his gaze feverish and piercing. 'What does Allah mean?'

'The House of God!' Muhammad's heart responded involuntarily.

'Where is this House of God?' Waraqa's thoughts were bent on inquisition.

'Inside me!' Muhammad could not help but repeat the song of his heart.

'No one else has seen it, then?' Waraqa prodded.

'No.' Muhammad's heart protested and thundered. 'I mean, it's in everyone's heart, and inside the heart of the Kaaba, and in the navel of Mecca, which is the centre and source of all Divine Light.'

'Have you seen the Divine Light, Muhammad?' Waraqa asked avidly.

'Yes, I have,' Muhammad murmured dreamily.

'Where did you see it, Muhammad?' Waraqa's voice shook with fear.

'Inside the emptiness of my soul, where longing and suffering had ceased to be.' Muhammad's eyes were unfolding a mirage of revelations. 'Suffering for the loss of something inside me, a nameless something, probing the wound of separation forever. And longing – the fiery need inside me to see the Face of God. Yes, I beheld that Divine Light inside the emptiness of my soul.'

'Are you sure, Muhammad, you didn't see this Divine Light anywhere else?' Waraqa asked softly, awed by the shimmering oceans of light in Muhammad's eyes.

'Inside the Cave of Mount Hira too!' The oceans of light in Muhammad's eyes reached out to Khadija. 'A vision most terrible and dazzling!'

'Did that vision bestow upon you the light of truth and wisdom, Muhammad?' Waraqa's gaze commanded absolute attention.

'Fear of God, and love for mankind, if that is truth and wisdom. Yes, that vision whispered to me, while my heart constricted with fear and expanded with love.' Muhammad reminisced aloud. 'Sweet injunctions all! To hold on to justice, whether in anger or calmness! To seek moderation in both poverty and affluence. Most of all, to join hands with those who break away from me, and give to those who deprive me. Foremost amongst all, to forgive those who wrong me. The silence in my soul murmurs again that my words and deeds should reflect the Love and Will of Allah.'

'The same vision, the same Allah! The One and Only God of the Jews and the Christians!' Waraqa sighed relief. 'Believe you me, Muhammad, the Torah and the Bible are in you, the pure scrolls inside the purity of your heart and soul. You are the Chosen One, have no doubt. The Comforter prophesied by Moses and Jesus. By the grace of Allah, your message will touch the hearts of the Jews and the Christians, and the polytheists. But under what name will you carry your message to the world?'

'Islam!' Muhammad's heart voiced his precious song from a memory. 'Gabriel thundered the name from the heavens above, as he stood towering over me from east to west, from north to south. Islam, meaning peace and reconciliation!'

'Unity in religions as foretold by the other prophets!' Waraqa smiled profoundly. 'I remember my parents worshipping all the gods of the Kaaba when I was a child, and I did the same. In my youth, I met certain Jews, and their reverence for the One and Only God, Yahweh, went straight to my heart. I adopted their faith and studied their Scriptures. During my travels, I came across Christians, and discovered that they too believed in the One and Only God of the Jews, Yahweh. The prophecy of the Jews came alive in Jesus, I learnt, and my very soul was moved by the message of love and peace as preached by Him. After studying the Scriptures of the Christians, I could not help but wonder when the promised Messiah would arrive, always hoping, always anticipating, always waiting. My wait is over, I am sure. Good timing, since Jews and Christians are at odds, fighting in the name of the same God, believing and disbelieving. I never thought I would see the Prophet of Unity in my lifetime. And now, you, Muhammad, are the One! I know I will die in peace now, knowing that peace will be restored amongst all. My end is near, I have this knowledge, and I will return to Allah.'

'How will I learn to believe in my message without your wisdom, Waraqa?' Muhammad cried. 'May Allah grant you a long life! Since I don't know how to read, I won't be able to study the old Scriptures. The Jews and the Christians, as you say, do they really believe in the One and Only God, Allah?'

'In Allah, the Lord Almighty, yes!' Waraqa was caught in his fever of recollection. 'In the Torah, Mecca is mentioned as Becca. The Bible calls it the valley of Becca. Abraham came here to sacrifice his son, but Gabriel came to his rescue, telling Abraham that his faith was the greatest of offerings, and that God had already accepted it, so need not sacrifice his son. Instead, a ram was given to him to perform his sacrifice to God. Then Abraham was commanded to pray to Allah, and to bless that spot as a holy place of pilgrimage. In the Book of Psalms, there is a beautiful prayer that I have memorised. *Blessed are those who dwell in Your House: they are ever praising You! Blessed is he whose strength is in You, whose heart is set on pilgrimage. As they pass through the valley of Becca, they make it a place of springs, and the autumn rains cover it with pools* (Psalm 84:4–6). This was Abraham's first prayer to Allah.'

'And Christ's too, I have heard.' Muhammad's eyes were ringed with shadows dark and profound. 'How can I be sure that the same God is speaking to me?'

'Allah has ways to dissolve all doubts.' Waraqa opened the book of knowledge he held in his memory. 'Almost six hundred years ago when Jesus walked on this blessed earth, preaching the message of love, peace and unity, he prophesied the coming of another prophet. In his mother tongue, which was Syrian, he named that prophet Munhamman, *the Praised One*. No doubt, you are that prophet. "For the earth shall be filled with the Knowledge of the Glory of God, as the waters cover the sea!" That one is from the Bible.'

'Though I long for truth and wisdom, and though I always seek the God of gods, I feel undeserving. Even now, when God has spoken to me through Gabriel, blessing me with revelations, I still doubt my sanity.' Muhammad smiled. 'I am afraid, I suppose, that if I tell the Meccans that I am the Messenger of Allah, they will consider me a madman, or worse yet, possessed by evil spirits. Perhaps they will forbid me to enter the sanctuary of Mount Hira, although they don't claim it as being holy. Only *I* know that it is holy; my very own gateway to truth and to Allah.'

'The Meccans will mock and persecute you, Muhammad, as I said earlier,' Waraqa declared. 'Didn't they scoff at Moses on Mount Sinai, and Jesus on the Hills of Galilee? But cast away all your doubts; Allah will guide you to dissolve the rifts between the Jews and the Christians. Allah's prophets and messengers remain under the shadow of His Grace and Mercy, succeeding in their efforts to deliver the message of Oneness. Blessed are the ones who heed this Call, striving towards making this world a garden of love, hope and peace. This, the burden of Grace, falls on the chosen few, who suffer, and do not exchange the pearls of truth for the pebbles of lies and distortion. But evil and injustice thrive when men forget the message. It's time! It's time! And a blessed time it is that Allah has chosen you to lead every nation on the path to unity.'

'The honour of this burden, I must accept then as the gift of Allah, guided by His will Alone!' Muhammad intoned reverently.

'Thy will will be done, Lord, as Jesus said.' Waraqa joined his hands in prayer, palms upward. 'Allah is already guiding you, Muhammad; my heart tells me so. Now I am at peace – and tired. I must go home and rest! Let Khadija write down those two revelations before they are lost to the world.'

'They will never be lost; I live to keep them alive!' Khadija's eyes fluttered open. Up on her feet, she glided towards her desk.

Khadija produced a clutter of leaves, tree bark and tanned leather as writing materials from under the debris of her business transactions. The reed-pen balanced between her fingers obeyed her will. She was quick to finish writing both revelations, and Waraqa announced his intention of leaving without further delay.

'Wait, Waraqa.' Khadija was back on her feet. 'Zaid will walk back with you.'

'Don't fuss, Khadija. Your old cousin can reach home without the intrusion of a chaperone.' Waraqa waved his bony arm, plodding towards the door.

Khadija edged closer to Muhammad, and they both stood watching Waraqa till he vanished behind the doors. Then Muhammad made her sit beside him.

'I hope you didn't catch the drift of Waraqa's predictions, dear Khadija. For if you did, you would wish a thousand times that I was not the recipient of those holy revelations,' Muhammad warned.

'I heard every word of your conversation, dear Muhammad!' Khadija laughed. 'Didn't you know why I stayed here instead of resting in my bed?'

'And you are not afraid, beloved' – Muhammad's eyes gathered stars of mirth – 'to watch your husband abused and maligned? Injured, too? And I am not talking about physical injuries alone.'

'With Allah as your helper, will you be afraid, dear Muhammad?' was Khadija's mock challenge.

'Since you won't mind my being tortured or persecuted, my Khadija, let's talk about something else which might invoke your sympathy,' Muhammad retorted.

'Yes, a lot has been on my mind lately,' Khadija admitted cheerfully. 'Your uncle Abu Lahab is insisting that Khultum and Ruqayyah be married soon. His sons, the restless bride-grooms-to-be, are behind it. Our daughters are getting old.'

'I wish they were old, beloved; then I wouldn't mind their being married.' Muhammad's tone was wistful. 'As it is, they are too young. Sweet Zainab, barely twelve, only a year older than Ali, already married. How I miss her—'

'My sister Hala is like a mother to her, dear Muhammad, and Abul As worships her.' Khadija was swift to console. 'Don't forget the Meccan custom. The majority of the girls around here are married between the ages of seven and nine. They mature early, many say; if that is a consolation?'

'This custom needs major changes, my Khadija, don't you think?' was Muhammad's shining proposal. 'One can't expect a custom to be changed overnight, but if one is to try, and keep trying, to change for the better, and even if it takes a hundred years to accomplish the change, isn't it worth trying?' He paused, adding sadly, 'Our Khultum is only seven and Ruqayyah nine; too young, our innocent babes! Abu Lahab, although he is my uncle, has no right to burden you with these things. He should talk to me about it. I will make sure he does, my Khadija.'

'Yes, he will, this very evening,' Khadija sang brightly. 'He has been coming here every day, and today won't be an exception.'

'I shall have to find shelter behind you, then, my Khadija!' Muhammad smiled cheerfully. 'He is short-tempered and I fear him greatly. Aggressive too! I might have to find refuge inside the Cave of Mount Hira, if he comes?'

'No, you won't!' Khadija declared passionately. 'This time I will follow you. More to be near you than to avoid the bad temper of Abu Lahab. Or to be near Allah. What was that experience like? How did you feel?'

'Frightened at first,' Muhammad began thoughtfully. 'But when Gabriel looked into my eyes, I could feel the light of joy piercing my heart. As he kept looking, the light became intense, and then increased with such violence that I thought my heart would explode, though it felt heavy, as if it contained all the worlds in each throb of joy and light. And yet, it seemed my heart didn't belong to me – the way it was expanding, drawing in tides upon tides of love and compassion, which could fill all the oceans of this earth for all mankind to drink or spill.

Strange, that feeling: I was no more! Consumed by the light of love, I was a part of everything. All were one whole. There was nothing to be separated from anything. We were all one, man and Allah, and child and woman, and king and beggar, they were a part of one whole. There were no distinctions under that lamp of understanding, only love, peace, beauty and harmony.'

'What else did you see?' Khadija's eyes gathered mists of tears.

'Nothing, my dear Khadija; I drifted away.' Muhammad's voice was low, his look distant. 'Though I could see veils upon veils of light, and my soul praying!'

'How did you pray, and to whom?' Khadija's heart was longing to know.

'O Allah, grant me Your love and to love those who love You. O Allah, make Your love more precious to me than cool water is to the thirsty,' Muhammad recited.

'Such a beautiful prayer, dear Muhammad! It is music to my ears; sweet music from the depths of your very soul.' Khadija sat there rapt and spellbound.

'Music to my ears too, dear Khadija! I heard it all the way from Mount Hira to home. Every atom in the world singing divine and inexpressible music, that I had never heard before.' Even Muhammad's eyes were singing divine songs.

'I wonder if you heard the same music, dear Muhammad, that I hear sometimes during the month of pilgrimage?' Khadija's eyes were lighting up like the stars in her memories. 'What I heard was like the tinkling of bells, far away.'

'The music in our souls, my Khadija: we can hear it when we befriend silence,' Muhammad asserted. 'You are blessed with the virtues of great love and purity of heart. Only the pure in heart, with love as great as the oceans, can catch the tunes of such divine music. The music is always present, not only at the Kaaba, or during the month of pilgrimage, but everywhere at all times. True pilgrimage is to our inner heart, and true the Kaaba is the sanctuary of our soul longing for the love of our Creator.'

'You are truly the Messenger of Allah, dear Muhammad! How else could you speak so eloquently, if not guided by—' Khadija's attention was diverted as Fatima bounded into the parlour, chased by Ali.

'Father!' Fatima bounced into Muhammad's lap. 'I told Ali he can't touch my dolls' house and he says he will beat me. Baraka made it just for me, with clay and sand, under my bedroom window. She made dishes for me too. I don't want him to touch them – he'll break them.'

'My sweet, you have to learn to share. And if he breaks some, Baraka will make you more.' Muhammad laughed, his gaze shifting to Ali. 'You are six years older than Fatima, Ali, and don't you know that boys are not supposed to raise their hands against girls, even if the girls beat them? That's the law around here.'

'Sorry, Muhammad, I didn't mean what I said. I was just teasing,' Ali murmured, flustered by Khadija's effort to control her laughter.

'Come here, Ali. Sit on my lap.' Muhammad hoisted Fatima on to one knee, tapping his other for Ali to sit.

Khadija got to her feet, unable to control her laughter. Baraka appeared on the scene, unleashing a string of apologies for letting Ali and Fatima escape her vigilance. Khadija was too happy to notice Baraka's consternation, and decided to accompany her to the kitchen, planning a great feast.

Muhammad was left with Ali and Fatima. Soon, Khultum and Ruqayyah skipped down the staircase, landing right in the arms of Zaid who had just come to take the dishes away. Fatima's dark eyes claimed Muhammad's attention.

'Why were you gone for so long, Father? May I come with you, next time, to the Cave?' she asked, tossing her curly hair right and left.

'Was it a long time?' Muhammad swept her hair back most tenderly. 'I might take you there next year, during the month of Ramadan. You don't have to fast though; you are too young. But you might learn to sit still, and pray?'

'Who would I pray to?' Fatima asked innocently.

'To Allah!' Muhammad murmured softly.

'But I have never seen Allah. Is He at the Kaaba? How would I know I am praying, and to whom?' Fatima chanted, rather profoundly.

'You don't have to see or know to whom you are praying, sweet Fatima.' Muhammad kissed her rosy cheeks. 'That's the beauty of prayer! All you have to do is imagine love, lots of love, for anything, or anyone. I mean, close your eyes and imagine you are bouncing over a carpet of stars, running straight into—' His effort to explain things simply was cut short by the arrival of Abu Bakr, led by Zaid.

Abu Bakr hugged all the girls. They fled as usual after this familiar profusion of love, chasing Zaid, who was goading them to race. Ali too slipped away. Muhammad stood greeting his friend with laughter in his eyes.

'Your face, Muhammad; it's brighter than a full moon in the Arabian sky!' Abu Bakr shook his eagle-like head. 'I know you are always happy to see me, and I have seen you happy before, but this, I can't explain. You look as if ... well, I don't know. And this perfume, it's different today? Don't tell me, this is the scent of love, as you always say. Let me see: this is the light of love; you are in love?'

'Yes, Abu Bakr, I am consumed by the fire of love. Allah is my love – and Beloved.' A beatific smile lit up Muhammad's eyes. 'If I told you, Abu Bakr, that the heavens will rain light, and that the rivers of love will wash away all the evils in this world, would you believe me?'

'Yes, Muhammad, because I have never heard you tell a lie,' Abu Bakr replied.

'How fortunate I am to have a trusting friend!' Muhammad confessed. 'If I were to tell others what I am about to tell you, they would call me a madman.'

'All the gods of the Kaaba would smite the head of anyone with angry blows, if they dared call you a liar,' Abu Bakr declared. 'I am dying to hear what you are going to tell me, Muhammad, and rest assured I will not be the one to doubt you, ever.'

'Even if you doubt me, Abu Bakr, I would have to tell you, since I can't contain this experience inside me – I need to share it with a friend,' Muhammad murmured. 'While I was inside the Cave of Mount Hira, the Angel Gabriel appeared to me. My whole being was suffused with light. I was seized with terror. And yet, I could feel myself dissolving into an ocean of love so profound and boundless that nothing else existed. Pure, ineffable love of inexpressible sweetness which my foundering self could neither contain, nor fathom. The agony and ecstasy of this supreme love churned and gurgled in the rivulets of my very soul, along with terror and bewilderment, against some nameless swirling of bliss and exaltation, and Gabriel commanded me to recite in the name of the Lord.' He closed his eyes.

'What did he make you recite, Muhammad?' Abu Bakr asked.

Read in the name of thy Lord who creates –
Creates man from a clot.
Read and thy Lord is most generous
Who taught by the pen,
Taught man what he knew not. (96:1–5)

Muhammad recited the words reverently, as if tasting their sweetness. 'I left the cave mad with fright and racked by doubts.' He opened his eyes. 'While I was running home, Gabriel overwhelmed me with his awesome presence, from one end of the sky to the other. His voice was clear and commanding, as he said: "Oh Muhammad, you are truly the Messenger of Allah, and I am His angel Gabriel."'

'You are, Muhammad, you are! I believe, I believe!' Abu Bakr threw his arms around Muhammad in a wild embrace, not even noticing Khadija approaching.

'He in whose hands stands the life of Khadija is my witness that you, Abu Bakr, are the blessed third to believe Muhammad,' Khadija sang joyfully.

'The first to believe was my own beloved Khadija,' Muhammad announced.

'And who was the second one?' Abu Bakr gasped for breath, his face on fire.

'Waraqa, my cousin.' Khadija lowered herself gracefully on the cushioned seat. 'Muhammad, did you recite the second revelation to Abu Bakr?'

'No, my princess!' Muhammad smiled in return. 'The first one to believe should have the honour and the privilege of reciting it to Abu Bakr.'

'I can recite it even in my sleep.' Khadija's dark eyes glowed with the warmth of her reverence. 'The second revelation came to Muhammad after he had slept for a few hours. I had gone to my cousin's house while Muhammad slept. When I returned with Waraqa, and went up to see if he was still sleeping, I noticed that he was just waking up, and then this revelation came pouring out of his lips in a voice that wasn't his own: *"O thou enwrapped in thy mantle! Arise and warn, and magnify thy Lord! Purify thy raiment and depart from all uncleanliness"* '(74:1–5).

'I will proclaim Muhammad as the Messenger of Allah to my own family and friends,' Abu Bakr announced beamishly.

'You are the closest of my friends, Abu Bakr, I know. But think and reason before you—' Muhammad's advice was left unexpressed as Zaid marshalled another visitor into the parlour.

This visitor was Amir, the slave of Abu Bakr. Amir's dark features glowed with excitement. His lips trembled with the anticipation of draining a fountain of joy he could not contain. Abu Bakr leapt to his feet.

'You are the father of a healthy daughter, Abu Bakr!' Amir sang suddenly. 'Aisha, the angel, Umm Ruman says. She is beautiful!'

'Blessed be the Lord, she is born a believer!' Abu Bakr exclaimed under some spell of fervour and exhilaration. 'And may the Lord bless Umm Ruman.'

'Congratulations, Abu Bakr.' Khadija expressed her joy by clapping her hands.

'Congratulations, Abu Bakr, and may God bless her always,' Muhammad murmured.

'It's a blessing to have daughters, and a greater blessing still to have the grace to love and cherish them in a land where many are buried alive,' Khadija could not help saying, watching the proud father float in a cloud of happiness.

'I must secure my fortunes and blessings then, before Umm Ruman decides to bury my little Aisha!' Abu Bakr cantered away, followed by Amir and Zaid.

'Little innocents!' The warmth of love in Muhammad's eyes caressed Khadija. 'May Allah guide me to pour love into the hearts of the men who are addicted to this vile custom of burying their daughters alive.'

'Allah will guide you all the way up to the heavens, dear Muhammad.' A sprig of a prophecy escaped Khadija's lips, her eyes brimming with love.

'My heaven is right here with me, beloved: you! I wouldn't dare covet another.' The poetry in Muhammad's eyes voiced more endearments than he could express. 'Your love and devotion are my heavenly gifts – my heart kneels in gratitude!'

'My own heart reaches out to Allah in gratitude for this angelic gift of a husband whom even Gabriel might envy.' Khadija's eyes were glinting poetry and profundity. 'What need is there for gratitude in our great love for each other? We should be grateful to Allah alone.'

'Allah is love, my Khadija.' Muhammad's eyes were closing. 'But if we are not grateful to others, how can we be grateful to Allah? Come, sit with me, beloved. I want to lay my head in your lap. Why am I so tired all of a sudden?'

'You probably haven't slept in the past three days, dear Muhammad, and those few hours of rest you just had are not enough.' Khadija slipped beside him, cradling his head in her lap. 'Sitting in the cave, praying and meditating!'

'But I don't want to sleep; I am afraid,' Muhammad murmured.

'You must sleep, dear Muhammad. I will sit here and dream happy dreams for you.' Khadija gently adjusted the mantle around his shoulders.

'But my shoulders are heavy like metal,' Muhammad murmured sleepily.

'I will share the weight with you, dear Muhammad,' Khadija murmured to herself, knowing that he had already drifted into the comfort of sleep.

The veil of gold against the window attracted Khadija's attention, as she stood watching. The red disc of the sun was suspended like a globe, cutting through the tapestry of the desert sunset in heliotropic colours. The face of the sun was obliterated, swallowed by a rainbow of colours, all of them bleeding through a golden haze, and painting the sky in lemon and violet streaks. Khadija's eyes were closing, her senses catching the celestial tunes of song and praise. The walls of the Kaaba were cradling her; her soul was being washed by the waters of Zamzam. Her heart knelt.

O Muhammad, truly thou art the Messenger of Allah, and I am His angel Gabriel. Khadija's very breath inside the bowers of sleep was singing this song.

Chapter 5
The Mountain of Pearl and Persecution
Year 613 AD

The floral rug upon which Muhammad was kneeling in his bedroom was soft and comforting. He was praying for love and guidance from Allah. Three swift years sprinkled with the magic of joy and pain had drifted past since his first divine call, and he was still reluctant to don the mantle of prophethood. After the advent of the first two revelations, the following six months of silence had been the longest for Muhammad. Khadija had become both his guide and his beloved during those six agonised months of hiatus and longing, when no revelations came to his rescue to dispel his fears and doubts. Her supreme love had kept him afloat, close to the shores of tranquillity, till the revelations commenced their surge as showers of mercy.

This evening Muhammad was to proclaim the message of Islam to a group of friends and close relatives. Khadija had sent invitations to dinner to forty families. Early that morning, Muhammad had received more revelations, commanding him to proclaim his message to all the tribes in Mecca. After consulting with Khadija, another invitation was sent through word of mouth to the major clans of Mecca, inviting them to the foot of Mount As-Safa. Before seeking the guidance of Allah in prayer, Muhammad had promised Khadija that his message at Mount As-Safa would be brief and that he would return before the guests arrived for dinner.

Muhammad's thoughts resurrected one scene from the folds of those agonised months when he was on the brink of despair; he was asking Khadija why she couldn't see Gabriel while he stood watching them both, holding him in thrall to his silence and majesty. Khadija, in return, pressed by her need to soothe and comfort, was struck by a bolt of inspiration. It was obvious. In a flash, she disrobed herself, as if guided by the divine hand of mercy, her lips moulding a strange question.

'Do you see Gabriel now, Muhammad?'

'No,' was Muhammad's dazed response.

Khadija was quick to explain and comfort him. Muhammad was seeing Gabriel for sure, she had stressed; since he was an angel, he fled at the sight of her nakedness.

With this recollection as his talisman, Muhammad's heart knelt at the altar of Khadija, his thoughts cradling his wife and his daughters in one loving embrace. Ruqayyah had married Utbah two years earlier, leaving behind a vacuum which had grown bigger six months ago when Khultum became the bride of Utabaibah. Muhammad's heart was throbbing with a sudden violence, as if aware of some sorrow awaiting his two daughters who were now married to the sons of his uncle, Abu Lahab.

The ripple of violence inside his heart was replaced by a shuddering ocean of love as he lit a candle at the grave of Waraqa, who had died shortly after the divine call.

Another candle was kindled in Muhammad's heart for the love of the Meccans. The gift of truth had come to Muhammad by the Grace of God, from within, not from without.

Allah meant the House of God, the God of all peoples and all nations. Islam was the birth and the promise of peace and reconciliation, and the ones endowed with the will to fulfil this promise would be called Muslims. And Muslims would be the ones who would learn to surrender to the Will of God. They would strive towards attaining such knowledge that surrendering to the Will of God meant, to surrender to the fruits of their own actions, whether sweet or bitter, and to accept them with gratitude as gifts from Allah. Allah would be their Guide and Beloved, the One and Only, their Healer and Sustainer...

Muhammad's thoughts were coasting along the shores of tranquillity, greeting a handful of believers who had welcomed his message. He could feel the presence of Gabriel close to his heart, his lips unfolding a song of prayer which he had repeated so often and with such devotion that he could never fail to taste its sweetness.

Allah, grant me Your love and to love those who love You and to love whatever brings me nearer to You. O Allah, make Your love more precious to me than cool water is to the thirsty. Muhammad's eyes opened, holding Khadija in their light of love.

'You should be on your way to Mount As-Safa, dear Muhammad.' Khadija's voice broke the spell of Muhammad's reveries. 'If you don't go now, you will be late coming home for dinner. Remember all those guests we have invited?'

'Yes, beloved, I should be going.' Muhammad heaved himself up reluctantly. 'Fear is clutching my heart again,' he murmured.

'Why fear, dear Muhammad, when Gabriel is always with you? He will surely guide you,' Khadija encouraged brightly.

'Yes. But I don't see him right now.' Muhammad's look was dreamy.

'I don't either, dear Muhammad.' Khadija's eyes twinkled mirth. 'But I feel his presence. Remember Waraqa's words: you are the Praised One mentioned in the Holy Scriptures of the Torah and the Bible.'

'That's my fear, beloved. Trial and persecution, as prophesied by your cousin.' Muhammad's eyes were shining with a subtle resolve all of a sudden.

'Allah will lend you patience and courage, I am sure,' Khadija laughed. 'I am not afraid, you see!'

'My beloved, brave and noble! I know I will persevere.' Muhammad joined her in mirth. 'Especially when Allah is the

Beloved of us both! And yet the weight of this honour upon my shoulders, this gift from Allah – why is it so heavy to be carried to Mount As-Safa? A mortal like me, weak and earthbound, how can I disobey, and yet not tremble with awe and fright?' He adjusted his red cloak as if ready to leave.

'I will share half the burden of your honour, dear Muhammad, and send my prayers over Mount As-Safa to shield and protect you from harm.' Khadija drifted closer. 'To tell you the truth, dear Muhammad, I am afraid too, but Allah will guide us.'

'Come, my Khadija, sit with me for a while before I leave.' Muhammad grasped her hands. 'I fear for our daughters. They have accepted Islam, but their husbands don't know.' He made her sit beside him on the sofa.

'Zainab is loved and adored by her husband Abul As. My sister Hala keeps me informed. He will respect her new faith, I am sure, when she is ready to tell him,' Khadija murmured soothingly. 'Khultum and Ruqayyah are happy and hopefully their husbands will respect their decisions too.'

'Zainab ascribes her happiness to the garnet necklace you gave her as a wedding gift,' Muhammad teased. 'It was a gift from me to you – your favourite piece of jewellery, my Khadija. And what did Khultum and Ruqayyah get? Only your gold and turquoise!'

'But you, dear Muhammad, squandered all my wealth on orphans and widows!' Khadija retorted, mirth dancing in her eyes and on her lips.

'And you, Beloved, hid all my golden revelations in your trunk!' A boyish smile washed over Muhammad's features, his look profound.

'They are written on the tablets of your heart, dear Muhammad! Better recite them before you go, and Allah's blessings will go with you.' Khadija's eyes were searching for the stars of profundity in the shimmering oceans of her husband's eyes.

'Yes, Quran, which is yet to be, all blessings from Allah.' Muhammad's eyes were lit up with the pearls of knowledge. 'To recite those revelations is like going on a mystical journey in search of the All-embracing Allah of all peoples and nations.

In the name of Allah, the Merciful, the Beneficent
Allah created you from dust, then from a drop of fluid. Then He made you pairs, male and female. No female will conceive or give birth except with His knowledge. And no one old will grow older, nor have his life shortened, but it is recorded in a Book. Lo! that is easy for Allah. (35:11)

He recited this verse as if it had been revealed to him that very morning.

'The one that I wrote down last week, dear Muhammad, pours joy and peace into my heart, so I can't help reciting it day and night.' Khadija was quick to speak:

In the name of Allah, the Merciful, the Beneficent
By the night enshrouding
And the day resplendent
And Him who hath created male and female
Lo! your effort is dispersed toward divers ends
As for him who giveth and is dutiful toward Allah
And believeth in goodness
Surely We will ease his way unto the state of ease. (92:1–8)

'Mystical journey, indeed!' Muhammad breathed profoundly.

In the name of Allah, the Merciful, the Beneficent
By the heaven and the morning star
Ah, what will teach thee what a morning star is?
The star of piercing radiance
There is no human soul that does not have a guardian over it
So let man consider from what he was created
He is created from a gushing fluid
That issued from between the loins and the ribs

Indeed Allah is able to bring him back to life
On the day when hidden thoughts will be searched out. (86:1–9)

'What a delight to listen to these revelations, dear Muhammad! I could sing them all my life.' Then Khadija's poppy-red lips spilled the perfume of another revelation.

In the name of Allah, the Merciful, the Beneficent
When the sun is wrapped up
And when the stars fall
And when the hills are moved
And when the pregnant camels are abandoned
And when the wild beasts are herded together
And when the seas boil
And when souls are reunited
And when the girl-child that was buried alive is asked
For what sin she was slain
And when the pages are laid open
And when the sky is torn away
And when hell is set ablaze
And when the garden is brought close
Then every soul will know what it has made.
Oh, but I call to witness the planets
The stars which rise and set
And the close of night
And the breath of morning
That this is the word of an honoured Messenger
Mighty, established in his presence before the Lord of the Throne. (81:1–20)

'I'd better heed the call of the Lord of the Throne, lest His message is left un-proclaimed.' Muhammad got to his feet, reciting another revelation.

In the name of Allah, the Merciful, the Beneficent
Say: I seek refuge in the Lord of the Daybreak
From the evil of what He created
From the evil of darkness when it is intense
From the evil of malignant witchcraft
And from the evil of an envier when he envies. (113:1–5)

He caught Khadija in a crushing embrace, his heart thundering. 'Pray for me, beloved.' He fled, neither looking back nor uttering another word.

The desert landscape was painted gold and scarlet from the heart of a volcanic sunset. But the slight incline on Mount As-Safa upon which Muhammad stood was bathed in a pearly evening haze. Below him was a throng of men in white robes and women in silk gowns, heavily veiled. All eyes were fixed upon Muhammad, and rills of curiosity flowed.

'O people of Quraysh!' Muhammad's voice was clear. 'Were I to tell you that an army was advancing to attack you from those hills over there, would you believe me?'

'Yes!' Voices billowed forth, with cheers and applause. 'We have always known you to be truthful.'

'Then hear me and believe!' Muhammad paused till the cheering subsided. 'I am commanded by Allah to tell you that Allah is the One and the Only God of the heavens and the earth, and He has chosen me as His Messenger to urge you to worship Him alone.' He paused, letting this revelation roll over the curtain of silence.

In the name of Allah, the Merciful, the Beneficent
Say: He is Allah, the One
Allah, the eternally besought of all
He begetteth not, nor was begotten
And there is none comparable to Him. (112:1–4)

This curtain of silence ripped open in a flash; the lips of the audience turned to flames, scorching the air with insults and epithets like hot coals. *Liar! Poet! Madman! Sorcerer! Soothsayer!* Muhammad stood there numb and speechless. Men were jeering and waving fists, their comments loud and threatening.

'He has surely gone mad! The gods of the Kaaba would be scandalised, and goddesses too!' Siba exclaimed.

'Why would al-Llah choose you as his messenger, Muhammad, regardless of the fact that he has been dead for ages? Now Hubal rules!' Khalid ibn Walid exclaimed.

'Allah knows best upon whom to bestow His Grace in choosing a messenger.' Muhammad's gaze was profound. 'Who knows, maybe I am the lowliest of His slaves in fear and humility? Or, the greatest of sinners daring to seek His Grace? And He, in His Great Mercy, has chosen me, this sinful mortal, to deliver His message of love, so that in contrast to me, His compassion can shine forth more radiant than ever before.'

'Where are the treasures, if any, which your al-Llah has bestowed on you to win our hearts? The robes of honour and the angels with golden wings?' Suhail ibn Amr was the next to shoot his daggers of anger and mockery.

Muhammad recited in response:

> *I do not say to you, "I have the treasures of Allah." Nor do I have the knowledge of the Unseen. Nor do I say, "Lo! I am an angel!" Nor do I say to those whom your eyes scorn that Allah will not grant them goodness. Allah knows best what is in their hearts. If I said those things, then indeed I would be one of the wrongdoers.* (11:31)

'This proves you are a liar, Muhammad, and you will burn in hell for fabricating such lies!' Umm Jemil, the wife of Abu Lahab, challenged. 'You think we are foolish enough to believe you, when you have no proof?'

'My own aunt, accusing me of lies?' Muhammad murmured. 'I am the servant of Allah, who sends me revelations, and many more are to follow as long as I live. He is the One who has chosen me as His messenger.'

'Where are your wings, Muhammad, and your chariot of stars?' Hind, Abu Sofyan's wife, taunted merrily.

'I am a mortal like any other man. And even if I stitched wings of gold over my robes, no one would believe me. Only the discerning and those willing to receive the grace of Allah will understand His message,' Muhammad replied calmly.

'Why would al-Llah all of a sudden decide to choose a messenger from Mecca?' was Abu Baseer's hypothetical question.

'There is no nation on earth into which a messenger has not been sent.' Muhammad's voice was extraordinary. 'Messengers with revelations. My revelations are to be recorded in a book called the Quran.'

'What is this book you are talking about, Muhammad?' fiery-eyed Hamza jeered from the back.

'A holy book, dear Uncle, which will confirm the Scriptures that came before, uniting us all as one large family of Allah,' Muhammad responded.

'We are the custodians of the Kaaba, Muhammad! Take care that your message doesn't reach the ears of our gods, or you will be lying face down into a pit of hot sand,' Othman ibn Talha challenged, pumping disdain from his lungs.

'The Kaaba belongs to Allah, as does the whole world!' Muhammad's eyes lit up with divine inspiration. 'Allah gave permission to Abraham to build this First House of Worship. Abraham and Ishmael worked together to erect the Holy House, and they were the first pilgrims of faith to walk around it. Praying, praising Allah. They dedicated this House of Worship to Allah. "Accept this from us, Lord. You are the One that hears all and knows all—"' His inspiration was reduced to cinders by the stormy approach of Abu Lahab, who came leaping forward, swinging his arms.

'Stargazer, my nephew! The bane of Quraysh and Banu Hashim!' Abu Lahab unleashed a big stone, which bruised Muhammad's arm before it fell at his feet. 'Why do you stand there stunned? Why don't you pick that stone up and hurl it back at me?'

'I am not stunned, only regretful, and I would not even think of striking a blow at my dear uncle.' Muhammad's voice quivered. 'My own personal injury could never move me to revenge. My heart is filled with so much love that there is no room left in there for anything else. You are invited to dinner this evening, I know, and you will find me as loving and respectful as before.'

'You can feed that dinner to the dogs! Don't ever speak to me until you empty your head of all those false ideas!' Abu Lahab turned on his heels, colliding with Abu Bakr, who was rushing towards Muhammad.

'As there is no darkness in the moonlit night
So is Mustafa, the well-wisher, the bright.'

This couplet tore out of Abu Bakr's heart, as he flung his arms around Muhammad.

A volley of stones was aimed at both men as they stood supporting each other, their faces illuminated by the light of love and compassion. More insults fluttered in the wind, but Muhammad's lips unfolded in prayer:

In the name of Allah, the Merciful, the Beneficent
Say: I seek refuge in the Lord of mankind
The King of mankind
The God of mankind
From the evil of the sneaking whisperer
Who whispereth in the heart of mankind
Of the Jinn and of mankind. (114:1–6)

The men of Quraysh were caught in a fever of rage, their insults more violent than the shower of stones. They were chanting. *Strike us, Muhammad, strike us back.*

'I have been sent in mercy to all peoples and to all nations.' Muhammad's eyes, radiant and sparkling, dissolved the challenge into a handful of ashes.

The crowds were dispersing, but a few scattered here and there were still laughing. Abu Lahab had joined them, goading them into hurling more stones and insults. His wife Umm Jemil, accompanied by her sister Maymuna, could be heard hurling a string of obscenities. Safwan bin Khalaf, the son of Ummayad ibn Khalaf, was the loudest amongst the gleeful, insulting stragglers.

'If you want to keep your head on your shoulders, O Messenger of Allah, do not dare to speak to us like this, ever again,' Abu Lahab warned, stomping away.

Muhammad and Abu Bakr stood still on top of the hill, facing each other in silence. Suddenly, Muhammad's face turned ashen, sweat breaking on his forehead. Abu Bakr watched helplessly. Muhammad trembled, slumping down the dusty hill in a white heap, only the red cloak over his shoulders throbbing with the colour of life. He sat shivering, his lips spilling words which didn't belong to him:

Let the hands of Abu Lahab perish, and let him perish
His wealth and his gains shall not help him
Burned shall he be at the fiery flame
And his wife laden with firewood
Around her neck a rope of palm fibre. (111:1–5)

Muhammad heaved himself up, dazed as if from under a spell.

'Not my voice, Abu Bakr, but Gabriel's. I am only the servant of Allah, and I obey Him alone,' Muhammad murmured, wiping the sweat off his brow with the sleeve of his robe. 'Let's go; Khadija is waiting.'

'You truly are the Messenger of Allah, Muhammad,' Abu Bakr could barely murmur, following his friend in his dreamworld of torment and mystery.

The dreamworld dissipated, leaving behind only the mists of silence and mystery, as the two friends sought the comforts of their homes. Muhammad, at this very moment, could feel darkness settled over the streets of Mecca, as he sat in his dimly-lit hall, teeming with guests. Darkness had entered his heart too, but he had donned a mask of cheerfulness, treating his guests with his usual warmth. Khadija beside him was guarding her own flood of sorrow, which had been released with tears and laments as soon as Muhammad had returned home from Mount As-Safa. Khultum and Ruqayyah had been sent home, divorced by their husbands.

The sons of Abu Lahab are not worthy of the love of our daughters, and our daughters will find better husbands soon!

Muhammad's thoughts absorbed the balm of his comments as he sat with Khadija, their hearts linked together in sorrow and courage. The guests were sated with food and drinks. The elite of the Quraysh were here, including those who had jeered and mocked Muhammad up on Mount As-Safa. Abu Lahab, of course, had stayed at home, probably to gloat over his act of vengeance.

Some semblance of gaiety was moving the guests to laughter – their need for gluttony and gossip-mongering was greater than their sense of pride and their desire for mockery. A group of men was caught in the fever of inquisition, their eyes glinting challenge.

'Don't you think, Muhammad, that perhaps someone has cast a spell over you? Planting this grand notion into your head that you are the Messenger of Allah?' Jubayr pretended kind indulgence, but his heart seethed with rage. 'You, an uneducated man, reciting poetry, the like of which we have never heard before?'

'I am uneducated, I don't deny it, but I am always truthful in word and thought. And no one has the power to cast a spell over me, for I do not believe in such things.' Muhammad's expression was kind and thoughtful. 'What appeared sheer poetry to you was but the breath of revelations by the will of Allah. The spiritual heart in my body is a fountain of knowledge, receptive to the words of Gabriel, and obedient to the commands of Allah, the One God of all religions, the Master of Truth.'

'What is truth?' As-Saib bin Abid asked, his fever of disdain mounting.

'Truth is the manifestation of a divine message from the One God, Allah, reaching out to us in all ages through the lips of the messengers whenever and wherever a need arises for the benefit of mankind,' Muhammad began profoundly. 'One such truth, the Word of Allah, touched Moses, who was endowed with a heart most pure and humble. The same truth shone like a noble light through Jesus Christ, the Virgin Mary its source and inspiration. This light is the gift of Grace, bestowed upon those who lose themselves in the purity of the Word, as if dying before dying, and existing in Allah.'

'All these stories! All that mumbo-jumbo from the tribes of Medina and Abyssinia!' Nadr declared. 'Some brandishing their cross, and the others fired by their zeal to cut it into pieces. What need have we for the Word when the Kaaba has its own gods and merchants, fetching all the wealth that the Meccans need? The Word, I hear, has been corrupted many times by many ambitious men to suit their ambition.'

'*Seest thou not how Allah coineth a similitude. A goodly saying, as a goodly tree, its roots set firm, its branches reaching into heaven. Giving its fruit at every season by permission of its Lord? Allah coineth the similitudes for mankind in order that they may reflect*,' Muhammad recited, concluding, '*and the similitude of a bad saying is as a bad tree, uprooted from upon the earth, possessing no stability. Allah confirmeth those who believe by a firm saying in the life of the world and in the Hereafter, and Allah sendeth wrongdoers astray. And Allah doeth what He will.'* (14:24–27)

'You surely are bewitched, Muhammad!' Abdallah ibn Jash, the Prophet's cousin, spluttered in awe and confusion. 'No man in his right mind with virtue as his only weapon of defence dare sing such powerful, incomprehensible verses. What is the source of your inspiration? What is the truth, and where does it lead? Do you gain from it at all? Is there any grain of reason in it? Acting like this, unlike any other man in Mecca, doesn't become you, Muhammad. You are a simple, uneducated man, and if you claim to possess any divine knowledge, which you do, be assured, it comes not from any god, but from evil spirits possessing you. And you will lose everything; your wealth and your reputation.'

'Meditation in Allah is my capital. Reason and sound knowledge is the root of my action. Love is the foundation of my existence. Enthusiasm is the vehicle of my life. Contemplation of Allah is my companion. Faith is the source of my knowledge. Sorrow is my friend. Patience is my virtue and clothing. Submission to the Divine Will is my wealth. Truth is my salvation.' Muhammad's eyes spilled light.

'The Kaaba is our guide, Muhammad, and its gods our guidance,' Al Abbas began indulgently. 'Merchants from far and wide flock to the Kaaba during the month of pilgrimage, paying homage to their gods, and bringing prosperity to Mecca. This new message which you claim to have received will unleash a storm of rifts and arguments, each clan vying for the supremacy of their own god or goddess. Those wealthy merchants are the pilgrims of the Kaaba. If their gods are subjugated under the power of one, they will refuse to come to Mecca, and our trade will suffer. We know our Kaaba inside out, and we know its gods too, and they guide us towards truth. What need have we of only

One God, and His angels and prophets, who will surely demand the destruction of our status, wealth, tradition?'

'The need for One God in Mecca is more urgent than ever before, more than it ever was in the times of Moses or Jesus,' Muhammad responded sadly. 'To right the wrongs done by man to man, to child and woman! To rescue the slaves, the orphans and the widows from the pit of degradation, where poverty and oppression abound. To end the vices of enmity and family feuds, and to make our roads safe for travellers and caravans! These are only a few of the ills in our society, which only God has the power to abolish. No single man can accomplish this difficult task of making our world a better place, but Allah can, with His Grace and Compassion. Allah is love, and he is offering to pour love into our hearts. We have made Mecca a pothole of cruelty and injustice; our hearts have hardened, and lack love. Injustice is even done to innocent infants; you are well aware of those babes buried alive through no fault of their own. And cruelty too! Are women not treated as chattels, beaten and abandoned by their husbands, and left with no means of sustenance when divorced?' He paused, noticing the fever of rage in the eyes of his guests. 'We have seen only the structure of the Kaaba. The true inner Kaaba is the Kaaba of the heart, the seat of love; love for Allah and mankind. When one learns to love Allah, one is guided by Allah's hand to love mankind. Then one becomes a vessel of virtue, justice, kindness, receiving these gifts from Allah with gratitude, and sharing them with others, while nurturing them always.'

'You are truly mad, Muhammad, to think that love alone could change this world to your heart's desire,' Zuhayar ibn Amr, the son of Muhammad's aunt Atika, protested with a sudden vehemence.

'We like the way we are!' Habbar declared with a gesture of impatience. 'Nothing is wrong with the lifestyle of the Meccans. It's tradition. Any change would be contrary to our ideas and beliefs. But, just for curiosity's sake, why do you think Allah loves you and has chosen you as His Messenger?'

'I don't know, but I am moved by His love,' Muhammad intoned thoughtfully. 'His love is bounteous, given to all His creatures great or small, freely and unconditionally. I was mistaken when I thought that I sought the love of Allah. Now I know otherwise, for in His Great Mercy and Grace, He has revealed to me that His love was always with me, though I didn't know that He sought me even before my heart could be opened to seek Him and His Love.'

'Where is this Allah of yours, Muhammad?' Imra al-Qais, the poet, asked.

'He lives in the temple of a humble and loving heart. Inside the heart of anyone who is consumed by the fire of love,' was Muhammad's mystical response.

'What does he say to our gods of the Kaaba, if he lives only inside the hearts of men?' another poet, Mistal, asked with a wide grin.

'Those gods of the Kaaba are created by men, since men have forgotten the Creator of this world and mankind.' Muhammad's gaze was kind, yet wearied.

'If your god is not at the Kaaba, Muhammad, how are we to worship him?' Imra al-Qais could not help flaunting his poetic glee. 'Tell us what he looks like, Muhammad, so that we can mould his face in the likeness of a god and build him a shrine at the Kaaba.'

'Wherever you turn, you can see the face of Allah,' Muhammad replied.

'My dear Nephew,' Abu Talib pleaded suddenly, his fingers stroking Ali's head. 'If you want us to believe in you as the Messenger of Allah, give us some proof.'

'I stayed with you a whole lifetime, dear Uncle, and amongst all my friends, and I have never lied,' Muhammad intoned patiently. 'Is that not proof enough?'

Suddenly, a symphony of angry protests was rippling forth, not only demanding proof, but branding Muhammad's claim to divine call as something bizarre and ludicrous. Muhammad's face was bright and luminescent. He raised his arms gracefully, requesting courtesy and audience from his guests.

'I don't know of any man among the Arabs who has brought you better than what I promise to bring you. I bring you the best in this world and the best in the next. So, who will support me in my cause as the Messenger of Allah?' Muhammad requested.

A funereal hush was all that followed Muhammad's request. He began reciting, as if inhaling the scent of joy with all his heart and soul.

In the name of Allah, the Merciful, the Compassionate
By the brilliance of the daybreak and the still of the night
Your Lord is with you and is not displeased
Indeed, your future is brighter than your past
Because your Lord will grant you what you wish and you will be pleased
Didn't He find you an orphan and care for you?
Didn't He find you lost and show you the Way?
And didn't He find you poor and provide for you?
Therefore, be kind to the orphan, gentle to the poor
And declare the Mercy and Blessing of your Lord. (93:1–11)

A beacon of desperate appeal lit up in Muhammad's gaze. 'Will no one join me to pour the light of love and truth into the hearts of the Meccans?'

Not a ripple of response from any of the guests to melt this shroud of silence which had frozen into a glacier, white and glittering. It was ripped open by the action of Ali, who leapt to his feet as if stung.

'I will, Muhammad, I will!' Ali bounded towards Muhammad as swiftly as his lanky frame could carry him. 'You will be my Messenger of Allah.'

'You, Ali! You, Ali!' Tears of joy and gratitude flooded Muhammad's eyes as he sat hugging his little cousin to his breast.

All the guests left in silence. Khadija breathed relief, her pent-up anguish finding release through warm and soothing tears. Zaid lingered behind, bewildered. His heart was flooded with anguish, and before he knew it he was kissing Khadija's hands and falling prostrate at the feet of Muhammad.

'Muhammad, I believe you are the Messenger of Allah! I do, I do with all my heart and soul,' Zaid wept joyfully.

'My son, my son!' Muhammad's hands, which had been drying the tear-streaked cheeks of his beloved Khadija, now reached out to bless and caress Zaid. 'You have a son of your own now; Usama. How old is he?'

'Only a few months,' Zaid could barely murmur.

Ali had thrown his head into Khadija's lap. Zaid's eyes did not feel the sting of tears any more, only the touch of grace and devotion, as he sat beside Muhammad. Muhammad's eyes brimmed with the warmth of love, as he recited.

In the name of Allah, the Merciful, the Compassionate
Praise be to Allah, Lord of the worlds
The Beneficent, the Source of all Mercy
Owner of the Day of Judgement
Thee alone we worship, thee alone we ask for help
Show us the straight path
The path of those whom Thou hast favoured
Not the path of those who earn Thine anger. (1:1–7)

'Never forget this revelation, Zaid. This revelation will be the first verse of the Holy and Blessed Quran, the Glorious and Living Quran. Now leave us, and take Ali with you. You both need rest, if not sweet dreams.'

Khadija and Muhammad were left alone in the rectangular haven of a hall, peacefully enveloped by the flickering shadows from the chandelier. Muhammad consoled her, and was consoled, clinging to the bliss of nearness.

'In blindness we stumble and fall, but by the Lamp of Grace we can soar aloft. The Divine Light lends us guidance on such a journey from heart to soul!' Muhammad's eyes unfolded more mysteries than he could voice.

'Yes; our hearts beat in unison, dear Muhammad, and our souls are linked together.' Khadija's perception had caught the light of mystery in her husband's eyes.

'Yes, beloved.' Muhammad smiled. 'Isn't it a strange evening? Joy and sorrow running parallel, never meeting, never yielding! Never crossing the bridge of separation, never reaching out to melt into each other's arms!' His voice seemed remote. 'Yesterday, our friends were friends, and today they have become strangers. Is truth itself the knife of persecution, cutting through flesh and bone? Heart bleeding, yet not ceasing its hymn of praise! Allah, Allah, Allah!'

'That's the glory of truth, dear Muhammad,' Khadija began dreamily. 'Sorrow does not crush it. It has a will of its own to rise again and again, no matter how many times it suffers tyranny and mutilation. And adversity is forever a fresh flame to the lamp of truth, lighting up peace and purity, effacing pride and prejudice and corruption. Meccans, steeped deep in such vices, are in dire need of befriending this lamp of truth.'

'Truth, my Khadija, has many faces, but there is only one face of God.' Muhammad gazed into her eyes reverently. 'I have seen but little, have tasted but one tiny drop of truth; my soul still hungers and thirsts for more. How can I be sure? Where did that light come from? Why was I swathed in darkness?'

'I form light and create darkness. I make peace and create evil,' Khadija murmured to herself.

'What are you saying, beloved?' Muhammad murmured back.

'These are the words of Isaiah, dear Muhammad, from the Jewish Scriptures. Waraqa was in the habit of reciting things like that when I visited him.' Khadija sighed.

'You have a great knowledge of those Scriptures, my Khadija. I have a longing to learn, but how and when?' Muhammad wondered. 'Already, I feel I need another lifetime to kneel before Allah in gratitude for bestowing upon me the riches of your love, beauty and grace.' Praise and adoration shone in his eyes.

'"I will be gracious to whom I will be gracious". That's from Exodus; Waraqa never failed to remind me.' A bittersweet smile flowered upon Khadija's lips. 'May Allah grant him peace in his grave!'

In the name of Allah, the Merciful, the Compassionate
O thou soul which art at peace
Return unto thy Lord, glad in His gladness
Enter thou among My slaves
Enter thou, My Paradise. (89:27–30)

Muhammad recited this old revelation with a renewed sense of joy and bewilderment.

'Your foot is on Jacob's ladder, dear Muhammad, as Waraqa would have said.' Khadija was lost in the mists of memories. '"That ladder is the axis of the entire Creation," he told me; "its steps rise higher and higher towards the Lote tree of the uppermost boundary." Waraqa loved Allah, and he proclaimed you as the Prophet of Allah before he died. And now these beautiful revelations are your faith and your truth, dear Muhammad; never doubt that. You have tasted more than a drop of truth, otherwise your strength would have abandoned you while confronting the blows of resentment and inquisition from your friends and family.'

'*Verily the righteous drink from a cup that is flavoured with camphor, flavoured from a fountain whereof drink the slaves of*

Allah, gushing it forth in copious draughts' (83:25–28), Muhammad recited in response.

'Who could recite those revelations with such passion, but the Messenger of Allah?' Khadija was inhaling the scent of love. 'Those revelations gush forth from the very fountain of truth, dear Muhammad. That pure fountain which strengthens the heart of the man who has surrendered himself to the will of Allah.'

'I wish I had as much faith in myself as you have in me, beloved.' Muhammad tried to be cheerful. 'Why can't my heart stop bleeding, carving fresh wounds at each little throb of memory for the grief of our daughters? Our little innocents! Flowers of my life! My little Khultum, and my little Ruqayyah!'

'Allah knows best. They will find better husbands, dear Muhammad, as you said,' Khadija consoled bravely.

'Since I am the slave of Allah, I will kneel at His throne. I will pray like a supplicant stricken with grief, for alms of joy and love for our daughters.' Muhammad grasped Khadija's hand, his own trembling. 'Though my heart, this moment, is praying that we sleep in peace and wake up in the morning with the light of hope in our eyes, our hearts washed clean of all hopelessness.' His eyes closed.

'And I, the slave of Allah's slave, will wrap your prayer inside the purity of my own heart, waking up joyful and hopeful.' Khadija helped Muhammad to rest his head on a pillow. 'In hope, we will kneel together at the throne of Allah, always.' Her own head was heavy, as she rested it on a pillow beside her husband.

A groan and a feeble murmur were all Khadija could hear from deep within the heart of her husband, her eyes shutting against a weight of sorrow and exhaustion. Something mysterious and astonishing was touching the harp of her soul, its strings singing a song of joy. It murmured *Prophet of Allah! Messenger of Allah!*

Chapter 6

Abyssinia, a Home for the Pilgrims of Islam From 615 to 616 AD

Kaaba, the centre of eternal life, was teeming with a horde of pilgrims and merchants. It was the last day of Hajj, and the pilgrims had come to the Kaaba from as far away as Egypt, Syria, and Persia. They had paid homage to their gods and were now trading rice and sugar and oils and hides, for pieces of gold and silver. But inside the walled sanctuary of the Kaaba, where Muhammad had retired to meditate, there was peace and quiet. His gaze wandered over the odes of the Meccan poets pasted on the wall. He couldn't decipher a word, not even the words of his own revelations gracing the walls of the Kaaba. Zaid was the one who had hung those revelations up there, copying the holy words from Khadija's treasure-trove.

Muhammad was grateful for the privacy in the sanctuary; all the poets had gone to Ukaz to flaunt their talents in a poetry competition. The competition was held every month, but a small voice in Muhammad's psyche was murmuring that the poets would be returning soon on this sultry afternoon.

Almost three years had passed since that resentful evening, and Muhammad was still the victim of persecution. He suffered a profusion of insults, and thorns were strewn in his path too, even within the precincts of holy Kaaba.

His thoughts swirled over the desert of pain where he could see Muslims suffering terrible torture. A handful of Meccans who had accepted the message of Allah as their one and only God had become the victims of persecution, especially the freed slaves. They were tortured mercilessly by the members of the Quraysh. To ensure the safety of the Muslims against the cruelty of the Meccans, Muhammad had sent forty of his followers to Abyssinia. They were to go to the court of King Negus, seeking the favour of asylum and friendship.

Amongst the exiles were his daughter Ruqayyah and her husband Othman ibn Affan, the cousin of Abu Sofyan. Othman ibn Affan had become a Muslim, and Abu Sofyan's rancour had doubled after he married Ruqayyah. His own daughter Umm Habiba had fallen victim to it; she had accepted Islam and married a Christian by the name of Ubaid-Allah, so both of them had also sought refuge in Abyssinia. Muhammad's thoughts turned to Jafar and his wife Asma, the youngest sister of Umm Fadal, and their young son, who were also amongst the forty self-designated exiles.

Suddenly, an ocean of voices drummed the walls of the Kaaba; the poets had returned from their poetry contest. Epithets like *dreamer, stargazer, village boy* grazed Muhammad's awareness, but he fixed his eyes on the revelation which Zaid had pasted on the wall. Right below it, a poet by the name of Labid was hanging his winning composition. As Labid stood proudly admiring his own work, his gaze was drawn to the revelation right above it, and he began to read it aloud:

In the name of Allah, the Merciful, the Compassionate
Praise be to Allah, the Lord of the Worlds
The Beneficent, the Merciful
Owner of the Day of Judgement
Thee alone we worship: Thee alone we ask for help
Show us the straight path
The path of those whom Thou hast favoured

Not the path of those who earn Thine anger, nor of those who go astray. (1:1–7)

'All the gods of the Kaaba be my witness, such words can only issue forth from the source of divine inspiration!' Labid swung around to face Muhammad. 'Everything but Allah is unnecessary. I believe in you, Muhammad. You are the Messenger of Allah, and Allah is the one and only God of the Kaaba!'

'*And this Quran is not such as could ever be invented in spite of Allah; but it is a confirmation of that which is decreed for mankind. Therein is no doubt – from the Lord of the Worlds*' (10:38), Muhammad recited in response, his eyes the shimmering oceans of love and light. 'Allah is the God of all peoples and of all nations.'

'Watch out, Labid, Muhammad is a sorcerer!' Mistal splintered the fabric of his silence. 'Tell us, Muhammad, why do you hate poetry?'

'Inside the ocean of my love for everyone and everything, there is no room for hatred.' Muhammad smiled. 'How can I hate poetry, when I say that Allah has treasuries beneath His throne, and the keys to them are the tongues of poets. And yet, to find those keys, one needs the light of wisdom. Some poetry is wisdom, and wisdom is like a lost camel; wherever his owner finds her, he still has the most right to her.'

'*Some* poetry?' Imra al-Qais asked. 'What do you mean, Muhammad?'

'Some, for sure! Poetry is wisdom if it inspires and enlightens, but when it wafts the odour of injury and mockery, not a grain of wisdom is to be seen in the whole husk of its inspiration.' He linked his arm into Labid's, and they both made a hasty exit.

'A mad, mad poet, lost to the madness of Muhammad!' Jubayr sang after them.

Labid and Muhammad stepped out into the white glare of the desert sun, followed by the poets, all taunting and cheering.

The poet and the Prophet left the cube-shaped shrine behind, their eyes upon the face of Abu Jahl, who had blocked their path. Stroking his beard, he seemed to be invoking the wrath of Hubal.

'Another apostate turning his back on the gods of the Kaaba, and accepting Islam. Is it true?' Abu Jahl peered into Labid's eyes, before turning his attention to Muhammad. 'Tell me, O Messenger of Allah: why do you revile our gods?'

'These accusations, Abu Jahl, tarnish your reputation as the leader of the Quraysh,' Muhammad began softly. 'How could I ever speak against the injunctions of the revelations bestowed upon me by the grace of Allah! *Revile not those unto whom they pray beside Allah, lest they wrongfully revile Allah through ignorance. Thus unto every nation We have made their deeds fair. Then unto their Lord is their return, and He will tell them what they used to do'* (6:109), he recited sadly.

'Liar! Don't you want to destroy our idols and gods, invoking the wrath of Allah to erase their names, aspiring to become the master of the Kaaba yourself?' The hatred in Abu Jahl's eyes flashed a challenge.

'Names that you have made up yourself, bestowing honour upon stones which you chose from the hills?' Muhammad's lips poured music. 'You mock your own gods when you are displeased, and only exalt them when fortunes greet you as a reward for your prayers. There are temples on this earth whose stone gods are revered, not vilified. But the Kaaba is not their home, though its light reaches out to them too. And those gods are revered because the devotees of those idols see the Creator behind what they have fashioned with their own hands. And the Kaaba can never be the home of those gods, because this is the House of Light and Oneness where no intercessor is needed to see the Face of Allah. This is the first House of God, its Black Stone the light of wisdom, radiating the purity of unity and Oneness. From this source of wisdom and knowledge itself, the light of truth journeys forth in all directions, illuminating holy places the world over wherever the name of the Lord is praised with sincere devotion. If you can show me any Holy Scripture where the names of any of your gods and goddesses are mentioned, I myself will pay homage to them in the name of Allah, to Whom we shall all return.'

'I was right! You, Muhammad, hate our gods and riches, and you are inventing your own sacred rites to drive all the merchants away from the Kaaba, bringing upon us the curse of ruin and poverty!' Abu Jahl's rage was mounting.

'*Unto each nation We have given sacred rites which they are to perform. So let them not dispute with thee on the matter, but summon thou unto thy Lord. Lo! thou indeed followest the right guidance*' (22:67), Muhammad recited wistfully.

'Right guidance, you say? New rituals, you mean! Urging us to discard the old ones, to satisfy your own vanity and madness!' was Abu Jahl's fiery inquisition.

'*And for every nation We have appointed a ritual, that they mention the name of Allah on the beast of cattle; and your God is One, therefore surrender unto Him. And give good tidings to the humble*' (22:34), Muhammad recited another revelation.

'Are you going to stand there, Muhammad, reciting poetry? Why don't you defend your honour by telling us why you continue to defile the holiness of the Kaaba with lies and warnings?' Abu Jahl challenged, his disdain inciting the spectators.

'*We have sent thee with truth, a bearer of glad tidings and a warner, and there is not a nation but a warner hath passed among them*' (35:24). Muhammad could not help but seek the aid of the revelations. 'Prophets and messengers have come to every part of this world, if you only knew. One hundred and twenty-four thousand of them have come and gone, but each and every one of them was scorned and rejected.'

'I pity you more than I hate you, Muhammad!' Abu Jahl exclaimed with a twinkle of mirth. 'Evil spirits have taken hold of you.' He stole a glance at the exorcist Daman. 'Daman is the man who can strike the demons dead in your head – let him assist you.' He beckoned Daman to step forward.

'I am the master of the demons, Muhammad.' Daman edged closer. 'Tell me about your malady. I will not only heal you, but I will find a cure for all the superstitious Meccans who hound you to the very gates of hell.'

'Praise be to Allah. We praise Him and seek help from Him. The one whom God guides, no one can lead astray. And to the one whom God sends astray, no one has the power to guide. I bear witness that there is none worthy of being served save Allah. He has no equal.' Muhammad smiled to himself, his look warm and indulgent.

'Oh, these words are snatched out from the deeps of the oceans! They are not the words of a conjurer or a soothsayer, like I was told,' Daman sang poetically. 'Give me your hand, Muhammad. I want to be a slave to the Messenger of Allah.'

'This stargazer has bewitched the sorcerer too!' Abu Jahl waved his arm.

'You are a fake and you spout drivel, Muhammad,' Amr ibn Aasi challenged menacingly. 'Why don't you keep your Allah to yourself, and stop disturbing our gods of the Kaaba, who are the keepers of our homes and fortunes?'

'Allah is the High God of the Kaaba, my God and yours. True love and beloved!' Muhammad responded. 'He is the same God worshipped by everyone; by the Jews and the Christians. *Say: we believe in Allah and that which is revealed unto us, and that which was revealed unto Abraham, and Ishmael, and Isaac and Jacob, and the tribes, and that which Moses and Jesus received from their Lord. We make no distinction between any of them, and unto Him we have surrendered*' (2:136).

'Are you the author of these revelations, Muhammad, or the author of madness?' Khalid ibn Walid gawked derisively. 'Our gods have been here for centuries; their divine names are grafted into our hearts. Why should we believe in your revelations, which urge us to bow before Allah alone?'

'I affirm the truth of every revelation; they have come down as a Holy Book from the source of truth. And that source is Allah, remembered by countless divine names, the God of all nations. Allah Most High will draw us together as we return home to Him, the source of love.' Muhammad's eyes confirmed the truth as he spoke.

'In the name of love! Wasn't Jesus crucified by that same message?' Abu Jahl's anger could not be contained. 'And where are the Christians now? Eating the dust of Abyssinia with their wicked tongues. And where is Jesus now?'

'He lives by the breath of the Holy Spirit; if you only knew!' Muhammad murmured. 'I am the closest of all people to Jesus, the Son of Mary, in this world and the Hereafter; for all prophets are brothers, with different mothers but one religion.'

'You profess to know everything, Muhammad, don't you?' Abu Jahl unleashed a handful of stones which grazed Muhammad's shoulders without causing much harm. 'Shunning reality, and causing rift and discord!'

'*The One Reality, Who calls Itself Allah Most High, is peaceful Unity and harmonious completeness*' (112:1–4), Muhammad murmured to himself.

'Your own uncles don't believe you, you imposter!' Abu Jahl hurled another handful of stones, before pouncing on him. 'If you were not under the protection of Abu Talib, I would have surely killed you by now!' He flung his mantle around Muhammad's neck, twisting and tightening it fiercely.

'Shame on you, Abu Jahl!' Abu Bakr intervened. 'You mean to kill a man merely because he says God is his Lord?' He stood guarding Muhammad.

'*Yours is the way of limited intelligence, O Quraysh, mine the limitless way of Islam*' (109:1–6). Muhammad gasped for breath as he walked away. 'Shake yourself free of error, and seek the treasures within your heart and inside the caskets of your imagination, plucking the stars of wisdom from the very heavens and bringing them back to earth as gifts from the Beloved.' He was drifting in the hazy sunshine mists, oblivious to the showers of dirt and stones following at his heels.

The poets and the politicians, jeering and applauding, had turned into a band of hoodlums. But Muhammad was homeward bound, not even aware that his white robe was muddy. Labid and Daman followed him, distraught and humbled.

'When the garment of flesh is torn open and the soul is released to its eternal abode, then men will know that Allah alone is the Beloved we all seek through different means and names.' A groan of longing escaped Muhammad's thoughts.

'Forgive me, Muhammad; I slandered you with my pen and in my thoughts.' Labid voiced his own low lament.

'Allah has treasuries beneath the throne, and the keys are the tongues of poets; haven't I said that before?' Muhammad was jolted to awareness.

'Teach us the ways of Islam, Muhammad,' Daman appealed dreamily.

'Learn to know yourself, Daman,' was Muhammad's tender response.

'How do I get to know Allah?' Daman's eyes were gathering the stars of urgency as Muhammad got closer to home.

'He who knows his own self, knows Allah.' Muhammad gazed, unseeing.

'But how?' both Labid and Daman asked in unison.

'Acquire knowledge. It enables its possessor to distinguish right from wrong. It lights the way to heaven. It is our friend in the desert, our society in solitude, our companion when friendless. It guides us to happiness, it sustains us in misery. It is an ornament amongst friends, and armour against enemies. With knowledge, man rises to the heights of goodness.' Muhammad was lumbering towards the entrance to his home. 'Be true to yourself, in the truest sense of the word. True in word, in deed and in thought! Now go home: may Allah guide you and keep you in His favour and mercy.'

'What makes a true believer, Muhammad?' Labid was quick to ask before Muhammad could disappear behind the door.

'No one is a true believer unless he desires for his brother that which he desires for himself,' Muhammad breathed softly.

Fatima, barely eleven, was the first to see her father entering the parlour. Her shock was great to see his clothes all muddy and frayed. Muhammad's eyes held the lamps of love, and like a wounded bird she fell into his loving embrace, sobbing and weeping. Khadija was next to witness this maudlin scene.

'Don't weep, my princess. Have you never seen your father after the camel racing?' Muhammad was murmuring, his gaze appealing to Khadija.

'Hush, Fatima, hush.' Khadija scooped Fatima into her own arms.

'Go and wash your face, Fatima, while I bathe and change,' Muhammad coaxed. 'Then we will eat and laugh, and I will tell you stories.'

Fatima fled to her room. Then he and Khadija sought the sanctuary of their bedroom, drawing comfort from silence and togetherness.

'Though I have seen you like this time after time, dear Muhammad, I can't help but fear and grieve.' Khadija smiled. 'Sweet prayers are my hope and salvation.'

'And I can't help but plead over and over again that you don't grieve, beloved.' Muhammad caressed her cheeks. 'This little discomfort of the flesh is but a gift of honour by the grace of Allah. Just remember, my Khadija: I have died to the world, and live only by the will of Allah. And when Allah's hand guides us, we learn to love everyone, nurturing kindness and compassion. Don't you feel the divine Hand guiding both me and you? You yourself tell me that we should be grateful for the bounties of love from Allah. Allah is love, and He is Beloved, our eternal wealth of truth and blessing.'

'Allah is our guide, and guidance comes from Him alone, dear Muhammad. I have faith,' Khadija sang with a sudden burst of joy. 'Hurry, dear Muhammad; don't take long in bathing. You will be rewarded with the gift of good news.'

'Sweetness, my Khadija.' Muhammad held her close to his heart. 'Anything coming from your sweet lips is good news to me.' He released her laughingly.

The bedroom itself and the little chamber with bathing facilities attached to it were Khadija and Muhammad's altar of holy secrets. It had attained this holiness with his first divine call, and they were wont to share their thoughts about the downpour of revelations there. Muhammad would clean the room while she was taking a bath, and vice versa. This particular afternoon was no different: Khadija bustled about putting things in order, her heart light, but her thoughts carrying the burden of fear and premonitions.

'What good news, my Khadija? My heart is longing to embrace it, no matter how small it is.' Muhammad's voice reached Khadija. She could tell he was polishing his teeth by chewing on a miswak stick.

'It is bigger than Mount Hira, dear Muhammad,' Khadija chirped. 'Our Ruqayyah and Othman are back from Abyssinia, so very happy, singing the praises of King Negus. Right now they are resting in Zainab's room.'

'Allah be praised!' Muhammad's prayer-song was clear and tinkling. 'I must bathe quickly. I want to know everything!'

'And they have a lot to tell, all good and encouraging,' Khadija sang joyfully.

'Do you see the timeless Oneness of Allah in this, beloved?' Muhammad's tone was heavy with the scent of mystical knowledge which only Khadija could catch.

'Yes; the message of Unity. My heart stands witness to the pulse of divine beauty in everything,' Khadija sang again with a mixture of joy and pain.

'You are blessed, my Khadija! Your heart reflects the beauty of Oneness, which the world has forgotten to behold and cherish,' Muhammad complimented.

'The secret between the seeker and the sought; you taught me that yourself, dear Muhammad.' Khadija stood hugging his white robe. 'The lover and the beloved, one and the same; isn't that right?'

'You didn't learn that from me, beloved, but through your love for me and for Allah; and you are rightly guided.' Muhammad's thoughts were hugging something too – the white purity of his recent revelation. '*O Prophet, you do not guide those whom you love. It is Allah who guides those whom He wills, and He knows best who receive guidance*' (28:56).

'Love, the highest paradise, as revealed to you, dear Muhammad.' Khadija laughed. 'But, ah, *thou soul at peace! Return unto thy Lord, content in His good pleasure! Enter thou among My bondsmen! Enter thou My Paradise*' (89:27–30).

'Love opens all hearts, my Khadija,' Muhammad intoned tenderly. '*I, who cannot fit into universes upon universes, fit into the heart of a sincere believer.*'

'I must stir the love of our family first, my dear Muhammad.' Khadija laughed again. 'I'd better wake up Ruqayyah and her husband, then check on dinner. Don't take long. Your robe and turban are laid out; we will be waiting.'

'Yes, beloved! This slave of Allah and of you will obey you directly,' was Muhammad's clear, mirthful response, as he followed his beloved at her heels.

The rectangular hall was a haven of comfort this evening as Muhammad sat with his family. Ali and Fatima were seated beside him on each side, and Khadija sat opposite. Her eyes were sparkling, gathering Khultum, Ruqayyah and Othman in their oceans of love. Muhammad's own gaze embraced them all.

'Tell us, Othman, how Jafar succeeded in befriending King Negus?' Muhammad asked. 'Especially when our Quraysh brothers had sent Amr ibn Aasi and Utbah ibn Rabia as their emissaries to oppose us in his court?'

'Jafar, though young and inexperienced, turned out to be brilliant in speech and manner,' Othman ibn Affan began passionately. 'He won the heart of King Negus with his eloquence alone, Muhammad. Against all odds too, since Amr and Utbah gained the audience of the king before Jafar did, and tried their best to prevent us from speaking to him. But King Negus granted us audience and Jafar was our spokesman. He wanted to know why this new religion of ours had generated such a flood of hatred and persecution. This was what Jafar said: "Great King, our religion is not new, but rooted deep in the Scriptures of the Jews and the Christians. But Allah has sent to us from amongst our own people a prophet, who can guide us to worship the One and Only, the same God Whom Abraham, Moses and Jesus worshipped. He tells us to speak the truth, to make good our truths, to respect the ties of kinship, and to do good to our neighbours. He teaches us to shun everything foul, and to avoid bloodshed. He urges us to treat everyone with love, to be kind to orphans and widows. He forbids us to bury our newborn daughters alive, and exhorts us to treat women with the utmost respect. Muhammad is the name of this Messenger, our Prophet of Allah. We believe in him, and for this belief alone, the Meccans have turned against us. They torture and persecute us and our Prophet, demanding that we worship not Allah, but only the deities of the Kaaba. So numerous and so overwhelming have become their means of torture that our Prophet has advised us to seek asylum in your country, hoping that no harm will come to us under your protection."' He paused.

'Don't stop now, Othman,' Muhammad prodded. 'What did King Negus say?'

'King Negus asked Amr if Jafar's assertion of torture and persecution was correct.' Othman ibn Affan's look was dreamy. 'Since Amr couldn't prove otherwise, he managed, skilfully, to bury the subject under a mound of lies, declaring passionately that Muslims hated Christians.' He paused again.

'Just tell us as much as you remember, Othman,' Muhammad encouraged. 'You have hypnotised us all, as you can see. Keep the stream of your recollections flowing; we welcome it with joy in our hearts.'

'I remember it all, Muhammad, but somehow the words are eluding me,' Othman ibn Affan intoned. 'After listening to Amr, King Negus asked Jafar if Muslims didn't believe in Jesus and hated Christians. Jafar recited this revelation in response:

> *So she pointed to him and they asked, 'How can we speak to a baby that belongs in a cradle?' The infant Jesus spoke miraculously and said, 'I am the servant of God. He gave me the Book and made me a Prophet. He hath made me blessed wheresoever I may be, and hath enjoined upon me prayer and chastity so long as I remain alive. He has made me kind to my mother and not overbearing. Peace will be on me the day I was born, and the day I die, and the day I shall be raised alive.'* (19:29–33)

'Then Jafar affirmed his belief in Allah, as taught by you, Muhammad, adding. "Muslims believe in Jesus as one of the holy prophets. They believe that Jesus did not die on the Cross, but was raised to the heavens by the command of Allah. He was received at the throne of God, and we believe that he will return triumphantly to bring peace, love and unity on the earth." King Negus was moved by Jafar's response, and traced an imaginary line with his staff. "The difference is no greater between us than the thickness of this invisible line," he said. Then he commiserated with the Muslims and granted them safe haven in Abyssinia. A just and generous king, Muhammad, who sighed to himself when he learnt about the tortures inflicted on the Muslims.'

'Tortures great and terrible! Did Jafar recount them all?' Muhammad murmured.

'As many as his heart could endure, without falling into a pit of grief and despair,' Othman ibn Affan murmured in response. 'He began with Bilal, since Bilal was born in Abyssinia. How his master Ummayad ibn Khalaf makes him lie flat under the heat of the sun, his chest bruised with heavy slabs. And then Yasir, whose legs were tied to two camels, and then the beasts were driven in opposite directions till his limbs were torn to pieces. He nearly cried when he was talking about Yasir's wife Sumayyah, who was killed in the same brutal way as her husband. Then King Negus almost wept when Jafar told him how Umar ibn Khattab beat his handmaid Lubainah at all hours of the day and night and only stopped for boredom, saying, "I leave you now not because I pity you, but because I am tired of beating you." At this point, King Negus raised his arm, declaring, "No more, no more, Jafar. Be comforted; the God of Abraham, Moses and Jesus is the one and the same Whom your Prophet calls Allah. Stay in my kingdom, you and your families, and you will live in peace. No one will dare raise a finger to harm you."'

'Allah bless King Negus and his kingdom,' Muhammad intoned in prayer. 'By the grace of Allah, all the prophets and believers, by virtue of their inner strength in faith and perseverance, are brought into this world to lead mankind towards the path of love and unity whenever mankind strays into the desert of cruelty and ignorance. Meccans, in this age and time, are in sore need of guidance, sightless to the golden reality right under their noses which they could claim as their ransom to gain liberty from the shackles of their own greed, cruelty, injustice and debauchery. May Allah have mercy on them, and on us. I suffer no injuries when the Meccans persecute me, but my heart suffers great agonies when other Muslims fall victim to their cruelty and persecution. The Muslims carry the burden and blessing of faith on their shoulders for the ultimate goodness of mankind in this world and the world hereafter. My cousin Zubayr, the son of my aunt Safiyah – after he professed Islam, his uncle threw matting over his head and made him inhale smoke, demanding that he renounce his faith. But it's no use recounting the cruelties of our friends and relatives turned foes. We should be grateful to Allah, who has opened for us the gateway to love in Abyssinia. Our message of unity will be nurtured on foreign soil, and from its seeds all peoples and all nations will reap the fruits of peace, justice and equality. The Meccans can jeer all they want to, behind my back and to my face, and they may inflict the worst of tortures upon me, but my message of love is still worth the bargain. It is the Rose Glory of the future, it is perfection, filling the earth with the scent of goodness and understanding.'

'And to think Zubayr is my nephew, dear Muhammad, since your aunt is married to my brother Awwam,' Khadija murmured. 'But you are right, Muhammad, it is needless to dwell upon the deeds of yesterday. The grace of Allah never leaves His prophets, dear Muhammad, be assured. Meccans jeer behind my back too, mocking me for not veiling my face. But since you came into my life as the emblem of wealth in truth and faith, what need do I have of a veil which women of wealth and status wear as a symbol of their pride? All wealth belongs to Allah, and in His sight we are all equal, regardless of our riches or poverty. Aren't I a good disciple of yours, Muhammad?'

'The first and the best, my Khadija,' Muhammad intoned reverently. 'A wealth of pride and an impoverished soul do not fit the character of any Muslim. We seek the jewels of love, justice and harmony, even when we are caught in sandstorms of hatred and humiliation.'

'Muslims are patient, Muhammad, but for how long can they endure the daggers of hatred and persecution?' Othman ibn Affan voiced his apprehension.

'I am the servant of Allah, and Allah knows best.' Muhammad's eyes were gathering sadness. 'We need to send more victims of persecution to Abyssinia. Allah will surely guide us, if we keep faith in His love and mercy.'

'May I go to Abyssinia too, Father?' was Fatima's abrupt plea.

'Why, my love?' Muhammad held her captive in his warm gaze.

'I want to see King Negus. He is so nice,' Fatima murmured.

'Kings don't talk to little girls, Fatima.' Ali rose to his feet, the light of sixteen springs dancing in his eyes, proclaiming him as a man of passion and perception.

'Now, Ali! She is not a little girl any more. She is a couple of years away from her teens, and she is going to be a young lady endowed with great wisdom. You should treat her with respect.' Muhammad's gaze searched the passionate eyes of Ali.

'Sorry, Muhammad, I didn't mean to offend.' Ali drifted towards the window.

'We should all go to Abyssinia, Father.' Khultum broke her silence with a little toss of her head. 'I am afraid. I fear someone will hurt you.'

'Hurt me! When Allah is my protector?' Muhammad breathed tenderly. 'Have no fear, my love! Learn to trust Allah. If you have a lot of love in your heart, my Khultum, you will have no fear.'

'I fear too, Father!' Ruqayyah followed suit. 'Khultum told me how your friends mock you and throw stones at you; they even try to kill you. They might succeed, Father!' She gasped for breath. 'I was afraid in Abyssinia too, of the Meccans coming there and wanting to kill us all. They went to the court of King

Negus, Umm Habiba told me, to try to convince him to drive all the Muslims out of his kingdom.'

'Fear is the root of all pain and hopelessness, my love, and trust is the flower of love and hope.' Muhammad's look was profound. 'Allah in His great mercy has promised me, His servant, and the servants of Islam great honours and great rewards. Soon, Mecca will embrace the glory of Oneness, and this beacon of love, peace and unity will dissolve all ignorance and oppression.'

'What is a beacon, Father?' Fatima asked bashfully.

'This beacon, my love, is the light of the heavens and the earth. It shines on all of us all the time, whether we see it or not.' Muhammad laughed, and his attention was caught by Ali.

'Are we having guests, Muhammad? I can see men out there, talking with Zaid. Am I allowed to stay if they come in?' Ali hung waiting for his response, his eyes pleading.

'We must always welcome guests, Ali. And you may stay with us, if you promise not to say a word.' Muhammad's gaze strayed towards his daughters. 'My lovely ones, run upstairs and stay there until all the guests are gone.'

The guests welcomed by Khadija and Muhammad were Utbah ibn Rabia, Abu Sofyan and Khalid ibn Walid. The three men seemed ill at ease, as if discomfited by the presence of Ali, Zaid and Othman.

'You know, Muhammad, by lineage you are our own flesh and blood.' Utbah ibn Rabia was the major spokesman. 'But your message of One God is weighing heavy on our shoulders. It is causing rifts amongst our own families, and toppling the balance of our trade during Ramadan. The merchants' hearts are filled with dread; they vacillate between doubt and belief in their gods. Their gods are the main reason that they come to the Kaaba; if they stop believing in them, they will not come, and our trade will suffer. After much thought and reasoning, the leaders of Quraysh have come to an agreement, and drawn up a proposal. Are you willing to listen to it?'

'Yes,' Muhammad murmured, his look piercing.

'You are wise, Muhammad, so pay heed. It is to your own benefit,' Utbah ibn Rabia began painstakingly. 'If you want riches, we are ready to give you enough wealth to make you the richest amongst us. If you want honour, we are ready to make you our leader and accept your verdict as final in our society. If you aspire to leadership, we are ready to crown you our king. If you like beauty, you can have the hand of the finest maidens, of your own choosing. And if all this is due to the influence of some evil spirit on you, which it is beyond your power to shake off, we are prepared to arrange for your treatment and bear the expense till you are fully cured. For sometimes an evil spirit can overpower a man, and he will only be cured when he is properly treated.'

'What wealth and prestige could compensate for the agony and longing of a soul to serve the Lord of the Worlds, and to proclaim His message of love and unity to all who are willing to receive it, to make this world a better place?' Muhammad responded. 'Are you finished with your proposal, Utbah?'

'Yes,' Utbah ibn Rabia could barely murmur.

'I don't want plunder or power, Utbah. I have been commissioned by Allah as a servant of mankind. I deliver His message to you and to all. Should you accept it, you shall have felicity in this life as well as in the life to come. Should you reject the Word of Allah, then Allah will decide between you and me. Here are the revelations for you to listen and ponder. You must think, and think again, before you accuse me of being possessed by evil spirits. Love alone is my shield and armour against any evil spirit within or without; it permits no darkness, only the light of divine inspiration.

In the name of Allah, the Merciful, the Compassionate

The revelation of the Scripture whereof there is no doubt is from the Lord of the Worlds. Or they say: He hath invented it? Nay,

> *but it is the Truth from thy Lord, that thou mayest warn a folk to whom no warner came before thee, that happily they might walk aright.*
>
> *Allah it is Who created the heavens and the earth and that which is between them, in six Days. Then He mounted the Throne. Ye have not, beside Him, a protecting friend or mediator. Will ye not then remember?*
>
> *He directeth the ordinance from the heaven unto the earth; then it ascendeth unto Him in a Day, whereof the measure is a thousand years of that ye reckon. Such is the Knower of the invisible and the visible, the Mighty, the Merciful.* (32:1–6)

He paused. 'These revelations are my answer to you, and to the Quraysh who sent you.'

'It is for your own good, Muhammad, that we brought this proposal to you!' Khalid ibn Walid breathed fire. 'If it was not for the protection of your uncle Abu Talib, one of the Quraysh would have killed you by now.'

'Allah is my guide and protector. And no one has the power to hurt even one lowly ant without His will, let alone me, the lowliest of His servants.' Muhammad responded humbly.

'Your own uncles don't believe you, Muhammad! How can you expect anyone else to listen to your message?' Abu Sofyan sneered. 'Even now, there are men out there, thirsting for your blood!'

'The same blood runs in their veins too, my friend!' Muhammad breathed kindly. 'Their thirsts will not be quenched by murder, but by the divine hand of love and forgiveness.'

'Well we can't say we didn't try.' Utbah ibn Rabia heaved himself up, regretfully.

'Try listening to the voice of truth, instead of crushing it with the rod of hatred.' Othman ibn Affan broke his silence.

'Only the gods of the Kaaba know the truth, and we need no poet to teach us about the one and only God, who challenges not only our rituals and customs, but even our lifestyles.' Khalid ibn Walid flashed a challenge. 'Guard your life well, Othman, lest Muhammad's daughter becomes a widow.'

'Life is a gift from God, and only He can claim it back whenever He wills.' Khadija could not help but toss in her comment. 'Family life, to Muhammad, is sacred, in wild contrast to how Meccans view it. So be cautious before attacking its sanctity, lest you offend your own gods whom you claim to worship.'

'Khadija!' Muhammad smiled after the men had disappeared behind the doors.

'If they had fear of Allah in their hearts, they would stop being hateful and insulting.' Khadija smiled back.

'Love for Allah, and belief in Allah's love for mankind, would do more wonders, my Khadija, than fear.' Muhammad laughed. 'I'm getting late to reach the sanctuary of Akram's house.' He got to his feet, his eyes shining with mock accusation. 'You didn't remind me, my Khadija, did you?'

'On purpose, dear Muhammad!' Khadija joined him in his mirth. 'Fear is clutching my heart.'

'Why, Khadija? Such weak trust in Allah that it crumbles at the mere thought of my leaving the house?' Muhammad teased. 'Look at Ali, Zaid, Othman, my shining guards, who will protect me at the risk of their own lives, I have no doubt.'

'If my mind and heart lacked even one grain of trust, Muhammad, I would never let you out of my sight.' Khadija sent this comment rolling after her husband. 'May Allah be your divine guide and comforter always!'

Akram had provided a large room in his house, lit by a few lamps on low stools, as a haven for Muhammad and his followers. The house was not far from Abu Talib's home, separated only by a dry ravine on the outskirts of Mecca. For almost a year, Akram's house had been a secret meeting-place for Muslims to learn about Islam.

This evening was no exception; almost forty men were gathered around Muhammad, longing for kernels of wisdom and knowledge. The best informed amongst them were Labid the poet, Zubayr ibn Awwam, the son of Muhammad's aunt, Safiyah, and Talha ibn Ubaidullah, the cousin of Abu Bakr.

'Most of you must migrate to Abyssinia, till the storm of persecution dies down.' Muhammad was saying. 'Abyssinia is a land where no one is wronged – a land of justice and harmony. Muslims can stay there without fear of harm, waiting for Allah's guidance. For surely, Allah will clear the way for them, and they will return home with joy and hope in their hearts.'

'It is so difficult, Muhammad, to be kind to the Meccans, who persecute us, though we provoke them not,' Zubayr ibn Awwam opined. 'And when Muslims leave Mecca, their riches and property are seized by the greed-mongers.'

'It isn't that difficult, Zubayr, if we realise that kindness is the most cherished of our riches, and love is more precious than gold – it can never be sold or bought in any bazaar,' Muhammad commented.

'You have taught us to be kind, Muhammad, but learning to be kind is as difficult as walking down a rugged road.' Zubayr ibn Awwam voiced his thoughts. 'Does prayer make such a path less tiring? What should we pray for?'

'Wisdom!' Muhammad's lips parted into a smile. 'If we can earn but one little grain of wisdom, it can illuminate the desert in our hearts with its own lamp of love, whose light no one can resist – well, only those forsaken by both man and God.'

'Where does that wisdom come from?' Talha ibn Ubaidullah was quick to ask.

'From the silence within your soul, which is the seat of grace by the will of Allah,' Muhammad began profoundly. 'When you befriend silence, you learn to be good to yourself and to others.

You can acknowledge the rights of others with the light of understanding, and hold on to your own rights with the warmth of humility!'

'Would such wisdom and knowledge make us great and virtuous?' Zubayr ibn Awwam's voice quivered under the weight of devotion and astonishment.

'The measure of a man's virtue and goodness, my worthy cousin, is that he can bow before his wife and child, and rise above his own pride by paying homage to his weakness.' The stars of profundity in Muhammad's eyes sparkled.

'To soothe our restless hearts and wandering minds, Muhammad, could you recite a few of your poetic revelations?' Akram requested humbly.

'The closest to my heart, Akram, is this one.' Muhammad commenced wistfully.

In the name of Allah, the Merciful, the Beneficent
Lo! We revealed it on the Night of Power
Ah, what will convey to thee what the Night of Power is
The Night of Power is better than a thousand months
The angels and the spirits descend therein
By the permission of their Lord, with all decrees
That night is peace until the rising of dawn. (97:1–5)

'I must confess, Muhammad, that when you recite your revelations, they touch my heart. But when I recite them, they sound alien and distant.' Othman ibn Affan sighed.

'Try it this way, Othman! When you recite them, imagine that you are embarking on a mystical journey to find the all-embracing Allah of all peoples and of all nations. That feeling of alienation will dissolve into a pool of the profoundest of loves, and your heart will surrender to that love and the Beloved.' Muhammad's eyes displayed a cluster of stars. 'Light the lamp of longing in your heart; kindle your soul with the flame of desire to seek the Beloved, the Ever and Forever Allah of Truth and Wisdom, who is all-perfect, commanding you to sing with joy and to dance the dance of unity.'

'Poetry to my heart, Muhammad! Your words and your vision!' was Abu Baseer's awed exclamation. 'If only the men who persecute you could hear you now. You could knock them dead with just your piercing look.'

'Allah has sent me as a mercy to all.' Muhammad's tone was urgent. 'My message to all of you present this evening is to pass on what you hear from me with the blade of truth, without the rust of lies and distortions. Allah will make manifest His mercy. Do not quarrel with one another like the disciples quarrelled over Jesus. He called upon them to spread the mission of truth, the same one which I am entrusting to you in the form of divine revelations.'

'Divine revelations, Muhammad! Could they speak to us the same way they do to you?' Zaid asked reverently.

'When you feel a cool breeze upon your cheek, my son, accept it as a gift from the hands of a divine revelation.' Muhammad laughed. 'Hold it and cherish it as the most precious of gifts from the bountiful treasures of Allah. Taste it and touch it. Kiss it, even. Feel its silken presence with the warmth of gratitude. Listen to its songs. It will sing for sure; sing to you alone the sweetest of melodies—' His thoughts were cut short by the sudden arrival of Abu Bakr, followed by Bilal.

'Finally, Muhammad!' Abu Bakr exclaimed. 'I have succeeded in freeing Bilal from the shackles of slavery. Ummayad ibn Khalaf was beating him more mercilessly than ever before, piling stone slab upon stone slab on his chest, and his son Safwan bin Khalaf was watching and laughing. How many times I pleaded with him to sell Bilal to me, I don't remember, but he agreed after much ranting and reluctance. Now, he is free. Free!'

'Allah will reward you with countless treasures, my friend, for this act of kindness; in this world and in the world hereafter.'

Muhammad's eyes were shining with gratitude. 'You have purchased the freedom of many already, with the purity of your noble and generous spirit. I am indebted to you for life. Thank you, my friend. Thank you! Words are too weak to express my gratitude.'

'You don't have to be grateful to me, Muhammad. All gifts of gratitude belong to Allah. Allah has favoured me with great opportunities to be the slave of His will, and never to aspire to be anyone's master.' Abu Bakr's features were flushed with joy.

'The man who does not express his gratitude to people will never be able to be grateful to Allah. It is a noble truth, Abu Bakr, which all of us should nurture and cultivate.' Muhammad smiled. 'The act of gratitude is a golden link, which unites loving hearts to the love of Allah.' He turned his attention to Bilal. 'Come, sit with me, Bilal. I want you to remember these words as a warning to all tyrants and oppressors who have made their means through slavery. Tell them that slavery is the worst form of human injustice; it corrupts the very essence of human dignity.'

'Yes, Prophet of Allah, yes!' Tears of devotion and gratitude swam in Bilal's eyes. 'Ummayad kept beating me, and I kept repeating, "Allah is One, and He saved…"' His voice choked up, and there was a sudden commotion outside the room.

Akram sprang to his feet, and dashed towards the doors in consternation. Soon he reappeared, claiming Muhammad's attention, almost whispering.

'Umar ibn Khattab is insisting on speaking to you, Muhammad.' Akram's eyes were glazed with fear. 'He's Abu Jahl's nephew – you know. I heard that he's after your life, so I can't let him see you.'

'Have no fear, Akram. If Allah has willed my return to Him through the hands of Umar, I surrender most willingly; I long to meet my True Beloved.' Muhammad's eyes were lit up with a deep smile. 'Let him in, he means no harm.'

'Muhammad, I will let him in because you say so, but I will watch him closely.' Akram plodded back towards the doors, his steps heavy and reluctant.

Umar ibn Khattab prostrated himself before Muhammad as soon as he entered, his gigantic frame awkward and shivering.

'I have come to enrol myself amongst the believers in Allah, Muhammad, accepting you as His Messenger.' Umar ibn Khattab professed his faith most earnestly.

'Now, Umar, you know you are not to prostrate yourself before any man, only Allah.' Muhammad shot a tender reproof. 'I have been told that you are after my life?'

'I was, Muhammad, it's true,' Umar ibn Khattab confessed passionately. 'Abu Jahl worked me up against you, and I promised him that I would bring him your head before the night was over. But that was before – not now, not ever.'

'So, what made you change your mind?' Muhammad prodded, beaming.

'Well, Muhammad, that's a long story,' Umar ibn Khattab replied.

'We have the time and the patience, Umar, to listen to your story, if you are willing?' Muhammad requested. 'Look how everyone is rapt with anticipation.'

'I have nothing to hide from you, Muhammad, or from the Muslims,' was Umar ibn Khattab's flustered response. 'I found out about the secret meetings at Akram's house, so I started out with the intention of murdering you. I was halfway when I met Urwah, and we got into an argument. In my anger, I blurted out that I was going to murder you, and he told me that first I should murder my sister Fatima and her husband Said, who have become Muslims. My anger was doubled, and I literally ran to their house with the intention of killing Said. I heard Fatima reciting something before I stormed in, but my anger was against Said. I confronted him with my sword drawn, and I was about to strike when Fatima got in the way, and the blow fell on her hand.

When I saw the blood on her hand, my anger vanished, and she said, "Why don't you kill me, Umar? I am a Muslim too. Your violence is not going to make me renounce my faith. There is no god but Allah, and Muhammad is His Messenger." She stood glaring at me. I begged her to let me read what she was reading, and she consented reluctantly. A few revelations inscribed on the lambskin spoke to me, but the one which moved me the most was, "*In the name of the most Merciful God! We have not sent down the Quran to inflict injury on mankind, but as a monitor to teach him to believe in the true God, the Creator of the earth and the lofty heavens*" (36:2–6). Such peace flooded my heart after reading that, Muhammad, that I couldn't wait to profess my faith.'

'Allah be praised.' Muhammad murmured. 'In this big frame of yours, Umar, lives an angel. And if the devil were to meet you, he would dodge into a side alley.'

'You are all kindness, Muhammad. Teach me about Islam. I will be your humblest devotee,' Umar ibn Khattab pleaded earnestly.

'Islam is very simple, Umar,' Muhammad began wistfully. 'Love, worship and surrender are the golden keys to unlock the doors of the heavens. These keys are no ordinary keys; they work in conformity with the law of the universe. *Love* means to love all Allah's creatures. *Worship* means to respect the holiness in each and everyone created by the Creator. *Surrender* means to surrender to the fruits of your actions, whether sweet or bitter, it doesn't matter – they are still gifts from Allah, your Beloved. To think otherwise would be faithlessness.'

'Merciful God! And I was nearly goaded by my hatred into—' Umar ibn Khattab was cut off as Hamza stormed in, followed by Akram's servants.

'A man comes here to profess his belief, and man and God's servants block his way!' Hamza surged closer, fiery-eyed and breathless. 'I believe in you, Muhammad, and in your One God, Allah,' he declared rather fiercely.

'How my heart sings with joy, Uncle.' Muhammad got to his feet, hugging him.

'The joy is mine, Muhammad, if you only knew.' Hamza squirmed out of this warm embrace. 'My wife Salma is expecting, and our child will be a Muslim.'

'May your wife and unborn child be blessed!' Muhammad exclaimed joyfully. 'Tell us, Uncle; what made you change your mind to believe? We need to share the sunshine of joy against all the gloom of persecution.'

'I was returning from my hunting trip when some men told me how Abu Jahl had treated you, almost choking you.' Hamza's eyes lit up with anger. 'So I rode headlong to the Kaaba where he stood boasting to a group of men about his heroic violence. My anger was doubled when I saw him like that, so I hit him over the head and knocked him down in the courtyard. "And I also do not believe in your gods of stone!" I told him, and I left him there to nurse his pride and injury.' Hamza paused and took in his surroundings. 'Why do you have to hide yourself like this? Are you afraid that the Meccans will kill you? It took me so long to get here!'

'Sorry, Uncle! Life is a gift from Allah to be cherished and preserved, but it is not because we fear for our lives that we have chosen this hiding place. Our fear is that Allah will smite the Meccans with His wrath because they won't stop corrupting their souls with the soot of hatred and ignorance, and we want to avoid them so that they can be saved from His wrath.' Muhammad's look was sad and thoughtful.

'We should let their corruption bleed on the streets of Mecca, Muhammad, if they don't stop persecuting you!' Hamza declared with a fresh burst of rage.

'No, Uncle. Islam teaches us to follow an evil deed with a good one, which will wipe out the former with its own virtue,' Muhammad intoned. 'All creatures of Allah are His family, and he who treats His creatures with love is the most beloved of

Allah. Those who are patient in adversity and forgive wrongs are the agents of excellence. Allah is gentle and loves gentleness, and He says that if people do good to us, we should do good to them, and that if they oppress us, we should not oppress them.'

'Who is to stop them from persecuting us then? And how? You know how their hearts are rusted with hatred, Muhammad, and nothing will take that rust off but the sword of action,' Hamza intoned with a desperate wave of his arm.

'Allah has the power to pour love into everyone's hearts, Hamza, and we must trust Him.' Muhammad smiled. 'There is a polish for everything that takes away the rust, and the heart's polish is the remembrance of Allah.'

'I have much to learn, then. What divine secrets Allah has entrusted to you, Muhammad?' Hamza's eyes glinted, agog with astonishment.

'Whatever He bestows in His mercy is for all to share,' Muhammad intoned contemplatively. 'I am commanded by Allah to revere Him externally and internally. To speak the truth with propriety, in adversity and prosperity; to practise moderation in poverty or affluence. To work for the benefit of my friends and kindred, even though it might not be of any benefit to me. To forgive him who injures me. To give alms to him who refuses me. I should spend my silences attaining knowledge of Allah. I should remember Him at all times, and I should be an example to mankind for Allah's mercy and forgiveness—' His gaze fell upon another intruder; Umm Hani.

'My father wants to see you, Muhammad,' Umm Hani breathed apologetically.

'At this hour, Umm Hani?' was Muhammad's astonished response. 'What could be so urgent?' He heaved himself up.

'I will come with you, Muhammad,' Hamza offered.

'My father told me he wants only Muhammad to come, and that he should not bring anyone else with him.' Another apologetic note escaped Umm Hani's lips.

'Better stay here, Hamza, and make friends with the brothers of Islam,' Muhammad appealed gently. 'Or you may leave. I myself will be going home after talking with Abu Talib. I told Khadija I would be home early.' He linked his arm with Umm Hani's, almost dragging her along, and both of them vanished behind the doors.

The curtains were not far from lifting on another scene, since Abu Talib's home was just a few steps away. Before she had entered the parlour, Umm Hani had broken her silence by commenting that her husband Hudayfah had gone to Taif with a caravan of merchants. The dimly-lit parlour where Muhammad sat with Abu Talib seemed oppressive and unwelcoming. Abu Talib had aged considerably.

'You know, Muhammad, I am growing old,' Abu Talib ruminated. 'How long can I protect you from the murderous designs of the Quraysh? My strength is dwindling, and I don't have long to live. What worries me the most is the danger to your life. You are very dear to me, and before I die I want some sort of assurance that you are safe from any harm.'

'Father! You have not invited Muhammad here to talk about death and—' Umm Hani's plea was cut short by an imperious wave of Abu Talib's arm.

'Now, my dear child, let me have my say. You must be quiet if you wish the privilege of spending a few moments with your cousin, as you requested.' Abu Talib returned his attention to Muhammad. 'I wish I was not the guardian of the Kaaba, for then the Meccans would not hound me with their demands that I restrain you from proclaiming the message of One God. As it is, they have already sent two deputations, and you know what they want. This evening, they sent a third one, challenging my resolve to keep you under my protection. They insist that if I can't prevent you from proclaiming Allah as the only God of the Kaaba, our whole clan of Banu Hashim will suffer dire consequences. My own brother Abu Lahab, unfortunately, is the chief instigator amongst the leaders of Quraysh. The other night, he brought Ammrah ibn Walid along with him, insisting that I adopt him as my son, and hand you over. I asked him, "You want me to take charge of Ammrah and to bring him up as my own son, Abu Lahab, while I hand over Muhammad to you to be killed?" That is how matters stand, Muhammad, and so my worries are multiplied. I am afraid they will kill you. Have you heard the latest accusations against you? That you are the one hurting them for the benefit of your own ambition and personal glory?'

'*Say: I have no power to hurt or benefit myself, save that which Allah willeth. For every nation there is an appointed time. When their time cometh, then they cannot put it off an hour, nor hasten it*' (10:50), Muhammad recited in response.

'Your message of one God, Muhammad, is making the men of Quraysh more angry and bitter than before, and they are unanimous in their opinion that this message alone is doing great wrong and injustice to all the clans in Mecca, and in fact to the whole of mankind,' Abu Talib murmured doubtfully.

'*Lo! Allah wrongeth not mankind in aught; but mankind wrong themselves*' (50:45). The gentle, profound mists of revelation were gathering in Muhammad's eyes.

'I don't understand you, Muhammad!' Abu Talib looked wearied. 'My own children understand you, no doubt, since they follow your belief. What puzzles me is this: why do you insist on hurling your message into the flames of hatred which burn like wildfire in the hearts of the Meccans?'

'I am the servant of Allah, Uncle, and I obey whatever He commands,' Muhammad replied. 'I am commanded to dissolve those fires of hatred into pools of love, so that the joy of Paradise can enter into their hearts.' From his lips poured another revelation: '*And if they deny thee, say: unto me my work, and unto you your work. Ye are innocent of what I do, and I am innocent of what ye do*' (10:42).

'What is this Paradise promised to the believers, Muhammad? Can't you hear the Meccans chanting and scoffing?' Abu Talib's look was feverish. 'They call you a madman and gloat with the slogans they've invented, laughing at the thought that anyone should ever despair of entering Paradise, just because he didn't heed the voice of a madman like you! Your madness; they insist it's ripping asunder the fabric of their religion.'

'If they knew the extent of Allah's mercy, even they wouldn't despair of Paradise!' The dreamy resolve in Muhammad's eyes suddenly flickered with passion.

'The gravity of the situation weighs heavy on my mind, Muhammad, and I must share that burden with you.' Abu Talib heaved a sigh. 'I am powerless against the demands of the Quraysh. They have given me an ultimatum that if I can't stop you from parading this divine call in front of the very face of Arabia, they will take strong measures to ostracise the entire Banu Hashim clan from social and political activities. It would be a social boycott, decided by the leaders of the Quraysh, forbidding intermarriage and commercial relations. As they have described it, it would force us all to stay within the boundaries of Shib, my estate outside the precincts of Mecca. Against such united opposition from the leaders of Quraysh, I can do nothing but submit. Have pity on me, my nephew, if you will. Renounce your claim as the Messenger of Allah. They are even willing to offer you riches in exchange for your silence and obedience.'

'They already have, Uncle.' Muhammad leapt to his feet as if stung. 'My dear, kind Uncle, even if they placed the sun in my right hand and the moon in my left to make me renounce my message, it wouldn't happen. I will never give it up until it pleases Allah to make it a triumph, or I will perish in the attempt.' His eyes were shining.

Abu Talib couldn't breathe as he watching his nephew; he was speechless with awe. Umm Hani rose to her feet, claiming Muhammad's hand in her own as a gesture of love and support.

Muhammad raised her hand to his lips, and imprinted a reverent kiss under a spell of pain and exaltation.

'Do whatever you will, Muhammad! Under no circumstances will I desert you,' Abu Talib said.

'Thank you, dear Uncle.' Tears of gratitude shone in Muhammad's eyes. 'Since Allah is all love, beauty and goodness, His mercy and forgiveness will drain out the envy, greed and hatred of the Meccans. And thank you, dear Umm Hani, for sharing the beauty of the silence in your soul. The eyes of my own soul have seen its love and purity, and its so very dazzling brightness.' He fled, his thoughts choked.

The night was dark and moonless; only the canopy of stars lit the way as Muhammad scurried home. He was a part of the cosmos, cradled in a dream-haze of nothingness, not even noticing the jungle of thorns strewn down the path leading home, which his foes had thrown down to hurt and intimidate him. His sandal-shod feet received prickly scars, and shot forth stinging appeals in tears made of blood.

Most exalted Allah! Ruler of the radiant expanse of earthly and heavenly realms! You reveal the potent secrets of your kingdom to whomever You will. As Pure Divine Mystery, You elevate whomever You will and limit whomever you will. Your Hands of Power and Goodness hold whatever is needed for the development of each living being, shaping as sensitive spiritual teaching every personal and every cosmic event, for through You alone all events become possible. You alone cause the night of ignorance to disappear into the day of knowledge, and the day of human knowledge, in turn, to disappear into the night of Divine Mystery. You alone cause the living to enter the sleep of death, and You alone awaken those who have died into Your own transcendent Life. Most Precious Allah, Your constant provision for the evolution of all being is subtle beyond my understanding (3:26–27). Muhammad's heart sang the revelation, and he was unaware that he had reached the comfort of his home.

The dimly-lit bedroom fanned Muhammad's senses into awareness of a stark, brutal pain in his body and soul. His feet, caked in blood, were stuck to the spot; his gaze reached out to his beloved Khadija on the bed. She lay sleeping in her own peaceful world, where all the doors to mortal suffering had closed shut. He stood caressing her pallor with his eyes, knowing full well the flood of pain and anguish inside her, which never escaped her lips or eyes, even when she comforted him. His own eyes flooded with love and tenderness, the agony of his spirit much more savage than the pain of his flesh. His mind was a swirling sand-dune of revelation – she suffered much more in her mute surrender to pain than he ever could with his fierce resolve and steely perseverance.

Beloved eternal! Muhammad's heart breathed the endearment.

Slowly and cautiously, Muhammad moved forward, drifting towards the bed in a dreamy, painful haze of memory. He abandoned himself on the floor at his beloved's feet. An overwhelming sense of loss and fatigue numbed his thoughts. His shoulders were heavy; his arms pillowed his head.

Allah, I submit my soul to You, and I entrust my affairs to You, and I commit my burden to You, longing for You, yet dreading You. I believe in Your Book which You are revealing to me, and Your prophets, whom You have sent… Muhammad's lips kissed the prayer-rug as he drifted into sleep.

Chapter 7
The Valley of Sorrow
Year 619 AD

The harsh desert wind whipped up Muhammad's black cloak as he paced outside the dungeon of his exile. This place of exile, called Shib, was a barren valley outside Mecca, where Muslims had been ostracised for the past three years on the authority of the Quraysh leaders. Muhammad, this particular evening, had ventured out to explore the heart of nature. His heart, pierced by countless shafts of grief, had persevered for three whole years, but now it was a cauldron of rebellion, unable to repel its agony since the illnesses of Abu Talib and Khadija.

An imperceptible shudder went down Muhammad's back as his pace dwindled and his gaze returned to the valley of Exile. Darkness from deep within his heart looped around his thoughts, which wandered into the alleys of time. Time itself was swallowed by eternity, scarred by hunger and digging deep trenches of death to lure the purity of life into its own dark, abysmal bosom.

Muhammad's inner eye fluttered open, watching the hour-glass of time. Abu Talib's fears had come true, and the Quraysh had succeeded in enforcing their decision to reject the clans of both Banu Hashim and Banu Muttalib. A proclamation had been written and signed by the leaders of the Quraysh, with the invocation *In Your Name, God.* This proclamation was drawn on vellum, with all the clauses of the various social and political bans highlighted. Then it was hung on the wall of the Kaaba as a legal document.

Soon, the leaders of Quraysh had gathered armed men to drive each and every member of the Banu Hashim and Banu Muttalib out of his home. Abu Talib was subjected to the same harsh measures, regardless of the fact that he still believed in the deities of the Kaaba, and had not become a Muslim. He was, though, allowed to retain his title as the Keeper of the Kaaba. The only former member of the two clans permitted to stay in Mecca was Abu Lahab, who had severed his ties with the Banu Hashim. He had become the greatest tormentor of the Muslims, joining forces with Abu Jahl.

Muhammad's feet came to a sudden halt, the face of Hakim ibn Hazan surfacing in his thoughts. Khadija had sent him to Mecca for food supplies, but he had been prevented from bringing anything back; Abu Jahl had confiscated every grain, all of it purchased with his own money.

The wind was whipping up Muhammad's cloak, and he pulled it tightly around his shoulders. He could feel the light of the Kaaba within him. His heart ached as he became aware of the children playing in the so-called courtyard against the background of tents and mud houses. These children were immersed completely in their own carefree world, chasing each other. Amongst them was Hamza's daughter Omara, now almost two years old. A little way apart from them, on a little sand heap, sat Aisha, combing the hair of her doll with the utmost absorption. Muhammad's feet were carrying him towards the hut of Abu Talib, but his attention was arrested by her.

'O Aisha, whatever game is this?' Muhammad stood watching.

'I am getting my doll ready to ride Solomon's horses,' Aisha chirped.

'The wisdom of Solomon is shining in your eyes, little Aisha.' Muhammad laughed, turning away quickly at the approach of

Aisha's nurse Burayrah. *Only nine years old, and who has been teaching her about Solomon?* he was thinking.

Muhammad jogged past the children; some dodged him, and others fell into his arms for hugs and kisses. By the time he reached the hut of his uncle, his lighthearted gaiety had fled. Abu Talib was resting on his bed of straw, frail and listless, his gaze feverish. Umm Hani, seated not too far away, was examining a length of coarse cotton, to be cut and stitched into garments for the children.

'Sorry, Uncle, for being the cause of all this discomfort and suffering.' Muhammad could barely apologise. 'I am an absolute slave of Allah, and guided by His loving hand – how could I not proclaim His message of love, unity and Oneness? If the Meccans could only feel and touch the light of love and brotherhood in Islam, they would leave behind the marshland of ignorance, and seek the...' His voice choked as he noticed the mist of tears in his uncle's eyes. 'Forgive me, Uncle. I shouldn't be talking about Islam, since you do not agree with me. All I want to do is love and comfort you, and I end up distressing you—'

'Have no regrets, my dear nephew.' Abu Talib made a feeble gesture with his arm. 'Islam is the light of the heavens I am not worthy to receive, since the gods of my ancestors have such a strong hold over my mind and body, which have both grown weak and will-less.' Tears poured from his eyes. 'These tears are for the ignorance of the Meccans, which you are trying to eradicate. They are cruel and arrogant, though they still accord me a little respect in deference to my being the guardian of the Kaaba, and send me the news of their deeds and greed. Little do they know that my servant Husein scouts the walls of the Kaaba undetected, bringing me all the news I need to know. Today it is hopeful, and yet the tears which you see in my eyes are for the little girl child born and buried alive by her own father in his drunken rage. If you could cure just this one Meccan evil, Muhammad, it would be a miracle.'

'Allah will guide them, Uncle, I have no doubt,' Muhammad consoled. 'Someday they will receive light through my revelations, and will repent of their sins for killing their innocent daughters. Each child comes into this world a flower of hope and innocence. To bury them alive is like killing hope and beauty. Ignorance guides the Meccans right now, but when the darkness is dispelled, they will desist from these acts of cruelty and injustice, and all hatred will dissolve.'

'Hope is not that far away, Muhammad. I might not live to see it, but it's coming.' A sprig of a prophecy escaped Abu Talib's lips. 'I am informed that the leaders of the Quraysh held a meeting today at the Kaaba. They want to retract our banishment. We might hear about it before this evening is over. We could all return to the comforts of our homes. What have they gained from ostracising us, anyway? Their aim was to stop you from proclaiming the word of Allah, and they have failed, since you continue to deliver your message during the months of truce. Your message is reaching far and wide, as far as the valleys of Medina, though their shafts of hatred and persecution try to prevent it from spreading. I fear my brother Abu Lahab, though. He thirsts for your blood, Muhammad. He is waiting for my death to wreak vengeance. I have not long to live, and I fear he will hound you to death.'

'Father!' A low lament escaped Umm Hani's lips, tears welling into her eyes.

'You are going to live, Uncle. For the sake of your grandchildren and for us.' Muhammad sprang to his feet. 'Don't cry, dear Umm Hani. You are lonely and suffering, much like my Zainab; both of you are away from your husbands. A great consolation, though, is that they are so loving and caring. I mean to say that they are the ones who are true Muslims, even in their disbelief, enduring this ban which is keeping them away from their wives. Does Hudayfah write to you?'

'Every day, without fail. His letters are a great consolation, for sure.' A beautiful smile sparkled through Umm Hani's tear-streaked eyes.

'That is much better, Umm Hani; your smiles will dissolve all the pain.' Muhammad returned his attention to Abu Talib. 'I must go, Uncle, and see Khadija. Then, as usual, I'll spend some time with my followers, talking about Islam.'

'I might surprise you, Muhammad.' Abu Talib's gaze shifted to his daughter. 'Dry your tears, my child; I am feeling better.' He returned to looking at his nephew. 'I might join you – my heart longs for the poetry of revelations.'

'Joys and blessings would be with us, Uncle, if you came!' Muhammad's eyes were shining. 'I would ask you to do all the talking, and we would benefit from your wisdom.' Then his feet guided him towards his hut.

The mud house where Muhammad sat holding Khadija's hand in his own was his haven and sanctuary. They were sitting on a reed mat. Muhammad had propped a pillow behind her back, trying his best to lend her ailing body the comfort of home, and Khadija was sitting bravely, smiling and talking. She suffered silently, succumbing to illness by the sheer weight of her inner torment.

'My Khadija, what can I do to alleviate your suffering?' Muhammad murmured tenderly. 'Besides Allah, there is no help.'

'Allah has been kind to us, dear Muhammad, bestowing upon us the well-preserved pearls of the revelations. They can never be destroyed by the fires of hatred or injustice.' Khadija's eyes were ablaze with love. 'I am not suffering, dear Muhammad; I am only too glad to shed all that extra weight. My body looks weak, but my heart is strong, forever lit up with your love, throbbing with the pulse of its own, and longing to lend you support in your great mission.'

'Without your love and support, beloved, I would surely perish.' Muhammad pressed her hand to his heart. 'Abu Talib just told me that the Meccans are relenting and this exile will end soon. We will be able to go home. The comfort of your own bed and good food will restore your health.'

'I can see the flowering of hope in your eyes, dear Muhammad.' It was blossoming in Khadija's eyes too. 'Zainab can rejoin her husband, and Umm Hani too! I hope that all hatred will end as well. How could the Quraysh continue to persecute you when your heart is filled with love for all mankind?'

'My Khadija!' Muhammad hugged her. 'You are my gift from the merciful hands of Allah Himself. And your gift of love is the greatest of all gifts. Now, I must share it with the believers, before they despair of Allah's mercy and grace.' He let go of her and stumbled to his feet. 'Rest, beloved; you must rest. We will return home soon, and you will get well.'

Muhammad sat presiding over his impoverished group of followers in the open courtyard. A poor lot they were, but their eyes sparkled with starry brilliance. The desert sunset was a golden haze above them, gilding the barren landscape in molten gold, and their voices were a medley of song and anticipation.

'Where is Allah, Muhammad?' Ali laughed. 'I am recalling the words of a Bedouin who confronted me during the pilgrimage last year. "I can see all the gods of the Kaaba, but where is the Allah of Muhammad?" I didn't know what to say.'

'You turned twenty this year, Ali, and you still don't know?' Muhammad joined him in his mirth. 'Wherever you turn, there is the Face of Allah. There is no refuge from Allah but in Him. *It is not their eyes that are blind, but their hearts. Verily we are Allah's and unto Him we shall return'* (22:46).

'As believers, what should we do to strengthen our faith, since doubts enter our heads now and then?' Abu Bakr asked thoughtfully.

'Doubts don't crumble your faith if you learn to honour the dignity of life in its entirety, my friend.' Muhammad smiled. 'Feeding the hungry and visiting the sick strengthens the faith. So does freeing captives if they are unfairly imprisoned, and assisting the oppressed, whether Muslim or non-Muslim.'

'Should we give alms to everyone who asks if we have enough to share?' Musaib ibn Omeir asked dreamily. 'I am proud of my wife Hamnah; she is very generous.'

'Being the daughter of my aunt Umaymah, she couldn't be otherwise! Why she named her after the poet, I still don't understand.' Muhammad smiled. 'Recognising the needy and giving without their asking is best, if you can afford it. But the best alms to give are those which the right hand gives and the left hand doesn't know about. And yet, another reason to give alms is to make peace between one another.'

'Is it true, Muhammad, that if we fulfil our duty to be faithful to Allah, to His prophets and to His revelations, that we need not turn to any other source for the improvement of our characters, since we need none by virtue of our duty to Allah?' Abdallah ibn Masud asked.

'Our duties to Allah are varied and countless, my friend. And if you wish to live your life to the fullest, you must perform them all according to your own capacity,' was Muhammad's kind response. 'The acquisition of knowledge is also a duty, incumbent upon every Muslim male and female. One must seek knowledge from the cradle to the grave, and venture forth to attain it from continent to continent.'

'All this suffering, Muhammad – what's its source? What's its purpose? Can any amount of knowledge explain things like that?' Bilal asked.

'The Merciful, Mysterious Source is All One, Allah! From Whom everything comes, even suffering, a gift of mercy to the soul, to learn and to grow towards perfection. To aspire to be united with the Beloved from Whom we have separated since birth. The minds

and hearts of those who can joyfully accept this astonishing truth, and who thereby turn in complete surrender to Allah, they will be guided by His Wisdom and by the Light of His all-embracing Love' (64:11). Muhammad's very eyes glowed with revelations.

'So, if Allah is truth and everything comes from Allah, then should we accept all injustice and imperfection as a part of His divine will?' Zaid was quick to ask.

'Those whose whole being is orientated towards the divine will, my son, perceive no injustice or imperfection in the boundless kingdom of the All-Merciful,' Muhammad intoned contemplatively. 'But human beings are granted free will to confirm or deny truth, and have the freedom to act to the dictates of their own souls, to distinguish between good and bad. The fruits of a man's actions can be sweet or bitter depending upon his intent, whether the actions themselves are vile or virtuous.'

'How can anyone miss the cruelty and injustice swarming all around us?' Hamza tossed his own missile of doubts, baffled.

'By changing your plane of existence, you are able to perceive the kernel of reality behind everything.' Muhammad's eyes were shining. 'And you cannot change your plane of existence, dear Uncle, if you cannot change your plane of actions. And that change comes with discipline, through the fire of love, from inside the purity of your own heart. It is a nameless, indescribable experience. No words can expound it. But when you experience the change within yourself, it transforms everything, dissolving each and every aspect of this world into an ocean of love, unity, perfection.'

'Teach us, Muhammad, how to attain that experience,' Othman ibn Affan begged.

'Love is a great teacher; it can accomplish anything,' Muhammad responded. 'Love turns your physical heart into a spiritual heart: the throne of God, the seat of truth; and its gates are thrown open to revelations when you can contemplate the self as one divine whole, not separated from anyone or anything.

In essence, you will see love's treasures within yourself, and experience the light of transcendent unity with the inner eye of the spiritual heart. Didn't God say "I desired to become known and I brought creation into being that I might be known?" And didn't He say, "My earth and My heaven contain Me not, but the heart of My faithful servant containeth Me?" Another way to experience the love and presence of Allah is to pray to Him as if you are kneeling at the feet of your beloved, and not to leave until your longing to see Him is fulfilled. You can pray like this, with the fire of love as your light. *Most exalted Allah, as each breath is drawn in, lead me inward in purity and strength to Your invisible life, and as each breath flows out, lead me outward with purity and strength to Your manifest creation. Most precious Allah, please grant me Your Direct Guidance along the subtle way of awakening*' (17:80–81).

'Such a beautiful prayer, Muhammad!' Othman ibn Affan murmured to himself.

'Many prayers like this have been bestowed by Allah to all His prophets since the beginning of time. All glory and praise to the powerful and wise Allah, Who makes possible what we accomplish.' Muhammad smiled.

'Such timeless, wise purity in prayer, Muhammad. Did any other prophet bring this?' Abd al Mottaleb commented, more than he asked.

'All of them did, Mottaleb; all the prophets old and young,' Muhammad responded. 'Even Abraham when he arrived in Mecca, after his initiation into the mysteries of life in Egypt. He brought the Black Stone with him, as many believe. *This stone I set here in memory of initiation, as a sign of God to be understood as One God.* He sang the praises of God while fixing that stone to the wall of the Kaaba. Now Allah has bestowed a song of a prayer upon me too, to be taught to the Prophet Abraham's descendants. *Most precious Allah, may we turn towards Your Divine Mystery in ever deepest trust and humility until we complete the immense journey, the conscious return into Your original Radiance. Most exalted Allah, divert from us please the negativity of those beings who turn away from the Source of Being, and liberate us from our own negativity with Your absolutely forgiving Love. You alone, Allah Most Sublime, are boundless Power and complete Wisdom'* (60:4–7).

'Prayers and poetry like that make me giddy, Muhammad, rather than lending me courage,' Abd al Mottaleb laughed nervously. 'I have been meaning to ask; may I seek the hand of Khultum in marriage?'

'Our family would be blessed if Khultum accepted your proposal,' Muhammad laughed in return. 'And I have the strong sense that she will.'

'You are a prophet, indeed, Muhammad.' Abu Bakr sought Muhammad's attention. 'And yet, somehow, this evening you look like a stranger amongst us. Not of this earth…' He couldn't continue against the blaze of love in Muhammad's eyes.

'Abu Bakr, and all my friends, please do not feel that I am a stranger amongst you,' Muhammad intoned. *'I am an ordinary human being, no different from your own selves. Humbly and gratefully, I have received the Revelation that all manifest Being emerges from and returns to the Single Source and Goal of Being, Who refers to Itself as Allah and by countless other Most Beautiful Divine Names'* (41:2–8).

'The beauty of your message, Muhammad! We lack the eloquence to impart it to the Meccans when they question us,' Akram commented shyly.

'The beauty of Islam's message, Akram, is that it's easy and simple,' Muhammad began cheerfully. 'Islam teaches love, equality and brotherhood. In the sight of Allah, no distinction exists between man or woman, or between Arab and non-Arab. Only the sincerity of one's own faith is pleasing to Allah, and this faith alone is the kernel of wisdom and understanding.'

'Guide us to strengthen our faith, Muhammad. It grows weak against adversity.' Musaib ibn Omeir heaved a sigh of regret.

'Love is the pillar and strength of faith, Musaib. Cultivate love in your heart, and it will lead you towards the riches of joy and peace,' Muhammad began contemplatively. 'Love has been everyone's guide forever. It is the dearest of our guides: our friend; our haven in times of joy and sorrow. Love is a divine gift, the crown of one's faith. The faith of a believer is not perfect unless one thousand sincere people bear witness to his infidelity. The faith of someone slow to believe is beyond the experience of love and understanding. Perfect faith is to serve people with perfect love for the sake of absolute love alone; for Allah. For if we are blind to divine love in this world, we will still be blind to it in the next. Love is true religion and true worship, melting blindness and lending sight to see the Face of Allah in everyone and everywhere. It was love which gave Jesus the gift of healing. Solomon too, with the gift of love, attained wisdom and understanding. Noah possessed the same love too: he fashioned the Ark with deliverance and fulfilment.'

'Isn't it difficult to love people, Muhammad, when they are bent on hurting you without provocation?' Abdallah ibn Jash aired his own doubts.

'Not if you die before dying,' Muhammad intoned with a glint of profundity. 'Not a physical death, but a purification of the soul, killing the roots of greed and hatred in the innermost recesses of one's being and living in the boundless ocean of Allah's love and grace. Such is the power of love that—' His thoughts were disrupted by the approach of Hisham bin Amr.

'You should be happy, Muhammad; the leaders of the Quraysh have decided to end your exile,' Hisham bin Amr announced. 'Now you can all return to your homes, and you are free to share the privileges of trade and social interaction.'

'Allah be praised! And thank you, Hisham, for being the messenger of such glad tidings.' Muhammad smiled joyfully.

'Allah has nothing to do with it! And you don't have to thank me, Muhammad, for the gods of the Kaaba have sent this edict in your favour.' Hisham bin Amr laughed.

'What do you mean?' Muhammad's voice was barely audible.

'When Al Mutam snatched the vellum off the wall of the Kaaba, everyone cried out in astonishment. All the injunctions inscribed upon the vellum had been eaten away by white ants, with the exception of one. *In Thy Name, O God,*' Hisham bin Amr expounded histrionically. 'Soon, everyone was shouting at each other, while the vellum crumbled in Al Mutam's hands.'

'Who was fighting?' was Muhammad's gentle enquiry.

'Many were there, Abu Lahab the foremost amongst them, joined by Abu Jahl,' Hisham bin Amr was only too happy to recount. 'Five of us, Zuhayar ibn Amr, Al Mutam, Al-Bakhtari, Zaman bin Aswad and me, had decided that your ban should be removed. We chose Zuhayar to be our spokesman. He addressed the leaders of Quraysh like this, if I can remember the exact words: "I can eat and put on clean clothes, while the Banu Hashim are starving. They can neither buy nor sell anything. By God, I will not sit idle until this cruel banishment law is destroyed and torn to pieces." Abu Lahab called him a liar and declared, "You shall not tear up this deed!" Then Zaman bin Aswad, on our behalf, said that we had never agreed to this deed, that Abu Jahl was the one who wrote it, and who had insisted on exiling you. Abu Jahl couldn't contain his anger after hearing this, shouting, "You are, by the gods, still the greater liar!" Al-Bakhtari intervened, insisting that we had never agreed to impose sanctions. All five of us, then, joined hands, chanting in unison that we spoke the truth. Livid with anger, Abu Jahl walked out of the sanctuary, exclaiming, "This is a scheme that was hatched in darkness!" So, the deed was no more, and all of us left behind inside the Kaaba were quick to decide that the Banu Hashim clan is not subject to the boycott any more.' He heaved a sigh of relief.

'May Allah grant you all peace and guidance.' Muhammad eased himself up thoughtfully. 'I am most grateful to you, Hisham, for what you have done. Please extend my thanks and gratitude to everyone who spoke in our favour. May your good actions and good thoughts always bring you peace and prosperity.'

'I can't understand, Muhammad, how you stay calm against all this flood of hatred and opposition.' Hisham bin Amr stood there in awe. 'You know, I assume, that a lot of men out there envy your perseverance? Some of them are moved by greed to seize your fortunes, and most of them are pressed by their own hatred to kill you. How can a man endure all this and not entertain any feeling of vengeance?'

'The lamp of truth which I see and hold melts anything negative I might feel, since I only wish to share the light of this truth with anyone who is willing to take heed,' Muhammad began indulgently. 'This lamp of truth is one's own spiritual heart. By polishing this lamp with the remembrance of Allah, the rust of ill feelings dissolves. Allah is all love, beauty and goodness, and sheer remembrance of Him takes away the rust of envy, greed, hatred or bitterness. By the very act of polishing this lamp with the light of love, we free ourselves from the prison of our lower selves, soaring aloft to reach the throne of the higher self. This higher self is the seat of all knowledge, where one begins to see the glory of transformation within one's own being as part of a cosmic whole. It is also a state of awakening to the mysteries and attributes of Allah, all reflected inside the mirror of one's own soul.'

All of a sudden, a great hush fell, as if the angels were hovering above. Since no one broke the silence – Hisham bin Amr was standing there rapt – Muhammad smiled, his gaze speaking volumes.

'Let's return to our own homes, my friends, and may we all live in the comforting arms of love and peace,' Muhammad announced. 'I must go and gladden my uncle's heart, though he knows already. My uncle is a prophet, I have begun to think.'

Muhammad's feet guided him towards his own hut instead of Abu Talib's, his heart a strange ocean of joy and grief. In his thoughts were gathering the clouds of doom and gloom. Reaching his hut, and catching the light of love in Khadija's eyes, his heart was quick to reclaim its share of joys and hopes.

'We are free to go home, beloved.' Muhammad caught her in his arms. 'You are going to get well. I can't wait to see roses blooming on your cheeks once again!'

'And I would give away all my wealth to buy back the colour of joy where pallor sits rudely on your cheeks, dear Muhammad.' Khadija was succeeding in ignoring the spasms of pain ripping through her stomach down her legs.

'No need for that, my Khadija! Had you told me before, I would have borrowed some colour from my wounded heart to splash on my cheeks.' Muhammad stood gazing. 'Let's share our joy with Abu Talib before we return home.' He linked his arm in hers, almost dragging her with him in his haste.

The pools of joy and hope inside Khadija's and Muhammad's eyes drained away as soon as they entered Abu Talib's hut. The old man lay groaning. Ali was pressing Abu Talib's hand to his breast, and Umm Hani was moistening her father's lips with a wet cloth. Muhammad could neither speak nor move, not even aware that his own beloved had turned white from trying her best to ward off the spasms of her own pain.

La Illaha illah Allah
Muhammad Ar Rusul Allah,

Muhammad stood murmuring to himself, a fevered, anguished look in his eyes.

'I can't hear you, Muhammad; what are you saying?' Abu Talib asked.

'I am reciting Kalima, Uncle,' Muhammad responded. 'It is the creed of Islam. I am reciting it to strengthen my own faith, and hoping to pour strength into your body.'

'I want to go home,' Abu Talib lamented feebly as he closed his eyes.

'Yes, dear Uncle, yes.' Muhammad was jolted out of the pool of his inner suffering, his gaze turning to Khadija. 'Zaid will help you and the girls – and, of course, Khalwa – to return home. I will help Uncle. It won't take long – soon I will join you.'

'Yes, Muhammad. Don't hurry on our account. We will be safe and comfortable.' Khadija smiled warmly. 'You stay with Abu Talib as long as he needs you.' She turned away quickly, willing the fresh violence of her pain to subside.

Muhammad was drifting into the mists of nameless doom and grief, though he did not know that his own beloved was succumbing to her own pain. He helped Abu Talib to leave Shib and reach the comforts of his home, oblivious to the march of time. Abu Talib lay moaning in his bed, his face ashen. A physician stood pouring some sort of concoction down his throat. Ali, Aqil, Rahmani, Umm Hani and Abu Talib's wives were all caught in a daze, their eyes riveted to the face of the dying man. Then suddenly his features attained some semblance of peace. The physician staggered back, then returned to the bedside and closed the eyes of the deceased. A heart-rending cry tore from Umm Hani's heart, her body racked with sobs as Ali and Rahmani caught her in their arms. Ali's own tears mingled with his sister's, but his grief was mute. Muhammad, in a state of utter shock, stumbled out into the silence of the night.

The cool air of the desert night was stinging Muhammad's eyes, his feet homeward bound, but his senses numb and sightless. He was weeping like a child, as if surfing on the turbulent waters of life's struggles, alone and defenceless.

Allah, Allah, Allah! Muhammad could hear the night-song of the wind. *O sweetness all, my Allah, I resign myself to You in my sorrow, and I believe in You. I trust You and to You I turn, and through You I prevail. Allah, my True Eternity, I take refuge in Your might, there is no God but You, lest You allow me to get lost. You are the living, who never dies, while spirits and humans do*. He was home at last.

A curtain of sorrow lowered over Muhammad's heart as he entered his bedchamber. Abandoning his head in Khadija's lap, he poured out all his grief, not even realising that the night was nearly over. Now, as Khadija sat whispering and consoling her husband, she couldn't fight the fresh violence of pain and nausea; her voice choked and she started shivering.

'Are you ill, my Khadija?' A cry of agony was wrenched out of Muhammad's very soul, his heart shuddering against the weight of nameless tragedy.

'A little, Muhammad.' Khadija gasped for breath. 'But I have returned home after so long – I just need a little rest and I will be fine.' She closed her eyes.

Muhammad sat holding her close, trying to infuse his own warmth into her shivering body, which grew limp in his arms. She had fainted, and he jumped to his feet as if stung, dashing down the stairs. Muhammad's frantic appeals stirred the whole house into awakening. Zaid was quick to fly out of the house to fetch a doctor, while Baraka stood there wringing her hands. Khalwa rushed towards the staircase, followed by Muhammad.

Muhammad did not leave Khadija's side for three whole days, his prayers mute and agonised. On the third day in a row of her ailment she succeeded in voicing her wish that she wanted to be alone with Muhammad, bidding her daughters to return later. Zainab was the first to leave, Khultum and Ruqayyah following reluctantly, and Fatima the last. Muhammad watched her in mute surrender to the violence of his own agony, his tortured spirit pleading with his beloved to live.

'Don't grieve, dear Muhammad.' Khadija gazed into his eyes, a pale smile hovering over her lips. 'I am leaving my body, but my spirit will always stay with you, watching you proclaim the glory of Islam from land to land, and from sea to sea.'

'You are the Mother of the Believers, my Khadija. My soul! My life! My very own beloved!' Muhammad murmured. 'You will be in Paradise, and the nymphs of Paradise will attend to you. Keep a place for me there; I will be longing to join you.'

'You have a great mission to accomplish, dear Muhammad.' Khadija's voice was barely audible. 'Never let any grief hold you back, not even my death—'

'How will I live, my Khadija?' Muhammad's eyes were glazed with living torment. 'Surely, I will be lost, and perish without you. My first believer, my own beloved, when no one believed in me. My friend! My disciple! My comforter! Who will believe in me when you are gone?'

'You won't lose heart in Allah, dear Muhammad. Your heart is so pure and noble!' Khadija murmured, fighting back the violence of pain. 'Hold me, Muhammad. Keep me in your heart's memory...' Her eyes were drooping shut.

Khadija was cradled in Muhammad's arms as he sat rocking her back and forth, her features washed by the purity of peace in death. His heart was numb with grief. He laid her down gently on the bed, kissing her eyes, face, hands. His own hands were trembling as he spread a sheet over her legs, his gaze never leaving her beloved face.

My beloved has left me. I will never hear her voice again. Her beautiful, loving eyes... Muhammad's thoughts pierced his heart and soul with the knives of grief.

He was weeping as he had never wept before. Much like a child, alone, defenceless. The eruption of his grief was volcanic, but he could feel the lava of pain and loss inside him, coiling around his heart and soul like a serpent of death and darkness.

Muhammad's shoulders were sagging under the weight of despair. His thoughts followed Khadija to the gates of Paradise. He could hear the sound of the falling leaves in the Garden of Eden.

In the name of Allah, the Merciful, the Beneficent
Those are they who will be brought nigh

In gardens of delight
A multitude of those of old
And a few of those of later time
On lined couches
Reclining therein face to face
There wait on them immortal youths with bowls and ewers and a cup from a pure Spring. Wherefrom they get no aching of the head nor any madness.
And fruit they prefer
And flesh of fowls they desire
And there are fair ones with wide, lovely eyes
Like unto hidden pearls
Reward for what they used to do
There hear they no vain speaking nor recrimination
Naught but the saying: Peace, and again, Peace
And those on the right hand; what of those on the right hand
Among thornless Lote trees
And clustered plantains
And spreading shade
And water gushing
And fruit in plenty
Neither out of reach nor yet forbidden
And raised couches
Lo! We have created them a new creation
And made them virgins
Lovers, friends
For those on the right hand
A multitude of those of old
And a multitude of those of later time
And those on the left hand: what of those on the left hand? (56:11–41)

Muhammad's thoughts proffered a tapestry of revelations. His heart bled white of all wounds, as he suffered still the agony of loss and loneliness.

CHAPTER 8

The Night Journey to the Throne of the Beloved From 619 to 620 AD

Muhammad's heart, bandaged in a prayer-rug of sweet, painful memories, was at peace, as he lay resting on the same bed where he had held Khadija in his arms during her peaceful last moments. A whole year had bounded past in a hurricane of tragedies since the death of Abu Talib and Khadija, and Muhammad had learnt to live with grief.

Now that Abu Talib was no more, Abu Lahab had become the protector of the Kaaba, pumping the bellows of his pride and hatred with a sense of vengeance. In league with Abu Jahl he had begun a fiery crusade of tortures against Muhammad and his followers. Muhammad had managed to send small groups of Muslims to Medina and Abyssinia. He himself had decided to stay in Mecca, praying for a revelation which would grant him permission to leave Mecca in search of a better place for the propagation of Islam.

Right at this moment, sleep was Muhammad's sanctuary, his thoughts suspended against mists swollen with memories. Khultum had married Abd al Mottaleb. The mists in his thoughts revealed another face, that of Swadah, now his wife. After Khadija's death, Muhammad's aunt Atika had suggested the match. Swadah was a middle-aged woman whose husband Sakran had died suddenly after his return from Abyssinia, and she had been left with no means to support herself. Atika had gone to console the grieving widow, and after listening to her plight had proposed that she marry Muhammad. Since Muhammad was immersed deep in grief, Swadah herself had approached him with the strangest of proposal pleas.

'Since you are the protector of orphans and widows, O Messenger of Islam, would you keep and protect me, a homeless widow, as your wife?'

This strange echo of a proposal was pounding at the gates of Muhammad's dreams. He had married Swadah in conformity with the law and virtue of his own purity of heart. She had become the sole mistress of his household, granting him the freedom to pray and contemplate. But Khadija was with him in his dreams, robed in stars from the garden of Paradise, and blessing him with the kisses of light.

My true love! Beloved! My All.

Muhammad could feel the dreamy ache within each fibre of his soul, which seemed to be reaching out to Eden in his dreams, longing to snatch his beloved from the starry heavens and bring her back to earth. His heart was empty and luminous; loss and grief had no names there, only the light of peace in unity. That light itself revealed one form, radiating the purity of truth, and reflecting the face of Gabriel.

What is a beautiful action, O Apostle of Allah? Gabriel was asking.

That one worships Allah, as if one saw Him. For if one does not see Him, truly Allah sees the one who worships Him. Muhammad's thoughts were trembling.

A beautiful answer from the beautiful heart of a prophet! Gabriel was smiling. *For your devotion to Allah, He has sent you a gift most precious.* In Gabriel's eyes was an image: Aisha's face. *She is to be your wife, Muhammad.*

A child of barely ten; how could she be my wife? In Muhammad's thoughts he shuddered with awe and disbelief.

Not a child, but a woman most noble and virtuous! Gabriel was saying. *She will be the light of your days, and the lamp of your nights. A beacon of hope amidst struggles and sorrows in your long journey towards the glory of Islam!*

That would be unfair. Why should Aisha marry an old man like me? I am already married to Swadah. Sadness gathered in his thoughts.

Aisha has already agreed; she longs to be the wife of a prophet, Gabriel insisted, *as many more would, seeking your love and protection.* Suddenly he was reduced to a speck of light, vanishing behind white mists.

Startled into awakening, Muhammad looked around for Khadija, but she had left home.

Muhammad visited her grave every day without fail. His obligations were hurling him towards the town of Taif, but his heart was aching for his daily pilgrimage to the grave of his beloved. Taif was calling him to proclaim his message of unity. The faces of Ali and Abu Bakr, the most persecuted by the Meccans, surfaced in his mind.

Allah, Allah, Allah. Muhammad's heart invoked the beloved name for strength and perseverance, as he scrambled to his feet. For a moment, he stood dazed, noticing, for the first time, the bare room stripped naked of all amenities, where he had spent twenty-four years of his married life with Khadija. He made his way towards the adjacent bathroom. A sudden realisation was dawning upon him that his business was suffering great loss, and that all these household items were sold to raise money for the expense of sending Muslims to Medina and Abyssinia.

Returning to his bedroom, he stood wrapping his turban with the utmost care and precision. His heart was throbbing all of a sudden, its wounds cankerous with grief. He flew out of his room, trying to flee the ghosts of grief, lest they prevented him from carrying his banner into the very heart of Taif.

The rectangular hall, now divested of all furnishings, seemed alien to Muhammad as he wandered into its vast emptiness. Swadah sat on a mat, brushing Fatima's hair. Both were content in a world of their own, Swadah telling a story, and Fatima sitting there rapt and wide-eyed. Swadah's plump figure, draped in a gown of green cotton, was most beautiful to Muhammad. And yet the pangs of grief did not take long to return. He smothered them before they could flower into a fresh wound.

'What wonderful story is this, Swadah, which has transported my little Fatima into a dreamworld?' Muhammad remonstrated.

'Muhammad!' Swadah exclaimed, startled.

'Father!' Fatima leapt to her feet, hugging him. 'Swadah was telling the story of Moses you told her. Why don't you tell me such stories, Father?'

'Because you are young and heedless, my love,' Muhammad teased. 'Besides, what you think of as stories are in fact revelations. Swadah commits them to memory, and all together they will become the body and soul of the Living Quran.'

'The Quran is going to be a book – Swadah told me, Father. How can a book be living?' Fatima's dark eyes were lit up with curiosity.

'Would you assist me in this, Swadah?' Muhammad appealed, flashing a smile. 'She understands better when you tell her.'

'The Quran is the tongue of truth, dear Fatima,' Swadah began thoughtfully. 'One can feel its living breath, if one recites its revelations with love and devotion. Quran is a holy book, a precious gift from Allah, already written inside everyone's hearts.' She couldn't continue, noticing the look of fear and confusion in Fatima's eyes.

'I recite revelations too, Swadah, but I only feel fear,' Fatima murmured.

'What do you fear, dear Fatima?' Muhammad held her captive in his gaze.

'I don't know, Father.' Fatima averted her gaze. 'When I recite, I start dreaming, and you are always there, with big wounds and bleeding.'

'My dear, dear Fatima; your imagination is far too wild! You need to forget the times when you saw me like that. And those memories are the ones coming back to haunt you.' Muhammad's look was profound. 'Things, most of the time, are not as they appear. If you see me wounded, remember that they are just the bruises of the flesh and I am not hurting. My heart is always whole and healthy, praying for those who injure others, and offering love to those who hate. We must learn to love, always; remember that, dear Fatima, then all your fears will dissolve. When you are a grown woman, you'll understand. You will feel the light and the breath of the Living Quran inside you, and no fear will ever come near you.' He returned his gaze to Swadah. 'Do you need anything from the market, Swadah, since I'm going out?'

'Sugar and cooking oil, Muhammad.' Swadah was quick to make a mental list of her daily needs, although she felt guilty. 'I can send Zaid to market if you don't have the time, Muhammad.' Swadah's heart was thundering. 'He is an angel.'

'Talking of angels, Swadah, here he comes, wearing the devil's cloak.' Muhammad laughed. 'And why are you grinning, my son?'

'I do that when I am happy, Muhammad; you should know by now.' Zaid's eyes were twinkling. 'Abu Bakr just came. He is waiting for you in the courtyard.'

'Why didn't you invite him in, Zaid?' Muhammad's gaze was piercing.

'He says he is in a hurry,' Zaid replied, enigmatically.

'I am in a hurry too.' Muhammad stood smiling. 'And don't follow me today. I want to go wherever I decide to go alone. Where is Ali?'

'He is helping Umm Hani to put everything in order; she and her husband have moved to Abu Talib's house.' Zaid was grinning again.

'If he comes here, tell him not to come looking for me. He won't find me at the Kaaba, for sure.' Muhammad turned with the intention of leaving.

'May I come with you to the market, Father?' Fatima raised a feeble plea.

'No, my love, not today! I am not sure when I will get to the market.' Muhammad kissed her on the head. 'Khultum and her husband are coming here this afternoon; you can help Swadah cook and clean.'

'They're going to Ruqayyah's house for something.' Fatima murmured disappointment. 'They'll come tomorrow, they promise, but I am not sure.'

'Even more reason to keep Swadah company then, my love, don't you think?' Muhammad consoled gently. 'She will tell you more revelations.'

'Don't make us wait for three whole days, Muhammad, like you did the last time. You go wandering without telling us where, and our hearts grow weary and restless.' In Swadah's possessive eyes gathered the mists of fear and doubt.

'Sorry, Swadah, I can't help it sometimes.' Muhammad's expression was contrite. 'But that was a few months ago. Those hospitable tribes! How could I tear myself away from the music of their insults and inquisitions?' He ran out hurriedly.

Abu Bakr, unable to wait outside any longer, had come into the front porch. He was pacing back and forth, and almost collided with Muhammad as he appeared in the high-arched entrance. One look at Abu Bakr's face, and Muhammad knew that his friend's heart was holding a fountain of joy which could bathe the whole world in its radiance of love and light.

'I knew I would find a way to bind myself with you in kinship, Muhammad!' Abu Bakr was quick to explain. 'Aisha is to be betrothed to you, my wife Umm Ruman and I have decided. Aisha was betrothed to Zubayr ibn Awwam, you know, but when Umm Ruman told her, she started crying and saying that she didn't want to get married. We talked to Zubayr's mother, your aunt Safiyah, to ask that the engagement be dissolved. Your aunt wouldn't agree, until we told her that Aisha would be marrying you.'

'A flower of a child! She'll break her little heart with tears when she is told that she has to marry an old madman like me!' Muhammad laughed.

'She is no child, Muhammad!' Abu Bakr exclaimed. 'You should have seen her dancing like an elf on her tiny feet when we told her that she was to be married to you. I have never seen her like that before, bobbing her curly head up and down, singing, "I am going to be the wife of a prophet!"'

'Gabriel was right,' Muhammad muttered.

'What? What did you say, Muhammad?' Abu Bakr stood in awe of the purity of the light in his friend's eyes.

'Nothing,' Muhammad murmured. 'Did my aunt Atika put you up to this?'

'No, Aisha herself did; and you think she is a child?' Abu Bakr confessed happily. 'You are betrothed to her, whether you like it or not.'

'I will like it when she is of age.' Streams of sadness formed in Muhammad's eyes. 'Right now, I will only kneel and offer my gratitude to Allah for the gift of her youth and beauty. Zaid told me that you are in a hurry. Where are you going?'

'Nowhere in particular. I didn't want to talk about this in front of Swadah,' Abu Bakr confessed. 'By the look of you, I can tell you want to fly away somewhere. I will come with you wherever you want to go. The Kaaba? Mount Hira?'

'I'm not going very far, Abu Bakr, and you wouldn't want to come,' Muhammad replied evasively. 'I am on my way to visit Khadija. I need to pray to forget my grief, since I can't forget her.'

'I'm sorry, Muhammad. May all your prayers be answered,' Abu Bakr sighed. 'I'll see you soon. Now don't go wandering around, carrying the weight of the divine call all by yourself. You know how cruel and heartless the Meccans are. The blades of persecution are easier to endure when a friend is there with you to support and console.'

'Your love and devotion, Abu Bakr, are always with me, even when you are absent.' Muhammad smiled wistfully. 'I should be forever grateful to Allah for His gifts of love, truth and friendship, rather than clinging to my grief and holding it as a pawn to win the mercy of His nearness. Am I being negligent in my duty towards Him, holding the flood of revelations to myself, fearing to pour them into the hearts of humanity lest their hatred and animosity consume me entirely?'

'No, Prophet of Islam, a thousand times, no!' Abu Bakr declared. 'Your love for Allah knows no fear, I stand witness to that. Go and pray, Muhammad, and absolve your heart of all grief. My only joy and prayer is to be at your side whenever you need me.' He turned on his heels, his eyes spilling the warmth of hope and peace.

Peace and quiet were Muhammad's companions as he sat praying at the grave of his beloved. The sun-baked earth under him was his prayer-rug, and a pewter-bright haze warmed his back. Muhammad appeared peaceful, his face a luminous white, but at his mind and heart were licking the flames of loss and grief.

I am sand and dust under Your feet, Allah, my Eternal Truth. Hold me in Your arms, My All, and make me whole with the bounty of Your grace. Muhammad's soul, not his lips, uttered the prayer. *Whatever joys and sorrows war within me, my Perfect All, take them away by the hand of Your love and mercy. Let only Your truth stay with me, my Profound, Infinite Sweetness. You have touched me with the sweetness of Your truth, and its fragrance is in my breath, for It alone I breathe. It is the breath of love and unity, longing, a Gift from*

You to be shared and cherished. My Precious All, let the hatred of others dissolve against the flood of my own love, and grant me the favour of seeing Your Face, even inside the hearts of the ones burdened with the weight of malice and ignorance. My grief is open to You, my beloved Allah. You can see all my wounds which I hide in vain inside my own breast. Heal these wounds, my True Sweetness. Have Mercy on Your servant. Pity this poor slave of Yours, whose agony of spirit still seeks the lost Beloved. Is my Khadija in Paradise, Allah? Is it not You, the Beloved of us all, Whom I am seeking? Did she not say, Beloved is One? Take away this hurt and this sickness, my Beloved Eternity, my One and Only Allah. Take away this agony of separation, this hunger and longing, this desire for nearness? Truth, my Truth, forgive… His prayers were sucked into the inner vacuums of his psyche.

Muhammad could neither move nor pray, as a dark cave in his memory threw open its portals of light, projecting the familiar form of Gabriel. Beside him, Khadija was emerging, radiant and youthful, holding a silver vessel.

Here is your Beloved, Muhammad. Gabriel was bathed in an aura of light. *She is carrying a vessel of Light and Truth, bestowed upon her by Allah. This Vessel itself has granted her the gift of drawing near you. Heed her words and be comforted.*

Dear Muhammad – Khadija's eyes were pouring the sparkling joy of love into his heart – *be of good cheer; Allah has given me a house in Paradise made of pearls, all smooth and glowing.* Her form vanished inside the cradle of the starry heavens.

Hot, scalding tears of pain and relief streamed from Muhammad's eyes, his head resting on Khadija's grave. He could see his beloved lodged comfortably in her own house of pearls, inside the purity of his heart. But this new vision of Khadija he had just seen was guarded by Gabriel. Gabriel commanded him to go on the road to Taif.

Time and events were riding on the wheels of eternity, shifting with such speed that Muhammad found himself in Taif, walled city of date palms and fruit trees, before he even noticed that he had travelled for half a day. The other realisation dawning upon him was that Zaid, seated beside him, was no phantom of his imagination. Two camels relaxing in a stream caught Muhammad's attention. He could see three men gliding out from the dusky haze. As they approached, one of them addressed Zaid.

'Who are you, and who is this man with moonbeams in his eyes?' The man's voice was stiff and threatening.

'He is the Prophet of Allah, and I am his servant,' Zaid replied boldly. 'He has come to deliver the message of Allah to the people of Taif.'

'I've never heard of this prophet,' the man scoffed.

'We are three brothers.' The tallest of the three introduced them. 'We are leaders from the tribe of Hawazin. We offer hospitality to everyone, whether friends or strangers. You are welcome to spend the night in our garden, and tomorrow you can have your share of breakfast here. If you have any favour to ask, now is the right time, before we go inside.'

'Would you be able to invite the people of this city to gather at the foot of that hill?' Muhammad's gaze indicated the spot. 'I would be forever grateful for the favour, and for the opportunity to talk about my message of love and unity as revealed to me by the grace of Allah.'

'The people of Taif are curious by nature; they're adventurous and superstitious. I promise you a great sea of an audience before you are even ready to face them.' The self-designated spokesman turned on his heel.

As the three brothers returned to their great mansion, Muhammad's eyes were closing, and his body grew limp on the grass in a soft heap. Zaid was quick to fold a sheet into a makeshift pillow and slip it under the Prophet's head, before dropping off himself.

What Muhammad had been unaware of during his journey to Taif, re-enacted itself in his sleep. In hushed tones, Zaid had informed Muhammad that Swadah had divined the intent and the danger of his journey to Taif, and that she had urged Zaid to follow him, supplying him with ample provisions and camels. In Muhammad's dreams unfolded a dark journey to the valleys of Taif. The valleys were dotted with the shrines of the goddesses. The shrine of the goddess al-Lat was the most imposing, since she was the consort of the god, al-Llah. A beautiful shrine to the goddess al-Uzzah nestled at the foot of the Nakhlah Valley, which housed another shrine on its shores, to the goddess al-Manat.

The goddess al-Huzza is worshipped as the Mighty One, and al-Manat is the goddess of fate. Zaid's words echoed in Muhammad's sleep.

Sleep was no more. Another day dawned as Muhammad stood at the top of a hill, below which sprawled the valley of Taif. Zaid, standing ramrod-straight beside him, looked anxious, but Muhammad's expression was all serenity. The denizens of Taif were brimming with excitement. The three brothers, who had succeeded in inviting half the town, were now urging everyone to silence so Muhammad could share his message.

'O People of Taif, my friends and my neighbours. Allah has sent me as an apostle so that I may demonstrate perfection of character, refinement of manners and loftiness of deportment.' From Muhammad's gaze poured loving libations.

In the name of Allah, the Merciful, the Beneficent
By the dawn and ten nights
And the even and the odd
And the night when it departeth
There surely is an oath for thinking man
Dost thou not consider how thy Lord dealt with the tribe of Aad
With many-columned Iram
The like of which was not created in the lands
And with the tribe of Thamud who clove the rocks in the valley

And with Pharaoh, Firm of Might
Who all were rebellious to Allah in these lands
And multiplied inequity therein
Therefore thy Lord poured on them the disaster of His punishment. (89:1–13)

'We need no rocks of punishments on our heads, Muhammad,' Ammrah ibn Walid interrupted. 'Tell us of our fortunes in this good city. Will we be the masters of our own health and wealth?'

'*In the name of Allah, the Merciful, the Beneficent,*' Muhammad's every thought was a revelation:

Nay, I swear by this city
And thou art are indweller of this city
And the begetter and that which he begat
We verily have created man in an atmosphere
Thinketh he that none have power over him
And he saith: I have destroyed vast wealth
Thinketh he that none beholdeth him
Did We not assign unto him two eyes
And a tongue and two lips
And guide him to the parting of the mountain ways
But he hath not attempted the Ascent
Ah, what will convey unto thee what the Ascent is
It is to free a slave
And to feed in the day of hunger
An orphan near of kin
Or some poor wretch in misery
And to be of those who believe and exhort
One another to perseverance and exhort one another to pity
Their place will be on the right hand. (90:1–18)

'And who will be on the left?' Shaiba bin Utbah's voice rang out loud. 'Who made you Prophet, Muhammad? If that's what your name is. Where do you get all these words of piety and exhortation?' His eyes were shining with a rude challenge.

'*In the name of Allah, the Merciful, the Beneficent*,' Muhammad resumed patiently, his heart feeling the pincers of premonition,

The Beneficent
Hath made known the Quran
He hath created man
He hath taught him utterance
The Sun and the Moon are made punctual
The stars and the trees adore
And the sky He hath uplifted. (55:1–7)

His recitation came to an abrupt halt against the shower of jeers and insults.

'Is your Allah the God of music and poetry, willing madmen to sing to us? Haven't we heard enough lies already? Diviners and would-be prophets deceiving us into believing, though lacking faith in their own beliefs, and hurling us straight into the marshlands of lies and error?' Otba bin Utbah challenged menacingly.

In the name of Allah, the Merciful, the Beneficent
By the Star when it setteth
Your comrade erreth not, nor is deceived
Nor doth he speak of his own desire
It is naught save an inspiration that is inspired
Which one of mighty powers hath taught him
One vigorous; and he grew clear to view
When he was on the uppermost horizon
Then he drew nigh and came down
Till he was distant two bows' length or even nearer
And He revealed unto His slave that which He revealed
The heart lied not in seeing what it saw
Will you then dispute with him concerning what he seeth

And verily he saw him yet another time
By the Lote tree of the utmost boundary
Nigh unto which is the Garden of Abode
When that which shroudeth did enshroud the Lote tree
The eye turned not aside nor yet was overbold
Verily he saw one of the greater revelations of his Lord
Have you thought upon al-Lat and al-Uzzah
And al-Manat, the third, the other— (53:1–20)

A hurricane of protests was spiralling up; a foaming ocean. The men were ready to strike this stranger who dared question the sanctity of their goddesses. Amongst them, Muhammad recognised two prominent chiefs: Malik ibn Auf of the Hawazin, and Abbas ibn Mirdas from the clan of Banu Sulaim.

'I would tear the curtain of holy Kaaba with my bare hands, if God ever made you His prophet!' Malik ibn Auf hurled a stone, but it missed Muhammad.

'What would happen to you, Muhammad, if we let you rave like a madman?' Abbas ibn Mirdas flashed his own threat of violence.

'I am the Prophet of Allah, but I do not know how I will die,' Muhammad responded patiently.

'Have you no fear of this mob? They will kill you if you don't desist from your claim of prophethood!' Zaid recognised Ibn Kami, who flung the warning.

'By Allah, the day is near when this faith will reach its pinnacle, and none will have to fear anyone except Allah!' A sprig of prophecy escaped Muhammad's lips.

A volley of stones was unleashed from the hands of the angry mob, and Zaid tried his best to shield Muhammad from the onslaught of violence. Muhammad, his head bent low, reached the foot of the hill, weaving his way out of this pandemonium, Zaid still trying to deflect the shower of stones. Muhammad could barely walk, blood dripping down his legs from large, throbbing wounds, and with a pain so savage and excruciating that he collapsed to the ground.

'This is no place for you to rest; keep walking.' One of the tormentors, by the name of Nadr, pulled Muhammad up to his feet and pushed him into the arms of Zaid.

The torture seemed endless, lasting the whole three-mile stretch, till the tormentors themselves were weak with hunger and exhaustion. Muhammad's shoes filled with blood as he staggered along, Zaid stumbling behind in a state of shock, oblivious to the ache and profusion of his own wounds. Muhammad too seemed unaware of his physical injuries, as he lumbered forward as if in a dream.

The valley of Nakhlah, flanked by the slanting shadows of the late afternoon, offered some sort of comfort to Zaid and Muhammad in their arduous journey towards Mecca. Muhammad's face lit up at the sight of an orchard stretching far back to a palatial house. Utbah and Shaybah were the names of the two young brothers who were seated not too far away in the courtyard. They saw Muhammad slump to his knees. Zaid fell into a stiff heap beside him. The brothers were attended by a Christian slave called Addas, and were quick to send him with a plate of grapes to offer to the poor strangers.

'Allah, help me. Do not leave me to fend for myself, my Infinite Sweetness,' Muhammad groaned, before catching sight of Addas holding out the plate of grapes.

'My masters have sent you these grapes,' Addas offered bashfully.

'May Allah bless you and your masters.' Muhammad scooped a bunch of grapes into his hands, giving half to Zaid.

'By God, I have not ever met anyone in this land before who invoked such blessings!' Addas exclaimed in astonishment.

'Where are you from? What gods do you worship?' Muhammad was concentrating on eating the grapes, his anguished features glowing with gratitude.

'I am a Christian from Nineveh in Iraq,' Addas muttered under his breath.

'So, you are from the town where good Jonah lived, the son of Matthew.' Muhammad looked at him in pain and intensity.

'How do you know that?' Addas could barely breathe, standing there perplexed.

'He was a prophet, and so am I,' Muhammad murmured.

'My heart tells me you are.' Addas fell to his knees, kissing Muhammad's feet. He bounced back up and fled before Muhammad could say anything.

'A sweet and agonising journey on the path to bewilderment, while seeking one's beloved.' Muhammad's eyes were searching Zaid's. 'And that Beloved is Allah, Zaid. There is a lesson to be learnt from this painful experience, my son. The march of time is swift and ephemeral, yet we carry its dregs on our shoulders and stumble and perish. During this brief journey, in barely half a day, we have experienced both rancour and hospitality. We were pelted with stones, then consoled with the sweet gift of grapes, and again blessed with the sweetest gift of knowledge that the devotion of one servant of Allah can heal manifold evils. Yes, ponder upon this, Zaid, and you will understand the cause of all afflictions.' He closed his eyes.

'I am sore and hurting, Muhammad, and I can't think,' Zaid groaned.

'Allah, my true Beloved. To Thee do I complain of the feebleness of my strength, of the lack of my resourcefulness, and of my insignificance in the eyes of the people! Thou art Most Merciful of all the Merciful. To whom do Thou entrust me, to an unsympathetic foe, who would sullenly frown at me? Or, to a close friend, whom Thou hast given control over my affairs. Not in the least do I care for anything except that I may have Your protection. In the light of Thy Face do I seek shelter – the light which illumines the heavens and dispels all sorts of darkness, and which controls all affairs in this world as well as in the hereafter. May it never be that I should incur Thy wrath, or that Thou shouldst be angry with me. There is no strength but through Thee.' Muhammad's agony lent sincerity to his prayer.

Zaid shadowed Muhammad to the very hearth of Mecca in a daze of exaltation. An astonishing sense of peace, with all its promise of joy and hope, had entered Muhammad's soul and psyche, holding out the lamps of love, not only to Zaid, but to the whole world.

'Go home, Zaid.' Even Muhammad's eyes commanded him. 'Don't tell Swadah about my wounds; she'll only worry. I'll spend tonight in Abu Talib's house, though it is Umm Hani's and her husband's now. Ali will be there too. It'll give me time to bathe my wounds before I see Swadah in the morning.'

The Prophet and his adopted son parted, drifting away in different directions. Muhammad's heart hummed strange tunes. Abu Talib was with him as he mounted the steps of the too-familiar home. The doors were thrown open. Ali held a lantern as he ushered Muhammad in with devotion.

'Umm Hani told me you were coming.' Ali intoned, his eyes dark and searching.

'Yes, I didn't plan to,' Muhammad swept past him, nursing a sudden pang of grief and loneliness, 'and yet, I knew I would.'

'Muhammad!' Umm Hani stood there aghast. 'You're all caked in blood! My vision unfolded such horrors, but I didn't want to believe them. Let me wash your wounds.'

'No, Umm Hani. I only need rest.' Muhammad collapsed on the mat. 'This suffering is insignificant as long as Allah's gift of remembrance stays, bestowing upon me the bounty of its love and mercy.' His agony was concealed behind his eyes.

'Go and sleep in my room, Ali; I will stay here in case Muhammad needs me.' Umm Hani sighed, sucking back her tears. 'If Hudayfah wakes up before you do, tell him that Muhammad came home wounded and I am keeping an eye on him.'

Ali had long since retired upstairs, and while Muhammad slept soundly, Umm Hani had dozed off in a corner by the window. The house itself was quiet when Muhammad's eyes were catapulted open by a sudden flood of light. Veils upon veils of shimmering light danced before him, revealing infinite, boundless vistas. They expanded into One Circle of Unity, its shining globe a bright mirror. Gabriel floated out of the mirror, clothed in a light so dazzling that it seemed to cut through the heart of the night, obliterating the darkness. His silvery thatch of hair was crowned by stars, and his wings were sprinkled with rainbow colours. Muhammad could not tear his gaze away, the fires of joy and bliss leaping through his soul into his shining eyes. Gabriel commanded him to rise, and he obeyed like the Pilgrim of Love, listening to the music of the night, which bade him to journey to the Throne of the Beloved.

The night was decked with brilliant stars, beckoning Muhammad to obey each and every one of Gabriel's commands. In absolute surrender to his senses, Muhammad had already followed Gabriel out onto the road. Gabriel drew his attention towards a beautiful mare, with glittering wings spread out like a giant eagle in flight. A jacinth-like fire and brilliance was contained in her eyes, and her golden hair was braided with moonbeams.

Her name is Buraq, Muhammad. Our heavenly mount to carry us on our Night Journey to the Lord of Power! Gabriel smiled, hoisting Muhammad up and slipping onto the horse's back himself with the swiftness of lightning. Buraq whinnied in delight, sucking in the cool draught of night air, and galloped over the wind towards the skies.

Muhammad felt light-headed, his eyes darting all over the expanse of the mountain upon which Buraq had planted her feet. Gabriel commanded him to dismount and offer his prayers, explaining that the ground under their feet was the summit of

Mount Sinai, where Jehovah had given the tablets of stone to Moses.

They travelled on. Muhammad was spellbound by his indescribable journey. Astride Buraq with Gabriel behind him, Muhammad could feel the silken sails of the wind caressing his face. Their next halt was at Bethlehem, and Muhammad prayed at the very spot where Jesus was born. Buraq was their holy guide, sailing up once again, and then swooping down in front of the temple in Jerusalem. Muhammad was commanded to enter this Holy Temple, where beside him Gabriel introduced him to Jesus and Moses. All three knelt in unison, offering prayers.

Muhammad had barely finished when he found himself outside the temple. Gabriel led Muhammad towards a ladder balanced on Jacob's stone, planted his feet on the first rung, and told him to follow in the footsteps of Light and Trust. They climbed the very rungs of the voids, each step light as a feather. In a flash, Muhammad was whisked into the mists of the ether, and stood face to face with Gabriel at the very gates of Paradise.

The gates of the heavens flung open at Gabriel's command. Muhammad entered the First Heaven, made of pure silver, suspended low under a canopy of stars, and balanced by golden chains. Adam was the first to greet Muhammad, embracing him and hailing him as the noblest of his children. He led him towards the Second Heaven where Noah stood welcoming him. Muhammad was embraced by Noah, Jesus and John the Baptist, before being whisked away by Gabriel into the Third Heaven. The Third Heaven was the abode of David and Joseph, Gabriel explained. In the Fourth Heaven, Enoch offered them a warm welcome before they were flown to the next. Muhammad had barely exchanged greetings with Aaron in the Fifth Heaven, when the Sixth Heaven, in all its splendour, started calling him, and he yielded to the glory of the angels standing singing.

O Allah, Who has united snow and fire, unite all Thy faithful servants in obedience to Thy Law.

Muhammad's senses were intoxicated by the sweetness of the music from the lips of the angels. His soul shuddered, a mirror of bliss and rapture so supreme that he didn't even realise that he had already been transported inside the shining vaults of the Seventh Heaven. He was absorbed into a flood of divine light, standing under the shade of a Lote tree, beyond which rippling waves upon waves of light concealed the many thrones of Allah. Muhammad was invited into the House of Adoration, embellished with rubies and jacinths, and his gaze searched for the face of the Beloved. The scent of Paradise was in his breath, the perfume of nearness; he was only two bow shots away from the Throne of Allah. The face of God was behind twenty thousand veils, and the glory which radiated from behind the veils was greater than fifty thousand suns caught inside the heart of one day. To the right of God's throne was a dazzling inscription.

There is no God but Allah, and Muhammad is His Messenger. The golden tongue of this inscription poured the music of ecstasy and exaltation into Muhammad's soul as he stood gazing, rapt.

O Muhammad, salute Thy Creator. One voice, imbued with all-encompassing love, pulsed with the caressing command.

Shafts of pain and bliss leapt from Muhammad's heart, his own fire of love an ineffable embrace. Sweetness upon sweetness from the face of his Beloved infused into every pore of his surrendered self, as he stood there annihilated, dazzled. His soul sang with ecstatic exaltation.

Glory be to Him Who carried His servant by night from the sacred temple of Mecca to the Temple that is remote, whose precinct We have blessed, that We might show him of Our signs. For He is the Hearer and the Seer (17:1).

Umm Hani, startled, woke up. Muhammad's face was transfigured with joy, as if the light of union with the Beloved had infused his whole being with the purity of love. Umm Hani could neither stir, nor speak, drowning in the shimmering oceans of his eyes, their diamond-like brilliance illuminating her, encompassing her. Muhammad was bathed in an aura of celestial light, the fire of rubies upon his trembling pomegranate-red lips.

'Dear, dear Umm Hani.' Muhammad's voice was pensive. 'This night – or was it dawn? – I was transported in an instant from Mecca to Jerusalem. I journeyed through the seven heavens, and expired in the presence of the Beloved. I have returned, Umm Hani, by the grace of Allah. I have seen the throne of the Lord, and He is my only Beloved. No one will believe me, Umm Hani; but my Beloved knows,' he murmured.

'I believe you, Muhammad,' Umm Hani could barely whisper.

'Bless you, Umm Hani. Khadija would have believed me too, if she was here.' Muhammad's gaze was dreamy. 'In heavenly reckoning, it took me seventy thousand years to reach Jerusalem from Mecca. And yet here I am, as if time stood still, and only my soul made the pilgrimage. It was a fleeting moment, but a moment enshrined inside the seed, the fruit and the flower of eternity.'

'Will you tell me about it, Muhammad?' was Umm Hani's prayer-like request.

'Yes, dear Umm Hani. I want to share this blessed, blessed experience with the world, and you are the first one.' Muhammad's thoughts were already kneeling before his pilgrim-soul, unwrapping the gift of union with the Beloved.

Umm Hani was Muhammad's lone audience. Muhammad's soul embarked afresh on his night journey. Dawn began to spill its lovely glow. The journey in words came to an end, but Muhammad's soul was entering the valley of earthly paradise where the Word of Allah could be heard from pole to pole, in continents upon continents.

Indeed he saw Him another time
By the Lote tree of the Boundary

Nigh which is the Garden of the Refuge
Where there covered the Lote tree which covered
His eye swerved not, nor swept astray
Indeed, he saw one of the greatest sights of his Lord. (53:13–18)

Chapter 9

The Caravan of Light to Medina From 620 to 622 AD

'I will race you, Prophet of Islam.' Aisha's eyes lit up with a bright challenge as she saw Muhammad on his way to her father's house.

Muhammad accepted the challenge laughingly, his gaze shifting to the house a few yards away where Abu Bakr stood watching. He was leading at first, but then Aisha bounded past him. She stood by her father on the front steps. Muhammad stood below them, humbled by the purity of her youth. Abu Bakr laughed and greeted him. Aisha slipped away, hearing her mother calling her indoors and obeying.

'Tell your mother, Aisha, that Muhammad is here to grace our home with his holy presence,' Abu Bakr commanded before she could disappear behind the doors.

'Now, Abu Bakr!' Muhammad protested, 'I am a man like you, or like anyone else. I don't have any saintly qualities to qualify me as a man of holiness.'

'Surely, Muhammad, your sense of humility itself proclaims you as a holy man!' Abu Bakr chanted happily. 'My Aisha, the tiny-footed elf, is ready to be married, don't you think? She's twelve years old! Besides, we need a reason to celebrate to dispel the doom and gloom of all this hatred and persecution.'

'All the more reason to wait till most of the Muslims are settled in Medina,' Muhammad murmured. 'Aisha is still young. A couple more years, and I won't be able to postpone my joy in marriage.' He smiled.

'That's what you said two years ago, Muhammad, after your night journey to Jerusalem and to the throne of Allah, remember?' Abu Bakr reminded him wistfully. 'And now you want to wait two more?'

'How can I ever forget?' Muhammad's gaze was piercing. 'Not even the sand-dunes of persecution could dim the light of that beautiful memory.'

'The Meccans haven't forgotten either, Muhammad. They are forever probing into the heart of this mystical experience,' Abu Bakr pointed out. 'They can't stop wondering how you can describe the Temple of Jerusalem with such great precision when you have never been there.' He jolted himself out of his thoughts. 'I have neglected the duties of a good host. Let's go in. Umm Ruman would scold me, I am sure.'

The large parlour with its rich rugs and colourful pillows enveloped everyone in its loving aura, as Muhammad sat talking with Abu Bakr and his family. Umm Ruman, Abu Bakr's wife, and their son Abdullah were longing to learn the meaning of the revelations. Aisha, seated by her eldest sister Asma, absorbed every word of the conversation. Asma noticed her aunt Quraybah helping in her father, Asma's grandfather.

'Father!' Abu Bakr rushed to help. 'I thought you had gone home.'

'You didn't tell me Muhammad was here,' Quhafah complained rather belligerently. 'I might as well get used to him, since he is going to be your son-in-law.'

Amir, the freed slave of Abu Bakr, materialised with an armful of tumblers, attending to the needs of the old patriarch before serving the others with the help of Burayrah. Another of Abu Bakr's sons, Abdal Kabah, trailed behind. The conversation resumed in snippets, shifting from religion to politics. Soon, both Abdal Kabah and Quhafah had lost interest and resigned themselves to listening. Quraybah, not interested in any topic, dozed off beside her father. Muhammad sat reciting a revelation in response to Abdullah's comment about race and equality.

'*O mankind! Lo! We have created you male and female, and have made you nations and tribes that ye may know one another. Lo! the noblest of you, in the sight of Allah, is the best in conduct. Lo! Allah is Knower, Aware*' (49:13). Muhammad turned to Amir. 'Come and sit with me, Amir. Let's learn the concept of equality by example. It is incumbent upon Muslims to treat the people of every race, colour or social status with equal love. There is no superiority of white over black, or black over white.'

'Yes, Muhammad.' Amir stumbled closer. 'Abu Bakr has told me often that we are all brothers, and that no man should be a slave to another. And the people who have slaves should free them, and if any of them are female, they should educate them and find good husbands for them, because those people are the best in the sight of Allah. I am learning, Muhammad, but I can't explain when people ask me one thing: what is a Muslim?'

'A Muslim is one from whose hand and whose tongue all people are safe,' Muhammad responded, kindly.

'People ask me about faith too, Prophet of Islam, and I get so deep into my thoughts that I can't…' Amir was content not to think or say more.

'Faith is to believe in God; in God's angels; in the messengers of God. Belief in meeting God is also faith,' Muhammad began profoundly. 'True faith is to worship Allah as if you actually see Him; and if you do not see Him, Allah certainly sees you. The believer with the most perfect faith is the one with the most decent character, and the most decent of us all is the one who treats his wife best.'

'This is the kind of faith most dear to my heart!' Umm Ruman exclaimed. 'There is hope yet for the jealous husbands who beat their wives mercilessly. A promise of joy and peace, if they listen.'

'No violence is permitted against women in Islam, and even slapping one's wife is punishable. For a husband who strikes his wife has not only hurt her physically, but has injured her heart, the temple of holiness which should never be desecrated!' Muhammad's eyes flashed with hope. 'Women deserve our utmost respect, for they are our wives, sisters, mothers, daughters, and the teachers of our children. I enjoin upon all Muslim men to treat their wives with love.'

'I do, and I believe in everything you say, Muhammad. Does that mean my faith is fair and complete?' Abu Bakr beamed, stealing a warm look at his wife.

'Your faith is not complete until you wish for your neighbour what you wish for yourself,' Muhammad spoke gently, 'and you are not a believer if you eat when your neighbour is hungry.'

'Our neighbours try our patience though, Muhammad, don't they, most of the time? These days, certainly.' Abdullah shook his head. 'They grow fat on anger and deem us weak, because we don't match their anger with angry words.'

'The strongest amongst us, my son, are those who control their anger.' Muhammad smiled indulgently. 'And the most patient amongst us are those who forgive others when they are strong enough to wreak vengeance on them.'

'Are they the ones who enter Paradise, Muhammad?' Asma asked.

'*And whoso doeth good works, whether male or female, and he or she is a believer, such will enter Paradise, and they will not be wronged the dint in a date-stone*' (4:124). Muhammad smiled.

'*And they, the women, have rights similar to those of men over them in equity. I, Allah, will allow not the work of any worker from among you, whether male or female, to be lost*' (3:195), Aisha sang.

'I knew you would remember that one, my Aisha,' Muhammad laughed.

'Of course, Prophet of Islam!' Aisha exclaimed. 'I want to work hard so that all women can live comfortably, and no one is allowed to beat them.'

'*Women shall have the same rights over men, as men have over them*' (2:228), Muhammad recited. 'This revelation alone should make you work harder, to achieve what you want to achieve. Patience and discipline, Aisha, and you will benefit the women of the whole world!'

'Aisha wants to be the centre of attention, Muhammad, but we have a mountainous task ahead of us.' Abu Bakr said. 'We will be comfortable to discuss the matters which need our immediate attention in the courtyard. We might as well do so before our meeting at Aqaba this evening. I have a lot on my mind, Muhammad.' He got to his feet.

'There's a lot in my heart too, my friend, which needs draining, if not purging.' Muhammad eased himself up slowly and thoughtfully.

'The sooner the better, Muhammad.' Abu Bakr turned on his heel, Muhammad following after bestowing a warm smile upon the hostess.

Air charged with a subliminal hush settled over the courtyard as Abu Bakr and Muhammad sat talking. The long, slanting shadows of the afternoon crept up behind them as Abu Bakr faced Muhammad.

'A great danger lurks over your shoulders, Muhammad. I am not talking about persecution, but about danger to your life,' Abu Bakr declared. 'The men of the Quraysh are plotting to kill you, even your own kindred. You should migrate to Medina as well. I myself would take care of everything.'

'Yes, you would, my friend, I have no doubt,' Muhammad affirmed. 'But how can I leave when Allah has not granted me permission? I obey only Him, and I am waiting for His command. He is my Lord and I am His servant, obedient to His will whenever He wills. You will be the first to know when

His will is known to me. You have spent half your fortune already, bearing the costs of migration to Medina for so many Muslims, and I am most grateful. All my funds have dwindled to nothing in the same cause, but Allah will open up the gates of His mercy for us. We should be grateful for the kindness of those Medinese men who carried my message from Aqaba to Medina, and offered a home and friendship to the Muslims who were persecuted here in Mecca. I am grateful, and yet I forget how long it has been since they left.'

'Almost two years, Muhammad: six men and two women,' Abu Bakr reminded him. 'Including those eight, seventy-five people have come here and they're waiting; they want to learn about Islam and invite you to Medina. You would be happy to see Musaib ibn Omeir this evening. He has been successful in Medina for the past two years, imparting the message of Islam. He says that the delegation from Medina whom you are to meet this evening have been reciting your revelations and are longing to meet you. They are all Muslims now.'

'Allah be praised! I long to meet them too!' Muhammad intoned joyfully. 'I saw a land of palm trees in my dreams, showering riches of love and hospitality upon me. Was it really only a dream?' He smiled. 'What else does Musaib say? He is not an idle son of wealth any more, even if he is married to Hamnah, my rich aunt Umaymah's daughter. But obviously now he is a devoted slave of Allah!'

'He has gained wealth in knowledge in Medina, Muhammad,' Abu Bakr was glad to confirm. 'All the members of this delegation belong to two major tribes, Beni Aus and Beni Khazraj. Medina has a diverse group of tribes, including the Jewish ones, the most powerful amongst those being Beni Nadir, Beni Kainuka and Beni Koreiza. They still have not forgotten the battle of Buath, almost two years ago. The Bedouin tribes claim that this war was incited by the Jewish tribes, but how the war started, no one knows. The Beni Aus tribe attacked the Beni Khazraj tribe, killing many of their men, burning their houses, and despoiling their orchards. Amidst this fury of death, a man by the name of Judd ibn Qays appealed to them: "O men of Beni Aus, why are you killing the men of Beni Khazraj? They pray to the same gods as you do. If you spare their lives, they will be your friends and good neighbours, better than the ones you have now; Jews and foxes." Upon hearing this appeal, the men of Beni Aus sued for peace. They were quick to choose a leader amongst them who could guide them, a man from Beni Khazraj, Abdallah ibn Ubbay. That was how the matters stood when we met the last delegation at Aqaba. After they returned to Medina, they told their friends that you are the same prophet the Jews are expecting. They want you to be their prophet before the Jews can claim you.'

'This prophet is the slave of Allah, and whoever accepts the message of His divine call surrenders to the will of Allah as the Lord of all peoples.'

'Yes, Prophet, I surrender to the will of Allah,' Abu Bakr sang brightly. 'But where do I find Allah in times of fear, conflict, and hopelessness?'

'Find Allah in the beauty of love, my friend; in beautiful actions.' Muhammad's look was distant. 'In friendship. In kindness, in giving and sharing. You will find Allah when you are sincere, much like the subtle scent of a rare flower – its colour is on display, wanting no reward, but it grows more perfumed and beautiful after you appreciate it. Allah is love and beauty, His ways are mysterious, but He is everywhere.'

'By Allah, then I have no cause to fear! Good thoughts guide me, and I follow them. Though, I need the light of understanding.' Fear and doubt were returning into his eyes.

'The light of truth, perhaps,' Muhammad comforted Abu Bakr. 'Look for it inside your heart, my friend, and it will reveal to you the love and mercy of Allah, where fear and hopelessness never enter.'

'The truth is, Muhammad, I fear your uncle Abu Lahab the most. He is the power behind all these persecutions,' Abu Bakr began reluctantly. 'Al Abbas, on the other hand, has a good heart. Though he is not congenial to your message, he still supports you and worries about you. He is coming to Aqaba to make sure you have the full support of this delegation.'

'Al Abbas, this dear uncle of mine, loves me, I suppose. After the death of Abu Talib, he has been a pillar of support to me.' Muhammad rose to his feet. 'We have been talking for hours, it seems. We must start right away – courtesy demands that we don't keep the men of Medina waiting for us at Aqaba.'

'And besides, I want to avoid the pilgrims throwing stones at the pillars of Satan near there.' Abu Bakr followed suit.

'I hope my uncle Hamza is coming? He has been twice as much support since he accepted Islam.' Muhammad took a side street.

'Definitely, Muhammad; and Umar ibn Khattab too.' Abu Bakr followed. 'And Othman ibn Affan; he is bringing along a few of his friends.'

The rocky hills, bronzed by early sunset, had claimed both Abu Bakr and Muhammad in their welcoming embrace, before they even realised they had reached their meeting place at Aqaba. With the Aus and Khazraj men were two women, Nasiba and Umm Sulaym. Hamza and Al Abbas were there, as were Ali, Umar and Othman. Also, a poet by the name of Kaab ibn Salma from the tribe of Muzaynah, and Saad bin Mudah, the Chief of the Aus, who had formerly belonged to the Jewish tribe of Beni Koreiza and has now become a Muslim. Bara bin Marur from the Khazraj was accompanied by his son, Bishr.

'The servants of the Merciful One are they who walk upon the earth softly, and when the ignorant speak to to them, they reply, "peace",' Muhammad was saying.

'I wish I could see the Merciful Creator, so that I could truly surrender to Him, knowing that He is with me!' Kaab ibn Salma exclaimed.

'If you can't see Him or His creation, then hold your heart still for just one moment and in it will be reflected His eternal glory.' Muhammad's lips spilled revelations. '*Lo! your Lord is Allah Who created the heavens and the earth in six days, then mounted He the Throne. He covereth the night with the day, which is in haste to follow it, and hath made the sun and the moon and the stars subservient by His command. His verily is all creation and commandment. Blessed be Allah, the Lord of the worlds! O mankind! Call upon your Lord humbly and in secret! Lo! He loveth not aggressors. Work not confusion in the earth after the fair ordering thereof, and call on Him in fear and hope. Lo! the Mercy of Allah is nigh unto good*' (7:54–56).

'If the bitterest of your opponents amongst the Quraysh heard this revelation, Prophet of Islam, they would surely believe you,' Saad bin Mudah declared.

'They already believed before it was revealed, though they have forgotten and don't know what they held sacred,' Muhammad responded. '*If you ask them, the Quraysh, who created the heavens and the earth, and controlled the sun and the moon? They will certainly say al-Llah. This was their belief of old, even before this revelation came to me*' (29:61).

'Are there any specific revelations, Prophet of Islam, which make women the recipient of truth, mercy or reward?' Nasiba's eyes shone.

'There are many revelations which not only speak directly to women, but bestow upon them the gift of holiness! Paradise lies under a mother's feet, and my heart holds all women in great reverence,' Muhammad replied. '*Lo! men who surrender unto Allah, and women who surrender, and men who believe and women who believe, and men who obey and women who obey, and men who speak the truth and women who speak the truth, and men who persevere in righteousness and women who persevere, and men who are humble and women who are humble, and men who give alms and women who give alms, and men who fast and women who fast, and men who guard their modesty and women who guard their modesty, and men who remember Allah much and women who remember – Allah hath prepared for them forgiveness and a vast reward*' (33:35).

'There are so many clans and tribes in Medina, Prophet of Allah! How do we behave towards each other, in a way which is pleasing in the sight of Allah?' Al Harith asked.

'With love and purity in one's heart,' Muhammad intoned kindly. '*O mankind! Lo! We have created you male and female, and have made you tribes and nations that ye may know one another. Lo! the noblest of you, in the sight of Allah, is the best in conduct. Lo! Allah is Knower, Aware*' (49:13).

'Jews in Medina argue with us, Prophet of Allah, that you have borrowed your revelations from their Holy Scriptures. And the Quraysh men make the same claim. Are we to believe them, or you and your revelations as the word of God?' Tabir sought assurance, as if to strengthen his faith.

'*And argue not with the people of the Scripture unless it be in a way that is better, save with such of them as do wrong; and say: we believe in that which has been revealed to us and revealed to you; our God and your God is one, and to Him we surrender. In like manner We have revealed to you the Scripture, and those to whom We already gave the Scripture will believe in it, and of those also there are some who believe therein. And none deny Our revelations save the disbelievers. And thou, O Muhammad, wast not a reader of any Scripture before it, nor didst thou write it with thy right hand, for then might those have doubted, who follow falsehood* (29:46–48). *Say unto them, O Muhammad: He Who knoweth the secret of the heavens and the earth has revealed it. Lo! He is ever Merciful, Forgiving*' (7:203).

'Our tribes fought with each other, Prophet of Allah, and our hearts are sore with grief,' Umm Sulaym contemplated. 'We blame the Jews for kindling the fires of cruelty and warfare, and the Jews are divided amongst themselves, blaming their own tribes for inciting each other. And our husbands talk about nothing but war and vengeance. How can we have peace in our hearts?'

'*Tell those who believe to forgive those who hope not for days of Allah; in order that He may requite folk what they used to earn. Whoso doeth right, it is for his soul, and whoso doeth wrong, it is against it. And afterward unto your Lord ye will be brought back. And verily We gave the children of Israel the Scripture and the Command and the Prophethood, and provided them with good things and favoured them above all peoples; and gave them plain commandments. And they differed not until after the knowledge came unto them, through rivalry among themselves. Lo! thy Lord will judge between them on the Day of Resurrection concerning that wherein they used to differ. And now We have set thee, O Muhammad, on a clear road of Our commandment; so follow it, and follow not the whims of those who know not*' (45:14–18). Muhammad's thoughts unfurled banners of peace in revelation form.

'We have come here to renew our pledge of allegiance, Prophet of Allah.' Bara bin Marur assumed the role of spokesman. 'We are inviting you to Medina to teach us the ways of Islam. In return, we will protect you and your followers from the persecutions of the Meccans. And to show you we have not forgotten our former pledge, I will repeat it for the sake of refreshing our memories. *We will not set up any associates with Allah. We will not steal, nor commit fornication, nor kill our offspring, nor bring false accusations against others. We will not disobey the Holy Prophet in anything that is right.* Now that I have repeated our promise, we entreat you to come with us to Medina as our leader.'

'Grateful as I am for this generous offer, will you also promise that if I come to Medina, you will protect all Muslims as you would your own wives and children?' Muhammad asked, his gaze profound and piercing.

'We will. With our lives, by Allah!' Bara bin Marur exclaimed.

'By God, I can't just sit here and let this pass without knowing whether your intentions are honourable.' Al Abbas waved his arm. 'O people of Aus and Khazraj, Muhammad, as you know, is my nephew. Some of our kindred, including me, have protected him as much as we can from the anger of the Meccans, who disagree with him over his religion. He is still under our protection. However, if he is willing to join you and become one of you, are you sure you will obey him and protect him from all opposition? If so, then feel free to bear this burden of responsibility. However, if you are going to betray or desert him after he decides to join you, it is better that you leave without him.'

'Be assured, Al Abbas, we will protect and honour Muhammad more than our own lives.' Bara bin Marur shifted his gaze to Muhammad. 'By the One who has sent you with the truth, Prophet of Islam, we swear we will protect you as we protect our own selves. Our pledge of allegiance is binding, Messenger of Allah, for we are a people who know how to fight, a knowledge that has been passed down among us from father to son.'

'Worthy sentiments, my friend Bara! I thank you and your men, and my heart is filled with gratitude, but Allah has not granted us the permission to fight,' Muhammad intoned thoughtfully. 'And He won't, save for the safety of our lives and for the sake of justice. For these reasons alone, if we are permitted to fight, we should defend ourselves with compassion and honour as our shields, not for the sake of vengeance. The Muslims who fled persecution and found homes in Medina through the generosity of your friends and kindred, left Mecca with courage in their hearts and without soiling their hands with the blood of their tormentors. I assisted and encouraged them to migrate, but Allah has not granted me, His slave, permission to leave Mecca as yet. But when Allah wills, I will join you, protected by you as well as protecting you, defended by you and defending you, even risking my own life.'

'We will wait patiently, Prophet of Allah.' Abu Ayyoub sought Muhammad's attention. 'But we are anxious to learn more about Islam. I have heard the expression *authentic faith*. Could you please tell us what it means?'

'None of you will have authentic faith until your hearts are made right,' Muhammad began eagerly. 'And your hearts won't be made right until your tongues are made right, and your tongues won't be made right until your actions are made right. Whatever you do, do it with love, and you will know what authentic faith is.'

'You have taught us the prayer of love, Prophet, and the prayer of praise.' Umar ibn Khattab broke his silence. 'Do these prayers bring us closer to Allah?'

'If they are offered sincerely, Umar, yes.' Muhammad smiled. 'Prayers with the incense of love and purity in one's heart reach Allah swiftly. Then Allah lifts the veils and opens the gates, so that His servant is standing in front of Him. Prayer is a beam of light at the entrance to Allah's reality, bringing together the devotee and the Lord. When the devotee takes one step towards Allah, Allah takes ten steps towards the devotee; and yet Allah is always with everyone, whether they realise it or not. *He is the one companion who remembers me*.'

'Our pledge to you remains solid and unshakable, Prophet of Allah. Guide us, and we will obey you in spreading the message of Islam.' Bara bin Marur offered his hand as a seal of the pledge between the Prophet and the delegation.

'Then Allah is witness that we are united in brotherhood and sisterhood.' Muhammad claimed his hand. 'Male and female, old and young, without the distinction of age, sex or wealth, in equality of love and friendship! Let this revelation guide you to the path of truth and unity. *O people, you are gathered to Allah Most High barefoot, naked and uncircumcised: As We began the first creation, so shall We repeat it; it is a promise binding on Us, and We will indeed do it*' (21:104). His gaze returned to Bara. 'Now, let us choose twelve men who can be entrusted with sharing the message of Islam.'

'Choose from amongst us, Prophet of Allah, and we will honour your decision,' Bara bin Marur requested.

'I hope my choice is acceptable to you all,' Muhammad began thoughtfully. 'From the tribe of Aus, Usaid bin Hudair, Saad bin Mudah and Rafi bin Abdul. From the tribe of Khazraj, Asad bin Zuraha; Said bin Ar-Rabi; Abdalah bin Rawaha; Raf bin Malik; Abdalah bin Amr; Ubadah bin Asmit; Saeed bin udadah; Almundhir bin Amr; and of course you, Bara bin Marur.'

'We shall return to Medina, cloaked in the message of Islam!' Bara bin Marur sang happily. 'We will await your arrival, Prophet of Islam, whenever it pleases Allah. We will set off at the first streak of dawn.'

'May Allah go with you,' Muhammad responded prayerfully.

In a chorus of farewells, the men of Medina dispersed in small groups as cautiously as they had assembled. Abu Bakr was the last to leave, protesting as usual that he should accompany Muhammad as far as the precincts of the Kaaba, but Muhammad was adamant in declining his offer to save his friend from the brunt of the persecution he would endure. Muhammad's companions were peace and silence as he abandoned the sanctuary of Aqaba, his thoughts guiding him towards the Kaaba.

Muhammad welcomed the blue-toned wall of the Kaaba in his sights. He could see Abu Jahl amongst a group of men by the shrine of Hubal.

'Here comes the stargazer to tell our fortunes on a moonless night! Is it going to be moonless?' Abu Jahl blocked Muhammad's way. 'And what does your God command us to worship this evening?'

I worship not which ye worship
Nor worship ye which I worship

And I shall not worship which ye worship
Nor will you worship that which I worship
Unto you your religion, and unto me my religion. (109:1–6)

So Muhammad recited in response, his pallid features awash with sadness.

'Another wise revelation, Muhammad!' Abu Jahl goaded.

These are revelations of the wise Scripture
A guidance and mercy for the good
Those who establish worship and pay the poor-due
Such have guidance from their Lord and have sure faith in the hereafter
Such are the successful. (31:1–5)

Muhammad's voice was dreamy and poetic.

'I agree with you, Muhammad! Even the men of Taif feel sorry now that they didn't let you finish speaking, to be guided by you when you recited *Have you considered al-Lat and al-Uzza? And al-Manat, the third, the other?*' (53:19–20), Abu Jahl mocked. 'They were so angry that they thought you were deriding their goddesses, while in fact they see now that you were offering homage to them. We would have embraced you for that revelation too, had you not countered it with a new fantastic one. *Indeed, they were near seducing thee from that We revealed to thee, that thou mightest forge against Us another, and then they surely would have taken thee as a friend. And had we not confirmed thee, surely thou wert near to inclining unto them a very little* (17:73–74). Your God lies, Muhammad – or do you? Why can't you tell us the truth?'

'God is truth!' Muhammad murmured reverently. 'Allah does not lie. And no lie has ever escaped my lips, not ever, you all know that. I am a mortal man just like you, subject to error, but not falsehood. When I recognise my errors, I admit them. If I make mistakes, I correct them. And if my old thoughts, by virtue of their goodness, find a better substitute for the goodwill of all, they conform themselves to the new ones by the grace of Allah. As He guided me in this revelation, *We sent not any messenger, or prophet before thee, but that Satan cast into his fancy; when he was fancying. But Allah annuls, what Satan casts, then Allah confirms His signs* (22:52). But this revelation does not confirm their conjectures; He only annuls what Satan had made them hear. If they had let me finish, they might have understood the truth of my message, which was clear. *And yours the males and His the females? That indeed is an unfair division! They are but names which ye have named, ye and your fathers, for which Allah hath revealed no warrant. They follow but a guess and that which they themselves desire. And now the guidance from their Lord hath come unto them'* (53:21–23).

'Ah! In your satanic imaginings then, Muhammad, you fancied that you went to the heavens?' Abu Jahl exclaimed. 'We can establish the truth with a simple test, if you agree. Will you cooperate, Muhammad? Lift one foot up, would you?'

Muhammad complied. Then Abu Jahl asked him to lift his other foot up, which he did. Then Abu Jahl asked him to lift both feet up.

'I can't,' Muhammad responded, puzzled.

'Ah! How can you, Muhammad, who can't lift both feet off the ground at once, claim that you went to the highest of heavens?' Abu Jahl snorted.

'I didn't say I went. I said I was taken,' Muhammad replied kindly.

An oppressive silence filled the air. The other men around him were stunned, but Ummayad ibn Khalaf waved his arms.

'What did you bring from the heavens, Muhammad, as proof that you really went up there?' Ummayad ibn Khalaf demanded.

'One simple command from the throne of the Merciful,' was Muhammad's unintimidated response. '*Become like a fruitful tree, sharing the fruits of your good actions with the world.*'

'Show us a sign, Muhammad, and we will believe.' Abdullah bin Arqat flung his challenge.

'Can you see the moon, ripped in two?' Muhammad's gaze was on the sky, where the moon was torn into equal halves.

'An illusion! Sorcery! Magic wrought by the words of a madman, a stargazer—' Angry voices entered Muhammad's awareness.

'*The hour drew nigh and the moon was rent in twain. And if they behold a portent they turn away and say: Prolonged illusion. They denied the Truth and followed their own lusts. Yet everything will come to a decision*' (54:1–3), Muhammad recited.

'You have nothing to prove the truth of your revelations, Muhammad!' Abu Jahl snapped. 'Don't defile the shrines of our gods; you're a slave to lies. Go home!'

Those on whom you call
Apart from Allah, are
Servants the likes of you
Call them and let them answer you, if you speak truly
What, have they feet wherewith they walk
Or have they hands wherewith they lay hold
Or have they eyes wherewith they give ear
Say: call you then, to your associates
Then try your guile on me, and give me no respite
My protector is Allah Who sent down the Book
And He takes into His protection the righteous
And those on whom you call, apart from Allah
Have no power to help you
Neither they help themselves. (25:17, 16:86, 10:28)

His senses reeled from a sudden assault by Abu Jahl.

'Who is going to help you, Muhammad?' Abu Jahl threw a jar of camel faeces at him from behind. 'I knew you would come here as usual in your madness, raving and preaching, so I decided to prepare a special reward for you which you would be proud to take home!' He poured the contents of the jar over his shoulders.

The foul odour which assailed Muhammad's senses intermingled faecal stench and the reek of hatred. He closed his eyes, fighting the assault of nausea. The gleeful tormentors left, their loud, booming voices growing muffled in the distance.

'Forgive them, Allah, they don't know what they're doing.' Muhammad's breath, scented with prayers, was driving the other odours away.

Muhammad had no idea how and when he had reached home, but Fatima was standing there wiping his cloak, a profusion of tears trickling down her cheeks.

'If Mother were alive, Father, she would have never let you go wandering in the night. And no one would have dared—' Fatima's voice was choked by tears.

'Don't weep, my child!' Muhammad abruptly cried, in agony. 'Allah has shown me your mother's beautiful abode; she is happy, I was there. No tragedy on earth could move me to despair now. Just remember that your mother is with us always. In her memory, dear Fatima, we must always be humble and loving. Allah, in His great mercy, has granted me, His obedient servant, this gift of a shining memory in which is reflected the beautiful face of Khadija. She lives in Paradise! I have seen her in the Abode of the Blessed, where I will be joining her.'

The face of dawn was pearly smooth as Abu Bakr and Muhammad rode side by side on their camels on the road to the south of Yemen. The reek of hatred was forgotten by Muhammad; Allah had granted him permission to migrate from Mecca to Medina.

Persecuted by the Meccans, Muhammad told Abu Bakr that he was feeling more and more like he was being tossed about on the ocean of time. The Quraysh had discovered about the pledge at Aqaba, and challenged the Muslims to fight. Failing in their attempt to goad them, the Quraysh had still succeeded in capturing one of the delegates. The victim was Saad bin Mudah. He was tortured for two days until Abu Bakr bought his freedom with a high ransom.

Abu Bakr had been so happy to accompany the Prophet from Mecca to Medina that he had asked no questions when Muhammad had asked him to make arrangements for the secret holy journey – the *Hijra*. One early morning, Muhammad had gone to Abu Bakr's house, telling him that Gabriel had warned him not to sleep in his own bed that night.

The scent of remembrance commencing this Hijra was enveloping Abu Bakr's thoughts. He had accomplished all the tasks requested by Muhammad. Taking Abdullah bin Arqat into his confidence, he had instructed him to bring the Prophet's camel, Qaswa, and another fast one to his home in the evening. Abu Bakr's son Abdullah had suggested that three miles south of Mecca, they should rest and take shelter in the cave of Thaur. He had devised a plan: he would go to the Kaaba in the morning to learn the Meccans' mood. In the evening he would meet them at the cave of Thaur, equipped with all the information they needed to decide whether they should wait or continue their journey. Asma too was part of this secret planning, instructed to bring food and provisions for the journey before her father and the Prophet left the cave. Also involved was Abu Bakr's freed slave, Amir, who was to bring a flock of sheep in the morning, and let them graze near the camels. This was to deflect suspicion from the cave, to make it look as though Amir was tending the herd of some rich merchant.

It was already dark when Abu Bakr reached Muhammad's house. He could see Ali in Muhammad's green cloak, pretending to sleep in Muhammad's bed by the open window in full view of the murderers-to-be, if any were around this early in the night. Fatima and Swadah were sleeping in the next room, Muhammad told Abu Bakr. Then Muhammad stepped out onto the porch, Abu Bakr following. In a flash, Abu Bakr saw the Quraysh men surrounding the house, vengeful scimitars drawn. Abu Bakr's heart was shuddering with fear, but watching Muhammad bound past them all murmuring something, his own heart was strengthened. He couldn't help noticing the men's glazed expressions, as if they were all blind.

'Of all the places on Allah's earth, beloved Mecca, you are closest to me and closest to Allah!' Muhammad's voice interrupted Abu Bakr's thoughts. 'If it wasn't for my people driving me out, I would never have left you, my Mecca.'

'You were murmuring, or rather reciting something, Muhammad, while leaving your home, and it seemed like all the men of Quraysh were turned to stone,' Abu Bakr thought aloud. 'What was it that you recited?'

'*We have covered them, so they cannot see*' (36:9). Muhammad was coaxing Qaswa to kneel at the mouth of the cave. '*I was also listening to the voice of Allah. And We have set a bar before them, and this has covered them, so that they see not.*'

'Forgive me, Muhammad, if you find my curiosity imposing, but I have been meaning to ask – how did you know the Quraysh would surround your house with the intention of murdering you?' Abu Bakr dismounted from his camel, his face flushed.

'By the grace of Allah, and with the flowering of a fresh revelation, how could I remain ignorant of their murderous plot?' Muhammad began to recite. '*And when the unbelievers plot to shut thee up or to kill thee or to drive thee out, they plot, but Allah plots also. And Allah is the best of plotters*' (8:30). He entered the cave.

'That revelation alone made you aware of all their plots, Muhammad?' Abu Bakr brushed the brambles aside before following him. 'Aren't you afraid that those men might hurt Ali, or Fatima, or Swadah?'

'It wasn't that revelation alone, Abu Bakr, but guidance from Allah.' Muhammad sighed. 'Allah in His mercy revealed their murderous plot to me in a vision. I could see myself amongst the men of the Quraysh, registering each and every word which escaped their scheming minds. I will tell you everything after I find a pillow to rest my head.'

The small cave's few needlepoint chinks admitted no light, though it felt cool. Muhammad found a corner to stretch his wearied limbs. Abu Bakr, too, sprawled his legs, trying not to think about the men who might be coming after them. Before he could voice his fears, Muhammad began to speak.

'This much you know: that after Umar, Zubayr and Othman succeeded in making their escape to Medina, the leaders of the Quraysh were furious, and tried their utmost to prevent more Muslims from migrating, especially Bilal. Hopefully, he has reached Medina safely.' Muhammad paused. 'Since they were failing to stop Muslims leaving, they held a meeting at Darun Nadwa, where the plot to kill me was hatched. Abu Jahl, Abu Sofyan, Jubayr, Utbah, Nawfal, Nabiah, Tuaiman, Al Nadhr, Omayya and Al-Bakhtari were there, to name a few. The chiefs from Najd were too, but the leaders of the Tehamah clan were not invited. The leaders of the Quraysh suggested that I should be chained up and abandoned in a cellar to be starved to death. A few argued that I should be exiled. Abu Jahl insisted that I should be murdered. The leaders of the other clans disagreed with Abu Jahl, fearing blood feuds amongst clans and families, but Abu Jahl's proposal was finally accepted after a plan was devised that one member from each clan would strike a blow, so no particular clan could be held accountable for the murder. That way the Banu Hashim could not avenge me: they couldn't possibly rise against all the clans in Mecca for the death of just one man. Now you know everything I've seen; it was as if I was with them. No harm will come to Ali: he has Allah to protect him. The Meccans think I am still at home, but they will find out when Ali wakes up… he might have already…' He drifted into sleep.

The prophet and his disciple slept blissfully inside the cave of Thaur. Just as it seemed that the desert was awakening, its silence was shattered by the sound of galloping. Abu Bakr was jolted awake. His hand reached out to claim Muhammad's. Muhammad was awake too, and he held his friend's hand tightly.

'How can they be hiding in this cave, you idiot? There's a spider web covering its mouth, as far as that acacia bush!' a Meccan voice jeered.

'There's a dove's nest here, and two eggs!' another flared.

'Those rock pigeons are looking at us! Can't you see them staring? No one's been here in years. Let's go back.' Drunken mirth sliced through the darkness.

'I'm afraid, Muhammad. They're going to kill us. There are so many of them out there, and only two of us. We're alone and defenceless,' Abu Bakr murmured.

'Don't worry, Abu Bakr. We're not alone. Allah is with us – we are three,' Muhammad murmured back, in a gentle, comforting voice.

Amidst gales of laughter, the men galloped away from the cave. Abu Bakr heaved a sigh of relief, shedding his fears, his heart still thundering.

'We are saved, Muhammad! What great trust you have in Allah. If I had only half as much…' Abu Bakr breathed freely.

'Your trust in Allah is more than you know! Otherwise you wouldn't be sitting here with me in a dark cave, hungry and unprotected,' Muhammad intoned softly.

'I'm not hungry, Muhammad. And I'm protected by Allah, as you say,' Abu Bakr confessed boldly. 'Are you hungry? Amir promised to leave some food at the back of the cave. He must have taken the camels back too. I wonder if he brought the flock of sheep here to graze? Should I venture out?'

'Trust is something, Abu Bakr, but caution another. Allah commands us to be wise and cautious. We don't know if it's day or night – those men could still be prowling around. We should wait a little while longer. I'm not hungry either.' Muhammad's voice was low and contemplative.

'Abdullah should be here. How long did we sleep?' Abu Bakr wondered.

'The time will pass quicker if we keep talking,' Muhammad suggested with a sudden burst of cheerfulness.

'Yes.' Abu Bakr was happy to seek advice and wisdom. 'I have so many questions I don't understand. What does *surrender to Allah* mean?'

'It's striving after righteousness, Abu Bakr, not sitting still and doing nothing.' Muhammad's voice was soft and dreamy. 'When one strives after righteousness, one is obeying the will of Allah, for Allah does not lead the doer of good into doing wrong.'

'I have been meaning to ask you about the issue of adultery since the pledge at Aqaba, but I keep forgetting,' Abu Bakr began, thoughtfully. 'One of the Medinese delegates told me that a Jewish woman was stoned to death in Medina for adultery. Isn't that a brutal punishment, Muhammad, even if it is their law? Is that just or unjust?'

'Allah's justice is different from the justice of man, which we fail to understand when we try to interpret Allah's laws in the light of our own limited intelligence.' Muhammad's voice sounded remote. 'Any punishment is brutal which falls short of Allah's mercy, and Allah is all merciful. Adultery is not the woman's fault alone; the man is equally guilty. And if punishment has to be meted out, it has to be to both the man and the woman. Allah, in His great mercy, has ascribed one hundred stripes for the adulterer and the adulteress, to teach mankind the virtue of noble living. And yet mercy is highly pleasing to Allah.

Didn't Jesus say to the angry, self-righteous group of men who were desperate to stone the adulteress, "Let he who is without sin cast the first stone?"'

'How do you know all that, Muhammad?' Abu Bakr asked, in awe.

'I listen to the voice of my heart, Abu Bakr, and know that Allah is most merciful and infinitely compassionate,' Muhammad replied. 'Anyone is capable of listening to their heart if they try, and its voice is the voice of the sages and the prophets who walked on the face of this earth before us. Didn't I tell you the story of the adulteress who passed by a well where a dog lay dying of thirst? The woman took off her shoe and, tying it to the end of her girdle, drew water for the dog. For this act of kindness, she was forgiven her sins.'

'You didn't tell me, Muhammad, but I heard it from Hamza before he left for Medina,' Abu Bakr murmured. 'Who are the most beloved of Allah's devotees?'

'I swear by Him who holds the soul of Muhammad in His hand that the most beloved of Allah's devotees are those who increase the love of Allah in others' hearts, and make them beloved of Allah, and who act with goodwill and sincerity towards one another,' Muhammad declared. 'Seek the verdict of your heart, Abu Bakr, even if men act as judges to decree otherwise…' His thoughts were silenced by the sound of footsteps at the mouth of the cave.

'The peace of Allah is with us,' Abdullah greeted them, holding before him an oil lamp.

'My son!' Abu Bakr was quick to relieve him of his burden of provisions.

'May Allah's love and peace be with you for all the days of your life, Abdullah.' Muhammad smiled, his eyes searching the youthful face of his friend's son.

'All is well, Muhammad,' Abdullah announced. 'I've brought you some food.'

'Thank you, Abdullah, but I am not hungry yet,' Muhammad murmured.

'I am not hungry, either.' Abu Bakr watched his son rather apprehensively.

'I know you must be dying to know the details, but all is well, as I just said,' Abdullah began thoughtfully. 'The men of the Quraysh kept vigil till dawn at your house, Muhammad. In the morning, they were ready to strike when Ali stirred in your bed. When they realised their mistake their scimitars fell limp in their hands. Ali got out of your bed, and stepped out onto the porch. When they recovered from their shock, they started pelting Ali with questions. Ali told them that he didn't know, that his cousin had not come home last night. They hastened towards the Kaaba, sounding the alarm that you had fled. Abu Jahl and Abu Sofyan were quick to organise several parties, who rode in every direction across the desert. But they all returned in the evening with not a clue where to find you. Now they're offering a hundred camels to any man who can find you and bring you back bound at the hands and feet.'

'Who can bind the feet and hands of a man whom Allah has granted the gift of escape, and freedom to proclaim His message of love and unity?' Muhammad sighed relief. 'Didn't they ask about your father, since he is the closest of my friends?'

'Yes, Muhammad; they came to our house while I was at the Kaaba,' Abdullah replied. 'I saw them ride out in search of you, while I stayed there till the evening. When I went home to get food, mother told me that the men questioned her and Asma, demanding to see father, but they told them that they didn't know where he had gone.'

'Poor Umm Ruman. She is a woman of wisdom and courage,' Abu Bakr murmured. 'Has Amir taken our camels back?' he asked weakly.

'Yes, father,' Abdullah assured gently. 'He is to bring his sheep here in the morning to graze and he'll leave fresh milk in the back of the cave. He will keep watch all day and return to Mecca in the evening.'

'We don't even know how long we slept. Or what time of the day it is – or is it night?' Muhammad asked. 'Is it safe for us to keep going towards Medina?'

'It's very late in the night, Muhammad,' Abdullah replied. 'You have only been here a day. I don't think it is safe to venture out as yet. There will be hunting parties scouting the desert tomorrow, I have heard. Tomorrow night I will bring you more news, and more food, and we can decide when it would be safe to leave.'

'A party of men were here at the mouth of the cave, Abdullah; we could hear them talking and laughing.' Abu Bakr's heart was thundering. 'We heard them say that there was a spider's web over its mouth. Did they talk about it at the Kaaba? Did you see a spider's web before you came in?'

'No, father, I didn't,' was Abdullah's astonished response. 'And I didn't hear anyone talking about it, but I must have gone home by then. I must leave now, before they come searching for me. This is a good time to get out of the cave. The desert is peaceful, and all the men in Mecca are asleep, drunk with wine and despair.' He bade them farewell with a look, which shifted from his father to Muhammad.

'Not right now, my son, my legs are weak; maybe a little later.' Abu Bakr attempted a pale smile.

'May Allah's great guidance keep you company.' Muhammad waved farewell. 'With Allah's blessings, you will guide my Qaswa and your father's camel back to us. Then we can fly to Medina on wings of joy and hope. Right now, we will do justice to the food you have kindly brought us. It will pour strength into our bodies, and hold Abu Bakr's legs firm under the canopy of stars when we venture out. Are the stars out tonight?' he asked thoughtfully.

'Yes, Muhammad, the stars were twinkling so bright that I could see my footprints on the sand,' Abdullah intoned happily.

'The camels will be here sooner than you can imagine.' After his prediction escaped his lips he turned on his heel. 'Asma cooked that food, and she would be greatly pleased if you finished it all.'

Two days after Abdullah's first visit, another star-studded night suspended itself over the cave of Thaur. Amir stood stroking Qaswa's hump while she knelt. Beside him Abdullah bin Arqat was busy loading provisions on Abu Bakr's camel. Abdullah was assuring Muhammad about the character of Abdullah bin Arqat, who was familiar with all the routes to Medina.

The Meccans, after three days searching the desert, had given up and gone home. Abdullah, as soon as he learnt of their decision, had taken Abdullah bin Arqat into his confidence and brought back the camels. Asma came too. Abdullah bin Arqat was to ride with Muhammad, and Amir with Abu Bakr. Asma was watching Amir, and, noticing that there was no rope left to secure the last sack of provisions, was quick to untie her girdle, tearing it in half lengthways.

'Quick, Amir – tie the sack with my girdle; it is strong enough.' Asma tossed half of her girdle to him, wrapping the other half around her waist without a thought.

'You will be remembered, dear Asma, She of the Two Girdles,' Muhammad applauded with a sudden burst of warmth and tenderness.

'Who would remember me, Prophet?' Asma argued. 'Allah loves you, I am sure, but why is He putting you through such an ordeal?'

'Future generations will remember you, dear Asma, and sing your praises,' Muhammad prophesied. 'As to your doubts, and my ordeal, remember this: whenever Allah loves a devotee, He subjects him to ordeals. If the devotee endures them patiently, Allah singles him out. If the devotee is content, Allah purifies him.'

'Why is Allah Him, not Her? Do all devotees have to be men?' Asma longed to know Allah's every aspect.

'Allah has no gender, dear Asma.' Muhammad laughed. 'Wherever you look you see the face of Allah, in everything. Devotees can be male or female; all nature sings the praises of Allah. Have you not heard the birds singing in the morning? Divine breezes from your Lord waft through every day of your life. Listen! Be aware of them.'

'How perfect your belief is, Prophet of Islam! I believe, but doubts keep surfacing.' Asma lowered her gaze.

'A believer is like a bee, which consumes only what is pure, and produces only what is pure,' Muhammad murmured. 'Come closer, Asma – feel Qaswa's ear. It was chewed up in a camel fight, but it is a mark of her wisdom and perception. Look into her eyes too. She has the gaze of a philosopher, concealing many secrets.'

'We must leave, Muhammad,' Abu Bakr cautioned. 'The Meccans might change their minds and send a fresh set of search parties after us.'

'Yes,' Muhammad murmured in response.

The bright stars throbbing in the bleak bowl of a sky carved a path for the four men, who rode forth into the very heart of the desert. Abdullah bin Arqat, riding with Muhammad, had chosen to go south from Yemen. Amir and Abu Bakr merely let their camel follow in whichever direction Qaswa headed.

'How long did it take Bilal and the other Muslims to reach Medina? I have been meaning to ask.' Muhammad's gaze sought answers from the stars, it seemed.

'Nine days, I was told.' Abu Bakr looked at Muhammad.

It seemed to Muhammad to be a journey into eternity, as he looked into the eyes of the second dawn since their departure from the cave of Thaur. The great rocks looming in the north were moving closer. A man astride an Arabian horse, fully armed with a bow and a quiver of arrows, could not be missed galloping towards them.

'Look out, Muhammad. This man might be seeking a hundred-camel reward. He could kill you.' Abu Bakr's warning was swallowed by the desert wind.

'Have no fear, Abu Bakr,' Muhammad chimed. 'The heart of the believer is held between the two fingers of the Merciful. He turns it about as He wills.'

The strange rider strung an arrow into his bow, and aimed at Muhammad. But in the act of shooting, his mount stumbled and he was unhorsed.

Truly, your Sustainer's grasp is strong
It is He Who creates from the very beginning
And it is He Who can restore
And He is Ever Ready to forgive, the Loving One
Lord of the Throne of Glory
The Unceasing Doer of all that He intends. (85:12–16)

Thus Muhammad gave thanks.

The assassin was quick to install himself back on his saddle. He strung another arrow into his bow, but his horse tossed him back to the ground once again.

And remember our servants Abraham, Issac and Jacob
Endowed with inner strength and vision
Truly We purified them
By means of remembrance of life to come
They were in Our sight, truly, among the elect and the good
And remember Ishmail, Elisha and Zul-kifl
Each of them was among the companions of the Good
This is a reminder:
And truly, awaiting the God-consciousness is a beautiful place of return. (38:45–50)

Muhammad sat combing the white coat of Qaswa with his fingers.

The young man tried to string another arrow, but the Arabian steed hurled him down, whinnying. The murderer-to-be fell at Qaswa's feet.

'What's your name, young man?' Muhammad asked kindly.

'Suraqah,' the young man could barely murmur. 'Forgive me, Prophet. I wanted to kill you – I wanted the prize of a hundred camels. But how can I? Allah is on your side.'

'You have my forgiveness, Suraqah. Go back in peace,' Muhammad murmured.

'Let me kill him, Prophet of Islam!' Amir was startled out of his shock. 'If we allow him to go back, he will tell everyone else. More men will be at our heels soon.'

'You have more to learn about Islam, Amir,' Muhammad intoned calmly. 'But right now, remember to be reconciled with the one who has fallen out with you. Pardon the one who has been unjust, and forgive the one who denies your belief.'

'Forgive me, Prophet,' Suraqah pleaded earnestly. 'I want to believe. I want to know Allah. Teach me.'

'Allah is inside everyone's hearts, and you indeed are forgiven,' Muhammad murmured. 'The heart of the believer is the sanctuary of Allah, and nobody but Allah is allowed access. Whoever desires to meet Allah, Allah desires to meet him.'

'I am still afraid, Prophet,' Suraqah pleaded. 'Can you give me a token of your assurance that you have forgiven me completely? When I return to Mecca, I promise not to tell anyone I saw you.'

'That piece of bone that you carry with you, Abu Bakr; make good use of it!' Muhammad sought his friend's attention. 'Your reed pen needs exercise. Give this young man a written token that I have forgiven him absolutely.'

'Yes, Muhammad.' Abu Bakr obeyed, procuring his reed pen and ink pot which he kept ready to jot down the revelations. 'You should be grateful to the Prophet for his kindness, Suraqah,' he advised, scribbling Muhammad's note of forgiveness hastily. 'Here, now go in peace and keep your side of the bargain.'

'Yes. I won't breathe a word.' Suraqah claimed the token of forgiveness, his gaze returning to Muhammad. 'Why am I still afraid, Prophet?

'Peace be with you, Suraqah. Be not afraid,' Muhammad consoled. 'A time will come when you will wear the gold bangles of the ruler of Persia.'

Dawns and starry nights dissolved into infinity, and Muhammad and his companions edged closer to Medina. The eyes of all four men shone with joy, much like the midday sunshine on this twelfth day of their journey. The deserted roads from Yemen south, then heading west towards the seashore, were coming alive in Muhammad's head. So deeply immersed was Muhammad inside the desert of his contemplations that he didn't even notice them entering the very heart of Medina.

A leader by the name of Baraida from the Sheekh tribe had seen Muhammad from a distance, and sounded the alarm that the Prophet was coming. Men and women were gathered on their rooftops, cheering and welcoming. The street was teeming with well-wishers, women in colourful attire, singing. An ocean of joy and applause parted, shimmering, as Qaswa padded along unperturbed. In a flash, a group of young girls had formed a circle, pirouetting on their toes and singing,

We are the girls of the Banu Najjar
O what a wonderful neighbour is holy Muhammad.

Tears of gratitude formed in Muhammad's eyes. Many men and women were edging closer, inviting him to stay with them. One man, introducing himself as Salool, seized Qaswa's reins, pleading with Muhammad that he stay in his home.

'Thank you all, and you, Salool, for the hearty welcome and these generous invitations, but I will entrust Qaswa with the decision as to who is going to be my host,' Muhammad announced laughingly. 'Qaswa is under Allah's command; wherever she stops, that's where I will stay. Then I will be able to humbly accept the generosity of my host, with profound gratitude.'

The assembled faces hushed for a brief moment in awe. The next, they were laughing, and clearing the way for Qaswa. Qaswa sniffed around, chewed on a leaf, backed up a little, and then padded forward. She headed towards a field bounded by palm trees, beyond which stood the house of Abu Ayyoub. Qaswa had finally decided. After making a bubbling sound she knelt down, her knees buckling under her. She stretched out her neck and her chin touched the ground. The girls were singing:

The white moon rose over us from the valley of Wada
Now we owe it to show the Lord thankfulness
Whenever a Caller calls to us
O you who have been sent among us
You come with a direct command
And you have brought to our city nobleness
So welcome to you
The best Caller of all
Medinatan Nabi, the city of Prophet.

'My noble Qaswa has chosen!' Muhammad alighted from his camel. 'Here I will stay. Here you will bury me. Here I will build a prayer-house for Allah.'

'This land is my gift to you, Apostle of Islam, to build a house and a mosque.' Abu Ayyoub embraced Muhammad. 'I am honoured to have you as my guest.'

'The honour is all mine!' Muhammad kept pace with Abu Ayyoub.

'Fresh goats' milk for the Prophet and his companions! Fetch all kinds of fruit!' Abu Ayyoub commanded, giddy and exhilarated.

'O ye who believe! Be steadfast witness for Allah in equity, and let not hatred of any people seduce you that you deal not justly. Deal justly, that is nearer to your duty. Observe your duty to Allah. Lo! Allah is informed of what ye do. Allah hath promised those who believe and do good works: theirs will be the forgiveness and immense reward' (5:8–9), Muhammad recited.

Chapter 10

The Sufi and the Prophet

Year 624 AD

Muhammad sat mending his slippers inside the little hut, absorbed in perfecting the skill he had learnt after coming to Medina. Two whole years had swept past since his arrival, but it felt like two centuries. A blessed shower of revelations had become his most precious treasure, infusing his soul with so much bliss that he sometimes thought he was in Paradise.

Paradise was Muhammad's abode at this moment too, though he was seated on a rough mat in his hut. The hut was his house in Medina, adjoined to the mosque, named Masjid Al-Nabi. Dressed in a white tunic, a black cloak gracing his shoulders, Muhammad looked half his fifty-four years. Youth had returned after his marriage to Aisha, a blossom of fourteen springs.

In his thoughts was the face of Ruqayyah, ravaged by pain and illness. Khultum was there too, mourning the sudden death of her husband, Abd al Mottaleb. Then Zainab surfaced. She had stayed in Mecca, since her husband was not a Muslim and he had no wish to migrate. Another Zainab followed; the Prophet's cousin, now married to Zaid. Muhammad had suggested the match for the sole purpose of abolishing distinctions between race, colour, or wealth, but the marriage had become a pothole of unhappiness. Muhammad's thoughts returned to his own sweet daughter.

How can I ever stop bowing to You in gratitude, my Eternal Sweetness, my beloved Allah, that Zainab and Abul As love each other despite their religious differences? Muhammad's thoughts marched back in time.

He had remained the guest of Abu Ayyoub, and they had found that the site chosen by Qaswa was owned by two orphans. Abu Ayyoub had offered the land to Muhammad for nothing, promising to compensate the boys by giving them his own share of lands. But Muhammad had declined, and requested Abu Bakr to buy it since he was the only one amongst the immigrants who had brought a large amount of cash to Medina. Abu Bakr was only too happy to secure the land for a mosque. Within seven months its construction was complete. Muhammad had assigned a title to the Meccan immigrants: *Muhajirins*: refugees. The Medinese Muslims were called *Ansars,* meaning simply 'the Helpers'.

The simple quarters for Muhammad's household were built next to the mosque. Muhammad had designed a way to prosperity for everyone by establishing a bond of brotherhood amongst the Ansars and the Muhajirins. Each Ansar was requested to accept one Muhajirin as his brother, making him a part of his household to work together. Muhajirins worked so hard that soon they were richer than the Ansars.

O Allah, there is no Felicity but the Felicity of Hereafter
O Allah, help the Helpers and the Refugees

The chorus surfaced in Muhammad's thoughts; the Ansars and the Muhajirins had never tired of singing it while they built the mosque.

Muhammad picked up another piece of leather to finish the slippers, letting his thoughts skip down the rungs of the past, when the Jewish tribes had chosen him as their guide and urged him to take up arms to settle issues which needed urgent attention. But Muhammad's shield of self-defence was his offering of peace with the gifts of love and brotherhood.

Jews and Muslims should live as one people. Each party should keep to its own faith, neither should interfere with the faith of the other. In the event of a war with a third party, each should come to the other's assistance, provided the latter is the wronged party, not the aggressor. In the event of an attack on Medina, both the Ansars and the Muhajirins should join hands to defend it. Medina should be regarded as sacred by all parties; all bloodshed within its walls is forbidden. The Prophet will be the final court of appeal in cases of disputes. Muhammad repeated the words of the pact in his thoughts.

And yet Muhammad was aware of the imminent threat of war from the very shores of Mecca. He dispelled any worry by recalling the peaceful resolutions reached between the tribes of Medina. A Jewish man by the name of Shas ibn Qays could not endure the idea of brotherhood. At one gathering where the men of the Aus and the Khazraj were making merry, he had caused dissension by recounting the scene of a battle between them at Buath. He taunted them by asking how they could laugh together when so many of their companions had been slaughtered there. Soon the men from both tribes had challenged each other to a fair fight. Fortunately, Muhammad was informed, and he had hurried there to get their anger in check before they could kill each other.

O Muslims, why are you behaving like you used to in the days of ignorance, even though I am with you, and Allah has guided you to Islam? He has honoured you with the light of wisdom, and he has helped you to abandon that spirit of enmity and vengeance, so that you can be united together as friends and brothers. Sheathe your swords, and weep for your folly for even thinking that you could shed the blood of any man who is bound to you by the holy oath of brotherhood!

Masjid Al-Nabi was calling Muhammad, but he was busy visiting scenes in his head as he mended his slippers. A few months after the construction of the mosque, Muhammad's followers had begun to wonder about a way of calling the faithful to prayer. Hamza started the discussion but had no specific ideas, except to name the mosque as the Cradle of Moses. Ali couldn't think of any suggestions, either. Abu Bakr suggested that they should choose between ringing a bell like the Christians or blowing a horn like the Jews. Zaid was quick to relate a dream in which he had seen a tall man calling the faithful to prayer in a clear, loud voice. Muhammad was moved to tears: the silence in his soul had confirmed that the vision had come to Zaid from Allah. Bilal was chosen as the first muezzin of Islam, calling the faithful to prayer morning, noon and evening. Bilal's voice, with all its fragrance of love, suddenly pervaded Muhammad's thoughts.

Allah is most Great, Allah is most Great
I witness that there is no god but God, I witness that Muhammad is the Messenger of God
Come to Prayer, Come to Prayer
Come to good work
Allah is most Great, Allah is most Great.

The portals of bliss were thrown open in Muhammad's eyes as his fingers worked magic on the leather to complete his pair of slippers. Fatima floated in his thoughts as the most beautiful of brides, from her marriage to Ali. Ali and Fatima had married a year earlier than he and Aisha, and Fatima was already mother to his newborn grandson, whom he had named Hasan.

He became aware of tart, crisp sounds, and couldn't help identifying giddy protests from the lips of Anas. Anas was only eight years old and had been the slave of Talha ibn Ubaidullah when he was presented to Muhammad. He was almost the same age as Usama, the son of Zaid. Now Anas was ten years old and Usama on the rungs of eleven. Muhammad had freed Anas and adopted him as his son, calling him 'my little Beloved'.

Aisha's sing-song voice surfaced above everything else. She was teasing Swadah, it was obvious. Muhammad abandoned the slipper with the intention of interceding on behalf of Swadah, but before he could get to his feet, Aisha pranced into the room, her tiny, bare feet lending her the appearance of an angel from the mists of Paradise.

'Why did you marry Swadah, Prophet? She is so fat and ugly.' Aisha pursed her lips tight to smother her mirth, while flinging herself on the mat beside Muhammad.

'Aisha!' Muhammad chided. 'Mark my words, Aisha, Allah will cut your tongue off for saying such mean things. When will you learn that every one of Allah's creatures is beautiful? Swadah cooks and cleans for you, while you indulge in making friends. Now, tell me, who is more beautiful in the sight of Allah between you two? Swadah, with all her devotion towards us? Or you, with your heart full of vanity?'

'Don't I make you laugh and relax in spite of all the burdens you carry on your shoulders, Prophet?' Aisha pouted and looked contrite.

'Yes, my heart's delight, yes,' Muhammad murmured pensively. 'It's such agony and torture for an old man, being married to a young adorable girl.'

'I will go to my parents' home, then, to save you from all this agony and torture.' Aisha resorted to teasing, her young heart aflutter with mischief.

'And to let me die of grief!' Muhammad's gaze was profound.

'Why do we have to live so poorly, Prophet, when you are the head of Medina?' was Aisha's flustered comment.

'Would you rather live in a palace, my little Aisha, wedded to some tyrant king, or to a Prophet blessed with the gifts from Allah's grace and bounty? Aren't you the envy of queens, endowed with beauty and wisdom, your young heart filled with the treasures of joy? Who gave you all that, my sweet tormentor?' He laughed.

'Allah, Allah, Allah,' Aisha chanted happily.

'And are you grateful, my pretty enchantress?' Muhammad chuckled.

'Yes, Prophet, all the time! And I'm even more grateful when you share your revelations with me. Have you ever wondered why I married you?' Aisha challenged.

'Yes, my sweet Aisha. I delude myself into believing that you find me handsome. Or you might like my sweet, charming manners?' Muhammad teased.

'I wanted to be married to a Prophet. Though, you are handsome.' Aisha's mirthful eyes shone with profound stars. 'That subtle fragrance from your body, it cradles me even when you leave; I can't explain. And my heart is always hungering for the joy in revelations. Such great treasures, I can't deny.'

'You are my joy and my wealth, sweet Aisha! Allah has blessed me with great bounty!' Muhammad exclaimed happily. 'To test your memory, and your love for revelations, recite to me the one which was revealed the night before last.'

Allah is the Light of the heavens and the earth
The similitude of His Light is as a lustrous Niche
Wherein is the Lamp, the Lamp in a Glass
The Glass as if it were a glittering Star
This Lamp kindled by a blessed Tree
An Olive, neither of the east, nor of the west
Whose oil will well nigh glow forth
Though Fire toucheth it not
Light upon Light
Allah guides to His Light whomsoever He wills
Allah sends parables to men
Allah knows all things full well. (24:35)

Aisha recited the words with the reverence and sweetness of a devotee.

'Your sweet voice brings it to life, my Aisha,' Muhammad breathed tenderly, his look pensive. 'Do you know its meaning?'

'No, my Prophet! But it is beautiful as it is,' Aisha murmured.

'The Holy Quran is still gathering pearls of wisdom, Aisha. There are countless interpretations for all its revelations, and no one knows the full wisdom of its words, save Allah,' Muhammad began thoughtfully. 'And yet the pure in heart will find the well-preserved pearls of love, mercy and compassion inside the shell of each revelation.' He smiled. 'The niche in this revelation is the inner soul, the glass our spiritual heart, and the lamp symbolises the very essence of our intelligence. Through this lamp we recognise the divine names of Allah, and the spark of divinity in all of us. The olive tree, as a symbol, is a sacred tree, the branching of our thoughts into virtue and goodness, loving all, accepting all, lending shade and comfort to the weary body and soul. Olive oil connotes purity of intellect, where the spirit of Allah resides. This intellect keeps itself alight; it needs no fire to feed its flame of imagination, and it is not restricted by the limitations of east and west to beholding the Face of Allah within the confines of our mortal sight—' His thoughts were silenced by the gusty arrival of Anas.

'Prophet! We are going to have a feast today! Our hearty meal of the day as early as this,' Anas declared. 'Swadah has cooked a fowl, all dripping with sauce and butter. She is inviting everyone to taste it, but won't let anyone touch it until you come.'

'A feast indeed, my son!' Muhammad heaved himself up, smiling. 'I haven't tasted meat since I came to Medina.'

'I was feasting on revelations, Anas!' Aisha sprang to her feet. 'You always choose the wrong time to intrude.' She began punching him on the shoulders.

'Aisha!' Muhammad restrained her. 'Allah will cut off one of your hands for striking Anas!' He laughed, dragging her along towards the kitchen.

The kitchen was as bare as Muhammad's room, with the exception of a brick hearth for Swadah's sole pleasure. She loved to buy her favourite supplies of food with the money Muhammad and Othman earned. They were the only earning members of the household; both were quite skilled at weaving mats and tending the orchards in exchange for figs and dates, even wheat and barley.

Love alone was the condiment for this feast for Muhammad's entire family, as they sat down together to share the meal cooked by Swadah's loving hands. Aisha sat to Muhammad's right and Swadah to his left. Opposite him were Othman and Ruqayyah. Khultum was seated next to Ruqayyah. Zaid and Baraka were at the fringe of this half-circle, across from them their son Usama, who was huddled close to Anas. Zaid was happy, since his second wife Zainab was visiting her friends. Muhammad commenced the ritual of carving the fowl, but decided to pray first.

'O Allah, bring me the creatures dearest to Thee to share this fowl with me.' Muhammad's prayer was answered, for he could see Ali trooping into the kitchen.

'I didn't know you were eating this early,' Ali apologised, 'but I wanted to talk to you, Muhammad. I took the liberty of lodging a few men in the mosque. They are from the tribe of Thaqif and have no place to go, so I promised them food and shelter. I am not sure of my decision, Prophet. They don't profess our belief.'

'All are welcome in the house of Allah, Ali. Are we not all His children? Your kindness has earned you a place in Paradise.' Muhammad smiled. 'To bring joy to a single heart is better than building many shrines for worship. And to enslave one soul by kindness is worth more than setting free a thousand slaves. Allah has answered my prayer, Ali, and we will share this meal together with joy and gratitude.'

The little hut's kitchen was filled with laughter while Muhammad sat talking. Ali had brought more joy to Muhammad than anticipated, for he announced that Fatima was again heavy with child. Swadah was proud to serve her favourite concoction of honey, wheat and barley, filling each earthenware tumbler with joyful diligence.

'Where's the goats' milk?' Othman ibn Affan asked. 'Didn't you receive a revelation, Prophet, that drinks like this are forbidden to us? Isn't it sinful to drink wine?'

'There are more than a thousand ways to interpret the revelations, Othman. Take care never to be guided by zeal.' Muhammad's eyes spilled reproof. 'Fighting is a sin too, and now that permission has been given to us in a revelation, it doesn't mean that we should fight. Only in self-defence, and only when all other means of peace are exhausted. As to the revelation about wine, Othman, listen carefully and think. *They ask thee concerning wine and game of hazard. Say: in both there is great sin and also some advantages for men, but their sin is greater than their advantages* (2:219). Ponder upon this one too: *O ye who believe, make not unlawful the good things which Allah has made lawful for you, and do not transgress. Surely, Allah loves not the transgressor*' (5:88).

'But this is not wine, Othman!' Swadah protested.

'I know, my dear Swadah,' Muhammad breathed tenderly, returning his gaze to Othman. 'I just wanted to stress the point, Othman, that each of us is tempted to interpret each revelation in countless different ways, but no one could claim knowledge of their true meaning except Allah. If you strive towards understanding, don't cling blindly to your own interpretation, since mortal intelligence is limited, but stay open to the voice of grace. Remember, Othman – when you asked me about worship and adornment, I recited this revelation: *O children of Adam! Look to your adornment at every time of place and worship, and eat and drink, but exceed not the bounds. Surely, Allah does not love those who exceed the bounds*' (7:31).

'Does that mean that we can eat forbidden foods, Prophet, as long as we do so in moderation?' Othman ibn Affan's eyes glinted in confusion and challenge.

'*Proscribed* and *forbidden* are words in the scale of one's own understanding; the measure of one's judgement to do good, and seek goodness, for the sake of one's own soul and for the soul of the world.' Muhammad's gaze was piercing. 'To understand things in a better perspective, Othman, hold this revelation as your guiding light: *On those who believe and do good works there shall be no sin for what they eat, provided they fear Allah and believe and do good works, and again fear Allah and believe. Yet again, fear Allah and do good. And Allah loves those who do good*' (5:93).

'At least we have enough to eat now, if this indeed is the reward for our good works!' Ali was quick to change the course of conversation. 'Remember, Prophet, our early days in Medina, when we suffered the pangs of hunger much too often? Do you remember that evening, when Abu Bakr was walking towards the mosque, not knowing that Umar was heading in the same direction? Finally, when they collided in the street, they both asked each other the same question: *why are you out in the street so late?* And they both confessed that they were hungry, and that there was no food in the house. Then they saw you, Prophet, asking the same question, and you too were hungry?'

'Yes, by Allah! How could I ever forget that?' Muhammad laughed. 'I was the one who suggested that we go to the house of Abu Ayyoub, and we did. He was as gracious and hospitable as ever, satisfying our hunger with dates and bread. That's when I said, "Bismillah – praise be to Allah who has satisfied our hunger".'

'The same Abu Ayyoub, Father, who was afraid to sleep on the upper floor while you were his guest?' Khultum's eyes lit up with the stars of curiosity.

'The same one, my child. You met him in the mosque.' Muhammad smiled.

'Why was he afraid, Prophet?' Anas was agog.

'Simply because their bedroom was right above where I slept!' Muhammad reminisced. 'I received quite a few revelations in their home, and they thought I would receive more if they didn't sleep above me, as if they were somehow blocking the flow of my revelations. He and his wife told me that they heard noises during the night and were sorely afraid. I assured them that I hadn't heard any sounds, and tried to allay their fears, but they insisted that I sleep upstairs and I agreed.'

'They were right in insisting, Prophet,' Baraka confirmed. 'They told me they had never slept better than when the Prophet of Allah slept above them.'

'When is Umm Mubad visiting us again, Father?' Ruqayyah queried. 'She tells me wonderful stories about you, and I love her voice, so soft and soothing.'

'What stories?' Usama's boyish features glowed with the fire of curiosity.

'Not just stories, but true accounts of what happened!' Zaid took up the challenge. 'Umm Mubad met the Prophet during his Hijra from Mecca to Medina. Abu Bakr was with him and their provisions had run out. They were looking for a place to rest when they came upon a Bedouin camp. That's where they met Umm Mubad, and she invited them in to rest. Her husband had taken the best goats to pasture, and she had no milk in the house to offer them. Kind and hospitable as she was, she apologised that the goats which were left behind were too weak to yield milk. Our Prophet then requested her to let him milk the goats. She agreed, and the Prophet invoked the name of Allah before milking. And by Allah, what a great miracle! There was so much milk that Abu Bakr and the Prophet drank their fill, and still there was a pail left full to the brim for Umm Mubad and her family.'

'No miracle, Zaid,' Muhammad chided. 'The only miracle is Allah's grace when one learns to trust in His will. Besides that, there are no miracles.'

'To me, your Night Journey to Jerusalem and the heavens is a miracle, my Prophet,' Aisha sang sweetly. 'Otherwise, how could you describe the details of the Temple Mount, where you have never been on foot?'

'My tiny-footed Aisha! Who told you about that?' Muhammad asked.

'My father, of course! Who else? You wouldn't tell me, since you don't want to talk about it. He told me about the Meccans who jeered, and that he'd asked you to tell them about the things you saw on the Temple Mount and around the city walls.' Aisha tossed her head, her golden eyes sparkling.

'Did Abu Bakr ever tell you, Aisha, that the Prophet helped a man find his lost camel that night in Jerusalem?' Othman ibn Affan began eagerly. 'The man had lost his camel and claimed that he heard a voice from the clouds, telling him where to find it – the voice of an angel or a prophet. When he found his camel, he noticed the seal of one of his water jars was broken, a sign from the clouds which he had seen, but he didn't know who had drunk the water. The rest the Prophet himself can tell you.'

'No, my father never told me!' Aisha sat there wild-eyed in awe.

'The details of my Night Journey are better guarded than paraded, Othman.' Muhammad's look was sad. 'The vision Allah in His great mercy granted me, His slave, I have no need to prove to others. Allah bestows His grace upon whoever He wants. And His grace most likely falls upon the lowliest of His servants, like me for one.'

'Temple Mount – what is it like, Prophet?' Anas appealed. 'I will probably never be able to visit Jerusalem. Can you tell me what it looks like?'

'You might, my little beloved.' Muhammad breathed indulgently. 'I will talk about it after all, then, in the hope that the eyes of your young heart will be opened with a longing to visit this holy city, Jerusalem. It is a city encircled by whispering palms and cypresses; its stones are tawny and golden against the curtain of sunset. The glory of its marble walls under the moonlit sky cannot be described. The temple itself, with its golden spikes, is the jewel of Jerusalem; the windowless inner sanctuary is the Holy of the Holies where the spirit of Allah dwells. A shining place flanked by thirteen offering boxes, and four corner-chambers for priests. The jars of oil and the offerings of wine—' He stopped, noticing Ruqayyah's pallor. 'Are you in pain, my love?'

'Not much, Father. Your voice is soothing, and I would love to hear more,' was Ruqayyah's faint plea.

Muhammad sat collecting his thoughts, his lips moving, but no words issuing forth. Before he could summon his voice, Bilal's call to prayer flooded the kitchen. All heads bowed in silence.

Allah is most Great, Allah is most Great
I witness that there is no god but God
I witness that Muhammad is the Messenger of God
Come to prayer
Come to prayer
Come to good work
Allah is most Great, Allah is most Great.

Bilal's voice was still soothing the hearts of the Prophet's family as they lifted their faces. Ruqayyah's face was pale. Everyone had scrambled to their feet with the exception of Ruqayyah, who couldn't trust her legs. They felt weak and ached.

'To the mosque for prayer, whoever is able and willing.' Muhammad was watching Ruqayyah. His gaze shifted to Othman. 'You must stay with your wife.'

'She needs rest, Prophet. I will hurry back straight after the prayer, and I will pray for her health.' Othman ibn Affan averted his gaze.

'Love for one's family and tending to their needs is better than a lifetime of prayers, Othman. Noble acts like that pave the way for Paradise,' Muhammad commented.

'Yes, Prophet.' Othman ibn Affan held her hand tenderly.

The little mosque with its walled-in courtyard was teeming with the faithful in prayer. More than a hundred men and women had gathered there this afternoon, kneeling and prostrating in unison, guided by Bilal. Men, women and children, including the Prophet's family, were a part of this congregation, all praying together.

After the prayers, Muhammad stood conversing with his friends, aware of a Jewish delegation stationed at the furthest end of the mosque, their women heavily veiled, the younger ones wearing only the head covering. Not far from them stood a group of Christian men. Muhammad floated towards his reed mat, where he was wont to preside while conducting discussions. Aisha and Swadah lingered behind, socialising with the other ladies, and oblivious to the arrival of the poets and the singers. The group of men from the Thaqif tribe whom Ali had lodged in the mosque joined the Prophet, and the Christian men began to ask questions.

'You profess, Prophet, that the religion of Islam is a confirmation of the religions of the Jews and the Christians?' Ukaidir ibn Malik began thoughtfully. 'And yet my Christian friends tell me that your belief is contrary to the beliefs of the Jews or of the Christians? How would you settle these doubts?'

'*Say unto the Christians, their God and my God are One*' (2:139), was Muhammad's only response; a revelation he had received not long ago.

'We have heard this revelation, Prophet, but it fails to address the rifts between the Jews, the Christians and the Muslims,' Yohanna ibn Ruba declared. 'Your claim is that Islam offers the gift of unity, yet the views of the Muslims have nothing in common with Jewish doctrines, causing many rifts; many conflicts which demand answers.'

'One finds the answers if one is willing to probe the hearts of the revelations, O Prince of Aila. The revelations proclaim the gift of unity, that is true, striving towards ending all rifts, and embracing everyone in the light of love, regardless of their views or beliefs, since all belong to Allah.' The sad look in Muhammad's eyes fell upon them all. '*We gave Moses the Book, We gave Jesus the Evangel, We gave Muhammad the Quran*' (3:3), he recited.

'The hearts of these revelations, Prophet, reveal nothing to us, and the believers who recite them persist in pounding fear into the hearts of all who do not profess their belief. Fear punishment, and the expectation of reward: are these the foundations of your belief?' Abu Amir, the monk, flashed his challenge.

'Good deeds are the only foundations for any pillar of belief that ensure its strength, my revered monk. Without them, it stands shortened from crumbling, weak and hollow inside and polished with the glitter of zeal.' Muhammad's gaze held his followers captive. 'O Muslims, I do not believe that you fill the hearts of your fellow men with the fear of reward and punishment, but if you do, it is my duty to warn you that such actions are against the precepts of Islam. You are strictly enjoined to memorise this revelation as your signpost for acting nobly and virtuously. *Surely, the Believer and the Jews, and the Christians and the Sabaeans, whichever party from among them, truly believes in Allah and the Last Day and does good deeds – shall have their reward with their Lord, and no fear shall come upon them, nor shall they grieve*' (2:62).

'Faith and forgiveness are two hands held together with the warmth of love and prayer, you tell us, Prophet.' Najiyal sought Muhammad's attention. 'But what is your advice to those who bandy derisive words about, thinking they're better than other people, and who lack respect and courtesy?'

'I would ask them to keep these revelations dear to their hearts, and to seek the light of understanding.' Muhammad smiled, reciting quickly:

'O ye who believe! Let not one people deride another people, nor call another names. Bad indeed is evil reputation after the profession of belief; and those who do not repent are wrongdoers. (49:12)

And again. Tell those who believe to forgive those who persecute them, and fear not the Days of Allah, that He may requite a people for what they earn' (45:14).

'Medina is a melting-pot of customs and alliances, Prophet, besides being a hotbed of intrigue between the Jews and the Christians. They do not take kindly to your message of Islam. Discord and dissension are rising,' Abdallah ibn Ubbay began. 'What punishment would a Muslim receive if he was provoked to wrong a Jew or a Christian?' He stole a glance at his reticent son, Abdullah, beside him.

'He who wrongs a Jew or a Christian will have me as his accuser, subject to the laws of justice and equality, regardless of his race, rank or belief.' Muhammad looked deep into his eyes, as if infusing the warmth of love into his soul.

'You should have your wives veiled, Prophet,' Zainab, the Jewess, breathed through her veil, her face turning to her giant hulk of a husband, Mahrab, beside her.

'Why? Why?' Muhammad could barely murmur, his gaze warm and wistful.

'You are the Prophet of God, Muhammad!' Zainab laughed. 'Far higher in rank and status than many who claim respect and reverence as their due! By veiling your wives, you would strengthen the claim of your religion as holy and sacrosanct.'

'And that is precisely the reason why my wives should not be veiled.' Muhammad lowered his gaze. 'Islam does not dictate how anyone should dress, men or women, with the exception that they should dress modestly. Islam is the religion of justice and equality for both sexes. It strives towards dissolving the barriers of rank, status, and supremacy. Veiling is a status symbol of wealth and royalty; it serves as a mark of noble birth and grand lineage, so it cannot be adopted by Islam, since Islam teaches equality for all. I am chosen as a prophet, but I am like any other man – in fact, I am the lowliest of Allah's slaves – and my wives can earn respect by virtue of their own deeds and actions, not by the adoption or discarding of customs which have been practised since time immemorial. And yet Islam teaches us to respect the customs and the religions of others; I am only a messenger, unfolding the message of Islam as it is revealed to me. That message is simple: Islam is the religion of love and unity, of peace and equality.'

'What equality is that, Prophet, when your latest revelation promises nymphs of Paradise for men and nothing for women?' Another heavily veiled Jewess threw in her blistering challenge.

'Before I attempt to explain or warn against literal interpretations of the holy revelations, please bear with me while I ask my scribe a question.' Muhammad turned his attention to Abu Huraira. 'Abu Huraira, answer me honestly. But before I ask, may I have your trust in my divine inspiration that words are gender-free, and a gift from our Creator to every creature?' Abu Huraira nodded. 'Now tell me, does the purity of the Arabic language permit you to ascribe any form to Allah?'

'No, Prophet.' Abu Huraira's eyes were beacons of devotion.

'You mould the revelations to perfection with your fingers, Abu Huraira! After you fashion the words, what do you see in those revelations?' Muhammad asked.

'A luminescent, formless light, that's all I see, Prophet,' Abu Huraira murmured devoutly. 'I see beautiful words addressed to the creatures of the world, devoid of any distinction between male and female, between high and low, between believer and unbeliever.'

'May the gift of Allah's guidance be with you always.' Muhammad returned his attention to the veiled lady. 'Nymphs of Paradise represent the heart's desires of any male or female, Lady Rehanna, if I may presume to guess your name by your speech and bearing? Paradise too, is a place for both men and women, where anyone's heart's desires come true if they have led a life of piety, loving Allah and His creatures and His creations from the profoundest depths of their own heart, where no seeds of envy, malice, hatred, cruelty or jealousy could ever find nourishment. Allow me to recite this revelation, which might show you a glimpse of how Paradise is suited to both man and woman.

Reclining there upon couches, they will find neither sunny heat, nor bitter cold. The shade is close upon them and clustered fruits bow down. Silver goblets are brought round for them, and glasslike beakers – as bright as glass, but made of silver, which they themselves have measured to the measure of their deeds. There they are watered with a cup whereof the mixture is of Zanjabil.

The waters of the spring there, named Salsabil. There youths serve them of everlasting youth, whom, when you see them, you would take for scattered pearls. When you see it, you will see there bliss and high estate.

Their clothing will be fine green silk and gold embroidery. They will wear bracelets of silver. Their Lord will slake their thirst with a pure drink.

And it will be said unto them: Lo! this is a reward for you. Your struggle upon earth has found acceptance. Lo! We, even We, have revealed to you the Quran, a revelation' (76:13–23).

'Are the fires in hell, O Prophet, described as vividly as the delights of Paradise in your revelations?' Abu Rafi, the Jewish leader, flashed a smile. 'Could anyone feel hell's horror and torment in words, as they do the bliss and pleasure of Paradise?'

'Before you witness the fires of hell, Rafi, be assured that a time will come when hell's gates will clash against each other, because there will be no one left in it.' Muhammad smiled. 'The fire in hell has many forms and degrees. One of them is the festering wound in one's own soul in this world, which one carries to the world beyond, if one has hurt the heart of even one person intentionally. By the same token, Paradise is part of this world too, if one has learnt to be guided by the virtue of love for all, cultivating the seeds of peace and unity, and nurturing them with kindness and compassion.'

'Tell me, Prophet, how will an old woman like me enter Paradise?' A poor lady with wrinkled face brought up her own doubts.

'You will be young when you enter Paradise,' Muhammad encouraged. 'The purity of your heart and the innocence of your youth are reflected in your eyes, and your youth and beauty will return when you enter Paradise.'

'I have a friend, Prophet; an old lady,' Asma began reluctantly. 'She still prays to her old Meccan gods. I am not sure if I am right in continuing the friendship, since Allah is not her God. Should I stay away from her?'

'Nay, by Allah's permission, nay, my Lady of Two Girdles!' Muhammad's features lit up with a beatific smile. 'Be kind and loving to your friend. She is set in her ways, and her devotion should be the envy of many who profess that they believe when they don't.'

'How can you sanction the idol worship, Prophet, of this lady who is set in her ways, when you proclaim the message of Oneness?' Abbas ibn Mirdas asked.

'Allah looks into the heart of the devotee, Abbas.' Rills of sadness crossed Muhammad's eyes. 'Idol worship and devotion are two different things. If one could only break the idols of hatred in one's own heart! Then you see no forms but Oneness. All idols vanish and only the light of devotion remains, and love becomes the object of worship, blind as faith, with no face or name! Islam teaches respect and tolerance for all faiths. I have made treaties with all the tribes of Medina, and with the Jews and the Christians. In the name of peace and friendship, we have to abide by the rules we have mutually agreed upon. Our actions speak louder than any treaties, and in order to do right we must remember the words of peace and friendship. So I'm taking this time, for everyone's benefit, to spell out the terms of our treaties once again.' He paused, his gaze dreamy. 'The Jews who attach themselves to our commonwealth shall have equal rights with our own people to our assistance and good offices. The various branches of Jews in Medina shall form one composite nation with the Muslims. They shall practise their religion as freely as the Muslims. The clients and allies of the Jews shall enjoy the same security and freedom.' His gaze swept over the Christian delegation from Najran. 'The revelation which says *There is no forcing anyone into this way of life, truth stands clear from error* (2:256), embodies that kernel of respect and tolerance for the religions of the world. Christians have the right to safety in their lives and property, and Muslims will respect their rights. No churches will be harmed, nor will any monasteries be closed, nor any priests impeded from their work. The religious symbols of the Christians are to be respected and protected, and they are not obliged to provide any supplies to the Muslims, if the threat of war looms over Medina. No Muslim will interfere with the Christians in the practice of their religion.'

'Can you tell us, Prophet, why the Meccans persecute you?' Malik ibn Auf was quick to ask, concealing his guile behind a sparkling smile.

'For offering them the gift of grace from Allah, who has dwelt amongst them since Abraham built the First House of Worship at the Kaaba!' Muhammad stroked his small beard, his look profound and piercing.

'No, Prophet, it's not for that, and you know it,' Malik ibn Auf declared. 'The Meccans persecute you because you challenge their gods. Why don't you sign a treaty of friendship with them, and give their gods of the Kaaba due reverence?'

'The Meccans have no gods, Malik, only the symbols of their own greed and chicanery.' Muhammad's gaze was one shimmering ocean of light. 'The Kaaba has been the House of

One God since Adam walked on the face of this earth. Abraham consecrated it by the command of Allah. And Allah is the God of the Arabs, of the nations, of the whole world. The Kaaba is the centre of divine presence, through which emanate all faiths, all religions. Allah's light shines in all the holy places, be it a temple, a church, a mosque, a monastery, or a synagogue, but the Kaaba is the holy of the holies, sanctified by Abraham, Moses and Jesus to such cosmic purity that nothing could stay except the seat of worship for one God alone, Allah. Our mortal sight can't envision this cosmic purity, nor can our limited intelligence comprehend the divine will and the divine presence. Allah is the light of the heavens and the earth; it has been revealed. Allah guides to His light whomsoever He wills. Meccans are persecuting us, my friend, for reminding them that Allah is still their God, and revealing to them His all-embracing grace and mercy, so that they can embrace the virtues of peace, justice, equality. And also for reminding them that they have turned this house of purity into a den of gain, power and oppression, moulding gods out of their own greed and hypocrisy, where love and goodwill are choked against their need to oppress and tyrannise.' He paused again. 'Yes, the Meccans don't desist from persecution, but ponder upon this revelation, my friends, and despair not of Allah's mercy, and practise tolerance even in your suffering: "*Those who have been driven from their homes unjustly only because they said 'Our Lord is Allah.' For had it not been for Allah's repelling some men by means of others, cloisters and churches and oratories and mosques, wherein the name of Allah is often mentioned, would assuredly have been pulled down. Verily, Allah helpeth one who helpeth Him. Lo! Allah is Strong, Almighty*"' (22:40).

'What does *surrender to one God* really mean, O Prophet?' Amr bin Mudah asked dreamily.

'It simply means to strive after righteousness, my son,' Muhammad intoned kindly. 'It means to be tranquil, to do one's duty, to pay one's debts, to be at perfect peace with one's own self and with others. To offer the fruits of one's good actions at the altar of Allah without expecting any rewards. We are the masters of our actions, free to refuse or accept the blessings of divine guidance, free to be responsible for our deeds, to set our own guideposts to determine whether we are to be rewarded or punished.'

'How can one be sure that one's faith in one's own God is true and strong, if that faith has never been tested?' Ukaidir ibn Malik seemed to be questioning his Christianity.

'The true test of any faith is love, which one must nurture and cultivate,' Muhammad murmured thoughtfully. 'No one can taste the strength of faith, if one has not learnt to love one's fellow men. For the health and prosperity of society as a whole, it is necessary to speak out about our love for each other, for love breeds peace and harmony.'

'Is reciting Kalima true surrender to the will of God, Prophet?' Hamza broke his silence, more for the benefit of the congregation than because he needed to understand.

'To recite Kalima is a spiritual discipline, dear Uncle, the beginning of real freedom from the tyranny of ego and pride.' Muhammad smiled. 'By reciting Kalima, one strives towards understanding the first phase of unity in spiritual discipline. *La Illaha illah Allah,* meaning, there is no God but God, affirms that Allah is everywhere and in everything. *Mohammed Ar Rusul Allah* affirms that I am the messenger sent by Allah to proclaim the message of love, unity and brotherhood.'

'The poetry of Kalima and the revelations, Prophet, touches my heart! But the countless interpretations of those revelations by Muslims are causing rifts amongst the Muslim Brotherhood. If you only knew!' Kaab ibn Salma lamented. 'How is anyone supposed to know the true interpretation of a revelation when so many interpretations are flying around?'

'By contemplating each revelation with love in one's heart,' Muhammad sang. 'Especially this one!' The stars of poetry gathered in his eyes. '*He is the One who caused the Book to descend to you. Part of it is clearly defined verses, which are "Mother of the Book", and others are symbolic. But those with error in their hearts follow the symbolic part of it, seeking dissension and seeking its interpretation. None knows its interpretation except Allah, and those who are firmly rooted in knowledge. Others say, we have faith in it, it is all from our Lord. But none recalls except those who possess the inner Heart*' (3:7).

'Ah, divine knowledge and divine inspiration!' Kaab ibn Salma exclaimed.

Love, like a venomous snake, has tormented my heart,
But for this illness there is neither physician nor sorcerer.
Only my Beloved,
With whom I am so much in love,
Can cure me;
For He possesses the medicines and incantations
For my malady.

The air in the courtyard seemed to filled with the fragrance of this song; everyone sat rapt and speechless. Muhammad's soul was moved to ecstasy, and he didn't even realise that he had leapt to his feet in a state of mystical abandon. He seemed oblivious to everything, his face revealing the deep-hearted mystery of his own self, where Allah was the Beloved and he the Lover, with a pure, sublime longing to be united with the Beloved. Muhammad's right hand had shot up, palm up towards the heavens, as if receiving blessings from the blessed Beloved. His left hand, palm down, was poised towards the earth, as if bestowing the gift of blessings upon the world. With the grace of a skilful dancer, he began to spin on his toes, his black cloak slipping from his shoulders and falling to the ground in a wave-strewn heap.

'You are part of me, Ali, and I am part of you!' Muhammad's voice kept time with the rhythm of his body, whirling and floating. 'Come, dance with me, and learn the art of receiving divine blessings and inspiration from Allah, the Beloved, with your right hand and bestowing them with your left hand upon all the world's creatures.'

Ali was quick to bounce to his feet, and join Muhammad. His movements were swift and ecstatic, his toes were spinning in unison with Muhammad's and his soul was sailing aloft to unattainable heights. Muhammad's lips were pouring forth another song, urging Ali's brother Jafar to taste the sweetness of this cosmic mystery.

'Come, Jafar, join us. You are like me in looks and character!' Muhammad was inviting everyone to participate in this cosmic dance of love and self-surrender.

Lit with the torch of divine love, the bodies of the three men were floating and swirling. They were spinning on their toes in unison as if attracted together to the centre of the earth, their bodies whirling like sparkling atoms to be consumed by the light of the sun. Then the cosmic dance came to a sudden halt, enveloping the three participants in the light of bliss and rapture. Muhammad retrieved his cloak, and stood splitting it into rags.

'This is the dance of Oneness.' Muhammad scattered the pieces of his black cloak over the heads of his congregation. 'My cousins are like the stars: whichever one of them you follow, they will guide you. Although Jafar is returning to Abyssinia with his family tomorrow, so you will be deprived of his guidance till he returns.'

'Was that enjoyable, Prophet?' Umar ibn Khattab asked, more aghast than awed, oblivious to the rapt expression of his wife Zainab and their daughter Hafsa.

'For sure, Umar! When the Beloved calls, the Lover can't help but be consumed by the fire of joy and ecstasy.' Muhammad's pomegranate-red lips spilled the fire of rubies. 'Allah the Beloved is inside the heart of every human being, but love is the key to unlocking the spiritual heart and seeing one's Beloved. Love, ecstasy and oblivion are the prerequisites to meeting our one and only Beloved, through the fire of longing, after we have reduced our ego to ashes and after our mortal attributes of wisdom are effaced.'

'This wild and ecstatic behaviour is not in keeping with your mission, Prophet!' A Jew by the name of Huyayy ibn Akhtab waved his arm in protest. 'Especially when the Meccans are ready to wage a war on Medina. Before you migrated to Medina, Prophet, you should have cut off the heads of your persecutors with a sword, and left behind the thunder of your vengeance as a warning not to dare follow.'

'Permission to fight was not granted to us then, not even in self-defence, my good man,' Muhammad murmured. 'With courage as our only weapon of self-defence, we came to Medina. By the grace of Allah, our souls remained pure and light during our flight from Mecca to Medina, not tainted by the blood of our kin. If we ever carry swords, it will be for the sake of justice, not for the sake of vengeance. Surely, we would be willing to defend Medina if its peace was threatened.' His gaze was settling on Aisha.

Aisha was assisting Swadah, but before Muhammad could voice his wish to seek the sanctuary of his hut, his attention was diverted by the arrival of a bold rider. Hakim ibn Hazan abandoned his horse and trooped straight towards Muhammad.

'Abu Jahl is at the head of a thousand men advancing towards Medina, Prophet.' Hakim ibn Hazan was quick to empty the quiver of his fear. 'They'll surround the valley of Badr, and they're all equipped with lances and javelins!'

Muhammad stood there speechless, no words escaping his lips until he turned to his wives, instructing them to leave and to keep Ruqayyah company. A subtle hush fell upon the courtyard after Aisha and Swadah vanished behind the mosque.

'I am seeking your advice, my friends; say what you will, and we will weigh the situation,' Muhammad began thoughtfully.

'Should we leave the safety of our homes behind, and march out to confront the Meccans, who are intent on seizing the lands and the villages of Medina? Are we prepared to fight in self-defence to fend off the assault on Medina – that is, when and if they come?'

'We have no choice, Prophet, since all our attempts at peace have failed,' Abu Bakr opined.

'We can't let the Meccans oppress our gentle hosts in Medina, who have offered us homes and friendship.' Hamza shot his own comment.

'All my resources are at your disposal, Prophet, for we must win or perish.' Talha ibn Ubaidullah's eyes gleamed with a firm resolve.

'We have believed in you, Prophet, and have confirmed that what you brought to us is the truth.' Saad bin Mudah rose to his feet. He was the first Jew from the tribe of Beni Koreiza who had accepted Islam upon the arrival of the Prophet in Medina. 'We made an agreement with you to hear and obey. So go ahead with whatever you decide, Prophet, and we are with you. By the One who sent you as a prophet, if you were to lead us into the sea, we would go with you without fear, and not one of us would stay behind. When we signed our agreement, we stripped ourselves of all fear, knowing that you might need our assistance in confronting the enemy in the near future. We will hold firm and stand our ground, and press forward against all odds in solid ranks. We hope that Allah will let you see us in action, and that you won't be disappointed; rather, that you will be proud of us. Lead us with Allah's blessings, whenever the Meccans come.'

'May Allah's blessing shine on you, Saad, and upon your family!' Muhammad's eyes lit up like gold stars. 'We will go forward, when the Meccans come, with love and trust in our hearts, begging Allah to grant in His mercy that bloodshed be avoided.'

'How are we to die as martyrs, if no blood is spilt on the battleground?' Abdallah ibn Ubbay mocked, pressed by his own need to cause rift and dissension.

'Before we tackle this subject, my friend, and before we march out as the champions of self-defence, I wish to make it clear that we must never plant the seeds of hypocrisy, stupidity or distortion.' Muhammad's eyes flashed his reproof. 'He is a martyr who exchanges his earthly life for life eternal, not by his own will to attain glory, but by losing his will to the will of Allah, where life is not offered, yet taken by the grace of Allah to nourish and propagate love, peace and justice. Without just cause, no one can receive the gift of martyrdom. So, long not for death, nor wish death upon others. Otherwise, in the first case it would be suicide, and in the second, a murder. Both these acts, and thoughts, are sinful.' He paused. 'Don't you remember this revelation? *O Mankind! Call upon your Lord humbly and in secret. Lo! He loveth not aggressors.* (7:55) And this one? *And if they incline to peace, incline thou also to it*' (8:61).

'How can there be peace in war, Prophet, when men invoke their gods and gird themselves with hatred to kill and mutilate?' Kinanah ibn Huqaiq could not stop the assault of his own warring thoughts, clutching the hand of his wife Safiya absently.

'By avoiding the shadow of death in war and by not making religion a weapon of cruelty and tyranny,' Muhammad intoned. 'If a person nurtures and creates hatred in the name of religion, be assured that he is guided by the devil. If one's piety allows one to seek peace and truth with an earnest desire to improve the conditions of mankind, then surely the hand of Allah is his guide and guidance.'

'How difficult and confusing this all is. Truth and Allah?' Bujayr, Kaab's poet brother, lamented.

'In our boundless planes of memory, we have caves and vaults.' The Sufic light in Muhammad's eyes sparkled. 'If we succeed in entering those caves and vaults, Allah in His infinite compassion will dissolve all our doubts. We will find nothing dark or complex in there, only a soothing light, radiant like a child's smile with all its purity and innocence. Every boundary would melt too against the glow of that radiance, no barriers between races, sects or religions—' His Sufic thoughts were interrupted by a song as Bilal's call to prayer pealed through the evening dusk.

Muhammad bowed his head, leading the congregation to prayer. They all stood facing north towards Jerusalem as was their wont, while Muhammad guided them through the ritual of prostration. His eyes were closed, and soon after the second prostration, he turned abruptly southward. The entire congregation followed suit, all baffled by this sudden move, but imitating obediently. At the conclusion of the prayer, Muhammad cupped his face between his hands, his eyes still closed.

'*Verily, We see thee turning thy face often to heaven. Surely, then, will we make thee turn to Qibla which thou likest. So, turn thy face towards the sacred mosque; and wherever you be, turn your faces towards it. And they to whom the Book has been given know that this is the truth from their Lord. And Allah is not unmindful of what they do*' (2:145). Muhammad lifted his hands up, as if still in prayer.

'What? We have always faced Jerusalem for prayers, and now you want us to turn towards the Kaaba?' Abu Amir protested. 'Are we to follow your whims, Prophet, whenever you change your mind?'

'The revelations are from the Lord, and I am only His humble slave,' Muhammad murmured. 'Turning inwardly towards the Kaaba is what matters, Abu Amir, not the outward act of prostration, or its direction.' The lamps of profundity in his eyes were flashing more revelations. '*The foolish among people will say: what has turned them away from their Qibla which they followed? Say: To Allah belong the East and the West. He guides whom He pleases to the right path*' (2:142).

'So, you claim to be the recipient of righteousness, Prophet, striving towards changing our Jewish laws, and inventing your own for power and distinction?' Abu Rafi's eyes blazed with fury.

'*It is not righteousness that you turn your faces to the East or West, but truly righteous is he who believes in Allah and the Last Day and the angels and the Book and the prophets. And spends his money for the love of Him, on the kindred and the orphans and the needy and the wayfarer and those who ask for charity! And who observes prayer and pays zakat! And those who fulfil their promise, when they have made one, and the patient in poverty and affliction and the steadfast in time of war! It is those who have proved truthful and it is those who are God-fearing*' (2:177), Muhammad recited.

'Where will you find Allah, Prophet, when you march to the valley of Badr, since you have abandoned our holy Jerusalem in favour of the Kaaba?' Shas ibn Qays, scarlet with rage, flashed his challenge.

'*To Allah belong the East and the West. So whithersoever you turn, there will be the Face of Allah. Surely, Allah is Bountiful, All-Knowing*' (2:115). Muhammad turned on his heel, drifting towards his own hut as if in a dream.

The Prophet's face was suffused with light as he wove his way out of the courtyard. The men were silent with awe. The congregation broke into little groups. The hearts of the women were touched with devotion and tenderness, it was obvious, their eyes glittering with awe following the Prophet before he could disappear behind the mud walls of his quarters.

Suddenly the Prophet became aware of Aisha, standing alone in perfect stillness, watching her hands with the utmost absorption.

'I was coming to the mosque to join you in prayers, Prophet,' Aisha murmured, her eyes still glued to her hands.

'The whole world is a mosque, my Aisha. There is no need to seek a special place for prayer.' A spontaneous gale of mirth escaped Muhammad's lips. 'And why are you looking at your hands so strangely?'

'I am wondering which one of my hands Allah will cut off for striking Anas, since I can't remember which one I used to hit him.' Aisha lifted her gaze up to him.

'Oh, my little angel!' Muhammad stood laughing with tears in his eyes. 'Allah forgives little girls much too quickly, just like He does the Prophet for saying bad things.' He linked his arm into hers, dragging her along towards the hut.

CHAPTER 11

The Song of Victory at Badr
From 624 to 625 AD

The sandy battlefield at Badr was enveloped by a night-time desert hush. Every peace talk with the Meccans had proven fruitless, and Muhammad had marched out of Medina at the head of three hundred and thirteen men to defend the lives of the Medinese against an army of one thousand Meccans. Muhammad could inhale the very breath of the night's silence as he lay resting in his palm-leaf hut. Swadah was sleeping beside him on her straw mat, but sleep was leagues away from him. Muhammad settled himself into a sitting position, willing his thoughts to prayer. But they were restless, hovering over Medina where Aisha had been left behind to watch over Ruqayyah. Ruqayyah's health was declining rapidly, and he had instructed Othman, too, to stay.

Fight in the way of Allah
Against those who fight against you,
Against those who drove you out of your homes.
Fight, but start no war;
For Allah loves not the makers of war,
And if your enemy cease his aggression
Then you may fight no more. (22:39–40)

Muhammad had received this revelation several months before the Meccans had turned up in the valley of Badr. Many rifts were dissolved by the sheer aura of this revelation, and many more by frequent expeditions with no actual fights, but harmless skirmishes. One of those expeditions was to Waddan to quell the rifts between the warring tribes of Darma ibn Bakr and Kinanah ibn Huqaiq. Other expeditions were against the caravans of the Quraysh, who were plundering villages near Medina. Muhammad had appointed eight men to scout the precincts of Medina. The leader of this group was the Prophet's cousin Abdallah ibn Jash, instructed by him not to engage in any fighting. Unable to obtain any information, Abdallah ibn Jash had left Medina, leading his companions as far as the Nakhlah Valley between Taif and Mecca. After two weeks in the desert sands, two of his camels were stolen. Then later, upon awakening, he discovered that two of his comrades were missing. Those missing, he was informed by the others, were two Medinese youths, compelled by their need to find the stolen camels. While waiting for their return he learnt that the Quraysh had captured them and taken them to Mecca. Abdallah ibn Jash had then headed for Yemen in fear of capture or assault. After two days of aimless wandering he decided to return to Medina, and seeing a caravan he ordered his companions to launch an attack. During the skirmish one Meccan man was killed and two taken prisoner. Abdallah ibn Jash was ecstatic, returning to Medina with his plunder and the prisoners.

Didn't I send you out with strict instructions not to fight, my bold cousin? Why did you? Especially during the holy month of Ramadan? Muhammad's thoughts repeated the same reproof which had made Abdallah ibn Jash wince.

Muhammad had treated the prisoners with the utmost kindness, and the bounty was well guarded, to be returned to its rightful owners. The Meccans were quick to send ransom for the freedom of their prisoners, but Muhammad declined it, requesting an even exchange. This was agreed upon, so Muhammad had appointed Saad bin Mudah and Abdallah ibn Rudafeh to take the bounty and the Meccan prisoners back, and to fetch the Medinese youths held captive in Mecca. All had ended well, but one of the Meccan prisoners, upon reaching Mecca, had confessed that he was so impressed by the kindness of the Prophet that he had become a Muslim. Hearing this confession, the Meccans had doubled their raids on the villages close to Medina.

In retaliation, Muhammad had dispatched an expedition to seize the rich caravan of Abu Sofyan bound for Syria, so that the victims of the plunderers could be compensated. This expedition failed due to the betrayal of a Jewish dissenter. Afterwards, Abu Sofyan swiftly hired a man by the name of Damdan, sending him to Mecca with the instructions that he, Abu Sofyan, needed the help of the Quraysh to wage war on Medina.

After reaching Mecca Damdan had torn open his shirt and cut off the ears of his camel, disfiguring its nose with a violent blow. He had turned his saddle around to signal his desperation, flailing his arms and shouting wildly: 'Help, help, Quraysh! Muhammad and his followers are attacking your caravan! You may yet be able to stop them!'

Muhammad's fingers knotted together at the assault of this recollection, as narrated to him by a Meccan trader. Through his head paraded the pride of the Meccan army, one hundred horses and seven hundred and fifty camels. His thoughts turned towards the rules he had dictated before leaving Medina.

You may not hurt children or women. You may not hurt fieldworkers. You may not hurt old men or take advantage of cripples. You may not cut down fruit trees. You may not take a drink of water without permission, or food without payment. You may not tie up any prisoner, or force him to walk while you ride. The enemy who surrenders to you must be treated kindly by you. No child is ever to be harmed under any circumstances.

Muhammad's head drooped over his chest. A lamenting prayer shuddered inside him.

Oh Allah! Fulfil Thy word and promise. O Allah, should this small group of ours perish, there would be none left to worship Thee.

The sands of Arabia shuddered in Muhammad's mind's eye, forming winged angels. Gabriel was their commander, ordering them to defeat the Meccans with the wands of their light, his smile radiant as he proclaimed laughingly, *O Messenger of Allah! Your prayer has reached Allah, and He surely will fulfil His promise.*

Muhammad was jolted to awareness. His eyes shot open, blinded by the dazzling light which flooded the palm-leaf hut with the brilliance of many suns.

'*I will help you with a thousand angels, rank upon rank. Allah appointed it only as good tidings, and your hearts thereby might be at rest. Victory cometh only by the help of Allah! Lo! Allah is mighty and wise*' (8:9–10). The song of victory caressed Muhammad's lips with warm sweetness.

The flood of dazzling light was washed away all of a sudden. Swadah had been awakened by this victorious song of revelation from Muhammad's lips.

'Another revelation, Prophet?' Swadah could barely murmur, her voice a little tremor of hope and wonder. 'That means we are going to win this war?'

'Yes, Swadah, be of good cheer. Allah's help is with us!' was Muhammad's response, the awe and profundity in his gaze rippling from his dream-reality.

'But our men are so few against so many Meccans, Prophet. Is Allah sending His angels to defeat the enemy?' Swadah's eyes shone with fright.

'Angels in our hearts, my dear, to lend us courage to defend ourselves. It is Allah's will that His truth and message may live and prosper,' Muhammad murmured.

'I pray that we win, Prophet,' Swadah murmured back. 'Yet my heart is full of fear and doubts. Did you hear how the Meccan army held the Shroud of the Kaaba over their heads and chanted this prayer before marching to Badr: *O God! may the people who amongst are better guided, superior in force, more honoured, and possess a better religion, win victory over their adversaries?*'

'They prayed to the gods of the Kaaba, but there is only one God of the Kaaba, my Swadah. And God has heeded their prayers – victory is promised to us, so Allah may reveal to them the message of Islam with all its purity of love, justice and compassion.' Muhammad heaved himself up slowly. 'Today we will defend ourselves, and we will be blessed with the gift of victory.'

The palm trees, their own leaves drawn like the swords, stood vigilant, overlooking the valley of Badr. Muhammad, astride his Arabian steed, faced his small band of men, pouring the light of courage into his followers' hearts.

One hillock separated the two armies, though it was no barrier, since both sides could see and hear the other if they were so inclined. The Meccans this morning were swathed in golden radiance, their casques and breastplates polished, their swords and scimitars naked and glittering. All night long they had feasted on the meat of ten camels which they had slaughtered. They had been entertained too, by dancing girls. The mighty palms carried the voices of the Meccans over to the Muslims.

'Why should we fight Muhammad and his companions? Are they not related to us one way or the other?' Ammrah ibn Walid's voice was shrill. 'Granted, their army is small, but even if we kill them all, what do we gain? Why don't we go back to Mecca, and forget about fighting?'

'We are fighting Muhammad because he is the prophet of lies! He is causing rifts between our clans and our families! What proof do you need? We are fighting amongst ourselves even on a glorious day like this when victory is near, instead of fighting with them and wearing the laurels of victory,' Abu Jahl was thundering. 'By al-Llah, we will not go back until we have killed Muhammad and his whole horde of followers!'

'By al-Llah, you will gain nothing by fighting Muhammad and his companions,' Utbah ibn Rabia was saying. 'If you kill him or them, every one of you will be loath to look into the eyes of the others, remembering that you have slain your nephew or a man of your nearest kin, who is still bound to you with family ties in a long line of patrimony?'

'You are a coward, Utbah, and…' Abu Jahl's voice was swallowed by an abrupt gust of wind, and no more voices reached the ears of the Muslim army. Muhammad, still astride his Arabian steed, examined the files of his men, bestowing upon them warm words and smiles for valour and courage. All of a sudden, he shoved a soldier back into line for the sake of discipline.

'Fall in line, Sawwad,' Muhammad commanded.

'You have hurt me, Prophet!' Sawwad protested.

'Sorry, Sawwad,' Muhammad murmured with all tenderness. 'I didn't mean to hurt or offend you. Here, push me back as hard as I pushed you.' He struck his chest with the same hand that he had used on Sawwad as the tool of discipline.

In a flash, Sawwad bounced out of the line, bent low and kissed the Prophet's feet. His eyes were filling with tears of shame and remorse.

'Get back into line, Sawwad,' was Muhammad's gentle command and reprimand. 'What are you doing?'

'I want to be a martyr in this holy war, Prophet.' Sawwad staggered back into the line, tears stinging his eyes. 'I want to receive your blessings before I die.'

'I have failed in my message, it is obvious,' Muhammad lamented. 'My friends and soldiers, listen carefully to what I say, and pay heed. Martyrdom is dying valiantly and honourably in self-defence. It is not martyrdom to wish death upon oneself, nor to will it upon others. And no one can claim martyrdom if they are motivated by the passion of hatred or vengeance. Always remember, permission to fight has been given to us because we have been persecuted and driven out of our homes. We will fight in self-defence only. We will not be the ones to incite the battle.' He paused, the sadness in his eyes replaced by compassion. 'And remember also: *Fight in the way of Allah against those who fight against you, but begin not hostilities. Lo! Allah loveth not aggressors* (2:190). *And if they incline to peace, incline thou also to it* (8:61). These revelations are your guides. Wear them as shields. There is no such thing as holy war. Anything which nurtures conflict, engendering death and devastation, can never claim the virtue of holiness. Peace is holy; cultivate it and nurture it and embrace it, even amidst the throes of war if it is forced upon you. By the law and virtue of this intention alone, the gates of victory will be opened for you, and joy and peace will be yours, if you purely desire love, justice and equality for all, fearing none but Allah. But don't ever forget that Islam means peace and reconciliation.'

'Is Jihad not holy war, Prophet? Fighting against evil, so that goodness could prevail?' Al Harith asked. 'Are we not here to fight in the name of Allah, and to kill these evil lords of tyranny and persecution?'

'Jihad is always an inward struggle, my friend. I thought I made it clear?' Muhammad lamented. 'Jihad is not a holy war, as you wish it to be, but a holy struggle to conquer the forces of evil within one's own self. To fight in the way of Allah is to fight the evil within, not to become the instrument of evil in propagating itself. We are here to defend ourselves against aggression, and that is a lesser Jihad: the greater Jihad is that while defending ourselves we succeed in keeping our hearts and minds pure of hatred, enmity or of a sense of vengeance, employing all means—' His voice was snuffed out by a sudden blaze of insults from the side of the Meccans.

The first phase of the battle had commenced. The insults of the Meccans were growing louder and louder. The Meccan army was a ripple of gold. The most prominent man amongst them was Utbah ibn Rabia on his red camel, with Abu Jahl beside him on his garlanded one. Abu Jahl could not miss Muhammad's warm scrutiny, his haughty features wrinkling into a smile.

'Why don't you reward our insults with curses, Muhammad?' Abu Jahl challenged. 'Surely your heart is simmering with rage?'

'*I have not been sent as a curse to mankind, but as an inviter to good and as Mercy. O Allah, grant guidance to my people, for surely they know not*' (7:199). Muhammad recited this revelation in response, with a look of compassion, not contention.

'Cry to Allah for mercy then, O Prophet of Lies, for you are doomed!' Abu Jahl flung his insult. 'Soon, your mode of loud worship in the mosque will be silenced.'

'*Say unto mankind: cry unto Allah, or cry unto the Beneficent, unto Whichever you cry, it is the same. His are the most beautiful names. And thou, Muhammad, be not loud-voiced in worship, yet not silent therein, but follow a way between*' (17:110). The revelation was torn out of Muhammad's heart as an appeal for a truce.

'Send your warriors onto the battlefield for single combat, Prophet. We want the satisfaction of hacking them to pieces before we get to you,' Abu Jahl challenged.

'Averse to war as I am, you won't see me fighting in this battle, but my men will defend their honour most valiantly,' Muhammad commented. 'If there is any good among your people, Abu Jahl, they should be heeding the advice of the man on the red camel—' His last appeal for peace was shattered as three Medinese youths stepped up to meet the challenge of the Meccans. Auf, Muawwidh and Amr bin Mudah had hurled themselves into the arena of combat, their swords drawn and their eyes shining.

'We have not come all this way to blunt our swords on the callow youths of Medina, Muhammad!' Shaiba bin Utbah from the Meccan lines jeered mirthfully.

'We have no quarrel with these young louts from Medina, Muhammad. We want the Meccan renegades!' Ammrah ibn Walid challenged.

'We want the heads of your uncles and cousins, Prophet! Not the limbs of these ugly colts.' Otba bin Utbah brandished his sword, his mirth strident and raucous.

The three Medinese youths retreated to their posts, as Ali raced his horse into the middle of the battlefield. Hamza was next to meet the challenge. Obaida followed suit, his gaze alone goading the Meccans to come forward. The Meccans raised a chorus of cheers as Otba bin Utbah, Shaiba bin Utbah and Ammrah ibn Walid let fly their steeds to pounce upon Muhammad's valiant team. The three duels were fast as lightning. The double-edged blade of Ali's sword cut off the head of Ammrah ibn Walid swiftly. Hamza too slew Shaiba bin Utbah before he could open his lips to pour out more insults. Obaida was still fighting with Otba bin Utbah, wounded in the leg. He was about to collapse when Ali and Hamza flew to his assistance. Hamza hurled himself at Otba bin Utbah, slitting his throat with one swift blow of his sword. Ali was quick to haul Obaida onto his own horse and to head for the safety of their encampment.

The sun itself seemed aghast at seeing three of the best Qurayshites slain. The Meccans were stunned, the fever of rage and hatred in their eyes chilled. An overwhelming weight of sadness pressed upon Muhammad's heart, but a fresh hailstorm of insults, followed by arrows, splintered the hush to smithereens.

'Why insist on shedding the blood of innocent men, my friends?' An agonised appeal tore out of Muhammad's lips, as he jumped down from his horse heedlessly. 'You are my family – we can trace our lineage back to our great-great-grandfather Abd Manaf, and—' He could not continue against the shower of arrows. 'May confusion light upon your faces!' With this heartrending appeal he scooped a handful of sand, scattering it in the direction of the Meccan army.

The desert sun seemed to snatch that handful of sand and mould it into a ball of a sandstorm. Muhammad jumped back on his steed, vigilant, commanding, yet not actively participating in the conflict. A fierce battle commenced in all earnest, the Meccans literally blinded by sand, if not figuratively by their hatred. Their arrows were rendered impotent against the swirling molecules of sand, carried away into the arms of whirlwinds.

'Even in this battle, my friends, cling fast to your compassion, as I appealed to you before. Do not kill indiscriminately, but with the sole intent of self-defence.' Muhammad's voice reached his followers as a beacon of courage and chivalry.

Amidst the whirlwind of chaos and confusion on the battlefield at Badr, the swords of the Meccans were powerless against the sandy bullets. Their mighty, splendid ranks were broken, crumbling like sandcastles. Their own well-bred mounts were stumbling and tossing them down to be slain and trampled.

Abu Jahl became aware of the flight of his soldiers. A flame of obscenities tore loose from the cauldron of hell within him in the wake of his searing insults.

'By al-Lat and al-Uzzah, we will not return to Mecca till we have killed Muhammad and his companions! Come back, you desert crows, and show your vengeful mettle!' Abu Jahl's lips let fly a string of curses.

The few Meccans still fighting were standing their ground, and some returned in response to Abu Jahl's laments, his son Ikrimah still guarding him like a young hawk. Amr bin Mudah's sword cut through Abu Jahl's loins, and a loud groan escaped his lips before he fell to the ground. Ikrimah was quick to strike the man who had felled his father, wounding Amr bin Mudah in the arm. Though swaying with the impact of pain, Amr bin Mudah used his sword to hack off his bleeding arm before raising the same sword to strike his assailant. The bloodied abomination of an arm rolled down to Ikrimah's feet, and he fled. Abu Jahl's pain was silenced by a merciful blow from Abdallah ibn Masud, who cut his head off and held it up as a sign of victory.

The Meccans, fleeing for their lives, didn't care whether their leader was dead; but amidst the pandemonium of the slain and the wounded, cries of victory soared on the lips of the Medinese. The victors were in hot pursuit of the enemy, taking captives and herding them together to bring them back to their encampment.

Amongst these captives was the ex-master and tormentor of Bilal, the rich merchant Ummayad ibn Khalaf. As the captives were being driven towards the victors' camp, he noticed Bilal and grew violent. Snatching a sword from the hands of his captor, he stood bellowing with rage, 'You bastard, you stinking slave!'

Bilal requested him to put down the sword. But Ummayad ibn Khalaf laughed, spitting on Bilal's face and raising his sword to strike him. His intended attack was thwarted by a swift thrust from Bilal's own sword into the chest of his tormentor.

No sooner had Bilal struck Ummayad ibn Khalaf dead than two more captives threatened violence, attempting to seize the swords of their captors. Jabir and Musaib ibn Omeir, with whom they wrestled, were swift to slay them.

The wind was abating, and another nameless storm was stirring in Muhammad's soul. He let his steed fly towards the battlefield. He looked into the hearts of his followers, and saw that their valour was tarnished by black, vengeful deeds.

'Didn't I say before leaving Medina that if Allah grants us victory, and if we take prisoners, we would treat all the captives like the members of our own families?' The sadness in Muhammad's eyes caressed the unfortunate dead.

The heads of men sank low, more because of the flood of sadness in the Prophet's eyes than because of his reproof. Anas was the first to lift his head up.

'Yes, Prophet, you did. But Bilal wouldn't have done it, if…' Anas could not discipline the riot in his young mind. 'Bilal told me all about Ummayad; how he used to torture him, bricks upon bricks on his chest under the hot sun, and beatings, and…' His thoughts evaporated in the blaze of sorrow and tenderness in Muhammad's eyes.

'Prophet… I…' Bilal could not explain, weighed down as he was by the burden of his own shame. 'Ummayad was my enemy; your enemy; Allah's enemy.'

'*O ye who believe. Lo! among your wives and children there are enemies for you, therefore beware of them. And if ye efface and overlook and forgive, then lo! Allah is Forgiving, Merciful*' (64:14), Muhammad recited. 'If I were to describe openly the enemy in your souls, even the bravest hearts would be shattered.'

'These two men you see slain, Prophet, are Nadr and Uqbah. They used to insult and persecute you in Mecca,' Zaid began feebly. 'They tortured the Muslims, and…' He couldn't speak when he saw the kindling of fresh grief in the Prophet's eyes.

'Have you learnt no lesson from this revelation?' Muhammad's heart was wounded; he longed to efface the splinters of vice rooted deep in their pious hearts. '*My Lord! Forgive and have mercy, for Thou art best of all who show mercy*' (23:118).

'They didn't believe in your message, Prophet,' Musaib ibn Omeir began his defence, agitated. 'Remember, these two sinners from Mecca pretended to be your friends, then betrayed you and disobeyed you after taking an oath of fidelity.'

'*My Lord! Lo! they have led many a mankind astray. But whoso followeth me, he verily is of me. And whoso disobeyeth me – still, Thou art forgiving, merciful*' (14:36). Muhammad's thoughts girded the armour of guidance. 'My friends, my heart rejoices over your valour and victory, but I must be stern to gild your valour with virtue, so that you don't tarnish it with the rust of hatred. Your captives have a right to fair and humane treatment, and a right to be set free upon payment of a fine by their relatives.' He elicited a smile. 'Let us tend to the wounded, and bury the dead. This is a rite of purification; it heals our souls with love and service to the dead and the living, and earns us the right to rejoice and celebrate.' He guided his horse towards camp.

The night had fallen early, the hot disc of a sun turning as red as the blood of the slain. This was Muhammad's vision as he tended the wounded and buried the dead. The prisoners were treated with the utmost respect; Muhammad had made sure of it before he retired to his tent.

Muhammad lay wooing the maiden Sleep, but his thoughts were visiting the shrine of death where all life was reduced to only a memory. Three hundred and thirteen ill-equipped men from Medina had claimed victory against one thousand Meccan warriors. Amongst the dead were fourteen Muslims and seventy Meccans. Seventy Meccans had also been captured alive.

The memory of digging the graves arose fresh in Muhammad's mind. When Utbah ibn Rabia's body was being lowered into the dark pit, Muhammad's attention had been claimed by his youngest son, Walid bin Rabia, who stood there groaning.

'Are you sad, my son, that your father is no more?' Muhammad had asked kindly.

'No, by Allah, no!' Walid bin Rabia had protested. 'No, Prophet, I am remembering my father as he was, trying not to tarnish his noble character with grief. I knew him to be wise, and endowed with the virtues of goodness. I had hoped that he would accept the message of Islam, but his devotion to the idols of the Kaaba was stronger than the wisdom he needed to accept a new faith. Perhaps I do feel sad. He didn't want to fight.'

'Your father was a great man, Walid,' Muhammad had consoled him. 'Wisdom and devotion are the keys to the doors of Paradise. If one could destroy the idols of hatred and mockery in one's heart, one would find Allah in every particle of the universe. The spiritual heart is the seat of Allah, and no mortal sight can ever behold Him except inside the purity of one's own heart, making Him visible everywhere. My prayers are with your father, Walid, and Allah will grant him peace and forgiveness. You too are in my thoughts and prayers, that Allah may grant you peace and courage to endure this great loss, and bestow upon you the gift of understanding. My thoughts and prayers are with your brother Hudayfah too; he has inherited the great spirit of your father, and though an idolater, his love for his wife Umm Hani is worthy of praise.

Muhammad was drifting into sleep, crossing the bridge into dreams. He was entering the abode of the prisoners. All the men were asleep, amongst them his son-in-law, Abul As; Al Abbas, his uncle; and Suhail ibn Amr, Swadah's cousin. A revelation in his head was removing the lid from his casket of questions.

Remember when you implored for help from your Lord and He answered you, 'I will help you with a thousand angels, ranks upon ranks'? (8:9) *It wasn't you who smote them, it was Allah. When you threw the pebbles, it wasn't your act, but Allah's, in order to test the believers by a gracious trial from Himself, for Allah hears and knows everything* (8:17).

Muhammad's dreams were leaving the deeps and soaring towards the glory of the heavens. Every particle of sand was lifting from the ground, mounting on the sky like a glittering star, and singing the praises of the Lord. *Allah, Allah, Allah!*

Permission to fight is given to you, because you are the victim of persecution. Our aim is to unite, not divide, and when victory is gained, our aim remains the same; not to oppress, but to befriend. For the purification of the Kaaba, you are not breaking the idols, but breaking the ideal of greed, injustice, inequality. For the Meccans mock their idols of stone, holding them in reverence only for the sake of trade and profit. The Kaaba is the House of Allah. He has been there since before time began, and will always be there when time is no more. You are appointed with the task of sanctifying the Kaaba once again, where peoples of all creeds and nations can come as the pilgrims of unity, wearing the robes of equality, and practising the religion of love; respecting what others believe, and believing that they all return to the One and Only True Maker, their Lord. The Kaaba is a world within and a world without. Purify it and purify the world with good deeds.

Muhammad's eyes jolted open. Swadah was already dressed, her hair coiled at the nape of her neck in a severe knot. She greeted Muhammad and fetched water for his ablutions, and pounded the prayer rug clean from dust. Soon, Muhammad was lost so profoundly in prayers that he didn't see Swadah plant herself by the door of the tent. She gasped when she recognised her cousin, Suhail ibn Amr.

'Shame of shames, Suhail! You surrendered too readily,' Swadah mocked. 'You ought to have died a noble death!'

'Swadah!' Muhammad was jolted out of his prayers, his gaze a blaze of reproof. 'Would you stir up trouble against God and His apostle?'

'Sorry, Prophet, I didn't mean it that way,' Swadah murmured contritely. 'I don't know much about wars and religion yet. The knowledge which you receive is easy for you to understand. I am not wise; I want to learn.'

'My dear Swadah,' Muhammad relented. 'Knowledge is vast and boundless within us, but understanding comes by the grace of Allah. Allah will guide you as He guides His most humble of servants. Love is the key to the gates of understanding, Swadah. Learn to be kind and loving, always.'

'But Suhail is our relative, Prophet. Is he an enemy? I don't understand,' Swadah ruminated, doubtful.

'Ponder upon this revelation, Swadah.' Muhammad smiled. '*Before long Allah will bring friendly relations between you and those whom you regard as your enemies. And Allah is powerful and Allah is forgiving and merciful*' (60:7).

'Suhail is a good man, Prophet, though an unbeliever.' Swadah smiled back.

'My Swadah, a true believer and a good nurse! Thank you for caring for me, and for bandaging the wounded. Now I must go and bandage the hearts of the prisoners, who are pining for freedom. You must never forget, Swadah: freedom is the right of every man and woman on the face of the earth.' He turned to leave.

'Wait, Prophet. Your black cloak!' Swadah hastened to snatch it from the floor. 'It is part of your dressing! You must never forget to wear it.' She laughed.

'I should sleep with it, if it has gained that much worth in your eyes, Swadah.' Muhammad joined her in her mirth before stepping out into the golden haze of the sun.

Seated on the sandy plain, Muhammad faced the prisoners, and so did his companions. Abu Bakr sat to his right and Bilal to his left. Zaid, Anas and Usama were on the periphery of the semicircle. The Prophet had been discussing the fair treatment of prisoners. Arguments were many and a fresh wave of them had flared, but Muhammad was quick to snuff them out with an abrupt wave of his arm.

'Cut those ropes of bondage, my friends. They are prisoners, not slaves,' Muhammad commanded. 'And even if they were your slaves, you would be commanded to grant them freedom. Islam has no room for slavery. It is incumbent upon Muslims to free slaves, as an act of essential righteousness.'

The guards leapt to their feet, obeying the Prophet without protest. The prisoners stood, haughty. Khalid ibn Walid stomped his feet and sneered.

'Why bother going through this charade of freedom, Prophet of Islam? You are going to kill us, aren't you?' Khalid ibn Walid was getting bold. 'You favour killers. Isn't Bilal still favoured by you, seated next to you, even though he slit the throat of his ex-master only yesterday? A freed slave! How could you forgive this murderer, and yet want us to believe that we will be granted freedom?'

'Doubts breed doubts, Khalid, and trust is the pillar of strength and success.' Muhammad turned his attention to Bilal.

'Would you, my beloved Bilal, tell our friend why you killed Ummayad?'

'I am no murderer,' Bilal began humbly. 'I am not worthy of the Prophet's forgiveness, but he forgave me when he learnt the truth which led to the unfortunate death of Ummayad. I didn't capture Ummayad, but he was captured just the same. I happened to witness it, and upon seeing me he grew violent, calling me a bastard, besides other expletives, and wanting me dead. He had a sword in his hand, which he waved at me, threatening to kill me. I asked him to throw his sword down if he wanted to live, but he spat in my face and called me a stinking slave. Before I could implore further, he lunged at me with the naked blade aimed at my throat. That was when I stabbed him. It was an act of self-defence, not murder.'

'But two more captives were murdered, Prophet,' Amr ibn Aasi challenged fiercely. 'Do you hold their killers in honour too, with their lies blacker than Bilal's skin?'

'Ignorance dusted with arrogance will smoulder like coals in your heart, Amr, kindling a conflagration of zeal and hatred,' Muhammad breathed kindly. 'Blow out that fire with the waters of reason and perception before it blights your youth and passion. In wars, there are no murders or murderers, only victors and the vanquished. The Muslims fought in self-defence. And those two captives who you mentioned were not defenceless, but armed with hatred and violence; they violated the honour of their captors by assaulting them, and succumbed to death much like Ummayad.'

'Is the Prophet telling the truth, my friends? Are we to believe in such lies, claiming them as good-luck charms, hoping that we will be allowed to return to Mecca alive?' Challenges throbbed on the prisoners' lips.

'Truth is not a commodity, my friends, to be paraded on the streets of pride and hatred,' Muhammad intoned patiently. 'Truth is. It suffices that truth is a precious and ethereal dream to be lived and experienced. Truth needs to be immersed in the baptismal waters of love to be purged of all the lies and misconceptions. Truth is purity, but when buried under a mound of lies it cannot be wrenched free, only by the grace and mercy of the all-compassionate Allah.'

'This all-compassionate Allah – is He the one commanding you, Prophet, to wage wars and destroy our idols?' Suhail ibn Amr grinned.

'These men have no right to address you like this, Prophet! Command them to silence,' Abu Bakr appealed, his face flushed.

'Let them speak, Abu Bakr. They might learn the difference between truth and lies,' Muhammad consoled. 'War is abhorrent to me, my friends. I chose exile for the sake of peace when you persecuted me. You brought this war to Medina, and we had no choice but to safeguard our lives and the lives of our kind hosts who befriended us in our plight, giving us homes and the gifts of friendship. Allah is the God of the Kaaba, my God and your God. Look into your hearts, my friends, feel and touch each grain of virtue inside you and each spark of goodness, and make them your idols. If your own idols have failed to reveal to you the kernels of nobility in your hearts, then what use is there in holding on to those idols, which you yourself mock and replace? Don't you spurn your idols and fashion new ones when they fail to satisfy your greed and incite your anger and mockery? Don't you wish to learn that the one worthy of veneration is not contained in any object, but inside the heart of mankind? Everywhere! He is not confined to any form, shape or colour.'

'You think you are the chosen one by all the gods to teach us how to worship One God, your Allah, so that He could destroy our idols? At least we have the choice to replace our idols with better ones! How could we worship One God when He is the author of all this bloodshed, killing all our hopes and aspirations for some other who could protect our lives and wealth?' As-Saib bin Abid shot the challenge.

'Surely God does not wrong anyone; they wrong themselves' (10:45). Muhammad's gaze spilled revelations. *'If you do good, you do good for your own souls. And if you do evil, it is for them* (17:7). We are the authors of our actions; we use blame and ignorance as weapons of self-defence to fulfil our own prophecies. When and if we attain wisdom and maturity, we learn the art of living by becoming responsible for our actions, and gain freedom by sloughing off the burden of blame, neither passing it on to others, nor searching for the One who would guide us in juggling blame from man to idol, from idol to God. To worship one God is to know the bliss in unity, and to return to the purity of the source where peace awaits us without the difficult journey of wandering on paths countless. All such paths lead to one, and each path unfolds before us the temptations of hatred, malice and injustice, while the source of Oneness guides the heart of the faithful, proclaiming love as truth for all nations, for all peoples, without the barriers of race, colour, or status. This Oneness from the ocean of its own boundless love seeks us, even when we founder in disbelief and ignorance. Wherever you turn is the face of God. It has no shape, no form, no colour, but the purity of love and light. Our mortal sight can't perceive this light, only the eye of the heart, not veiled by ideas and forms. God is love, the lover and the beloved. Light and mercy! The one and only source of holiness to lead mankind to the path of unity in this life. Allah's message is made manifest through our own acts of love and kindness. Strive towards experiencing and sharing this light of love. It will guide you in this life and in the life hereafter. *Whoever does good benefits his own soul; whoever does evil, it is against his own soul. And your Lord will not deal unfairly with His servants'* (41:46).

A great hush had fallen. Muhammad waited for the shower of protests, but since none came, he began to speak with the authority of a commander.

'We will be returning to Medina with all these prisoners, but they must be treated with respect and all due consideration. They will be fed and clothed as our own brothers. Once in Medina, we will send letters to their relatives asking for ransom in exchange for their freedom, and grant them safe return to Mecca.'

'If we treat our captives with kindness, Prophet, won't they turn upon us and kill us? A few tried yesterday, and now we are rewarded with the epithet of murderers.' A false sense of righteousness was bleeding though the gentle concern of Baraida.

'Put your trust in Allah, and look for guidance in these revelations, Baraida.' Muhammad held him captive in his gaze. '*O ye who believe! Be steadfast witnesses for Allah in equity, and let not hatred of any people seduce you that you deal not justly. Deal justly, that is nearer to your duty. Observe your duty to Allah. Lo, Allah is informed of what you do* (5:8). *For that cause we decreed for the children of Israel that whosoever killeth a human being for other than manslaughter or corruption on earth, it shall be as if he has killed all mankind, and whoso saveth the life of one, it shall be as if he has saved the life of mankind. Our messengers came to them of old with clear proofs of Allah's sovereignty, but afterwards, lo, many of them became prodigals in the earth*' (5:32).

'If they return to Mecca, Prophet, won't they renew their assaults and launch another attack on Medina?' Dinah Kalbi asked with genuine concern.

'We must renew our own faith then, Dinah! Nay, multiply it ten times, for the blessings of hope in this revelation.' Muhammad smiled. '*Work not confusion in the earth after the fair ordering thereof, and call on Him in fear and hope. Lo! the Mercy of Allah is nigh unto good*' (7:56).

'How are we going to decide upon the amount of ransom, Prophet?' Umar ibn Khattab sought the Prophet's attention.

'It depends upon the means of the captives. The wealthy can pay more compared to those who have little to spare,' Muhammad responded thoughtfully.

'What if some of them can't afford any?' Abu Bakr ruminated.

'Those unfortunate ones can earn their freedom by teaching at least ten children each to read and write for a whole year.' Muhammad was quick to make the decision.

'What if some of them are poor and illiterate?' Usama asked anxiously.

'They will have to be freed without ransom, then.' Muhammad smiled.

'Should we not convert them to Islam, so that they can pay their ransom too?' Saad bin Mudah could not help voicing his opinion.

'No one must ever hold on to such an intention of converting anyone to Islam!' Muhammad commanded. 'Remember always, Islam forbids conversion by force, threat or coercion. The very thought of such a conversion is demeaning, hurling one towards the rungs of tyranny and cowardice. Muslims must, through their own example of love and kindness, be worthy to embrace those who join their fold freely, without any constraint of fear or burden. Allah's message is for all of us, but everyone has free will to accept or reject it.' His eyes were gathering the stars of revelations. '*There is no compulsion in religion* (2:256). *No soul can believe except by the will of Allah. Will you then compel mankind against their will to believe?*' (10:101).

'Are these revelations for the Jews and Christians, Prophet, who pretend to be your friends?' Abul As declared. 'What about for us idolaters? Does "no compulsion in religion" apply to us?'

'My Zainab should have exposed you to a little of our religion, my son; then you would not have felt compelled to flaunt your misery,' Muhammad breathed tenderly. '*Lo! those who believe this revelation and those who are Jews, and the Sabaeans and the Christians and the Magians and the idolaters – Lo! Allah will decide between them on the Day of Resurrection. Lo! Allah is witness over all things*' (22:17).

'Shame on you, my nephew!' Al Abbas blustered forth, his eyes hurling accusations. 'Treating your son-in-law and me, your old uncle, as base prisoners!'

'May I cut his tongue off, Prophet?' Umar ibn Khattab leaped to his feet.

'Would you strike the Prophet's uncle, Umar?' Muhammad heaved himself up slowly, his eyes flashing not anger, but sagacity.

'Ah, the apostle of Allah!' Al Abbas bellowed with rage. 'You and your talk of love and truth. Where is the spirit of jihad now? What does it mean to be a martyr? All those sand-scorched words! What is Islam, anyway?'

'Islam means peace and reconciliation, dear Uncle, if you didn't know,' Muhammad intoned kindly. 'And jihad is not war, but an inner struggle to conquer the forces of evil within oneself. And a martyr is one who dies valiantly and honourably in self-defence. No doubt you'll be asking about martyrdom next, so for your own good and for the benefit of everyone here, try to remember what martyrdom is not. Martyrdom is not killing unarmed, defenceless people, and it is absolutely not shedding even a drop of blood if one is guided by deceit and hatred. In Islam, such a cowardly manner of fighting or killing is in stark defiance of the laws of love and justice.'

'What justice, Muhammad? Do you know what the Quraysh call you now? *The Dark One*! No more *the Praised One,* or *the Pure One,* as your name suggests,' Al Abbas raved. 'What kind of ransom are you going to settle on my head, my nephew?'

'A heavy one, Uncle, since you are the wealthiest,' Muhammad murmured.

'No! I have not a dinar left to my name,' Al Abbas lamented, waving his arms.

'Even if you convinced me of your poverty, Uncle, you would still have to pay,' Muhammad began calmly. 'The ransom will be exacted from the wealth you have left in safekeeping with your wives. You will pay not only for yourself, but for your cousins and nephews, using the gold which you left with your wife Umm Fadal.'

'May you be cursed by Hubal, al-Lat and by all the gods and goddesses of the Kaaba, my nephew!' Al Abbas exclaimed. 'You are a sorcerer, sent by another even bigger one, your Allah! No one knew about that gold but me and Umm Fadal!'

'If I were a sorcerer, Uncle, I would scrape out the rust of hatred from everyone's heart and transmute it into the gold of love. Then I would infuse the gold back into the cleansed hearts till it flowed, molten, leaving no room for anything else,' Muhammad laughed.

'Zainab was right, Prophet, to praise you as she did, but no praises could do justice to your character as I see it now,' Abul As murmured contritely. 'How can any man be so kind and forgiving, rewarding curses with such lighthearted gaiety?'

'*Keep to forgiveness, O Muhammad, and enjoin kindness, and turn away from the ignorant*' (7:199), Muhammad murmured, averting his gaze lest he weep.

'Go, find my ransom in the rich bounty left behind by the Meccans.' Al Abbas admitted defeat, waving his arms at Muhammad's back as he turned to leave.

'Bounty still! The crumbs of greed ...' Muhammad murmured to himself.

'The proceeds need to be distributed, Prophet.' Zaid sought Muhammad's attention. 'Men have been talking about the plunder all morning. Some say it belongs to those who captured it, and some argue that it should be given to the most valiant. Others are claiming that everyone should receive an equal share.'

'Why quibble about the pebbles of earth?' Muhammad murmured again. 'Equal shares for all, I should say, even for those left behind in Medina to safeguard our wives and homes. *They ask thee, O Muhammad, of the spoils of war. Say: the spoils of war belong to Allah and the Messenger, so keep your duty to Allah, and adjust the matter of your differences, and obey Allah and His Messenger, if you are true believers'* (8:1). Little beads of perspiration were glistening on his brow. 'Zaid, my son. You are the father of a daughter now; a little sister for Usama? Take my Qaswa and ride back to Medina. Bilal will accompany you. As soon as you reach there, spread the news of our victory.' He drifted in the direction of his own tent.

'Prophet…' Abu Bakr's lips were forming expressions, but no words were escaping.

'Sorry, Abu Bakr, not now. I am very tired. I must rest,' Muhammad murmured.

The Prophet rested indeed, inside the hot bubble of his tent, dreaming. Zaid, astride Qaswa, with Bilal seated behind him, were announcing that the Muslims had won the battle of Badr. *Muhammad is dead!* Some of the Jews shouted, quick to spread the rumour. Some merchants from Badr were confirming the victory of the Muslims. A Jewish leader, learning the merchants' claim, was wailing histrionically.

Death for us is better today than life! What kind of life can we live now that the best men of Mecca, their lords and kings, are dead and defeated?

Medina was draped in festive colours on this particular day, as Muhammad sat with his family to celebrate the festival of Eid-ul-Fitr. Almost seven months had elapsed since his victory at Badr and return to Medina. The joy of victory was tainted with his grief at Ruqayyah's death, which had occurred as soon as Muhammad had set foot back into his house.

Eid-ul-Fitr, Muhammad had told his followers, was to commemorate the birth of Islam on the tenth month of Hijra when the new moon could be sighted at the end of the month of fasting. Another festival was named Eid-ul-Adha, the feast of sacrifice, and it fell on the tenth day of Hijra after the yearly pilgrimage to Mecca. This feast of sacrifice was in honour of Abraham's faith.

Muhammad's thoughts were diverted by a sudden rippling of song and music. Aisha, seated next to him, was enamoured by the dance of spears. Fatima, the young mother of one-year-old Hasan and four-month-old Zainab, and again heavy with child, was enjoying the recitations of the poets. Hasan, swathed in a tunic of Yemeni silk, was sleeping on the straw mat beside his little sister. Khultum, followed by Othman ibn Affan, was wending her way towards her father.

'Where did you go gallivanting, Othman? And taking my daughter along too!' Muhammad chided, his black eyes pouring mirth.

'Eid is a festive and joyous occasion, Prophet – you told us so! So, I took the liberty of showing Khultum the stalls decked with bright friezes. We bought some sweets.' Othman ibn Affan stood smiling, rather flustered.

'How could anyone think of more sweets, after our feast of date pudding and Swadah's vermicelli cooked in milk?' Muhammad teased, laughing.

'Sweet versification of the poets, more sweet, Prophet, and tempting?' Othman ibn Affan's smile widened. 'Besides, Khultum wanted to see the jugglers.'

'And no scholars to guide the wayward and the heedless!' Muhammad cried a mock lament. 'Come, my dear Khultum, sit by me. Othman, you sit by Ali – he is a scholar, and he will teach you the art of wisdom.'

'I am not a scholar, Prophet, but a scribe,' was Ali's quick retort.

'Your loss then, my dear Ali!' Muhammad quipped. 'The ink of a scholar is more precious than the blood of a martyr.' His eyes flashed deeply.

'He is a scholar, Father, I assure you!' Fatima interceded on behalf of her husband. 'But compared to your fountain of knowledge, he thinks he knows nothing.'

'If I am the city of knowledge, then Ali is its gate,' Muhammad intoned.

'I am a better scholar than Ali, Prophet!' Aisha sang with a spurt of jealousy. 'Yes, I am, since your holy knowledge is closer to me than to anyone else."

'You are my star, Aisha,' Muhammad laughed. 'All the scholars of knowledge on this earth, and especially you, my Aisha, are like stars in the sky, by which one is guided amidst the shadow of darkness over land and sea.'

'I write poetry, Father. Am I a scholar too?' Khultum asked bashfully.

'You are the queen of the stars, my love,' Muhammad breathed tenderly.

'More scholars are tumbling your way, Prophet.' Swadah was quick to draw his attention to the boy somersaulting his way towards them, a girl behind him giggling.

'Why, Hashim, my son!' Muhammad held out his arms, into which fell the laughing brother and sister. 'I thought the ransomless captives were teaching you reading and writing, not somersaulting.'

'I can read and write, Prophet.' Hashim squirmed out of the Prophet's warm embrace. 'I somersault only when I am happy. Today is Eid, and I got so many gifts! I am happy, I am happy.' He chortled with glee.

'Good, my son. May happiness be with you all your life.' Muhammad laughed. 'What have all you learnt so far?'

'About lands and trade, Prophet,' Hashim boasted, eyeing his sister with suspicion as she perched snugly in Muhammad's lap. 'Syria, Yemen, even China. I know about the people in those lands and how they live and work so very hard.'

'For knowledge, one must go as far as China, I have said before; but you don't need to go there, Hashim, since you have already been there in your head,' Muhammad teased, as he stroked the girl's hair. 'Have you learnt to read and write yet, little Vashima?'

'Yes, Prophet,' Vashima chirped. 'I can read and write better than Hashim.'

'What have you learnt about, my dear?' Muhammad's eyes were shining.

'All the herbs, Prophet; I know where to look for them. My mother had a fever once, and I found the ones I was looking for, and I ground—' Vashima's boast was silenced by the stormy arrival of Umar ibn Khattab, his look fiery and his face flushed with anger.

'Now, Umar, why must you charge in like that? Look how you have frightened my little Vashima!' Muhammad arched his eyebrows. 'The blaze of anger in your eyes doesn't suit this festive occasion. Today is Eid, if you have forgotten.'

'How can I think of festivities, Prophet, when my family roasts me alive on a pit of threats, and my friends spurn me with the brands of rejection?' Umar ibn Khattab's huge frame swayed. 'My daughter Hafsa is so young, and widowed already! I offered her hand in marriage to Othman and he refused. Then I asked Abu Bakr to marry her, and he did the same. Now my wife and daughter have made my life a living hell. They taunt me for the—' His anger was sucked back into his lungs by another stormy arrival, his own young daughter Hafsa, piercing the air with her laments.

'Are you not the protector of the orphans and the widows, Prophet?' Hafsa flung herself at Muhammad's feet. 'My father won't find me a husband! No one will have me. I am scorned and repulsed by all! Won't you marry me, Prophet?'

'Now, child, you are only eighteen. You're young and beautiful! Why would you want to marry an old man like me?' Muhammad murmured.

'Just admit you don't want to marry me, Prophet. You are rejecting me too,' Hafsa challenged. 'I am four years older than

Aisha when you married her. You just don't want …' She could not continue, tears of shame stinging her eyes.

'I would be honoured to marry you, dear Hafsa.' Muhammad closed his eyes. 'Your late husband Hudhafa was a fortunate man, no doubt,' he murmured sadly.

'Come, daughter! Eid will be a day of festivity after all. We will turn the day into the eve of a wedding feast!' Umar ibn Khattab snatched Hafsa to himself and fled lest Muhammad change his mind, almost carrying his daughter out in his arms.

Muhammad opened his eyes, his gaze reaching out to Aisha, but before he could speak Abu Bakr landed upon the silent tapestry with as much haste as Umar had fled in. *This festival of Eid has turned into a festival of magic,* Muhammad was thinking. Abu Bakr's demeanour was demure as his gaze fell on Muhammad.

'Did you not notice Umar abducting his daughter in unseemly haste, Prophet?' Abu Bakr appeared to falter, as if trusting not his own voice.

'He abducted my fiancée, Abu Bakr, since you refused to marry her,' Muhammad confessed. 'Hafsa is betrothed to me.'

'Allah be praised, Prophet,' Abu Bakr sighed in relief. 'But may Allah have mercy on His Prophet too, since Hafsa's temper is as fiery as her father's, and her tongue sharper than a naked blade, wounding and stabbing even when sheathed.'

'I never despair of Allah's mercy, my friend; you should know that by now.' A thin smile hovered over Muhammad's lips. 'Can you feel the shadow of sadness lurking behind you, Abu Bakr? Your soul is heavy. What are you concealing in there?'

'The ransom for the last prisoner came, Prophet. Could that be the reason for my sadness?' Abu Bakr wondered, stealing a look at Aisha.

'Any news from Mecca?' Muhammad asked softly, thinking of Zainab, whose husband was this last prisoner.

'Your uncle Abu Lahab, Prophet. He died.' Abu Bakr released this bit of news.

'How? He was in good health!' Muhammad's voice was barely audible.

'He couldn't believe that the Meccans had been defeated,' Abu Bakr began thoughtfully. 'And his pride was frustrated further when my son, Abdal Kabah, described the scene of battle at Badr and said that the Muslims were not those fighting, but some beings robed in white on piebald horses. Upon hearing this, your uncle's slave exclaimed that such beings could be none other but angels. Abu Lahab was so incensed by his comment that he began beating him till his own wife came to his rescue. She cursed her husband. A week later, his body broke out in boils as large as plums, and he was in great agony before he died.'

'May Allah grant him peace and forgiveness in the afterlife,' Muhammad muttered in prayer. 'Abul As can return to Mecca now that his ransom is here. Will I see Zainab again, and her newborn daughter? Umamah, that's what she named her.'

'I almost forgot, Prophet.' Abu Bakr snatched a pouch out of his pocket and held it out to Muhammad. 'This is the ransom Zainab sent.'

Muhammad took the pouch, untying its string with the utmost concentration. Suddenly, his face was as white as death, as his fingers closed over a garnet necklace.

'Khadija. My beloved.' A tremor of prayer was silenced on Muhammad's lips. 'Give this to Abul As, Abu Bakr. Tell him to return it to Zainab as soon as he reaches Mecca. Also, ask him to send Zainab to Medina for a visit.' Two large tears slipped down his cheeks as he lumbered to his feet. 'This necklace was my gift to Khadija. She gave it to Zainab.' He let go of the pouch into the hands of Abu Bakr.

Aisha, blind to the Prophet's grief and aware only of her own bitterness at her husband's betrothal to Hafsa, leapt to her feet.

'Khadija! Khadija! You love her more than me, Prophet!' Aisha wailed.

'My Aisha.' Muhammad turned to face her. 'Why are you jealous, my love, as if she is still alive?' He dried his tears with the hem of his cloak.

'Yes, yes.' An anguished lament broke from Aisha's lips. 'She is more alive than any of us. Khadija! Khadija! You talk about her as if she is always with you. Why can't you forget her? She was old and fat, and I am young and beautiful! Why—'

'She loved me, my Aisha, when I was an orphan, unloved and homeless. She believed in me when no one else did. She consoled and comforted me when I was persecuted.' Muhammad's eyes sparkled against a mist of fresh tears.

'But how can you keep loving someone who has been dead for years?' Aisha murmured, fascinated.

'The tears and sorrows we shared purified our love for each other, dear Aisha. You are too young to understand the holiness of such a love. Even one moment of agony and exaltation, which is ephemeral as well as everlasting, can't describe the…' He became aware of Hasan watching him and he snatched him into his arms. 'Come, Hasan. We will pray together. Your innocence, and my sheer joy of holding you close, will wash away the rivers of sorrow.' His feet guided him towards his quarters.

Chapter 12

The Soul of Arabia

Year 627 AD

The white hollow of dreams was Muhammad's sanctuary this afternoon, as he lay cradled in the comforting arms of sleep. He was inside his mud hut of a home in Medina. Almost three years since the victory at Badr and it was still a canker in the Meccans' hearts, though they had avenged themselves at the battlefield of Ohud, defeating the Muslims, and mutilating the bodies of the slain.

Muhammad lay wrapped in the mantle of sleep, dreaming. All his wives were with him except Zainab, whom the Prophet had married after her husband Hobeida had died at the battle of Badr; she had died after eight months. His wife Hafsa was there, greeting Khultum as the bride of Othman. Umm Salmah, the widow of Abu Salama, whom the Prophet married after her husband died at Ohud, was talking with Aisha. Another Zainab, who had been divorced by Zaid and had married the Prophet, was befriending Swadah. Juwairya, a captive from the tribe of Beni Mustaliq whom he had married, was opening wide more dream-portals.

Abdallah ibn Ubbay had accepted Islam. Zainab, Muhammad's daughter, had reached Medina, but at the cost of a miscarriage when her carriage was overturned by the raiders of Abu Sofyan. Fatima was the proud mother of another son, Husain, almost a year old now.

Meanwhile the tribal Jews were caught in a ripple of enmity. A Muslim girl from the Beni Kainuka tribe was seated in a shop, waiting to be served. She didn't notice that a Jewish man had crept up behind her and pinned her skirt to her blouse. Ignorant of the prank, she had walked out on the street with her posterior exposed, gullies of laughter trailing after her. A Muslim watching the scene had killed a man, but had been stabbed by another.

Countless provocations from the same tribe, Beni Kainuka, were invading Muhammad's sleep. Its leaders had entrenched themselves in their fortress, but had been defeated and forgiven for their offences against Muslims and were now settled in Syria. An assassin by the name of Omeir was emerging in Muhammad's dreams. He had been sent by Abu Sofyan to murder the Prophet, pretending to bring a ransom for his son Wahb. He hadn't succeeded, since Muhammad received him with every mark of kindness, asking why he was hiding a sword under his clothes.

'By Hubal, Messenger of Allah! You couldn't have discovered this secret from anyone but God!' Omeir prostrated himself at his feet, pleading forgiveness.

A vision of the battlefield at Ohud was forming in Muhammad's sleep. The bodies of the slain jolting back to life. The Muslim army had shrunk at the caprice of Abdallah ibn Ubbay, who had deserted halfway to Ohud, leading his band of three hundred men back to Medina. The mists of doom and betrayal were looming over the heads of seven hundred Muslims, confronted by three thousand Meccans.

The battlefield at Ohud with its prickly-backed lizards scrambling for shelter inside the crevices was unfolding its arid landscape inside Muhammad's dreams. The barren rock of Ohud was crimson with blood. The clattering of swords and the neighing of horses were muffling the cries of the wounded, the slain and the slayer reduced to insignificance by the fists of fate and time.

He could see Hamza fighting with Siba, the son of Umm Anmar, known as the circumciser of Arab women for her unmatched skill in mutilation. Hamza had wounded Siba, his sword poised for another blow, but Washi, Hind's slave who darted forth unobserved, was quick to strike a severe blow to Hamza's heart with his javelin. Hamza was swaying and staggering, while Washi tried to yank out his javelin. Hamza's heart was a cascading fountain of blood, bathing him in the scarlet shroud of death, the ostrich feather on his helmet stringing its own necklace of ruby beads straight from his heart. Outnumbered and overwhelmed, the Muslims defended themselves till their standard-bearer Musaib ibn Omeir succumbed to death at the hand of Ibn Kami. The Meccans were victorious and jubilant.

The very fabric of dreams behind the closed shutters of Muhammad's eyes was bloodied. Hind was fluttering over the bodies of the slain, her face glowing with the fire of ecstasy. She gouged out the slain Hamza's eyes with her nails, and sliced off his ears and nose with a knife. Laughingly, she plunged the knife deep into Hamza's side, scooping out his liver with her hands. Sinking her teeth into it, she sat rolling in mirth. More Meccan women appeared on the battlefield, singing and dancing. They joined Hind in a wild spree, mutilating the bodies of the slain, fashioning bracelets and necklaces with ears, noses and fingers severed from the bodies of the dead.

While the Meccan women danced and mutilated, the men, drunk with the soma of victory, shifted their efforts to capturing the Prophet. The Meccan assailants who surrounded the Prophet and his small band of followers were being repulsed most furiously, when Ibn Kami dashed over brandishing his sword. Talha ibn Ubaidullah was the first to see Ibn Kami, and he planted himself in front of Muhammad as a human shield, poised to defend him. Ibn Kami came charging up, and as Talha ibn Ubaidullah was deflecting the blows of his opponent, Bilal and Abu Bakr flew to his assistance. Ali and Umar too carved their way towards them amidst showers of arrows and javelins. Ibn Kami, fighting desperately, succeeded in striking two violent blows, one landing on Muhammad's mouth and the other on his forehead. Ibn Kami was swift to flee. Muhammad's companions were haze and darkness, the metal strap of his helmet driven into his cheek, and a crimson pool of blood gushing forth from the deep gash on his forehead. Muhammad was carried to the safety of his encampment, while Ibn Kami could be heard proclaiming, 'I have killed Muhammad!'

Muhammad was not dead, only stunned from pain and shock. Fatima had cauterised his wounds with ashes before bandaging them in clean strips of muslin. Muhammad was quick to regain his strength. Gathering his followers behind him, he led them towards the battlefield, silent and contemplative.

The Meccans, after conducting a thorough search of the battlefield, had retired to their encampment. They had no proof of Muhammad's death. They didn't know that Muhammad and his followers had ventured forth. Abu Sofyan, under the impact of a sudden impulse, had torn open the curtain of silence, his voice shrill and booming:

'Anyone there? Muhammad? Umar, Abu Bakr? Answer me! If you don't answer me, then we know you are all dead. It's a pity you can't gather the bones of your dead and feed them to the dogs!' Abu Sofyan's voice was punctured by a ripple of laughter.

'Even the dead are alive in our hearts, Abu Sofyan!' Umar ibn Khattab could not resist the temptation of a challenge. 'When you are ready to fight, come down the hill. We will show you how to mutilate the living.'

'Glory be to Hubal, victory is ours! You can't claim it back. We will fight you in a year, at Badr!' The challenge from the throat of Abu Sofyan was deep and hollow.

More scenes unfolded in Muhammad's sleep. The tribe of Beni Mustaliq, in secret alliance with the Quraysh and instigated by Abdallah ibn Ubbay, had planned a massive attack to destroy the Prophet's leadership. Fortunately, the plan was disclosed to Muhammad and he sanctioned a surprise attack. The victory was swift; Harith Abi Dirar, the leader of the Beni Mustaliq, had fled, but his daughter Juwairya, along with a band of his soldiers, was captured. Harith Abi Dirar was a wealthy man, as generous as his friend Hatim Tai. Upon learning of this, Muhammad had freed all six hundred of his prisoners without ransom. Juwairya was freed too, but she wished to marry the Prophet.

A scene of betrayal linked to Abdallah ibn Ubbay was surfacing in Muhammad's dreams. After the Prophet's victory at Muraisi, Aisha was left behind as a result of some confusion. On their journey towards Medina the Prophet's army set up camp in a little valley for rest. When they were preparing to resume their journey, Aisha had left her camel's howdah, where she had been seated waiting to leave, and wandered into the heart of the valley to look for her lost necklace. By the time she found it and returned to the camp, it was deserted. Overwhelmed with fatigue, she had fallen asleep. A night scout from the Prophet's army, Sufwan ibn Muattal, who happened to be scouting the area, spotted the Prophet's wife and brought her back to the Prophet's next resting spot. Abdallah ibn Ubbay, upon learning of the incident, had begun circulating rumours to soil Aisha's noble character. Muhammad was the last to learn about the slander. Aisha's suffering was great, but she was rewarded with the gift of a revelation affirming her chastity, and silencing the base and insidious gossip.

There was silence in Muhammad's dreams too. Now the Meccans were planning to march to the very gates of Medina. The Muslim army was marching towards the valley of Ahzab, as he had planned, but Muhammad was waking up and the dream was breaking apart.

Sitting resting against the mud wall, Muhammad's eyes shot open. A ripple of noise from his wives' lips had reached his awareness.

'Guess which one of us will accompany the Prophet to this war with the Meccans?' Aisha's voice rose above the others with mirthful poetry.

'You think you will be the one going for sure, Aisha, since you are the Prophet's favourite?' Hafsa's voice, spiced with sarcasm, invited laughter from the others.

'Why would any of us want to go to these wars, or even feel privileged to go, when the Prophet himself abhors wars?' Zainab's reproof cut through the giggles.

'Does it matter if the Prophet wants to fight or not? He has to defend himself and his followers. They are coming to Medina to kill us all, isn't that obvious?' was Juwairya's loud and passionate declaration.

'Lower your voices, you young brides! The Prophet is sleeping and he surely needs rest,' Swadah appealed gently. 'We'll draw lots anyway, so why quibble?'

'Yes, the wisdom of Swadah should teach you all to be obedient to the Prophet, and to take care not to disturb him in his sleep!' Muhammad stole upon them.

'Obedient, Prophet!' Aisha protested. 'Didn't you say yourself that your wives were free to speak their minds without compunction?' She tossed her curly head in defiance. 'And I did, several times, didn't I? Especially when you married Zainab! I was angry too, since you justified your marriage to her with a revelation.'

'Your anger and your jealousy! How could I ever forget, my Aisha?' Muhammad laughed. '"Truly, thy Lord makes haste to do thy bidding." Isn't that what you said? And the revelation prompted by your anger – have you forgotten?'

'I rarely forget, Prophet,' Aisha responded merrily. '*And when thou saidst unto him on whom Allah hath conferred favour and thou hast conferred favour: Keep thy wife to thyself, and fear Allah. And thou didst hide in thy mind that which Allah was to bring to light, and thou didst fear mankind whereas Allah hath better right that thou shouldst fear Him. So when Zaid had performed the necessary formality of divorce from her, We gave her unto thee in marriage, so that henceforth there may be no sin for believers in respect of wives of their adopted sons, when the latter have performed the necessary formality of release from them. The commandment of Allah must be fulfilled* (33:37). So Allah favours you over us, and you tell us that we are all equal in the sight of Allah?'

'Are we not?' Muhammad murmured. 'All equal in the sight of Allah, I mean. Have you forgotten Allah's favour when He sent a revelation about you against that slander? *Why did they not produce four witnesses? Since they produce not witnesses, they verily are liars in the sight of Allah*...' (24:13). He couldn't finish reciting the entire revelation, noticing a subtle flush on Aisha's cheeks. 'Has Allah not favoured another woman in another revelation? The Virgin Mary, when she carried the Holy Child in her chaste womb and her chastity was doubted. *And because of their disbelief and of their speaking against Mary a tremendous calumny*' (4:156).

'How could we not be jealous, Prophet, even of your love for Allah?' Umm Salmah's eyes were spilling mirth. 'Jealousy keeps us entertained, don't you think?'

'How well do I know, dear Salmah!' Muhammad smiled. 'Didn't you try to escape the fetters of wedlock by recounting three of your afflictions? Jealousy, for one; the burden of your family; and your youth in decline!'

'I remember your answers well too, Prophet!' Umm Salmah declared. 'Regarding jealousy, you said you would pray to Allah for the removal of this affliction. Families, you said, are a blessing not a burden. As to my age, your answer was that you too were afflicted with the same problem, so we would have a common affliction.'

'Allah be my witness, I am not jealous!' Juwairya exclaimed. 'I wish you would stop roasting yourselves with jealousy over Zainab's wedding feast. How tiring it is to hear about it day after day! The feast, the celebrations, how grand it was – it has been more than a year, and you all still talk about it.'

'They are not jealous of Zainab, Juwairya, though her wedding feast was the most sumptuous, I agree.' Swadah interceded on behalf of the younger wives. 'They are jealous of you; of your pride. Well, you are beautiful and rich…' She could not continue against the flood of sparkling intensity in Muhammad's gaze.

'You all bask in the riches of her stories though, I can't help but notice.' Muhammad breathed indulgence. 'She has a wealth of stories to share about Hatim Tai, since he was her father's friend. More like a brother to him, I should say, and famous for his kindness and generosity. She may seem proud to you, but she is humble at heart. Rich in wisdom alone!' He fixed his smiling gaze on Juwairya. 'Did you ever tell them how Hatim Tai became rich in virtue and wisdom?'

'Tell us. We want to hear. We are jealous, because you reserve the best stories for the Prophet. Please, Juwairya, we will be your friends, we promise.' All the Prophet's wives were eager and pleading all of a sudden.

'You don't have to plead! I am willing to tell this story a thousand times over,' Juwairya began avidly. 'Hatim Tai's grandmother was poor and widowed, when a grand miracle came her way. She was standing in the middle of the street one day when she heard a great cry. The villagers were streaming out onto the street too, astonished by the shifting scene up in the sky, where the birds, clouds and rainbows appeared to dance up and down. Some said it was just a big, strange cloud, and the others that it was Izrael. Some said they could see a king on a carpet of silk, his throne made of pearls and rainbows. Amidst this flurry of conjectures, something came swirling down to earth. Everyone was disappointed, because it was only a gourd. The grandmother of Hatim Tai picked up the gourd, recalling an old story about Solomon, how, after the completion of the

Temple in Jerusalem he had journeyed to Mecca on a carpet of silk, carried by the wind, while the birds, the spirits and his friends accompanied him. She took the gourd home. Her surprise was great when she broke open the gourd, finding three seeds in there. One red like a ruby, another blue as sapphire, and the third green as emerald. A mystical voice whispered to her that she should make an amulet, hiding the seeds inside, and tie it around the neck of her grandson, Hatim Tai. While she sat sewing the amulet she heard another voice, saying that this amulet would make her grandson wise, virtuous, generous and—' Her speech was silenced against a flurry of noise.

One Jew stood grinning by the door. He planted one foot inside, and shouted a greeting, 'Assam o Alaikum!' *Death upon you.* He stood gloating, much too confident in his assumption that no one in the household of the Prophet would catch the meaning of his greeting, which sounded so similar to the one used by the Muslims. But Aisha was quick to catch its import.

'Assam o Alaikum to you!' Aisha chanted, and the Jew fled in all haste.

'Aisha!' Muhammad was up on his feet, his eyes flashing rebuke and regret. 'Control your tongue. Speak gently, for Allah likes gentle speech.'

Before Aisha could speak, another Jew appeared at the door. Umar ibn Khattab at his heels couldn't stop him from flaunting his authority.

'I have come to collect my dues!' the Jew demanded boisterously. 'You, the Banu Hashim, never pay anything back once you get what you want.'

'You filthy liar!' Umar ibn Khattab raised his hand to strike the intruder.

'Put your mighty arm down, Umar!' Muhammad thundered a command. 'Strength lies not in striking out, but in taming your anger and temper. Pay the good man more than he is owed. Why was I not informed of this?'

Umar ibn Khattab's hand fell limp to his side, and his other hand groped for his pouch. Counting out the sum demanded by the Jew, he added a few extra silver pieces as commanded by the Prophet.

'Wasn't it after my wedding, Prophet, when the men became riotous, lingering over the feast unwilling to leave, that you received a revelation which forbade them to enter the Prophet's home?' Zainab's eyes were flashing. 'How can you condone these men's rude behaviour? Have they not heard that revelation? How dare they come to our door, or speak to you or to us without permission?'

Before Muhammad could respond, Umar ibn Khattab began reciting the revelation mentioned by Zainab, his eyes lowered and his face shining.

'*Believers, do not enter the houses of the Prophet for a meal before waiting for the proper time, unless you are given leave. But if you are invited, enter, and when you have eaten, disperse. Do not engage in familiar talk, for this would annoy the Prophet, and he would be ashamed to bid you go. But of the truth, Allah is not ashamed. If you ask his wives for anything, speak to them from behind a curtain. This is more chaste for your hearts and their hearts*' (33:53). Umar ibn Khattab raised his eyes to Muhammad, adding dolefully, 'That man had no right to come to your door without your permission, Prophet. You don't have the riches of the kings, but you are the King of Medina as it stands. That's why I prevented him from entering your home. For his rude and insulting behaviour, he should be banished, not rewarded with more than his due!'

'By Allah, Umar, if Satan chanced to meet you, he wouldn't take your path!' Muhammad began to laugh. 'Since this king is too poor to buy a curtain to prevent intruders, why don't you get me one, and hang it over the door.' His mirth was dwindling. 'Come, Umar, be of good cheer! Haven't I stressed enough that God will not be kind to he who is not kind to God's creatures and to his own children? Kindness is a mark of faith, and whoever has not kindness, has no faith.'

'Yes, Prophet.' Umar ibn Khattab smiled. 'And here is another injunction of yours about kindness, which I can never forget: *Whoever is kind to His creatures, God is kind to him. Therefore, be kind to man on earth, whether good or bad; and being kind to the bad is to withhold him from badness, thus in heaven you will be rewarded kindly.*'

'Make these words the rosary of your actions, Umar.' Muhammad smiled. 'My heart longs for peace, but Medina must be defended. To the mosque then, to discuss the strategies of war. How well I know why you came here!'

'Which one of us will be going with you, Prophet, if there is a war?' Aisha could not keep her silence, stalling him as he tried to leave.

'All of you, my Aisha,' Muhammad intoned thickly. 'We need the help of women as much as men against this colossal Meccan force. Talk to as many women as you can, who might be willing to come. Asma will come, for sure. And my aunt Safiyah. My daughters too, but not Zainab, she is ill…' His gaze held them all in a warm embrace, before he stepped out into the open, followed by Umar.

'What a day, Prophet!' Umar ibn Khattab exclaimed as they walked towards the mosque. 'I have been confronting rudeness all morning, it seems. First, as I came out of the mosque, I noticed a Bedouin shamelessly relieving himself by the wall. I whacked him soundly before I threw him out on the street.'

'You shouldn't have done that, Umar,' Muhammad murmured regretfully. 'You must bring him back. Be kind to him. Apologise.'

'Apologise? When he defiled the sanctity of the mosque?' Umar ibn Khattab protested.

'Anything which is holy can never be defiled that easily, Umar,' Muhammad murmured. 'Covering that spot with water would have made it holier than ever, and shown the man that our wish to keep the mosque clean is the best way to teach holiness. He would surely listen to you if you were kind enough to show him by your example – he might even come to the mosque for prayer and worship.'

'Are you lenient with offenders, Prophet, even when they hurt you personally?' Umar ibn Khattab could not conceal his bitterness.

'Especially when they hurt me personally. As long as they don't hurt others,' was Muhammad's gentle response. 'Fear Allah and make peace in yourself, for Allah! May He be blessed and exalted. He will make peace among the faithful on the Day of Resurrection. Make sure, Umar, that the nine mosques which we have built in Medina for our children to learn the lessons of love and kindness don't become dens of zeal and hatred in the name of holiness. Maths, science, medicine, reading, writing…' He stopped suddenly, noticing a funeral procession carrying an open bier.

Muhammad stood still with his head bowed, his eyes closed and his lips murmuring prayers. Umar ibn Khattab stood beside the Prophet, curious and impatient, watching the mourners and recognising most of them. After the funeral procession had inched past the groups of vendors and stragglers, Umar tossed a muttered comment.

'That was just the bier of a Jew, Prophet.'

'Was he not the holder of a soul, Umar, from which we should take example and fear?' Muhammad murmured to himself, his eyes still closed.

'The Jews are after your life, Prophet,' Umar ibn Khattab murmured back bitterly. 'Didn't they try to poison you? Fortunately they failed – but then they tried their hand at assassination, and failed in that too. And now they have sought the help of the Quraysh, and aren't the Quraysh planning an attack in great numbers, hoping to accomplish the very same thing which the

Jews have failed to achieve so far? That Jew on the bier – he might be the one who tried to assassinate you.'

'Do not speak ill of the dead, Umar.' Muhammad's eyes were wide open. 'If you happen to be sitting down when anyone's bier passes by, whether Jew, Christian or Muslim, you must get to your feet as a mark of courtesy and reverence to the dead.' He resumed his walk towards the mosque, words tumbling from his lips. 'And when you pass a graveyard, take a moment to stand still and offer this prayer: *Peace to you, oh people of the graves. May Allah forgive us and you. You have passed on before us, and we are following you.*' He sprinted into the courtyard of Masjid Al-Nabi.

The courtyard was rippling with wave upon wave of joy, as if no clouds of war hung low over the valleys of Medina. Amongst them stood Bilal, more flushed than his bride; although only her fair cheeks glowed, his own Nubian features were flushed with the warmth of an inexpressible joy. Muhammad's heart leapt with joy at the sudden realisation that his efforts in making this nuptial match possible had finally materialised. Umm Sofia was the happy bride, whose parents had been against the match, though Muhammad had tried to convince them, appealing to their sense of love. Love shone in his eyes now, as he approached the happy couple.

'Allah be praised, Bilal! It is obvious that her parents have dissolved their prejudice against other races and other colours, and have given you the gift of joy!' Muhammad locked Bilal into the warmth of his embrace. 'They have earned a wealth of joys in return, on this earth and in the heavens; you must tell them, and be grateful.'

'After heeding your words of wisdom, Prophet, they couldn't help but give their consent.' Bilal's voice had the murmur of a distant waterfall, sweet and wistful.

'And what wisdom was that, Bilal, of which the Prophet himself knows nothing?' Muhammad flashed him a happy challenge.

'They told me, Prophet, that the last time you were with them you had said, *Isn't it enough for you that Bilal is a man of Paradise?*' Bilal beamed, humble and devoted.

'We will celebrate your wedding this evening, Bilal. The war can wait.' Muhammad's gaze was a shimmering ocean of tenderness. 'Go, fetch my wives and daughters so that they can share this joy – and hear a few words of wisdom, which they might remember and treat me kindly.'

Bilal scuttled away happily, while Muhammad settled himself amongst his congregation on the bare floor. Even before Muhammad's wives could join, Safiyah, in league with the other Medinese women, claimed Muhammad's attention.

'If Islam stands firm on the foundations of equality, Prophet, then are we not strong enough to stand beside our men to defend Medina? To tend to the wounded and to pour strength into the hearts of those burdened with fatigue and sorrow?' Safiyah's eyes held Muhammad captive in an ocean of profundity.

'Women are as strong as men, dear Aunt; strong enough to assist the men and to defend Medina if they choose to do so.' Muhammad's eyes lit up with an enigmatic smile. 'I have already been humbled by doubts from my wives concerning this issue. Women are strong, and equal in all spheres of life; free to study, to teach or engage in business, or even to lead men on the path to righteousness by the virtue of their own love.'

'*For believing men and women, for devout men and women, for patient men and women, for humble men and women, for them Allah has prepared forgiveness and a great reward*' (33:35). Bilal approached, followed by the Prophet's wives.

'Their strengths make us men weak though, Prophet, don't you agree?' Umar ibn Khattab looked at his daughter Hafsa. 'My wife, who has only ever been obedient to me, now stirs up a storm over petty disagreements. Just yesterday she waved her fists to my face, saying, "You forbid me to criticise you, even though our daughter is allowed to criticise the Prophet of God himself, may Allah bless him! Hafsa talks back to the Prophet so much at times that he spends the rest of the day angry, though no word of reproof escapes his lips!"'

'Men are fortunate, Umar, when they discover their weaknesses through women's tongues. And it is a bitter taste indeed, because the truth is bitter – it only becomes sweet when it becomes manifest!' Muhammad declared mirthfully. 'We fall conquered if we hide our weaknesses behind the pretence of our strengths.'

'Talking of conquering, Prophet, is it true that after the conquest if a Muslim forces a conversion, he risks the fires of hell?' Abdallah ibn Ubbay asked.

'He doesn't just risk the fires of hell, my friend; he is sure to fall into them!' Muhammad declared prophetically, his lips unfolding the blooms of a revelation. '*Will you then compel mankind against their will to believe? No soul can believe, except by the wish of Allah*' (10:99–100). To set an example by virtue of your own noble character is the only way to win converts, not by force or coercion.'

'What virtues should a Muslim cultivate, Prophet, to polish their noble character?' Fatima asked shyly.

'Thanking Allah for every blessing is a virtue, dear Fatima.' Muhammad's tone was tender all of a sudden. 'When there is a disagreement, judging without favour or partiality is a virtue. Being kind and loving is a virtue. Removing obstacles from a path which might cause injuries to others is a virtue.'

'Your own virtuous discipline, Prophet: could you expound more on that so that we all could benefit?' Umm Hani asked quickly, her heart longing for wisdom.

'My virtues are not my own, Umm Hani; I obey only the commands of Allah.' Muhammad smiled. 'And Allah has commanded me to be sincere, openly or in secret. To be fair when I am calm or angry. To be thrifty in poverty, or in good fortune. To forgive the one who has wronged me, and to give to the one who has taken from me. To build relations with whoever has severed them with me. To let silence be my meditation. To let speech be my prayer, and to let whatever I observe act as a lesson to me.'

'What would be your advice to us, Prophet, if we are tempted to sin?' Othman ibn Affan asked abruptly, as if compelled by the voice of some inner torment.

'If one becomes the victim of that sinful temptation, then one must follow it with a good deed,' Muhammad murmured kindly. 'What darkness do I see lurking behind your eyes, my son, when you are the Possessor of Two Lights?' He smiled at Khultum beside him before continuing. 'Indeed, that name is true, since you married two of my daughters! One lends you light through the heavens and the other holds it out to you on earth, even now.'

'I am fortunate indeed, Prophet.' Othman ibn Affan smiled a thin smile. 'Yet the people who betray us and our friends, and who thirst for our blood, make me sad and weary. Maybe the darkness in my soul is what you see in my eyes.'

'Happy are those who find fault with themselves, instead of finding fault with others,' Muhammad breathed cheerfully. 'Dwell upon that, Othman, and you will chase all your sadness away. Be gentle and loving with your own soul, and love others, and watch the miracle of joy unfolding within you and all around you.'

'I am trying to learn from my mistakes, Prophet, but I have learnt that I am not good at learning.' Ali voiced his own doubts. 'Wisdom eludes me, especially when I think too hard. And I have been thinking; how are we to act wisely when the enemy is sitting at the gates of Medina with every intention of annihilating us?'

'Asking good questions is half the learning, dear Ali,' Muhammad intoned kindly. 'Acting wisely is to do what you should do when you do it. To refuse to do what you should not do. And when it is not clear, wait until you are sure. Listen to your heart – it is the sanctuary of Allah, and nothing but Allah is allowed access, and Allah guides the believer on the path to love and wisdom.'

'Is faith alone the safeguard of our religion, Prophet, or are there any outer forces which can destroy faith as well as religion?' Abu Huraira asked.

'Faith might survive against all the odds, Huraira, but there are forces which corrupt religion,' Muhammad began profoundly. 'The most dangerous of them all are the ill-tempered scholar, the tyrannical leader and the ignorant theologian.'

'How should we keep our faith strong, Prophet, against all these threats of assault and persecution?' Anas asked, a mixture of devotion and confusion shining in his eyes.

'*Oh you who have attained to faith! Always be steadfast in upholding justice, bearing witness to the truth for Allah's sake! Even though it may be against your own selves or your parents and kinsfolk. Whether the person concerned be rich or poor, God's claim takes precedence over the claims of either. Do not, then, follow your own desires, that you might not turn aside from that which is just. For if you distort the truth, witness: Allah is indeed well aware of all that you do*' (4:135). Muhammad recited this revelation in response. 'Remember this revelation, my son, and your faith will not waver, no matter how overwhelming the blows of assault or persecution.'

'Yes, Prophet. And this one too!' Anas bowed his head. '*And for those who have faith in Allah and His messengers and make no distinction between any of them, to them, in time, will He grant their recompense. And Allah is indeed Ever Ready to Forgive, Most Merciful*' (4:152).

'There is no justice in this world, Prophet, only hatred and enmity!' Abdallah ibn Masud declared. 'Even now as we sit here talking about faith and religion, the Meccans are almost upon us to kill us. Is there any use suing for peace still? Where lies the justice?'

'Justice resides in the will to do right, and Allah guides those who strive for understanding,' Muhammad breathed profoundly. 'To recite the revelations is the first step towards wisdom and understanding. *O you who have attained faith, stand firmly in devotion to Allah, bearing witness to the truth in complete fairness! And never let hatred of anyone lead you to make the mistake of deviating from justice. Be just: this is the closest to being God-conscious. And remain conscious of God: truly, God is well-aware of all you do*' (5:8).

'Jews and Christians here, Prophet, have different ways of worship than ours. Each faith asserts that theirs is the right way. Are we to profess that ours is the right way?' Najiyal unleashed his own arrows of doubt.

'*To every community we have appointed ways of worship which they ought to observe. And so, do not let others draw you into arguing about it. But invite them to your Sustainer. For you are indeed on the right way! And if they argue with you, say: Allah knows best what you are doing. Indeed, Allah will judge between you on the Day of Resurrection concerning everything about which you used to differ*' (22:67–69). Muhammad's gaze was dreamy. 'Does this revelation answer your question, Najiyal?'

'Will there be more revelations, Prophet, to lead us towards understanding?' Abu Bakr appealed, noticing that Najiyal had bowed his head, his lips sealed.

'Memorise this one as your talisman, my friend.' Muhammad's pomegranate-red lips throbbed with poetry. '*And if all the trees on earth were pens and the oceans were ink with seven oceans behind to supplement them, still the words of Allah would not be exhausted. For Allah is exalted in Power, All-Wise*' (31:27).

'What answers should we give to the Jews and the Christians who argue that we worship a different God than theirs?' Usama voiced his own concern.

'I look to Allah for guidance, my son, and the revelations which I receive are the answers to every dissension.' Muhammad's eyes sparkled. '*And call out to them. And stand steadfast as you have been commanded. And do not follow their likes and dislikes, but say: I have faith in the Book which God has bestowed from on High: And I am asked to judge justly between you. God is our Sustainer and your Sustainer. To us belongs the responsibility of our deeds, and to you, your deeds. Let there be no argument between us and you. Allah will bring us together, and with Him all journeys end*' (42:15).

'All arguments aside, Prophet, are we to let the Meccans come to Medina without any opposition? Or are we to march forth to defend our land?' Saad bin Mudah's impatience shone in his eyes.

'You are rushing to the fire like a moth, and I am pulling you back!' Muhammad gazed at him profoundly. 'Indeed, we will march forth to defend ourselves, as soon as every attempt at peace has been exhausted. And victory will be ours.'

'How can you be so sure of that, Prophet?' Saad bin Mudah arched his eyebrows, doubt flickering in his eyes.

'My faith in Allah grants me this knowledge. Perseverance is half of faith; certainty is all of it,' Muhammad murmured to himself.

'But we were defeated at the battle of Ohud, Prophet,' came the feverish challenge from Saad bin Mudah.

'That was not a defeat, but a test, if you recall the revelation which I received after the battle,' Muhammad intoned kindly. '*What you suffered on the day the two armies met was ordained by Allah. He tested you that day in the strength of your belief. And He tried you in your faith*' (3:166).

'The Messenger of Allah must know, Prophet, I agree, but how do we comfort our poor hearts?' Saad bin Mudah's faith was clearly being tested.

'Your Lord has gifts of mercy for you throughout the days of your life, so expose yourself to them,' Muhammad replied. 'Be aware of Allah; He will teach you.'

'A man's heart clings to despair, Prophet. I look to the past, and fear the future. But I can still hope, if I can feel victory as a kernel of certainty,' Saad bin Mudah said zealously.

'Be certain then, Saad; you take your knowledge from the dead, but I take my knowledge from the Living Who does not die.' Muhammad's eyes spilled compassion. 'Follow your heart, Saad, even if religion offers you a different opinion. The only solution is to find a way out of the darkness, which breeds fear, zeal, despair!'

'And if we die, we enter Paradise anyway!' Zaid sang, his hands stroking the hair of his almost-three-year-old daughter, Salima, who lay sleeping in his lap.

'The best of my people, my son, will enter Paradise not because of their valour in wars, but because of the mercy of Allah, and because they are satisfied with little of themselves and because of their extreme generosity towards others,' Muhammad chided.

'Tell us, Prophet: are there certain rules which we must follow to enter Paradise, as well as to escape the fires of hell?' Salman broke his silence.

'You are wise, Salman, and your thirst for knowledge is great.' Muhammad's eyes lit up with sudden interest. 'Anyone who fulfils any oath to Allah they make will enter Paradise, including those who feel slighted and powerless. Anyone who stays away from hatred, violence and arrogance will be saved from the fires of hell.' His gaze enveloped everyone in a gentle embrace. 'It is only your deeds, my friends, that I hold in account, and then I set them out before you in full. So whoever meets with good should praise Allah, and whoever finds anything else should blame none but his own self. Be patient and generous, loving and prayerful.'

'To offer prayer and to praise Allah: do they strengthen our faith, Prophet?' Umm Ruman asked suddenly. 'Do such acts keep one inside the boundary of religion?'

'One stays within the boundaries of one's religion, Umm Ruman, as long as one does not shed forbidden blood,' Muhammad began softly. 'Praising and glorifying Allah fills everything between the earth and the heavens with love and harmony, in order that we may share these gifts with the world. Prayer is light, charity is the evidence of light, and patience is its radiance. The Quran is an argument for us, or against us. Everyone starts his or her day selling his or her soul, and either frees it, or ruins it.' He heaved himself up.

'You are not leaving us yet, Prophet? I thought we were going to discuss strategy?' Abdallah ibn Ubbay challenged subtly.

'I intended to do that, Abdallah, but somehow the talk drifted towards faith. In honour of Bilal's wedding, I guess,' Muhammad murmured soothingly. 'After evening prayers, we can get to the matters which are on everyone's minds.'

'Before we do that, Prophet, could you tell us precisely what *jihad* means? There are so many different opinions here,' Abdallah ibn Ubbay asked with some urgency.

'The precise meaning of *jihad*, my friend, is an inner struggle against one's own lusts and greeds, weaknesses and shortcomings,' Muhammad began reluctantly. 'Jihad is a war to fight evil within one's own self, and to fight injustice for the sake of justice in the world. Jihad on the battlefield is an outward war against the evils of injustice, tyranny and oppression, after every attempt at peace has been exhausted, and if the intent to fight is noble and honourable, not corrupted by the poison of hatred or vengeance.' He paused, his gaze distant and wandering. 'I know your hearts are heavy with the thoughts of this war, so near and so imminent, but be assured we will devise a way to defend our lives, our homes and our Medina.' He paused again, and his gaze stopped at Salman. 'From the twinkle in your eyes, Salman, I gather you have some mighty proposal up your sleeve? Or rather, a great plan to defeat the enemy. What is it?'

'A strategy from the very heart of Persia, Prophet!' Salman exclaimed with a burst of enthusiasm. 'We can dig a large trench like the Persians do, so the enemy men and horses die before they even reach the battlefield!'

'A wicked plan!' Abdallah ibn Rudafeh jeered disdainfully. 'It's harmful, besides being dangerous and impractical!'

'A fool does more harm through his ignorance than the wicked do through their wickedness,' Muhammad murmured under his breath. 'Let's take a little time to rest before we meet again.' He drifted towards his wives.

'Will we ever see the gates of Paradise?' Abdallah ibn Ubbay struggled to his feet, laughing to himself. His laughter was checked when Muhammad turned suddenly, a revelation cascading from his lips.

'*When the Sun shall be folded up! And when the stars shall fall! And when the mountain shall be set in motion. And when the camels shall be neglected! And when the wild beasts shall be huddled together. And when the stars shall boil! And when the souls shall be paired with their bodies. And when the girl-child that was buried alive is asked 'For what sin was she slain?' And when the leaves of the Books shall be unrolled! And when the heavens shall be stripped away like a skin. And when hell shall be made to blaze! And when Paradise shall be brought near. Every soul shall know what it hath produced*' (81:1–14).

Chapter 13

The Prophecy of the Prophet From 627 to 628 AD

The palm fronds in the distance flapped their wings like the guardians of Medina as Muhammad's army marched towards Mount Sal, where the Meccan army of ten thousand had gathered. *The rugged rocks will protect the holy city on one side*, Muhammad was thinking, astride Qaswa, *and the exposure on the other side is guarded by the fortifications of the Jews who have promised to safeguard the inhabitants of Medina.* Al Abbas, though still opposed to the Prophet's views, had informed him of the Meccan plans, for the safety of his nephew.

Could I still snatch a promise of peace from my kinsmen? Muhammad's thoughts were clinging to hope. Suddenly he coaxed Qaswa to kneel, becoming aware of Saad bin Mudah, who was whipping his mount and cursing.

'Fear God in these dumb animals, my friends! And ride them when they are fit to be ridden, and get off them when they are tired.' Muhammad sat down on the ground.

'We are all tired, Prophet!' Salman was the first to squat beside the Prophet. 'Who is going to dig this trench to ward off the assault of the Meccans?'

'We will all dig, with Allah's help, as Allah wills.' Muhammad smiled wearily.

The men alighted from their mounts, some flocking around him, the others nursing their wearied limbs on the solid ground. Muhammad was watching Safiyah, but his attention was diverted by a loud comment from Abdallah ibn Ubbay.

'The air is heavy with warning! Can't you smell the reek of death in here?' Abdallah ibn Ubbay abandoned himself on the ground in a heap, his face flushed.

'Why must you invite death into this garden of life, Abdallah?' Safiyah stood towering above him. 'The scent of Paradise is in the air – can't you smell it? Its fragrance delights the heart, and it comes from the body and soul of the Prophet. Anas's mother knows how precious it is; she gathers it secretly from the Prophet's bed after he leaves.' Her gaze shifted to the Prophet. 'Do you know, Prophet, what Umm Ayman says after she gathers the scent of your perspiration? "No scent in Arabia can match this heavenly perfume." Those are her own words, Prophet!'

'Safiyah, my aunt, the poetess!' Muhammad teased. 'Umm Ayman claims that, does she? Secretly gathering what? Dust and sweat? The sweetness of incense from Masjid Al-Nabi is still with you, dear Aunt, and you are only breathing memories. The air is cool and fresh here, and I am not perspiring, as you can see. Your poetic fancy alone is conjuring up a heavenly fragrance.'

'By Allah, I too inhale this subtle fragrance, as Safiyah does,' Abu Bakr confessed happily. 'The perfume of love, as you told me once – or was it the scent of gratitude, you said? Deny it as much as you will, Prophet, but this scent is much too real, delighting the senses of those who are fortunate enough to catch a whiff.'

'All your wives profess the same truth, Prophet, that this scent is a part of your body and soul.' Safiyah's eyes were shining with the sparkle of love.

'My wives, and my dear aunt, are the victims of their own wild imaginations!' Muhammad commented. 'You have left them to the luxury of gossip again, and they are sure to wreak havoc with their imaginations.'

'Women are the twin halves of men, didn't you tell us, Prophet?' Safiyah retorted. 'I predict that, right now, your wives are planning a siege in protest at this long journey.'

'The Prophet is already besieged, dear Aunt, by doubts from within and without himself.' Muhammad smiled. 'Tell my twin halves to be brave and forgiving. They should pray for peace, and have patience. A little rest, and then we will be marching again.'

'They are brave, Prophet, I assure you. But forgiving? I am not sure,' Safiyah teased. 'Before I leave I want to let all the men assembled here know that I myself am braver than any man and could kill a whole horde of the enemy, if they dare threaten our safety.' She turned on her heel, leaving behind the aura of her grace and strength.

'Brave and mighty are those who control their anger, not those who make it a weapon of violence.' Muhammad's gentle comment followed at her heels.

'How should we treat our enemy, Prophet, if they make us angry?' Saad bin Mudah was quick to unburden his quiver of doubts.

'Your enmity towards a group, Saad, who make you angry should not force you to stray from the path of justice. For only justice is next to piety,' Muhammad replied.

'Piety is prayer as well as justice and much more, you told us, Prophet, and yet we know not what true piety is,' Zaid murmured, absorbed in writing down each word.

'If you are able, keep your heart free from malice towards anyone, from morning till night and from night till morning. That's true piety,' Muhammad murmured back.

'We have faith in you and in Allah, Prophet, which has brought us together in our resolve to defend Medina.' Othman ibn Affan assumed the responsibility of chief spokesman. 'Guide us so we may be worthy of our duty towards Allah.'

'Be careful of your duty to Allah, my friends,' Muhammad began earnestly. 'The faithful slaves of the Beneficent are those who walk upon the earth modestly. Whoever becomes humble for Allah's sake is elevated by Him.'

'For Allah's sake, we will follow the right path,' Ali intoned passionately.

'*Whoever chooses to follow the right path follows it but for his own good. And whoever goes astray, goes but astray to his own hurt*' (45:15). Muhammad closed his eyes. 'We must resume our journey soon to avoid the arrows of time and regret.'

The Muslims had moved swiftly towards Mount Sal before the Meccans could reach it to claim this vantage point over the hills. They had been digging the earth for the past six days to carve a mile-long trench, and it was almost complete. Muhammad was wielding his shovel with great agility, singing a couplet for the sole pleasure of his companions:

This beauty not the beauty is of Khaiber
More innocent it is, O Lord, and purer.

The refrain was picked up by other men, and Muhammad's gaze turned to the man digging beside him, a Darmite from the clan of Beni Damrah. His name was Juayl, which meant literally *little beetle*, and he was much teased by his friends. Muhammad, after noticing his plight, had changed his name to Amr, meaning *spiritual well-being*. Muhammad glanced at Salman, who was lowering an empty date-basket at the feet of Amr, and his lips sang inspiration.

His name he changed, Juayl to Amr
Give the poor man this day his help.

This song too was snatched by the others, exploding forth into a chorus of mirth.

'Salman is ours,' the Immigrants were chanting.

'Salman is one of us,' the Helpers vied with the Immigrants.

'We are the people of one House, and Salman is one of us, where no distinction is made between the Ansars and the Muhajirins,' Muhammad commented. 'O God, no life is but the life hereafter. Have mercy on the Helpers and the Immigrants.'

These words too were multiplying, carried on the chords of passion.

'Lord but for Thee we never have been guided. We had never given alms, nor prayed Thy prayer. Send then serenity upon us. Make firm our feet for the encounter. These foes oppressed us, sought to pervert us, but we refused,' Muhammad prayed aloud.

'Come! Help, someone! I can't dislodge this rock,' Jabir appealed.

Muhammad was the first to pay heed, racing towards him. Wielding his pickaxe he struck the rock, which did not yield, but emitted a spark.

'Allah-hu-Akbar! I have been awarded the keys to the palace of the Syrian King!' Muhammad exclaimed prophetically.

Another mighty stroke, and this time a flame erupted forth.

'Allah-hu-Akbar! Now the keys of the Persian kingdom are in my hands.'

This gleaming pickaxe had become a part of Muhammad's body, working with the strength of his bare arms. In a flash, the heart of the rock was split open.

'Allah-hu-Akbar! Now the keys of Yemen are in my possession.'

'What does this mean, Prophet?' Anas's voice splintered the silence.

'The first spark, my son, showed me the palace of Caesar.' Muhammad's face was transfigured with joy. 'The second one, that of the Chrosoes of Persia! And the third one, the white palace of Kisra at Yemen. Allah has bestowed upon us these kingdoms, the gifts of His grace for future generations. Be of good cheer, my friends, the victory is ours. Now, let us share a wholesome meal, and stay vigilant.'

No joyful songs were stirring the Muslims' hearts this particular day, as they sat with Muhammad. It had been a month since the Meccans had laid siege. The cold weather had descended early. The Muslims were suffering the most, since the Meccans, in secret alliance with the Jewish tribes, had succeeded in blocking the main routes, so that no supplies of food or fodder could reach the Prophet's besieged army.

Abu Sofyan was the chief plotter, whose guile was extended to a Jewish chief by the name of Huyayy ibn Akhtab from the clan of Beni Nadir. Huyayy ibn Akhtab, in return, was quick to win support from two more major tribes, Ghatafani and Beni Koreiza. Beni Koreiza were to attack the Muslims from behind, while the allied army of Beni Nadir and Ghatafani were to surround them from one length of the moat to the other, allowing Meccans the opportunity to slaughter the Muslims if they dared to try to escape.

That day will never dawn – Muhammad's faith in Allah had granted him that knowledge. His first concern was for the safety of the women, so he had sent them to the neighbouring village to be lodged in the homes of the peasants, and Zaid was advised to ensure their safety. Time was precious to Muhammad, and he had sent his envoy to the Chief of the Ghatafanis, promising them one-third of Medina's date harvest if they were willing to desist from siding with the Meccans.

Pressed by the urgency of impending doom, Muhammad had chosen a Medinese youth by the name of Nuaym as his emissary to carry his messages to the leaders of the Meccans and of the Jewish tribes. First he went to the leaders of the Jewish tribes, warning them that the Meccans would abandon them to their own fates if Muhammad was to emerge victorious, and urging them not to attack unless they could secure a promise from Abu Sofyan of perfect alliance. Then the same night he gained audience with Abu Sofyan, cautioning him against his new alliances with the Jewish tribes, saying that their leaders were already regretting betraying their former oath with the Prophet, and were vacillating in their decision to attack.

After Nuaym had returned from his night mission, and had shared his comments with the others, nothing more was said or planned by the Muslims. Muhammad had prayed a lot during those hours of darkness and uncertainty, even binding his stomach under a weight of stones when the hunger became unendurable.

'We should never have sent that offer to the Ghatafanis,' Saad bin Mudah protested. 'They never got our dates before without paying, so why should we offer them now when they spurn our faith?'

'If you doubt the judgement of the Prophet, Saad, why don't you ask him?' Umar ibn Khattab was losing patience, his own anger flaring.

'By Allah, I will!' Saad ibn Mudah turned his eyes to Muhammad. 'Was that offer, Prophet, the command of Allah? Or was it your own idea?'

'If it was the command of Allah, Saad, I would not have sought anyone's advice,' Muhammad murmured sadly. 'We were in a dangerous plight, and still are. They didn't accept my offer, so why think about it? Why such bitterness, Saad?'

'Why, you ask! Don't you know, Prophet?' Saad bin Mudah exclaimed. 'Didn't I tell you what the Ghatafanis said, when I went to them with the plea for peace? "Who is Muhammad?" they jeered. "And who is this Apostle of God, that we should obey him? There is no bond or compact between us and him."'

'Your anger towards them is stronger than your devotion towards me, Saad,' Muhammad breathed tenderly. 'Absolve this anger with the waters of forgiveness, and you will feel the bliss of soaring above the marshlands of fear and anxiety. Fill your heart with love and faith; these tender saplings are two of our best friends in times of despair and darkness, leading us on the path to hope and success.'

'What puzzles me the most, Prophet, is why the Jews sided with the Meccans when they don't believe in their gods, while our God and theirs is one and the same.' Abdallah ibn Ubbay was gloating inwardly at his secret alliance with the Jews.

'Worldly gains and ambition have guided their spirits, Abdallah.' Muhammad smiled. 'Didn't the Jews tell the Quraysh that the idolatry of the Meccans is indeed better than what Muhammad has brought to them? If they had sought guidance from their God in this matter, they might have escaped the vice of hypocrisy.'

'We are hemmed in from all sides, Prophet. If the Jewish chiefs stick to their plans, we are doomed,' Tabir lamented aloud.

'Have you no faith in—'

Muhammad's mild rebuke was left unfinished against the sudden flurry of voices and commotion outside his tent.

Bilal stumbled into the tent flustered, gasping for breath.

'The warriors of Beni Koreiza are descending from their fortress, Prophet, and occupying the houses close to where our women are lodged,' he said, finding his voice. 'Your aunt Safiyah, Prophet, saw a Jewish scout lurking in the alley. She informed the owner of the house, and pleaded with him to kill the intruder before he murdered all the women. But the man was afraid, and hid himself in the corner, even when the Jewish warrior broke open the door. Meanwhile, Safiyah had grabbed an iron rod, and she swiftly hit him on the head before he could wield his sword. Stunned by the blow, he died instantly. Since then, all our women have armed themselves with whatever they can find in their quarters, even knives. Now they're taking turns during the long hours of the night, shouting *God is Great* to frighten the Beni Koreizans.'

'Allah is our faith and salvation. No harm will ever come to them,' Muhammad affirmed. 'The women warriors of Islam!

Allah has bestowed upon them—' His speech was truncated once again as a thunderous fury of challenges from the throats of the Meccans, hurled across from the moat, invaded the tranquility of the tent.

The large moat at the foot of Mount Sal appeared to be sprinkled with gold-dust from sunshine. Arrayed gorgeously in their armour, and astride their Arabian mounts, the Meccans were waging a psychological war, flinging insults and chanting the cry of battle.

'Look at you, Muhammad, telling lies to your little horde of hooligans!' Abu Sofyan jeered. 'They are about to be wiped off the face of the earth, and you still fill their hearts with false hopes that they are going to possess the lands of the Caesars and the Chrosoes. And the fools believe you.'

'Prophets do not lie, Abu Sofyan.' Muhammad's voice carried over the breeze. 'Even if you don't live long enough to benefit from the gift of love and unity in Islam, your children and their children will.'

'This trench won't keep us from killing you, Prophet.' Nawfal, in a fury, spurred his horse into the mouth of the trench, brandishing his sword.

Nawfal had barely reached halfway inside the moat when he was confronted by Zubayr ibn Awwam. With one violent blow of his scimitar, Zubayr ibn Awwam succeeded in slitting Nawfal's throat. The Meccans stunned. Ikrimah charged from amongst them, letting his horse thunder into the deathly trench. Saad bin Mudah from the Muslims' side entered the fray, but his unerring aim accomplished only half of what he intended, for Ikrimah was seen fleeing to the safety of his own troops, clutching his wounded arm. Meanwhile, Saad bin Mudah himself was injured in the leg by an arrow from the enemies' side, finding refuge on his side of the trench.

'Come, cowards! Let us engage in duels, and determine who is valorous before we pound you all to dust!' Amr ibn Aasi jumped into the moat, laughing hysterically.

'If you can kill me, Amr, even Muslims will praise you for your valour.' Ali darted forward, his sword, which he called Zulfiqar, glittering in his hand.

'I'd hate to kill the likes of you, Ali,' Amr ibn Aasi mocked. 'Your father was a wonderful companion of mine. Go back, you are but a stripling.'

'You are afraid of the Lion of Arabia then?' Ali sailed closer, his eyes flashing.

'We will see who is the Lion of Arabia!' Amr ibn Aasi lunged forward.

'May you find peace in death.' Ali ducked away from the sudden assault, and plunged his own sword into the leg of his foe.

'Oh Arabs, death is better than this!' Amr ibn Aasi cried out in agony as he fell, but not before flinging his severed leg towards Ali.

The Meccans were stunned and horrified once again. Ali returned to his side of the trench. Muhammad closed his eyes, his hands clutching the red cloak over his shoulders involuntarily, and his lips moving as if uttering prayers.

'We will meet you, Muhammad, another day, another time!' Abu Sofyan's voice was heard above the furious gusts of wind. 'It will be a great day of battle for us, and you will not escape – you'll fall into a moat of your own digging!'

That great day of battle had not yet arrived, though time had slithered onward for five days now since Abu Sofyan's challenge. The weather had turned cold and Muhammad spent most of his time praying. Even this particular night, on the verge of another bitter dawn, his heart was unfurling its own foreknowledge.

'Allah, my Beloved. Revealer of Books. Swift Caller to account, turn the enemy to flight…'

Muhammad sighed to himself, unwilling to open his eyes. But a sudden gust of wind rushing through his thoughts forced him to, and before him stood his beloved friend, Abu Bakr.

'Where does this light come from, Prophet? And this overpowering fragrance?' Abu Bakr stood in awe of the light flooding his tent.

'This light, Abu Bakr, you have brought with you; it is the essence of your own noble character, and Allah in His great mercy has blessed us both with the light of love.' Muhammad's eyes emanated the warmth of prophetic knowledge. 'And as to the fragrance, remember, we are the descendants of the Scented Ones? When the keys of the Kaaba were entrusted into the hands of the Banu Hashim – our tribe – Hashim and his brothers dipped their hands into a bowl of perfume which the women of their family had placed by the Kaaba. Then they rubbed their hands all over the walls of the Kaaba, swearing a solemn oath that they would guard and protect its sanctity with their lives. That scent which they rubbed on the stones of the Kaaba is our legacy, Abu Bakr; the legacy of all Arabs. But to claim that scented legacy, one needs to purify one's heart.' His look was profound. 'But no need to talk about such things which rest in the past. Tell me, what prompted you to visit me? Did the storm keep you awake all night?'

'Despite the storm, I slept quite well, Prophet. But I was anxious to be the first to bring you the good news. And yet I wanted to wait to make sure…' Abu Bakr could not continue, noticing the dancing stars of perception in Muhammad's eyes. 'But you already know, Prophet … there's no need to repeat what has been revealed to you.'

'Yes, Abu Bakr, but your voice will sweeten the lips of truth, which are now silent in my breast,' Muhammad murmured. 'Even prophets are beset by doubts, and words of glad tidings lend peace to vacillating thoughts. So, tell me all that you have heard, and I will match it with what I have seen with gratitude and thanksgiving.'

'The secret embassies of Nuaym have proven to be successful after all!' Abu Bakr began. 'Abu Sofyan would have launched an assault yesterday, Prophet, if his plans had not been thwarted by the coalition's refusal to comply. The envoys whom he had sent to the chiefs of the Koreiza and Ghatafan tribes returned with a similar message from both the chiefs that they couldn't possibly fight on the day proposed since it was the Sabbath. Upon hearing this, Abu Sofyan's suspicions were aroused. It was an added blow to his despair, since the cold winds hit them harder than us because their camps are high up the mountains. He has been heard saying he wants to leave this accursed place. All we have to do is to wait. Now if the Jews challenge us, we will match them in numbers as great as theirs.'

'There won't be a next time, Abu Bakr,' Muhammad murmured. 'What you didn't hear or discover, I have seen with my mind's eye. Remember the night before last? The rain and the storm? Remember how the wind howled and groaned, and cut through the scrub and pelted the date palms? It wrought havoc in the Meccan encampment; it blew out their fires and uprooted their tents. Many of their soldiers have died of cold, their beasts too. Last night, my friend, they left: this morning they will be wending their way back, whipped by harsh, merciless winds. Before leaving, Abu Sofyan addressed his troops in a feverish strain. "The camels and horses are dying. The Beni Koreiza have broken their word, and so did the Ghatafanis. Look around you at how we have suffered from the violence of the storm: no fires, no tents, no cooking pots. Be off, be off! I am going. Follow me, follow me!"'

Muhammad looked out of the tent through the open flap. 'Look, Abu Bakr, have you seen such a dawn before? It's so lovely. The storm is no more.' His thoughts were silenced by the sweet music of a call to prayer from the lips of Bilal.

The Muslim soldiers were abandoning their tents in droves, clutching their weapons, goaded by one thought alone: the day of great battle had arrived. Abu Bakr and Muhammad followed the soldiers, but armed only in the mists of serenity, they had failed to notice them. A sudden burst of sunshine had made the sky mirror-bright, replacing the blush of dawn with molten gold at the sound of the invocation *Allah-hu-Akbar,* throbbing on Muhammad's lips.

'Glory to Thee, O Allah. And Thine is the praise. And blessed is Thy Name. And exalted is Thy Majesty, and there is none to be served beside Thee,' Muhammad prayed. 'Peace be unto you, and the Mercy of Allah.'

'Victory is ours! Allah-hu-Akbar!' Men sang the chorus.

'The Meccans have left, my friends, but we are still hemmed in by hordes of Jewish warriors, who are intent on barring our way to Medina,' Salman warned.

'By Allah's grace, nothing can block our way to Medina but the weakness of our own faith,' Muhammad began thoughtfully. 'Those who betrayed us and broke their oaths must be chastised. We will deal with each tribe in succession. We will march against the tribe of Koreiza first, since they have entrenched themselves not far from Medina.' His gaze came to a rest on Ali. 'Ali will be our commander to lead us back to Medina, and if the tribe of Koreiza rise against us, they will have to defend themselves against his valour and judgement.'

The stronghold of the Koreiza on the borders of Medina, though not a giant roadblock, stood before the Muslim army like a rock. It had been twenty-five days since they had laid siege to the Jewish camp, demanding surrender as a ransom for the tribe's acts of betrayal and treason. But their leader Huyayy ibn Akhtab was defiant. He had lured the Medinese poet Kaab ibn Salma to his side to gain support from his tribe of Muzaynah. On this particular evening Muhammad, as he sat with his companions inside his tent, had decided to prove to the chiefs of the Jewish tribes that he was the leader, striving towards maintaining peace in Medina by plucking out all the seeds of treason and betrayal.

Betrayals were countless, Muhammad knew, and his eyes this evening were clouded by his inward anguish as he sat with his chosen companions. One man in particular by the name of Abu Lubadah from the tribe of Beni Nadir was invading Muhammad's thoughts. Abu Lubadah, oppressed by the burden of his own guilt, had tied himself to one of the mosque pillars, chanting a revelation:

> *Verily, we are for God, and verily unto Him we are returning.* (2:156)

Muhammad recited the same revelation aloud, involuntarily.

'Abu Lubadah is still on your mind, Prophet?' Zaid commented.

'Why do you say that, my son?' Muhammad murmured absently.

'Because Abu Lubadah recites the same revelation you just recited, Prophet. And he is still tied to the pillar of the mosque, I am sure,' was Zaid's astonished response.

'I did?' Muhammad's eyes sparked with realisation. '*Verily we are for God, and verily unto Him we return.* And what else does he say besides reciting that? You must know, since you visit him day after day.'

'He raves and prays, Prophet,' Zaid began. 'He never tires of repeating *I have betrayed God and His Messenger.* When he sees me coming, he groans, *I was aware that I had betrayed the Messenger of God! That's why I tied myself to this pillar, and my feet have not moved since then.*'

'Abu Lubadah is truly penitent, Prophet,' Abu Bakr smiled. 'He says, *I will not stir from this place until God relents unto me for what I did.*'

'If he had come to me, I would have prayed to God to forgive him. But now that he is doing penance on his own, it is not for me to free him until God relents towards him,' Muhammad murmured. 'You have been visiting him too, Abu Bakr? How long is he going to stick to this ritual? Has it been ten days? I have lost count.'

'I am not sure, Prophet.' Abu Bakr smiled. 'He shared his dream with me yesterday. He saw himself sucked into a bog of foul slime. He tried to pull himself out, and nearly died from its stench. Next, he found himself near a clear stream where he bathed, and the air around him was filled with a sweet, intoxicating fragrance. He asked me if I knew how to interpret his dream, and I offered him an interpretation as best as I could.'

'What did you tell him?' Muhammad asked.

'I told him that, in the dream, his body represented his soul,' Abu Bakr began dreamily. 'And that once he realised the state of his soul, he would be bewildered, but then a great sense of relief would come to him from that same state of bewilderment.'

'You have given him hope, Abu Bakr, and he is sure to find relief and salvation soon,' Muhammad breathed tenderly. 'As for the tribe of Koreiza—' His thoughts were disrupted by the sudden appearance of Anas, who stood gasping for breath.

'The Koreiza have capitulated, Prophet!' Anas could barely contain his joy. 'There was another little skirmish, and Ali picked up a door as his shield, ready to charge, and then their leader announced that there was no choice left but to surrender.'

'Allah be praised. Now we can return home.' Muhammad stood up.

'Not before we punish them for their betrayals, Prophet?' Umar ibn Khattab leapt to his feet. 'We must do that, Prophet, for the sake of our future safety, and for the peace and safety of Medina. Otherwise, they will never learn to honour their peace treaties, and they'll keep breaking them whenever they wish, assured of our forgiveness.'

'They will choose their own punishment, Umar. Exile, or a sacred oath of utmost obedience to my authority as the leader of Medina.' Muhammad's features were washed over with sadness.

'We will convene a meeting, and the verdict of the majority will serve as the mode of punishment for the tribe of Koreiza.' His words were greeted by cheers.

The evening was thick with clouds of doom suspended over the date palms as Muhammad stood facing the vanquished, his followers silent behind him. Muhammad, cloaked in pallor and compassion, stood oblivious to the march of time, immersed in thoughts of the past three days, silent and ominous.

The vanquished had sealed their hearts with the bands of doom themselves. Muhammad had sent Abu Bakr as his envoy, offering them the gift of peace and forgiveness if they were willing to go into exile like the other Jewish tribes who had violated their peace treaties with the Muslims. But their leader Huyayy ibn Akhtab rejected the offer, demanding that he should be given the right to choose one Muslim man to judge. Muhammad had no objection to this demand, confirming his concession with an oath that he would neither oppose his choice, nor interfere in any way with his decision. Huyayy ibn Akhtab chose Saad bin Mudah as an arbiter. Saad bin Mudah, who had been wounded at the battle of the Trench, had gone to his home in Medina, so Muhammad sent Usama with an urgent message, summoning him to the stronghold where the Koreiza had surrendered. Usama had returned that morning, informing the Prophet that the wound in Saad bin Mudah's leg was infected, but he had promised to come in the evening, saying, '*They have chosen me as their arbiter, have they? After they foreswore the oath of their peace treaty with the Prophet? Bent on killing the women and the children of the Muslim soldiers, and siding with the Meccans? They have the audacity to insist on their rights when—*' Muhammad's thoughts broke off at the sight of the slow approach of Saad bin Mudah.

Saad bin Mudah, wrapped in blankets, riding a donkey padded with cushions, looked like a phantom from the nether worlds. One look at Saad, and Muhammad's heart sank. Saad bin Mudah halted his mount beside Muhammad, his lips sealed and his gaze feverish. Suddenly, the silence was shattered.

'Huyayy ibn Akhtab, will you, your men, women and children, bind themselves by the covenant of God, that whatever I decide, you will accept?' Saad bin Mudah's gaze was singeing the air over the heads of the Jewish compound.

'By our own request, Muhammad has appointed you as our judge, O Saad, the father of Amr. So we will accept your verdict without a protest.' Huyayy ibn Akhtab's voice quavered, his eyes shining with dread.

'Then I will judge you by your own law of the Torah, the Mosaic Law, as you well know. What is the punishment for betrayal in the Torah?' Saad bin Mudah asked.

'No – you, betraying us—' Huyayy ibn Akhtab's voice was choked as he saw the dance of death in Saad's eyes.

'Have you forgotten the law of the Torah, Huyayy, which commands death as the punishment for betrayal?' Saad bin Mudah emitted a snort of mirth. '*And when the Lord hath delivered into thine hands, thou shall smite every male thereof with the edge of the sword. But the women and the little ones and the cattle and all that is in the city, even all the spoil thereof, shalt thou take unto thyself and thou shalt eat the spoils of thine enemies which the Lord thy God has given thee*. I shall judge you by the same law. In conformity with Jewish law, I command that the men be put to death, the women and children sold into slavery, and the spoils divided amongst the soldiers of Islam.'

A wail of lament ripped through the limbs of the date palms, it seemed, and the wind itself shuddered. The Jews stood stunned, no words escaping their lips.

'Had I not forsaken the right to intervene, I would have split my own heart into two; one to plead with God for forgiveness and the other to long for the crumbs of mercy.' Muhammad's love reached out to Huyayy, before he turned on his heel.

'I don't blame myself for opposing thee, Muhammad; but whoever forsakes God, they shall be forsaken!' A cry of pain ripped through the agonised soul of Huyayy ibn Akhtab. 'The command of God cannot be wrong! A writ and a decree and a massacre, which God hath set down in His book against the Sons of Israel!'

'Don't look to the blackness of the letters, but to the whiteness of purity in our hearts,' Muhammad muttered over his shoulder, racing towards his tent.

Muhammad staggered into the sanctuary of his own tent. Cradling his head into his hands, he sat weeping as he had never wept before, not even after the death of Khadija. Abu Bakr had stolen in behind him, unable to offer a word of consolation. Slowly, he too slumped down beside the Prophet, the violence of his own anguish finding voice.

'Why are you weeping, Prophet?' Abu Bakr pleaded.

'My back hath been broken by these pious fools, Abu Bakr, and you ask me why I weep?' Muhammad lifted his tear-streaked face towards the heavens.

'They chose Saad as their arbiter, Prophet. You are not to blame,' was Abu Bakr's feeble attempt at consolation.

'I would take such blame a thousand times over, Abu Bakr, if it could save the lives of seven hundred Jews from this fate.' Muhammad's voice was racked by sobs. 'Have I not been sent as a mercy to mankind? I have failed, failed in my message. Have I not taught Muslims to shun zeal and tyranny? Yes, I have failed, my friend, I have failed terribly. Leave me, Abu Bakr. I want to be alone, to pray to Allah for understanding.' He closed his eyes.

The day was crisp and bright, the date palms in the distance glistening innocently as if no blood had been shed during the night, as Muhammad rode towards Medina with his followers. He was still carrying the burden of the massacre on his shoulders, burying the dead in his thoughts. Umar ibn Khattab had been the first to greet him in the morning, suggesting that he accept a Jewess by the name of Rehanna as his concubine. But Muhammad had dismissed him, commenting that the hand of death was reaching out to her with the promise of releasing her from her own burden of grief and suffering.

Muhammad's thoughts were evading the pincers of the tragedy by recalling snippets from the scandal when Aisha had lost her necklace.

Verily who brought forth the lie are a party amongst you. When ye took upon your tongues, uttering with your mouths that whereof ye had no knowledge, ye counted it but a trifle. Yet in the sight of Allah, it is enormous. Why said ye not when ye heard it. To speak of this is not for us. Glory be to Thee. This is a monstrous calumny. God biddeth you beware of ever repeating the like thereof, if you are believers (24:11, 15–17).

This is all a lie, Prophet; Aisha is blameless, Usama had exclaimed.

By Him that sent thee with the truth, Prophet, I only know good of Aisha, and if it were otherwise, God would inform His Messenger. I have no fault to find with Aisha, but that she is a girl young in years, and when I am kneading dough and I bid her to watch it, she falls asleep, and her pet lamb comes and eats it. I have blamed her for that more than once, Burayrah, Aisha's maid, had attested.

Suddenly, half the burden of grief from Muhammad's shoulders slid away, as in his heart he knelt in gratitude for the victory and for the safe return of his family and troops to Medina. Zaid, Bilal and Abu Bakr were riding ahead of him, on each side of them the graceful riders, Asma and Umaymah, the Prophet's aunt. The mosque was coming into view, and Muhammad could not help seeing Abu Lubadah still tied to the pillar.

'Is Abu Lubadah not forgiven, Prophet?' Umaymah asked.

'He is, dear Aunt. Yes, he is forgiven,' Muhammad chanted.

'May I be the one to give him this gift of good tidings, Prophet?' Umaymah was racing ahead of the trio of men to reach the pillar of penance.

'Yes, sweet Aunt, yes!' Muhammad's features were lit up with the light of love.

'Be of good cheer, Abu Lubadah; Allah has relented towards you!' Umaymah announced. 'The Prophet himself says you are forgiven.'

'Not until the Messenger of Allah sets me free with his own hands, will I forgive myself,' was Abu Lubadah's low lament.

'And the Prophet is at your service, my friend, since Allah has accepted your offering of penance,' Muhammad confirmed wistfully, dismounting with the agility of a young man. He was swift to loosen the bonds, his eyes bright and shining.

'How could you forgive him, Prophet?' 'He has wronged us, Prophet!' 'He even went after our women to kill them and to violate their honour – you know that, Prophet?' 'His own Scriptures condemn him to death for all these betrayals!' 'Your own revelations, Prophet, don't they brand such men hypocrites, not to be forgiven?' A flurry of protests rippled forth from the lips of the men who had gathered around him.

'Is it not revealed: *Keep to forgiveness, O Muhammad, and enjoin kindness, and turn away from the ignorant*? (7:199). Do not forge weapons of zeal from my revelations, my friends. Do not fashion lies, which will sit on your tongues like burning coals. I would rather you mould a blade of pure gold from my words, and plunge it deep into your souls to know the bleeding truth within. Then you will be able wrench it out, much like a blood-soaked babe from the loving womb of its mother. This truth will serve you as a loving gift from the very hands of divine love. Do not be like those who are blind and ignorant, cultivating seeds of hatred; those who are sightless to the light of mercy from their Lord, neither knowing the grace of joy in love, nor tasting its sweetness.' He plodded towards his humble quarters, his pallor growing more intense, and his pomegranate-red lips glowing like a crescent wound.

Chapter 14

The Lote Tree of Peace
Year 628 AD

That afternoon Muhammad was at Abu Bakr's house, and he lay resting, or rather dreaming. It was a month short of a year since the battle of the Trench, and the Medinese had proclaimed him as their sole sovereign to safeguard their lives, lands and properties. Muhammad's dreams were peace-loving as he lay enveloped in the mists of time. Fatima was with him, now the mother of another son, Mushin.

The scent of peace in Muhammad's dreams suddenly split into a crater of rifts and raids, revealing the grave where Saad bin Mudah lay buried. He had died two nights after the massacre. This dream scene faded into the mists of a skirmish between the tribal chiefs Ghifar and Juhaynal, both allied with the tribe of Khazraj. The chiefs were fighting over a bucket of water, as both factions laid claim to well-watered territories. Peace had been restored through the intercession of Muhammad, but the comments of Abdallah ibn Ubbay were surfacing in his dreams.

Oh, these rags of the Quraysh! Who gave them the authority to rule over us? Feed fat thy dog and it will feed on thee! By God, the higher and the mightier of us in Medina would drive the lower and the weaker out of our holy city.

The scene was swallowed by dream-mists, alive and palpitating. One dream which he had not been able to efface since the night of the massacre had nothing to do with that tragedy. He had forgotten the slander against Aisha, but every time he closed his eyes, it erupted forth in musty, frayed visions.

'May God cut the tongue of Mistah, your cousin, Abu Bakr! He is the first one to air this slander against our daughter,' Umm Ruman had said.

'He is not the only one, Mother! Zainab's own sister Hamnah carries this slander in her eyes and upon her lips wherever she goes,' Aisha had commented.

'It's time you forgot this slander, my little daughter,' Abu Bakr had interceded. 'There is seldom a beautiful woman married to a man who loves her, who does not find that his other wives and outsiders are full of gossip about her. Then friends and relatives pick up that gossip and toss it around till it grows out of proportion. You need to swallow your pride, my dear Aisha, and profess your innocence to the Prophet. Then the burden of sorrow will be expelled from your dainty head.'

'Have I not done that already, Father? And the Prophet believed me, before the lies muddied the streets of Medina. Or did he? I know what everyone is saying. I also know I am innocent, but who believes me? Not even the Prophet, otherwise he would come to comfort and console me. Doesn't he know I am sick, half mad with crying and praying? God alone is my refuge and salvation. I have confessed to Him, and He has comforted me and assured me that I am guiltless. I have no need to confess to anyone else, not even to the Prophet. As Jacob the father of Joseph said, *Beautiful patience must be mine, and God is He of Whom help is to be asked against—*'

'O Aisha, praise Allah, for He has declared you innocent.' Muhammad was present in his own dreams.

'Allah be praised indeed, Prophet.' Abu Bakr urged Aisha to welcome her husband.

'Nay, by Allah, I will not get up and go to him. He should come to me. Allah be praised indeed, for He alone believed me, while others doubted my innocence.' Aisha's eyes challenged her parents and the Prophet.

'Forgive me, Aisha. I am the slave of Allah, doubting or believing as He wills or guides.' Muhammad grasped her hands.

'May Allah forgive you, Prophet, but I can't.' Aisha was skipping away.

'What can a man do with a woman like that, Abu Bakr?' Muhammad was saying.

'Beat her to obedience, Prophet.' Abu Bakr was laughing.

'Nay, my friend, women are the twin halves of men. If one were to beat one's own precious half, the other half would revolt.' Muhammad's eyes shot open, and he fled the room, to flee his dreams. He almost collided with Abu Bakr in the parlour.

'I thought you were sleeping, Prophet! I was going to wake you up.' Abu Bakr was leading him towards Aisha, where she sat petting her lamb.

'I was, Abu Bakr.' Muhammad attempted a pale smile. 'But that dream, have I ever told you about it? It has been more than a year since that slander against Aisha, and I still dream about it. It won't go away.'

'That dream might go away, Prophet, if the slanderers were to pay a penalty for their lies!' Abu Bakr declared. 'I, for one, have been supporting Mistah because of his poverty, although he shares a major part of the guilt in airing that scandal. I have decided, Prophet, that never again, by God, will I give him any money, and never again will I show him any favour, for what he said against my Aisha.'

'All those base accusations. Hassan and Hamnah, and all the others too, they must be punished somehow!' Umm Ruman could not help airing her old bitterness.

'Allah in His great mercy forgives all, while we tend to be harsh towards our own fellow beings,' Muhammad opined aloud. '*Let not the men of wealth and dignity among you swear that they will not give unto kinsmen and unto the needy and unto those who have migrated for the sake of Allah. Let them forgive and let them be indulgent. Do ye not long that Allah should forgive you? And Allah is Forgiving, Merciful'* (24:22).

'Indeed, I wish that Allah would forgive me,' Abu Bakr murmured contritely. 'Forgive me, Prophet, for hoarding this anger in my heart. I promise I will not withdraw my favours from Mistah.'

'Allah will reward you with bounteous gifts, my friend.' Muhammad smiled again, his gaze resting on Aisha. 'Come, my Aisha, it's time I proclaimed your innocence in front of the entire congregation in the mosque.'

'No matter what you do, Prophet, I will never forgive you.' Aisha leapt to her feet, her eyes shining with mirth and mischief. 'You doubted my innocence?'

'I never did, dear Aisha! I only waited for guidance from Allah to stop the gossip.' Muhammad snatched her hand into his own, turning. 'Come Abu Bakr, and Umm Ruman, you can witness the art of removing tarnish from one's character.'

The balmy golden afternoon appeared jubilant, as Muhammad strolled towards the mosque. They were joined by more of the Prophet's wives. Hafsa and Juwairya were talking at the same time, as if trying to restrain Aisha. Zainab and Umm Salmah were trailing at their heels, Swadah and Umm Ruman left far behind. Muhammad was about to step into the courtyard of the mosque when he caught sight of Suhayl the freedman, bending double to repair the mud wall. Muhammad crept behind him, covered his eyes with his hands, and challenged him to guess who he was.

'This can be no other but the Prophet himself! Who else could extend such affection to a lowly person like me, to brighten my day?' Suhayl laughed.

'Allah has chosen me to be His Prophet, because I am the lowliest of His slaves, Suhayl! Never forget that.' Muhammad laughed in return, his eyes lit up with love.

More men and women were joining this happy group. The Prophet became aware of Umar ibn Khattab.

'Permit me, Prophet, to behead this traitor, Abdallah?' Umar ibn Khattab whispered. 'His tongue offends me more than any Meccan treachery.'

'Would you rather, Umar, that even more tongues rise in unison, proclaiming that Muhammad slays his companions?' A quick reproof escaped Muhammad's lips.

'Everyone knows he is a traitor and a hypocrite, Prophet!' Umar ibn Khattab murmured heedlessly. 'Didn't Saad ibn Waqqas challenge Abdallah that he would cut his throat if he dared speak a word against the Prophet again?'

'And didn't I advise him to deal gently with all God's creatures?' Muhammad intoned sadly. 'Have you not heard me say that the strongest amongst you is the one who controls his anger? And to you, Umar, I say that if a man gives up quarrelling when he is in the wrong, a home will be built for him in Paradise. But if a man gives up a conflict, even when he is right, a home will be built for him in the loftiest part of Paradise.'

'And even so, Prophet, Saad ibn Waqqas has not withdrawn his challenge,' Umar ibn Khattab persisted. 'He went to Abdullah, the eldest son of Abdallah, repeating his threat and—'

He couldn't finish, as Abdullah himself appeared suddenly.

'O Messenger of Allah, I am told that you want my father slain,' Abdullah began urgently. 'By Allah, if you want his head, I will bring it to you. All the men of Khazraj know that there is no man amongst them who feels his filial duty more than I do. And I worry that if you assigned this deed to someone else, my soul would not let me see my father's killer walking amongst men without me slaying him.'

'You have heard wrong, my son,' Muhammad began gently. 'Hold fast to your filial piety, and be forever kind and respectful to your father. He is not mighty who has the strength to kill; he is mighty who has the strength to control his anger.'

'Allah commands you to deal with justice, Prophet; I have heard you say it often. Now deal justly with me!' Muawwidh stormed upon the scene. 'They accused me of theft because I am a Jew, isn't that right, Prophet? The Muslim who accused me of theft, after concealing the armour of another Muslim in my house, has been proven guilty. Didn't you think, Prophet, that I was the guilty one?'

'I would be guilty in the sight of Allah, if I thought so, Muawwidh,' Muhammad breathed profoundly. 'Like any other man who believes in justice, I try to do my best. And justice can't be done until evidence is sought and truth ascertained. You are innocent of the crime you are accused of, as I discovered just this morning. And the Muslim who tried to sully your name is commanded to pay half the income of his harvest, and to ask your forgiveness. Allah's justice and mercy do not distinguish between Jews, Muslims, or Christians, or between men of different creeds.' He let his gaze sweep over his congregation. 'O Lord of us and of everything, I give witness that all human beings are brothers unto each other.' His poetry was swallowed by the music of the call to prayer from the lips of Bilal.

Prayer time this particular afternoon was prolonged, since the Jews from Khazraj and the Christians from Najran were honoured guests, housed inside the mosque. At the conclusion of the Muslim prayers, the Christian and then the Jewish prayer rites were observed. Muhammad prayed with the Jews and the Christians with as much devotion as he exhibited in his own Islamic prayers. Afterwards, he seated himself at the head of his congregation, his thoughts bent upon washing out the stains which had soiled the name Aisha.

'My family has long been purged of all lies, since Allah revealed Aisha's innocence to me, but I want to talk about the slander against her for reasons other than my own family,' Muhammad began gently. 'I am kindling the embers of past lies to prevent more fires in the future. The revelations which I received concerning that slander have never reached the ears of the slanderers. Now, I wish to share those revelations to guide anyone who might be tempted to taint the reputations of the innocent and the virtuous. *Lo! who spread the slander are a gang among you. Deem it not a bad thing for you; nay, it is good for you. Unto every man of them will be paid that which he hath earned of the sin; and as for among them who had the greater share therein, his will be an awful doom. Why not the believers, men and women, when ye heard it, think good of their own folk, and say: It is a manifest untruth? Why did they not produce four witnesses? Since they produce not witnesses, they verily are liars in the sight of Allah. Had it not been for the Grace of Allah and His Mercy unto you in this world and Hereafter, an awful doom had overtaken you for that whereof ye murmured. When ye welcomed it with your tongues, and uttered with your mouths that whereof ye had no knowledge, ye counted it a trifle. In the sight of Allah, it is very great. Wherefore, when ye heard it, said ye not: It is not for us to speak of this. Glory be to Thee, O Allah! This is an awful calumny. Allah admonisheth you that ye repeat not the like thereof ever, if ye are in truth believers. And He expoundeth unto you His revelations. Allah is Knower, Wise'* (24:11–18).

'Women are believers as well as men, Prophet; why then do the revelations address only men?' Umm Salmah, in league with the Prophet's daughters, asked quickly.

'Words have a life of their own, dear Salmah; look into their hearts and you will discover every child, every man, every woman, every creature living by the Breath of God in everything, everywhere.' Muhammad smiled enigmatically. 'Men and mankind are merely expressions, and yet the revelations at times specifically address women to stress the truth of equality between genders. Did you not hear the words of the revelation I just recited? And this one, you know by heart, if I am not mistaken? *Lo! men who surrender unto Allah, and women who surrender, and men who obey and women who obey, and men who speak the truth and women who speak the truth, and men who persevere and women who persevere, and men who are humble and women who are humble, and men who give alms and women who give alms, and men who fast and women who fast, and men who guard their modesty and women who guard their modesty, and men who remember Allah and women who remember Allah – Allah hath prepared for them forgiveness and a vast reward'* (33:35).

'O people, I give protection to my husband Abul As!' Zainab appealed loudly. 'You know my husband was with the caravan you raided, and yet he escaped. But he didn't go back to Mecca without seeing me and our daughter, so he is in my house.'

'Did you hear what I heard?' Muhammad stared in disbelief.

'Aye, we heard!' Several voices rose in unison, some confirming his whereabouts and others only concerned about the bounty left behind by the Quraysh. 'The merchandise entrusted to him by the Quraysh is rightfully ours – he carried some into hiding and the rest we claimed. He escaped, but we heard he found safe haven in his wife's home—'

'By Him in whose hands my soul is, I knew naught of this!' Muhammad stared at Zainab. 'My child, what kind of protection do you seek for him?'

'He is afraid, Father, that he will end up a prisoner again in the hands of the Muslims, and he wants the promise of a safe return to Mecca,' Zainab appealed. 'He also begs a great favour; that the bounty captured by the Muslims be returned to him so that he can carry it back to its rightful owners for the sake of his clear conscience, since he was responsible for it all.'

'What do you say, my friends?' Muhammad's eyes swept over his congregation. 'Abul As is my son-in-law and the most honest of Meccans, held in great esteem by the Quraysh.' He could barely control the tremor in his voice. 'Are you willing to grant him the favours he is requesting?'

'He should become a Muslim. He could claim a share of the bounty for himself, and be one of us.' Khira voiced his opinion with a mixture of arrogance and bitterness.

'Converting anyone by force or even suggestion is forbidden in Islam, Khira; have I not said that before?' Muhammad began gently. '*O mankind! Lo! we have created you male and female, and have made you tribes and nations, that ye may know one another. Lo! the noblest of you, in the sight of Allah, is the best in conduct. Lo! Allah is Knower, Aware*' (49:13).

'People of Medina, Abul As has chosen to become a Muslim,' Zainab announced. 'But he wants to do so with a clear conscience, not by betraying the trust of the Quraysh. That's why he wants to return the goods which were entrusted to him; then he can return to Medina and embrace Islam free of all obligations.'

'I am willing to return my share of the booty: the water-skins, the leather bottles and the wooden utensils,' Abu Khaythamah offered generously.

More men followed his lead, offering their share, as Muhammad sat listening. Although seemingly attentive, he was overwhelmed by some scent of inner joy and peace. Mecca was inviting him to its sanctified bosom. He became aware of the silence; his mental journey came to an end.

'Thank you, my friends. Your generosity is more precious than all the goods which you offer to return,' Muhammad said. 'However, they belong to you. God gave them to you, and you have the right to dispose of them as you will, though it gladdens my heart to know that your spirits are endowed with the virtue of generosity.' He shifted his gaze to his daughter. 'Be comforted, dear Zainab; the safety of Abul As is assured. Now, let your father deal with more weighty matters.'

'What weighty matters, Prophet?' Abu Rafi asked. 'Medina is blessed with the light of peace and harmony since God sent you to us as our prophet.'

'A weighty matter, indeed!' Muhammad laughed. 'As pilgrims of peace, we will carry it as a gift to Mecca.'

'How? When?' Several voices rippled forth in a chorus of disbelief.

'Clear as daylight, I have felt and experienced all of us going to Mecca on a pilgrimage, clad in white and rejoicing.' Muhammad smiled.

'Tell us more, Prophet. Tell us! When are we going on this wonderful pilgrimage?' Another chorus sliced through the air with notes of joy.

'You shall enter the Holy Mosque, if God wills, in security. Your heads shaved, your hair cut short, not fearing' (48:27), Muhammad recited. 'With this revelation as our song and guide, proclaim to everyone in Medina that we are going on a pilgrimage, and everyone is invited to come with us, if they are willing. Within a week, we will be on our way. Now, time to rest till we meet in the evening.'

The entire courtyard was flooded with songs of joy as Muhammad finished speaking. His wives had floated ahead, and were already disappearing behind the walled parlour, making their own plans for the promised pilgrimage. Muhammad had barely left the courtyard when Anas tugged at his mantle, wishing to speak with him in private.

'You are grinning from ear to ear, my little beloved!' Muhammad teased. 'What sweet secrets are you holding in your eyes and in your hands?'

'A letter from King Negus, Prophet,' Anas chirped. 'You are always happy to receive letters from him, and it makes me happy too to know that you will be happy.'

'Why so secretive then? And why you are whispering?' Muhammad goaded.

'Aisha is so jealous, Prophet, and I thought—'

Anas couldn't continue against the sudden reproof in Muhammad's eyes.

'So, you have read it already?' Muhammad chided.

'Just a little, Prophet,' Anas admitted, contrite and flustered.

'Then read it to me quickly, before Aisha's jealousy throws me out of Medina, even before I embark on this pilgrimage of peace,' Muhammad laughed.

'Jafar informed me of your intention to marry Umm Habiba, the widow of Ubaid Allah,' Anas began hastily. *'It has been four months since her husband died, and the period of mourning is over. I have conveyed your proposal to her, and she is most willing. Umm Habiba told me that she had a dream, in which she saw herself as the Mother of the Faithful. So she expresses her joy and willingness to become the wife of the Prophet. If you agree, this marriage can be arranged by proxy in Abyssinia. Her kinsman Khalid is here, who has promised to act as her guardian, and to be a witness to the marriage contract. He approves of this marriage with such great delight, that he is talking about holding a wedding feast in my own palace. A great honour, if you consent, Prophet? May God's peace and guidance be with you. King Negus.'*

'Of course, Anas, I give my consent for this proxy marriage with Umm Habiba.' Muhammad breathed low. 'Her father Abu Sofyan would be unhappy to see his daughter married to the Prophet, but it can't be helped.' He paused, his gaze unseeing. 'Send a letter to King Negus, conveying my thanks and gratitude, and my consent. Also, a letter to my cousin Jafar, requesting him to come to Medina. I haven't seen Jafar and his family for four years, since they went to Abyssinia. It's hard to imagine! Umm Habiba will feel safe travelling with him and his family – yes, send a letter immediately.'

A sea of pilgrims, fourteen hundred in all, clad in seamless white, were nearing the well of Usfan, about twenty-five miles north-east of Mecca. Muhammad, astride Qaswa, was thinking about the two weeks they had spent preparing for the pilgrimage, and the two weeks on the road since they had left Medina. He was aware of the three women in his entourage, Nasiba, Umm

Hani, and his own wife Umm Salmah, all dressed in traditional Arab white, their faces tanned and their hair secured with scarves as protection against the violence of the sandstorms.

'Here I am, O Lord! Here I am at Thy service!' the pilgrims were singing.

Muhammad's thoughts were in the valley of Dhul Huleifa, where he had sent a man by the name of Budail with a message to the Meccans that the Muslims were on their way, with the sole intention of performing a pilgrimage. The thought was coming alive as Muhammad watched a rider racing towards them; it was none other than Budail himself, with another man holding on to his waist.

'Prophet, I bring only disturbing news.' Budail jumped down from his mount, the other rider claiming the reins. 'The Quraysh have posted a cavalry of two hundred men, ready to fight under the command of their leaders, Ikrimah and Khalid ibn Walid. They have taken an oath that they will never let you enter Mecca.'

'Didn't you tell them, Budail, that we have no intention of fighting?' Muhammad asked. 'Don't they know we are pilgrims of peace?'

'They say they don't believe what you say, Prophet,' Budail muttered with genuine regret. 'Their message to you and the pilgrims is that you must all turn back. Prepare for fighting, they say, if you wish to enter Mecca.'

'We will fight, we will fight! Jihad, jihad!' A handful of angry voices were spiralling forth, balanced on blades of zeal.

'We will not fight!' A thunderous command escaped Muhammad's lips. 'Jihad, as I said before, is to conquer the forces of evil within one's own self! A war maybe, but only if fought in self-defence, not for the sake of warring. Jihad is the noble and virtuous soul of our actions, and the most merited action amongst them is to fight against the base and selfish desires in one's own heart. And the next is to strive towards bringing peace and harmony into all facets of your life.' He returned his attention to Budail. 'Is there any other route open to us, so that we can avoid the warring lords of Mecca, and still perform the pilgrimage?'

'There is one, Prophet,' was Budail's flustered response. 'Down the mountain track there. It leads you to a place called Hudaybiyah, about three miles away from the Kaaba. I dare not be your guide, for if the Quraysh found out, they would flay me alive. But Aslam ibn Akwa can.' He indicated the silent rider on his mount. 'He belongs to no particular clan, and is free to choose as he wills. Besides, he is virtuous.'

'A noble man indeed, and a worthy guide.' Muhammad smiled, thanking Budail and accepting the services of Aslam ibn Akwa.

The desert dusk had deepened to the colour of pewter as Muhammad's caravan trampled over the sands of Hudaybiyah. *We are pilgrims of peace and reconciliation, not soldiers of war and destruction.* Muhammad could barely catch the murmur of his thoughts, as his gaze fell on the Egyptian thorn tree where Qaswa had decided to halt all of a sudden. *We ask God's forgiveness, and we repent towards Him.* He coaxed Qaswa to proceed, but she sank to her feet.

'Hal! Hal!' The special expression, used to urge camels to their feet, chorused from the lips of the pilgrims, who had seen Qaswa's capricious halt.

'Is she tired? Is she lazy, or just stubborn? Hal! Hal!' More voices were joining the chorus, loud and impatient.

'No, she is not tired. She is not stubborn either.' Muhammad's voice rose above the chorus. 'It's not in her nature to be lazy. She is led by the divine guidance of Allah, who created us all. Guided by the One who stopped an elephant from entering Mecca. If you could only recall the Year of the Elephant when Abraha the ruler of Yemen came to Mecca with the intention of war and destruction, but his elephant wouldn't budge. Our intentions are pure, and our guidance comes from Allah, so we will make camp right here. I will accept any offers of peace that the

Meccans make, or any concessions that they might ask; all shall be granted to them by the will of Allah.'

'You are half a day's journey from here to Mecca, Prophet; on horseback it is only a few hours,' Aslam ibn Akwa murmured. 'Since you have decided to set up camp, I must go.'

'Thank you for your friendship and guidance, Aslam. May Allah's peace and mercy go with you.' Muhammad's eyes were beacons of love. 'And if you see the men of the Quraysh, extend our message of peace. And remind them that the pilgrimage to the Kaaba is a privilege that should never be denied, even to their worst enemies.'

'I will, Prophet.' Aslam ibn Akwa bowed his head before letting his mount fly.

'Come, sit over here.' Muhammad turned his attention to the three ladies, spreading his cloak on the ground. 'I will help the men to pitch the tents.'

'Is there going to be a fight, Prophet?' Nasiba could not help asking.

'No, Nasiba, not so close to the holy grounds of Mecca,' Muhammad reassured her. 'We are too close to its heart, where the ground is sacred and no violence is permitted, and the Meccans are well aware of it.'

'Will we be able to perform the pilgrimage rites?' Umm Salmah asked.

'God willing, yes, dear Salmah,' was Muhammad's tender response.

'Any stranger or wayfarer is permitted the rite of pilgrimage – why should we be barred from doing so?' Umm Hani murmured to herself.

'The Meccans are the guardians of the Kaaba, Umm Hani, and they think they have the right to change their minds if they wish, especially when…' Muhammad tailed off, noticing the breezy approach of Najiyal.

'Prophet, this area is dry and barren,' Najiyal began hastily. 'Abu Bakr found a well, but it is filled with sand. I've been nominated to plead with you not to camp here. They're saying we will all die of thirst – and our beasts too.'

'Come with me, Najiyal. Show me the well.' Muhammad turned on his heel. 'Find me a stick or an arrow.' He was already making his way towards the group of men where they stood ranting and complaining.

Muhammad was quick to reach the site of the sand-filled well. He punctured its heart with the arrow in one bold stroke. To everyone's astonishment, a fountain of clear water gushed forth. The pilgrims rejoiced and chanted: '*A miracle!*'

'This is no miracle,' Muhammad declaimed. 'It is but God's mercy to the servants of peace,' he continued, plodding back to where he had spread his cloak. The early afternoon gilded the newborn fountain – it sparkled and gurgled.

Seated under the Egyptian thorn tree along with his followers, Muhammad thought about the derisive comments of Abdallah ibn Ubbay, which Zaid had recounted to him that morning.

'What tree is this, Prophet?' Othman ibn Affan asked suddenly. 'I have looked all over, and there is none other like this in Hudaybiyah?'

'The sacred Lote tree, I should say, though it is also known as an Egyptian thorn,' Muhammad responded dreamily. 'This is the Tree of Peace, and the generations after us will remember it as *Bait-al-Ridwan*, meaning *the Pledge of Good Pleasure*.'

'Only a Prophet of God could look into the heart of the future and see prophecies which our mortal sight could never behold!' Abu Bakr's eyes shone with devotion.

'Divine breezes from your Lord waft through every day of your life. Listen! Be aware of them.' Muhammad's lips spilled poetic nectar.

'I hear them not, Prophet, and I remain ignorant.' Abu Bakr laughed suddenly.

'The most ignorant among you is the one who does not learn from the cycles of changes in time and place.' Muhammad's eyes sparkled with new parables.

'Doesn't belief in one God dissolve the mists of ignorance, Prophet?' Umar ibn Khattab voiced his own doubts. 'This belief alone, I am sure, eases the burden of our difficulties, grants us success, and lends our hearts the fulfilment of our wishes.'

'Surely it does, Umar. As long as you wish for others what you wish for yourself. Belief is the knowledge of the heart, the words of the tongue, and the actions of the body,' was Muhammad's Sufic response. 'There is an organ in the body that, if righteous, ensures that the whole system will be righteous, and if corrupt, makes the whole body corrupt. This organ is the heart: the spiritual heart. And the heart of the one where love abides, leaving no room for anything else, is called a Sufi, the spiritual heart of anyone whose creed is love alone.'

'There comes the hypocrite,' Zaid hissed under his breath, noticing the approach of Abdallah ibn Ubbay, accompanied by his son Abdullah.

'Happy are those whose own faults preoccupy them so much they have no time to think about the faults of others,' Muhammad reproved.

'I have brought water for your ablutions, Prophet.' Abdallah ibn Ubbay lowered an earthen bowl at Muhammad's feet.

'Have you ever seen, Abdallah, the like of what you have seen today?' Muhammad smiled, temporarily ignoring Abdallah's comment.

'I have never seen anything like it, Prophet,' Abdallah ibn Ubbay responded.

'Then why did you say what you said last night?' Muhammad asked genially.

'I was misunderstood, Prophet. But I have asked forgiveness of God for what I said,' Abdallah ibn Ubbay murmured contritely.

'Forgive me, Abdallah, for presuming,' Muhammad murmured. 'The Prophet too must beg Allah's forgiveness for—'

His thoughts were sucked into a whirlwind of sand, out of which galloped an impetuous rider – no other than Urwah from the Banu Shemite clan.

'Here we meet again, Muhammad!' Urwah alighted from his steed. 'I have come straight from an assembly that the Quraysh are holding. Their decision is plain and simple: they don't want you and your rabble to enter the city of Mecca. They say you'll have to cut your way through a wall of swords.'

'Surely you must have received our message, Urwah, that we have come as pilgrims of peace.' Muhammad dipped his hands into the bowl of water to wash them. 'We seek permission from the Meccans to enter the city peacefully. All we wish is to perform our pilgrimage rites and then return to Medina.'

Everyone present was awed by the warmth of the love in Muhammad's gaze. Othman ibn Affan was seated to his right. He pressed the edge of the Prophet's cloak, with which he had dried his hands, to his lips. The bowl of water, too, was passed from hand to hand like some holy relic; the pilgrims took small sips from it, as if tasting the purity of his holiness. Urwah, watching the devoted scene, was jolted out of his stunned silence. His voice exploded forth with sudden violence.

'You call these pilgrims, Muhammad? All these dolts and cowards?' Urwah jeered. 'The winds of calamity will whip them like swirling sands. We will cut you all to pieces if you dare to come near the holy grounds of Mecca.'

'Might I repeat, Urwah, that we have no intention of fighting,' Muhammad began calmly, as before. 'We are pilgrims of peace, but if the Meccans bar our way, we will be forced to fight. This is my message to the pious guardians of the Kaaba: that my offer of peace is sincere, and if they want it they should make sure they leave the way clear for us.' His eyes shone with a mixture of challenge and warning.

'Pilgrims of peace, you say, Muhammad?' Urwah leapt forward, grabbing Muhammad's beard.

A canopy of arms pinned Urwah down in a flash. More than a hundred pilgrims circled around him with their hunting swords unsheathed. Muawwidh was quick to strike a blow to Urwah's face with his fist before Muhammad could say a word.

'Take your hand off his beard, while it is still yours to take!' Muawwidh's eyes flashed murder.

Overwhelmed with sadness, Muhammad commanded his followers to sheathe their swords, and waved Urwah farewell. Urwah could barely murmur 'Forgive me, Muhammad' before he fled. The Muslims stood spewing rage, as he galloped away as if pursued by demons. Muhammad closed his eyes and spoke.

'*Lo! the first Sanctuary appointed for mankind was that at Becca, a blessed place, a guidance to the peoples; wherein are plain memorials of Allah's guidance, a place where Abraham stood to pray, and whosoever entereth is safe. And pilgrimage to the House is a duty unto Allah for mankind, for him who can find a way thither. As for him who disbelieveth, let him know that, lo! Allah is Independent of all creatures*' (3:96–97). Muhammad opened his eyes, his gaze meeting Umar ibn Khattab's.

'Are we expected to just sit here, Prophet, ignoring the emissaries from Mecca who come here armed with insults? Is it your wish for us to be slaughtered without defending our honour?' was Umar ibn Khattab's desperate appeal.

'No, Umar, no,' Muhammad murmured sadly. 'But remember this: the one who wields his sword with restraint conserves his energy, while the one who hacks away is quickly wearied. It's the same with time. He who submits to its dictates will be saved, and he who chafes restlessly under its blade will go astray. Much is gained by peace, and much is lost in war. Only when every effort for peace is exhausted is fighting permitted. We will sue for peace once again.' He looked at Khira. 'Take a swift horse, my noble Khira, and fly to Mecca. Convince the Meccans of our peaceful intentions with the spears of your wisdom and eloquence.'

'Yes, Prophet,' Khira murmured, tramping away to find the fastest horse.

'These Meccans are malicious sinners. They don't deserve your compassion. We should not forgive, nor should we sue for peace!' Umar ibn Khattab intoned bitterly.

'*Say: O My servants who have transgressed against their souls! Despair not of the Mercy of Allah. For Allah forgives all sins. For He is oft-Forgiving, Most Merciful*' (39:53). Muhammad recited the revelation in response, and got to his feet wearily.

'Surely, Prophet, they will not agree to peace. They prefer to subject us to hardships and difficulties,' Bilal commented.

'I know otherwise, my Bilal.' Muhammad embraced him. 'Success follows patience. Opportunity follows hardship. And ease follows difficulties.' He turned on his heel, seeking the refuge of his tent. 'Time for rest and prayer. Keep your swords sheathed, you pilgrims of peace,' he commanded over his shoulder.

Three whole days of patient waiting followed in Hudaybiyah. Muhammad, along with a few of his followers, sat under the Lote Tree of Peace and hoped. Khira, who had been sent as an emissary of peace, returned, though he had nearly been killed by the angry mob while escaping and his horse had been hamstrung by Ikrimah.

'My wisdom and eloquence didn't win us peace, Prophet, but a man better protected than I am may yet succeed!' was Khira's cry of despair on his return.

Muhammad dispatched Othman ibn Affan, entrusting him with another message of peace, hoping that the Meccans would relent. The same night, the pilgrims' camp was attacked by a group of marauders. They were captured, then released when Muhammad forgave them. Othman had still not returned, and his absence was causing fear that he might have been murdered.

And then Abdallah ibn Ubbay was visited by the Meccans' secret envoy. The envoy made him his confidant purely to win his support.

'Urwah is chastened, I tell you. He is supporting our cause and is in favour of peace, though he is hounded by wild and violent objections,' Abdallah ibn Ubbay was recounting. 'It is hard to imagine Urwah saying the things he said. *I have seen Chrosoes of Persia in his kingdom, Caesar in his court, and Negus in his palace, but never have I witnessed even a semblance of the devotion Muhammad commands.*'

'May Allah keep us firm in our devotion to the Prophet, even if we disagree – and we do,' Ali sighed to himself.

'Your devotion, my friends, must never become veneration. For Allah alone is worthy of veneration, and we worship only Him.' Muhammad flashed a warm look at Abdallah ibn Ubbay. 'Though your devotion to me, Abdallah, is praiseworthy, after your secret tryst with the envoy from Mecca. He offered you alone the privilege of pilgrimage; and your response? Won't you share it with everyone gathered here now, my friend?'

'I declined, of course,' Abdallah ibn Ubbay murmured bashfully. 'I told him I couldn't think of performing this pilgrimage without the Prophet himself leading.'

'After this act of deceit on their part, Prophet, and their causing rifts amongst us, how can you still insist on suing for peace?' Umar ibn Khattab protested. 'Yesterday you named this Lote Tree of Peace *Irak*, Prophet. What would you name it today?'

'If not Iron-wood, then Shajar, or better yet, Shajar-Rizwan,' Muhammad murmured.

'What if Othman is…' Umar ibn Khattab's concern was checked by the sudden thundering of hooves. All eyes turned to see the bold riders coming into view.

The sand-swept desert was caught in a whirlwind of dust-clouds. The four riders were quick to dismount, Othman at the front. Next to him was Suhail ibn Amr, followed by Mikraz and Huweidib.

'I have failed to change the minds of the Qurayshites concerning the pilgrimage, Prophet,' Othman ibn Affan confessed. 'But they insisted on sending their emissaries to discuss the terms of a peace treaty. I have read its terms. It reeks of pride, favours their greed, and imposes unjust restrictions on us.'

'Now, now! Is this the way to offer hospitality to your own kinsmen?' Suhail ibn Amr interceded with a complacent smile.

'Hospitality, you say?' Othman ibn Affan cried angrily, avoiding the disapproving look in Muhammad's eyes. 'After what you did to Khira and his mount? Would you like me to repeat the story of how our pilgrim escaped the brutality of your mob?'

'Ikrimah was the one who hamstrung Khira's horse. Ikrimah's father was killed at Badr, as you know. Any man of reason would weigh this act of his somewhat kindly in comparison to his great loss,' Suhail ibn Amr offered, smiling to himself.

'Reason? The men of the Quraysh don't even know what reason means!' Othman ibn Affan's rage was mounting. 'Did the Quraysh heed the reason of the leader of the Hulays, the only man of sense? What he said, I want to repeat in front of my brethren. *You men of Quraysh, it was not for this that we made an alliance of agreement with you. Is a man who comes to do honour to the house of al-Llah, to be excluded from it? By Him who holds my life in His hands, either you let Muhammad do what he has come to do, or I shall take away my troops to the last man.*'

'Those alliances are our private concern, not to be discussed,' Suhail ibn Amr began thoughtfully. 'We are here for the sake of a peace treaty. Let your Prophet decide, Othman, whatever he deems right. I have brought two witnesses with me, Muhammad, if you are willing to sign this treaty of peace.'

'Read the terms of this peace treaty, Suhail, and may the Hand of God guide us all.' Muhammad intoned.

'Yes, Muhammad.' Suhail ibn Amr unrolled the parchment of tanned leather. 'The Muslims will go home this year without performing the pilgrimage. Next year, they can come, but they cannot stay in Mecca longer than three days. They cannot take any of the Muslims with them who already live in Mecca. On the other hand, they will not stand in the way of any of their own who might wish to remain behind. Should any Meccan man defect to Medina, the Muslims will hand him over to the Meccans. But if any of the Medinese Muslims rejoin the Meccans, the Meccans will not restore them to the Muslims. The Arab tribes will be at liberty to enter into alliance with whichever party they choose.'

'I agree to the terms proposed,' Muhammad consented. 'Lend your pen and inkstand to Ali, Suhail, and he will write my consent to the terms proposed. Write this, Ali: *In the name of God, the Merciful, the Compassionate*—'

'I've never seen any treaty written this way, Muhammad!' Suhail ibn Amr interrupted. '*In Thy name, O God*, is the proper expression, as practised by us.'

'Write that then, Ali. *In Thy Name, O God*,' Muhammad dictated. 'Under that, write *These are the terms of peace between Muhammad, the Messenger of Allah, and*—'

'If we believed you to be the Messenger of Allah, Muhammad, there would be no need for this peace treaty,' Suhail ibn Amr scoffed.

A rumble of protests was let loose from the pilgrims' lips, but Muhammad was quick to silence them with a gentle wave of his arm.

'Write this then Ali. *These are the terms between Muhammad ibn Abdallah and Suhail ibn Amr*,' Muhammad commanded.

'I dare not erase *Messenger of Allah*, since I have already written it, Prophet,' Ali appealed.

'Then point out where you wrote it, and I will erase it myself, Ali.'

After this inscription was blotted out by Muhammad, Ali finished writing the treaty as dictated by the Prophet. The Lote Tree of Peace itself seemed to be watching, wafting forth a heavy scent all of a sudden. Ali sat making a copy of this peace treaty in the perfumed air. Both copies were signed and witnessed by members of each party. The treaty was accepted by Abu Bakr, Umar ibn Khattab and Othman ibn Affan on behalf of the Muslims, and by Suhail ibn Amr, Mikraz and Huweidib on behalf of the Qurayshites.

No sooner was the treaty signed than Suhail's son, whom he had imprisoned for becoming a Muslim, was seen approaching, dragging his fetters behind him as if carried by the fury of invisible sandstorms.

'Take me with you to Medina, Prophet,' Abu Jandal could barely plead. 'Look at my body, the scars of torture and beating – I will die in Mecca.'

'This agreement was signed before my infidel of a son came here, Muhammad, and you have no right to take him with you.' Suhail ibn Amr waved the peace treaty before the stunned eyes of all present, dragging his son towards his mount.

'Am I to be betrayed to this tyrant of a father, Muslims?' Abu Jandal cried, unable to struggle against the mighty grips of three men – Mikraz and Huweidib had joined Suhail. 'Am I to be returned to the unbelievers?'

'Be patient, Abu Jandal. Allah will soon provide relief and means of escape for you, and for those of you who are helpless and oppressed,' Muhammad consoled him, his gaze following the horses as they raced back towards Mecca.

'Why did you make us sign and witness this deplorable piece of paper, Prophet?' Umar ibn Khattab was the first to protest. 'It's so unfair and degrading to us all!'

'Because, Umar, insight into the future is denied to most of us, yet I have seen it clear as daylight,' Muhammad responded tranquilly. 'Have you forgotten the revelation? *And if thy enemy incline to peace, incline thou also to it*' (8:61).

'Didn't you say before we started from Medina, Prophet, that we would be performing the rites of pilgrimage at the Kaaba?' Abdallah ibn Ubbay cried haughtily.

'But I never said that we would do it this year, did I?' Muhammad intoned.

'Are you not the Messenger of Allah, Prophet?' Umar ibn Khattab stood defiant.

'Yes, I am,' Muhammad affirmed, the light of prophecy in his eyes smouldering.

'Are we, the Muslims, not those surrendering to the will of God?' The flames of inquisition were kindling in Umar ibn Khattab's eyes.

'We certainly are, Umar.'

'Then why have we compromised our religion for injustice and unfairness?' Umar ibn Khattab was swept along in the storm of his inner rage and bitterness.

'We have not, Umar. We have surrendered to the will of Allah in conformity with our faith and belief.' Muhammad's voice was tender, though his eyes flashed a mild rebuke. 'You are raving, Umar. Be silent and be comforted.'

'How can I be comforted, Prophet, after this treaty of injustice and humiliation? Why did you agree? I can't understand,' Umar ibn Khattab protested.

'Allah exalts the humble, and humbles the proud,' Muhammad intoned sadly. 'Understanding comes through the humility gained after much suffering. If you practise the art of humility you strengthen your own belief. The simple reason for signing this peace treaty, if you must know, is that I am the servant of Allah, and as His messenger I obey only His commands, and He will always be my guide and protector. We will perform the traditional rites of pilgrimage right here on these sands in Hudaybiyah. Go, shave your heads, then we will slaughter the sacrificial camels.'

A sullen silence confronted the Prophet. Muhammad repeated his appeal to them to shave their heads, this time loud and commanding, but no one spoke or stirred.

'You won't shave your heads, my friends?' Muhammad murmured to himself, sensing the fire of mutiny and defiance in his followers.

Muhammad turned on his heel. He was barely aware that he was entering his wife's tent, his features ravaged by sorrow.

'I have failed, Umm Salmah; I have failed. Did you see what happened? I can't make them understand. They won't listen. Now that I'm so used to their devotion and obedience, I have forgotten the art of purifying their hearts of all bitterness and resentment. Where do I begin?' Muhammad closed his eyes.

'I have heard and watched, Prophet,' Umm Salmah consoled. 'Didn't you tell us there is no such thing as failure, only the ladder of learning one must keep climbing? They are still devoted to you, Prophet, and will obey.'

'Will they?' Muhammad smiled, tears shimmering in his eyes, while his thoughts painted Umm Salmah in the semblance of Khadija, as if his beloved had returned.

'Have you lost faith in Allah, Prophet?' Umm Salmah smiled back. 'Didn't you teach me, there is a polish for everything to take away the rust, and the polish for the heart is the remembrance of Allah?'

'My heart is much like any other man's, dear Salmah, and I have suffered.' Muhammad's look was sad. 'And yet, the sufferings of my followers are greater than mine, for I can't appease their fears and doubts. The burden of wisdom is too heavy for their shoulders, and understanding comes only by the grace of God.'

'You can't make fourteen hundred men do something they don't want to do, Prophet, but you can make them look silly.' Umm Salmah's eyes twinkled with mirth. 'Go out and perform the rites of pilgrimage on your own, then slaughter your garlanded camel on a spot where everyone can watch you offering the sacrifice, and, be assured, they will all be watching. They will join you. That's my prophecy, Prophet.'

'By Allah, Salmah, you are wise beyond your years!' Muhammad's face was transformed with joy. 'The Prophet kneels before your beauty and wisdom.'

The blaze of early dusk crept down the hillside, as Muhammad emerged from his tent. The pilgrims, though pretending to be indifferent, were watching him. His feet came to a slow halt under the Lote tree, and he began the rites of pilgrimage.

Muhammad clipped his nails, then slowly began shaving his head. He chose the camel which Abu Jahl had lost at the battle of Badr, and drove his sword into the back of its head. Then Muhammad abandoned himself to his ritual of prayers and prostrations.

Something was stirring inside the hearts of the pilgrims. They could hear Muhammad offering thanks to Allah, and their hearts longed to join him in performing his rites, even outside the Kaaba.

'Here I am, O Lord! Here I am at Thy service!' Bilal's deep-throated song was picked up by others, who thundered down bolts of joy and exhilaration.

The desert came alive, witnessing the obedience of camels being sacrificed. A prayer of blessing flooded from Muhammad's heart.

'May Allah have mercy on those who shave their heads!'

'What about those, Prophet, who shaved the heads of the others?' A flurry of happy protests rippled forth.

Umm Salmah, accompanied by Umm Hani and Nasiba, had ventured out to watch. The pilgrims were protesting still, chanting their own refrain, and demanding the blessing for those who had shaved the heads of the others.

'Allah have mercy on the cutters too!' Muhammad granted them a blessing, his features glowing with the warmth of joy and gratitude.

'Why did you pray only for the shavers first, Prophet?' Khira asked.

'Because those who shaved their heads on their own had no doubts.' Muhammad's voice was snatched by a gale of wind. It scooped the pilgrims' hair into the bowl of a whirlwind, and carried it beyond the gullies of Hudaybiyah.

'Look, Prophet, the wind is carrying the hair to Mecca!' Nasiba cried in astonishment, snatching a handful as a token.

'*Verily, We have won for thee an unbounded victory. In token that God forgiveth thy earlier and thy later faults. And fulfilled His goodness to thee, and guided thee on the right path*' (48:1–2), Muhammad recited.

An astonishing sense of peace descended upon them all, as if time itself had come to a standstill. Muhammad was the first to stir, sailing towards Umm Salmah.

'*It is He who sent down the Sakina into the hearts of the believers. That they might add faith to their faith*' (48:4). Muhammad claimed Umm Salmah's hand.

'*When the unbelievers set in their hearts the fierceness of pagandom. Then God sent His Sakina upon His Messenger and believers, and fastened to them the word of God-fearing*' (48:26). Muhammad's voice was reaching the heart of Hudaybiyah, it seemed.

Chapter 15

The Lamp of Love in Arabia
The End of 628 AD

Muhammad's heart was light this particular evening, as he sat with his followers in the courtyard of Masjid Al-Nabi. He had closed his eyes, contemplating his recent marriage that afternoon to the sister of a prince from Najd to strengthen their alliance. His wives had whisked the young bride away after the feast, offering to get her ready for the nuptial bed. But the Prophet was not deceived; he could see the mischief in their eyes.

His thoughts had strayed down the alleys of the past four months since the signing of the peace treaty in Mecca.

Abu Bakr's wife, Umm Ruman, had died suddenly. Abu Baseer, who had contrived escape from Mecca and sought refuge in Medina, had been pursued by the Meccan envoys. They had come demanding his return under the terms of the peace treaty. Muhammad had no choice but to hand him over, as he had done before with Abu Jandal. He had comforted him with the same words: *Be of good cheer, Baseer, God will surely find thee a way out.* While Abu Baseer was being escorted to Mecca under guard, he had seized the sword of his captor and killed him. The other guard, a freedman by the name of Kawthaur, had followed him back to Medina. Muhammad had been seated in the mosque when Kawthaur stormed in, declaring that Abu Baseer had murdered the guard. Abu Baseer was the next to materialise.

'O Prophet of God, you fulfilled your promise to the Meccans. You returned me to them, and Allah has delivered me out of their captivity,' Abu Baseer confessed.

'Alas for your mother, Abu Baseer! What a firebrand you are!' Muhammad remembered his own words, peeling afresh the scene of that conversation.

'The arms and the armour of my deceased captor are in my possession too, Prophet! A great bounty, and camels too,' Abu Baseer had boasted. 'All this is yours, Prophet, for you to divide into five parts, and distribute amongst the Muslims.'

'Sorry, Abu Baseer, but you must go back with your plunder, lest the Meccans accuse me of breaking the terms of the peace treaty.' Then Muhammad had turned his attention to the terrified freedman. 'Abu Baseer is in your custody, Kawthaur. Take him back to the people who sent you, and return all the bounty to them too.

'I value my life, Prophet!' was Kawthaur's cry of agony. 'My strength is no match for Abu Baseer's. I dare not take him back.'

'If you refuse to take him back, he is free to go wherever he chooses,' Muhammad had advised. 'You can't stay in Medina, Abu Baseer, but go wherever providence takes you. May Allah guide you and keep you under His mercy and protection.'

Abu Baseer had found a home on the shores of the Red Sea. Soon, Abu Jandal had contrived escape and joined him. More than seventy Meccans had embraced Islam voluntarily and made their sanctuary there. They were surviving by looting passing rich Meccan caravans.

Othman ibn Affan's half-sister had escaped Mecca too and sought asylum in Medina. She was adamant on staying and declared she wouldn't return to Mecca, whatever the Prophet said.

Muhammad's thoughts were reaching deep into his soul now. He remembered how he had decided to extend his message of Islam to the leaders of the neighbouring kingdoms. He had made his green agate ring into a silver seal with the inscription *Muhammad, the Messenger of God* to be stamped on letters dispatched to the leaders of the various nations. The words of that letter came alive in his thoughts.

In the name of Allah, the Merciful, the Beneficent. Say: O People of the Book, come to an equitable word between us and you, that we shall serve none but Allah, and that we shall not associate aught with Him, and that some of us shall not take others for lords beside Allah (3:64). *We strive towards welding various systems into one universal religion, and humanity into one universal brotherhood. In order to eliminate all differences, we should take whatever is common to all religions and build the foundations of a superstructure in harmony with the fundamental truth. This way, all religions of the world can meet on common ground, and settle their disputes in an amicable manner.*

The names of the kings to whom this message was sent were Heraclius, the Caesar of Rome; Muqawqis of Egypt; Chrosoes of Persia; and Negus of Abyssinia. The silent parade came to a sudden halt in Muhammad's thoughts with the drumming sound of arguments so very familiar to his senses, even when his eyes were closed.

'How can we benefit from your wisdom, Prophet, if you spend all this time contemplating, not teaching us about faith and prayer?' Abdal Kabah asked.

'An hour of contemplation is better than a year of prayer, Abdal.' Muhammad opened his eyes. 'None of your faith will be rectified unless your hearts are made right. Nor will your hearts be rectified unless your tongues are made right. Nor will your tongues be rectified unless your actions are made right.'

'But Muslims suffer such trials, Prophet. In Mecca, I mean; how can that be rectified?' Abdal Kabah appeared to be questioning his own faith.

'Whenever Allah loves a devotee, Abdal, He subjects him to ordeals. Should he endure patiently, Allah singles him out;

should he be content, Allah purifies him.' The Sufic light in Muhammad's eyes was bright and shuddering.

'Are we not patient, Prophet, when our brethren are dragged back to Mecca? This peace treaty imposes torture and suffering upon them.' Abdal Kabah could not be pacified. 'I myself will have to return now that the mourning period for my mother is over. Do we still have to be kind to the Meccans, as you tell us to be?'

'Have trust in Allah, and be comforted, Abdal. You will not have to go back to Mecca. Be kind to people whether they deserve your kindness or not. If your kindness reaches the deserving, good for you. If your kindness reaches the undeserving, take joy in your compassion. Allah will not show mercy to him who does not show mercy to others. Remember always, the believer is a mirror to the believer.'

'With our doubts and weaknesses, Prophet, how can we seek Allah's mercy, nurture piety, and worship Him with all devotion?' Abdallah ibn Ubbay asked.

'Have mercy on people, Abdallah, so you may receive mercy. Forgive people so you may be forgiven.' Muhammad smiled. 'Do not commit yourself to lengthy discussions on religion. Such talk succeeds only in making religion an arena of conflicts and complexities. Allah has made religion easy and simple for us. We should avoid greed, jealousy and arrogance. Piety lies in purifying your body and soul by shunning evil actions and evil thoughts. If you have behaved badly, then do a good deed right away to cancel out the bad one. Do not make yourself a judge between two people.'

The dusk's peace was splintered by men on horseback coming into view. Emissaries from Mecca were cantering towards the congregation. Suhail ibn Amr, and Muayiya, the son of Abu Sofyan, were soon recognised by most of the congregation, and the two men following them were also identified by some as the brothers of Umm Khultum.

'We have come to take Umm Khultum back to Mecca, in accordance with the terms specified in the peace treaty at Hudaybiyah,' Suhail ibn Amr demanded.

'It is almost half a year since that peace treaty was signed, Amr…' Muhammad left a pause before voicing his decision, 'and still you are not familiar with its terms? Surely you have not forgotten those terms, and none of those apply to Umm Khultum. She is free to stay in Medina.'

'How so, Muhammad? Are you refusing to honour this peace treaty?' Suhail ibn Amr exclaimed. 'I know the wording of that treaty. It states that anyone who leaves Mecca and becomes a Muslim must be returned into the custody of the Meccans.'

'Specifically, it says "any man", Amr,' Muhammad intoned kindly. 'There is no mention of women in any clause. So Umm Khultum is not bound by this treaty.'

'But…!' Muayiya exclaimed. Suhail stood there aghast. Muayiya began again, scornfully. 'You have made a mockery of every clause in that peace treaty, Muhammad, to suit your own purpose. All those men who escaped from Mecca to Medina? You let them go free, Muhammad, and now they have turned into bandits, looting our caravans. The chief culprits amongst them? Abu Jandal and Abu Baseer.'

'I handed them over to the Meccans, didn't I, Muayiya?' Muhammad began kindly. 'Since your own men failed in their duty to guard the victims of that peace treaty, who is to blame, tell me?'

'Victims, you say, Muhammad! They are renegades—'

Muayiya's fury was checked by a desperate appeal from the lips of Suhail. 'No need to argue, Muayiya! We are more in need of peace than Muhammad.' Suhail ibn Amr shifted his attention to the Prophet. 'It is true, Muhammad, that this peace treaty, though designed by us, has benefited you the most. It's also true that you honoured every word, and we failed to protect our interests. Considering all this, the leaders of the Quraysh have proposed amendments. If it is acceptable to you, Muhammad, they wish to cancel the clause which forces Meccan men to return to Mecca if they choose to flee and become Muslims.'

'Any offer of peace is always welcomed by me, be assured, Suhail. My message to your leaders is that I accept the amendment,' Muhammad consented.

'Well, I must return straight away with this message of peace.' Suhail ibn Amr turned on his heel, urging his stunned companions to follow.

'May the peace of God go with you,' Muhammad muttered. 'This amendment allows us the freedom to call our men to Medina; those who couldn't stay here and have turned fugitive.' He looked at Zaid. 'Send a letter to Abu Baseer, my son, to say that he and his companions are free to return to Medina. Allah's blessings are with us, and we must nurture the spirit of love and peace amongst all.'

'How can we nurture the spirit of peace, Prophet, when Beni Nadir of Khaiber is plotting to wage war on us?' Abdallah ibn Ubbay exclaimed.

'Allah is your trustworthy friend, Abdallah. Have faith in this revelation.' Muhammad smiled enigmatically. '*Before long Allah will bring about friendly relations between you and those whom you regard as your enemies. And Allah is powerful. And Allah is Forgiving, Merciful*' (60:7).

'What things in the world appeal to you most, Prophet, besides love, peace and friendship?' Abdallah ibn Ubbay asked.

'Little children, women and beautiful scents. Those all appeal to me, but I have found complete contentment in prayer.' Muhammad's eyes were shining.

'I pray continuously!' Wahb boasted. 'I do not eat meat, and I am unmarried.'

'Praise be to Allah!' Muhammad laughed. 'I eat meat, I fast, I keep vigil, and I sleep, and I am married. Marriage is incumbent upon Muslims, and whosoever does not marry is not one of us.

With this little injunction to ponder upon, I must leave, and welcome my new bride before—'

His words were disrupted by the sudden arrival of Dinah Kalbi, who had been sent to Rome with the message of Islam to Caesar.

'Rome is a mighty kingdom, Prophet. Its people are proud, yet courteous,' Dinah Kalbi murmured hastily. 'The Emperor Heraclius read your letter with great interest. He shared our message of Islam with his viziers in an open court, and compared it with the Christian doctrines of their own, but his men were not interested in similarities or comparisons between Islam and Christianity. So, Emperor Heraclius entrusted me with this message to you, Prophet, that he respects the teachings of Islam, but he will not be able to share it with his Christian subjects, lest they turn against him.'

'An honest and honourable emperor!' Muhammad applauded cheerfully. 'Our God and the God of the Christians is one and the same. Next time, anyone delivering the message of Islam should not forget to stress that Islam is not a new religion, but an extension of the faith practised by the Jews and the Christians. Allah is the creator of all the created. Love is our religion, peace our creed, and unity our belief, proclaiming the Oneness of one God in all faiths.'

'How do we glorify Allah, Prophet, if people do not accept our message of Islam?' Umar ibn Khattab arched his eyebrows, baffled.

'Don't we all glorify Allah, consciously or unconsciously?' Muhammad sang joyfully. '*The seven heavens and the earth and all that is therein extol Him, nor is there anything which doth not glorify Him with praise, yet we understand not their glorification. Lo, He is ever Clement, Forgiving* (17:44). Speak to everyone at their own level of understanding, Umar, and you will—'

His train of thought was disrupted once again by the breezy approach of Zubayr ibn Awwam. He laughed. 'Allah is testing my patience this evening, as all my envoys are returning at once, from different parts of the world!'

'Glad tidings, Prophet.' Zubayr ibn Awwam announced. 'King Negus of Abyssinia has accepted Islam. Jafar was there to witness the miracle. And King Negus is sending him to Medina as a worthy escort for Umm Habiba.'

'Allah be glorified! Another bride on the way.' Muhammad's joy was boundless. 'Though I can't get to the one who is already married to me.'

'That reminds me, Prophet,' Dinah Kalbi began hastily. 'Umm Habiba's father, Abu Sofyan, was at the court of Emperor Heraclius when I was there. The emperor questioned him about your character, Prophet, and his enmity towards us didn't stop him from telling the truth. He said that you came from a noble family, and that your followers were daily growing in numbers. That you always tell the truth, and that you have never broken a promise.'

'His heart is being purified, it is obvious. May Allah guide him towards love!' Muhammad murmured a prayer, spotting another envoy as he'd predicted.

'I thought I would be the first to return to Medina,' Hindal muttered.

'All are first who arrive this evening, my son. They are all endowed with grace and eloquence,' Muhammad breathed tenderly. 'Come; Zubayr is making room for you to sit with me. Success is shining in your eyes, but we need to drink it from your lips.'

'I was received by Muqawqis in Egypt most cordially, Prophet,' Hindal smiled. 'He read your letter with enthusiasm. I am not sure about his views on Islam, but he told me he is sending his own envoys with a letter and precious gifts. Before I left, the Egyptian governor told me that the gifts which he promised include Egyptian linen and jewellery, mules and horses, and two Copt sisters.'

'Allah is beautiful and bountiful! May He bestow wealth upon Muqawqis.' Muhammad joined his hands, offering a silent prayer.

'I saw my Lord in the most beautiful forms!' Hassan the poet sang happily.

'Everything perishes except the face of God!' was Muhammad's mystical refrain. 'Heaven and earth contain Me not, but the heart of My faithful contains Me!'

Everyone was enveloped in an aura of mystical light; the dusk lowered a peaceful veil of silence. No one noticed the slow approach of three men.

Ali was the first to see them, recognising only Abdallah ibn Rudafeh.

'Forgive me, Prophet, for not returning alone, but rather being escorted by these Persian guards,' was Abdallah ibn Rudafeh's murmur of apology. 'Chrosoes of Persia took offence at your letter, tearing it to pieces. Then he commanded that I be accompanied by two guards, who would deliver his message to you, Prophet.'

'Be comforted, Abdallah. Chrosoes didn't know what he was doing. Yet I know his intentions, and the intentions of these men. And yet again, no harm will come to us.' Muhammad's eyes shone with love. 'The king was incensed because he couldn't bear to see the name *Allah* above his name on the letter.' His gaze shifted to the Persian guards. 'Am I correct in guessing the cause of your king's rage?'

'Yes,' one guard could barely murmur.

'Our king has commanded us to arrest you, and to bring you back to Persia, as our—'

The other guard managed to deliver only half of the message, his heart thundering.

'Your King Chrosoes is no more.' Muhammad got to his feet. 'When you return to Persia, pray over the grave of your king, so that Allah may forgive him for his pride and arrogance.' He left for the sanctuary of his humble quarters.

The Prophet approached the bridal chamber of his new wife, Esma. He stood there waiting, listening to the litany of his thoughts. Esma was the sister of a princely desert chief from Najd. Even before Muhammad had seen his bride, he had learnt from the fits of jealousy shown by his wives that Esma was young and beautiful. Now, as he stood outside the bridal hut, he wondered if he had succeeded in quelling their envy.

Seemingly, the wives of the Prophet were reconciled to the idea of welcoming another bride, but secretly they had devised a plan to send this princess back to Najd. Aisha had combed her hair, while Hafsa hennaed her feet and hands. Sweetly, they had offered her advice. 'When the Prophet comes near to embrace you, you should resist, and he will think highly of you. Say to him, "I take refuge from thee in Allah."' Esma, the gullible bride, overwhelmed by their attentions, had memorised that phrase, not realising that by uttering it she would be stating that she had no wish to have physical relations with her husband.

Ignorant of the plot concocted by his wives, Muhammad approached Esma trancelike, holding out his arms, his eyes shining.

'I take refuge from thee in Allah!' Esma sang, her face flushed.

Muhammad's arms fell limp to his sides, as he stood gazing at her. He thought he heard wrong, and took another step, holding out his arms once again.

'I take refuge from thee in Allah!' Esma repeated her litany.

Muhammad staggered a step further, his eyes smouldering with anguish. He edged closer, holding out his arms a third time, but was buffeted by the same chant of rejection. Abandoning himself over the mat in a dejected heap, he closed his eyes.

'If that is your wish, Esma, you will be escorted back to Najd tomorrow,' Muhammad murmured, hugging his cloak, welcoming blissful sleep.

Muhammad drifted towards his quarters after a solitary walk. Three months, punctuated by more weddings, had floated past since Esma had gone back to Najd. A week after Esma's departure, Jafar had arrived, bringing with him Umm Habiba. The Prophet married her, since she was already his wife by proxy. Another week and the gifts from the King of Egypt arrived, including the Copt sisters, Mary and Shirin. They were sent as slave girls, but Muhammad freed them, taking Mary as his own wife, while Shirin was married to the poet, Hassan.

Muhammad had to divide his time into slices, allotting a cyclical day, hour or night to each wife in succession. He was immersed in his contemplations when Hala, Khadija's sister, greeted him. Hala was chirping as usual, singing the praises of her son Abul As and of his wife Zainab, the Prophet's daughter, and of their daughter, Umamah. Muhammad didn't know how long he stood there, but he realised with a sudden jolt that Hala was gone. He did not even notice Aisha standing not too far away. His gaze met hers as she sailed towards him. Her eyes were flashing and he braced himself for another bout of jealousy.

'Hala reminded you of Khadija, Prophet, didn't she?' Aisha flung this accusation. 'By the Lord of Abraham, Prophet, why do you always think about that old, toothless woman? She's been in the grave for a whole decade, if not more!'

'Oh, Aisha, how can you say such cruel things about Khadija? They don't mar her beauty, but they wound me most deeply,' Muhammad appealed. 'Why are you so angry?'

'O dearer than my father and mother, how do you know I am angry?' Aisha tossed her head, defiant and smouldering.

'Because when you aren't angry, you say, "By the Lord of Muhammad", not, "By the Lord of Abraham",' Muhammad murmured soothingly.

'By the Lord of Muhammad, then – didn't Allah replace Khadija with someone better?' Aisha challenged, her cheeks flaming.

'No, indeed, my little fair one!' Muhammad intoned dreamily. 'Allah has not. She believed in me when I was rejected. When the Meccans called me a liar, she proclaimed me truthful. When I was poor, she shared her wealth. There can never be another like Khadija. Allah will cut your tongue off, Aisha, if you keep saying bad things about her.' He smiled.

'I am not a child any more, Prophet, like I was when you convinced me that Allah would cut off my hand for striking Anas. And I believed you!' Aisha declared. 'I am a grown woman now, and I am jealous, yes! More of Khadija than of any of your living wives. You think about Khadija, and you mention her name so often, as if she is still living, and as if no other woman exists for you! Every time you sacrifice a sheep, you send a generous portion to her friends.' She paused. 'Tell me, O Messenger of God, if you were between the two slopes of a valley, one of which had not been grazed, whereas the other had been, on which one would you pasture your flocks?'

'The one which had not been grazed, my little prophetess,' Muhammad murmured, looking piercingly at her.

'Yes, and I am not like your other wives!' Aisha exclaimed, her eyes shining. 'Each one of your wives had a husband before you, except me. Now, tell me, Prophet, who do you love the most?'

'You, of course, Aisha!' Umm Salmah came charging over, loaded with the ammunition of her own jealousy. 'Isn't the Prophet happiest when he is with you?'

'Umm Salmah,' Muhammad could barely murmur.

'We know who is the Prophet's favourite!' Hafsa mocked.

Muhammad drifted away, colliding with Mary as he went. Involuntarily, he pressed her close to him, as if seeking solace. Hafsa was quick to raise a cry of outrage, proclaiming that it was her turn with the Prophet that night, and how dare he embrace Mary? Soon, a pandemonium broke forth among the wives, Zainab and Juwairya joining in. Muhammad swung back to face them all.

'You women are more contemptuous of Allah than of me!' Muhammad's eyes flashed rebukes. 'I shall not visit you for a month.' He stalked out of his courtyard, aiming straight for the mosque, his refuge and sanctuary.

The morning was cool as Muhammad sat meditating inside the turret of his mosque. It had been three weeks since he had chosen this turret as his living quarters, and the populace of Medina was swollen with conjectures. He had adopted silence as his friend. Umar, as was his wont, visited the Prophet every morning, noon and night, and this morning was no exception. He entered the turret, seating himself opposite the Prophet as he had done for the past three weeks.

'Have you decided to divorce your wives, Prophet?' Umar ibn Khattab asked. Getting no response, he continued, 'I am not the only one asking this question, Prophet. Every man in our congregation wants to know. Rumours are multiplying. Do you want your enemies to get hold of the gossip, and use it as a weapon against you, waging wars and creating havoc? Some of them are plotting already, if you want to know.'

Muhammad's lips remained sealed, his eyes hermetically shut, gloom and pallor glistening vividly upon his noble features. He didn't stir or speak.

'If you could answer just one question, Prophet, all the rumours in Medina would stop,' Umar ibn Khattab tossed another appeal. 'Are you so upset that you are willing to divorce your wives?'

Muhammad shook his head, his eyes still closed. Encouraged by this mute sign, Umar ibn Khattab was quick to deliver his news bulletin.

'Abu Bakr will be relieved, Prophet,' Umar ibn Khattab began hastily. 'You wouldn't speak to him, so he has become a pilgrim of the bazaars. He wanders around, forlorn and distraught, searching for something, or going in circles, as if he's circumambulating the Kaaba.' He paused, as Muhammad opened his eyes. 'You must know, Prophet; the Jews of Khaiber are not honouring the peace treaties any more. They are gathering large forces with the intention of launching an attack on Medina. Abdallah ibn Ubbay is covertly in league with them. He's encouraging them to fight, telling them that the Muslims are weak and an easy target, and that they will have no difficulty in conquering Medina. Our spies have confirmed that they have sought the alliance of the Ghatafani tribes. Even the leaders of the Quraysh are in touch with them, inciting them to rebellion, and promising huge funds to help them launch a massive assault. Won't you leave this turret, Prophet, and check their spirit of insurrection before it is too late?'

'In time, Umar, in time.' Muhammad broke his silence. 'Meanwhile, get our men ready. If the reports are true, we can surely defend Medina.'

'That means you are coming home, Prophet!' Umar ibn Khattab exclaimed.

'I didn't say I was going home, Umar,' Muhammad sighed. 'Not until my heart is purified of all the fires of my ego. Not until I fill my heart with love, making sure that there is no room left in there for anything else, not even for a grain of anger. Now leave me – I will return when I return.'

'You shun the comforts of home, Prophet, I know that. But in this turret you have chosen discomfort, and welcome sorrow and solitude. How my heart breaks to see the impression of your rush mattress on your blessed cheeks!' Umar ibn Khattab appealed again. 'Why on earth wouldn't Allah allow His messenger a few comforts? After all, the emperors of Persia and Byzantium live in great opulence.'

'They seek the comforts of this world, Umar. Let that suffice as an answer for the time being.' Muhammad closed his eyes. 'Now leave me. I need a lifetime to ask forgiveness of Allah. My sins are countless, and His mercy boundless.'

Just two days short of a month, Muhammad abandoned his dark hole of a turret, and marched home. Barely had Muhammad's feet touched the mud floor of the courtyard leading towards his quarters than he spotted Aisha sailing towards him.

'I thought you told us you were going away for one whole month?' Aisha teased, smothering her relief and mirth inside her heart.

'This month only has twenty-eight days.' Muhammad cradled her in his arms.

'What made you leave us, Prophet? And who was the one to convince you to come back?' Hafsa floated closer, followed by more of his wives.

'Your jealousies drove me away, and your loves brought me back.' Muhammad stood laughing. 'But save yourselves the trouble of further jealousy, for it would slide over me like water over a smooth pebble.'

'To test that smooth pebble, Prophet, won't you admit you prefer Aisha over all of us?' Umm Salmah challenged.

'Not in the way you think, Salmah.' Muhammad smiled. 'I love you all.'

'How can you say that, Prophet, when your preference for Aisha is known to everyone?' Zainab protested. 'Even the men who request a favour from you – they time their requests on the day you allot to Aisha.'

'Have you ever heard me tell a lie, Zainab?' Muhammad challenged genially. 'My love is boundless, given to you all equally, and unconditionally. If the tongues of the gossip-mongers accuse me of favouring Aisha over others, then know this amongst you: that Allah multiplies my love for everyone a thousand times over when I am with Aisha, simply because of His gift of revelation, which comes to me when I am with Aisha alone.'

'Surely fair curly-haired Mary is the Prophet's favourite, not me?' Aisha's sing-song voice was infused with mirth and mischief.

'Let's not stir the fires of jealousy any more,' Umm Habiba cautioned.

'You are too young to advise us, Habiba,' Juwairya chided her happily. 'But you could extend your wisdom to your father, who keeps saying unkind things about the Prophet since the Prophet married you.'

'I am most eager to hear the unkind words concerning me! What did he say?' Muhammad asked amusedly.

'Her father, Prophet, wrote her a letter, right after you married her. His comment – well, should I...' Mary ventured forth bashfully. 'Well, Prophet, concerning you, he wrote: *That camel is so rampant that no muzzle can restrain him.*'

'A worthy compliment to a Prophet who became the son-in-law of Abu Sofyan!' Muhammad laughed. 'He is not angry with me, and this fact alone is revelation to me.'

'And no revelation came your way, Prophet, after you abandoned us?' Swadah edged closer, her eyes lit up with motherly affection.

'Amongst several, dear Swadah, this particular one is just for you, if not for your jealous brood.' Muhammad's eyes shone with warm tenderness.

Men and women who have surrendered
Believing men and believing women
Obedient men and obedient women
Truthful men and truthful women
Enduring men and enduring women
Humble men and humble women
Men and women who give in charity
Men and women who remember God oft
For them God has prepared forgiveness
And a mighty wage. (33:35)

'Allah be praised, Prophet, that you have come home!' Abu Bakr appeared upon the scene, followed by Umar. 'And also for the gift of revelation – I caught a few words.'

'Is there any revelation about the Jews of Khaiber, Prophet, since they are without a doubt allied with the Ghatafanis and the Qurayshi to disrupt the peace of Medina?' Umar ibn Khattab was quick to voice his concern.

'*Ill feeling is rife amongst them. You count them as one whole, but their hearts are divided*' (59:14). Muhammad's eyes spilled the light of a prophetic vision. 'We march to Khaiber within a week, if all is in readiness?'

'It is, Prophet. Everything is ready,' Abu Bakr confirmed.

'Which of your wives is to accompany you on this campaign, Prophet?' Aisha asked, her eyes flashing a subtle appeal.

'To whoever the lot falls, my Aisha. Draw well, this time,' Muhammad murmured, knowing her thoughts.

'I have tried, Prophet, but the lot never falls in my favour,' Aisha lamented quietly.

'Give me your mantle, Aisha.' Muhammad looked at the black cloak over her shoulders. 'We will march to Khaiber carrying a standard. Our standard will be a black eagle cut out of your mantle. That way, you will be with us, regardless of whether the lot favours you or not.'

'It's all yours, Prophet.' Aisha gave her mantle to him. 'Any other revelation, Prophet, for our sole consolation, that Allah has forgiven us?' she teased.

'No.' Muhammad's eyes creased in mirth. 'But I did hear a voice. It said: *Be charitable to women sprung from your ribs. If you try to straighten a rib, you will break it. Accept women as they are, with all their curvatures.*' He tossed the cloak to Abu Bakr. 'Your daughter's. Make a black eagle out of it!'

'Glory be to Allah and Islam, Prophet!' Abu Bakr exclaimed. 'This mantle will serve us as a lamp of victory.' He bounded out of the courtyard, Umar following.

Umar ibn Khattab, carrying the Black Eagle, was at the head of the Muslim army. They were fifteen hundred men, entering the precincts of Khaiber. Muhammad, astride Qaswa, could hear them splintering through his thoughts, as he reflected on his two weeks of journey from Medina. The lot had fallen in favour of Umm Salmah, and she was a part of this cavalcade, along with the wives of the other soldiers.

'God, but for Thee we never had been guided,

Never had given alms, nor prayed Thy prayer.'

The voice of Aslam ibn Akwa, rising above others, could not be mistaken.

'Allah be praised, Aslam, you have a beautiful voice,' Muhammad complimented over his shoulder. 'Why don't you sing us some camel-songs like the Bedouins sing? They would reach the heart of the hills and the heavens!'

'I did, Prophet, but you didn't hear them! How could you, when no voice can penetrate the gates of your divine contemplations?' Aslam ibn Akwa laughed. 'I sang those old melodies, but Umar told me they were sad and monotonous.'

'With eloquence like that, Aslam, you can open the very gates of Paradise,' Muhammad laughed. 'Don't listen to Umar, his fervour banishes him from the pleasure of enjoying good songs.'

'Prophet!' Umar ibn Khattab could barely protest. His gaze followed the Prophet's, where it had settled on Abu Abs.

'Why are you wearing that ragged cloak, Abu Abs?' Muhammad wondered aloud. 'Didn't you come to me, lamenting that you had no means to join us in this campaign since your cloak was ragged, and you had no camel to ride? Didn't I give you a fine cloak and a camel? How come this cloak of yours looks poorer than the one you were wearing before? What did you do with the cloak I gave you?'

'I sold that cloak for eight dirhems, Prophet,' Abu Abs admitted. 'I left two dirhems with my family, and two I spent to buy dates as provision for the journey. And I paid four for this ragged cloak.'

'Oh, father of Abs, I didn't know you were that poor!' Muhammad laughed. 'But by Him in whose hand is my soul, you shall have an abundance of provisions and leave an abundance for all the members of your family. You shall have so many dirhems that you won't know what to do with them!' His gaze sailed up to the moon. 'We will camp here and resume our journey tomorrow.'

The citadel of Zubayr in Khaiber was bathed in the dew-drop silence of morning, as Muhammad sat talking with his companions outside his tent. Six whole days had slithered past since they had laid siege to the fortress, but their hopes of conquest were as distant as on the first. The leader of the Jews, Kinanah ibn Huqaiq, had been killed and many Muslims wounded. Muhammad looked towards the high mass of the citadel prayerfully.

'Oh Allah! Lord of the seven heavens and of all the things they cover! Lord of the seven earths and all which they sustain! Lord of the evil spirits and of everyone they lead astray! Lord of the winds and of all whom they scatter and disperse! We supplicate Thee to deliver into our hands this city and the riches of all its lands. To Thee we look for aid against these people and against all the perils by which we are encircled.' Muhammad's lips closed, and the red upon his lips glistened vividly.

'Amen, amen!' several voices chanted. 'Allah-hu-Akbar, Allah-hu-Akbar!' The chorus reached the gates of the citadel.

'Make ready for a decisive assault,' Muhammad commanded. 'We will use those palm-tree battering rams we built.'

In a flash, the entire camp was full of activity. The soldiers filed into ranks, heeding the commands of their generals with utmost devotion. Ali was the most prominent amongst them. His horse was invested with the Black Eagle standard, and his scimitar, Dhul Fikar – a gift from the Prophet – was slung proudly at his waist.

The battle began with the fury of a hurricane. The Flower of Judaism, the elite army of the Jews, was intent on guarding the gates of the citadel, chanting, 'Great Jehovah! Great Jehovah!'

'I am Ali the lion! And like a lion howling in the wilderness, I weigh my foes in the giant's balance!'

Ali flung his challenge at a Hebrew warrior called Mahrab, whose size alone would have intimidated the Goliath of Gath. Before Mahrab could land his intended blow, Ali deflected it with an unerring stroke of his scimitar. Mahrab's trident was dislodged from his hands. Ali swiftly struck a mortal blow to his head, cleaving his skull into two equal halves. The Goliath of Khaiber crashed from his horse with a terrible groan.

Ali lost no time in galloping headlong towards the gate of the citadel, which Umar-al Khattar had succeeded in breaching, but who now found himself trapped against a fresh assault from a handful of Jewish soldiers. Ali wrenched a door from its hinges with the strength of a lion and used it as his shield, laughing with relief at the fleeing horde of soldiers. Umar-al Khattar, beside him, liberated from the fear of death, could neither speak nor move, awed and humbled.

'Victory is ours!' the Muslims were chanting.

The Jewish soldiers were laying down their weapons. The citadel gates were flung open to release a flood of men and women, pouring out into the open, their eyes glazed and their lips sealed. Some of the men broke their vows of silence, and sued for peace and protection. Muhammad was quick to divine the intentions of his men, so he raised his sword in appeal, and commanded them.

'Sheathe your swords, my friends! They sue for peace, and peace and protection are gifts from Allah to be shared with all.' Muhammad slung his sword at his waist. His men followed.

As he stood amongst the suppliants, the compassion in his eyes was bright.

'Our leaders are dead, Prophet. Please do not punish us for their folly in breaking the peace treaty!' A venerable man sought Muhammad's attention. 'We will agree to any conditions of peace, and we'll remain forever obedient – just let us stay in our homes. Please don't drive us out of Khaiber.'

'You are wise, my friend. Peace is the only treasure worth gaining and cherishing,' Muhammad murmured. 'If we could learn to love one another, the whole world could live in peace. We'll offer you peace and protection. You are allowed to stay in your homes, and free to cultivate your own lands. Make it known to everyone, whether they are in the city or the wider citadel, that anyone who sought to harm us is forgiven. As a guarantee of this pact between us, we ask in return that you deliver half the yearly harvest of Khaiber to Medina. This earth is God's palace. We are His servants, and He has assigned us certain tasks, which we must perform with devotion, forever obedient to His will, so when we return to Him we are not counted as wayward or negligent. Yet, remember: if we do our jobs well, we do it for the benefit of our souls; if not, it's God's will, whether He punishes us or rewards us.'

'O Prophet of Islam, would you grant me the honour of having dinner at my home tonight, with a few of your friends, of course?' Zainab, the recent widow of Marab, requested. 'I will cook it with my own hands to earn your blessings. I am Zainab, if you are wondering, the unhappy widow of Mahrab. But your generosity towards us all has touched my heart, and I want to show my gratitude.'

'The honour is ours, Zainab,' Muhammad breathed kindly, wondering about the Jewess beside her. 'I accept your generous invitation.' He paused, his gaze falling on the young Jewess. 'Is she your daughter?'

'No, Prophet.' Zainab slipped her arm around her waist. 'She is Safiya, the daughter of the late Huyayy ibn Akhtab, who was the Chief of the Beni Koreiza. She is a widow too; her husband Kinanah ibn Huqaiq died just—'

She didn't continue, as Muhammad had snatched his cloak off his shoulders, and wrapped it around Safiya's.

'She is under my protection. Might she consent to be my wife?' Muhammad looked into the eyes of Safiya. 'Would you be willing to marry me, Safiya?'

'Yes, Prophet,' Safiya murmured in awe.

'My camel Qaswa will kneel before you, Safiya, and bring you to my tent.' Muhammad shifted his attention to his soldiers. 'Allah has granted us this victory, my friends, along with the gifts of peace and forgiveness. Let us retire to our tents to pray for our hearts to be healed, making everyone whole for the love of Allah and mankind.'

'Allah-hu-Akbar! Allah-hu-Akbar!' The symphony of praise was borne aloft, where angels sang their hymns of joy, peace and forgiveness.

The evening arrived too soon, gilding the tent of the Prophet in molten gold. He sat talking with Safiya. Qaswa had kneeled at her feet, as prophesied, and had brought her to his tent as his bride. His gaze was warm, soothing the large welt on her cheek with the intensity of prayer and devotion.

'Is this a birth-mark, Safiya, or did you get hurt somehow?' Muhammad asked.

'It's the mark of man's cruelty, Prophet,' Safiya said. 'I had a dream. I saw a moon hanging in the sky, beneath which lay the city of Medina. The moon began to move towards Khaiber, and fell into my lap. I told this dream to Kinanah, and he slapped me, saying, "You desire Muhammad, the King of Hijaz?" That was two weeks ago.'

'There are many sins in this world, Safiya, but the worst of them all is striking a woman.' Muhammad stroked her cheek tenderly. 'May Allah forgive him.'

'You forgive men more readily than God does, Prophet! Where is God's will?' Safiya murmured to herself.

'This act of forgiveness comes from God, Safiya. It is God's will; He has sent me as a mercy to mankind.' Muhammad averted his gaze. 'And did you desire me, as your unhappy husband accused?' he asked.

'A long, long time ago, Prophet, almost seven years now,' Safiya smiled, 'when I was ten years old, my father and uncle returned from Quba. It was late in the evening, and they started talking about you, discussing your character and features. I was in the room, pretending to be asleep. From their conversation, I could gather you were a prophet, noble and handsome. I immediately adopted you as my idol. I was puzzled on one account, though; that after recounting all your qualities, they said you were an impostor and that they were intent on opposing you.'

'All prophets, since time immemorial, have been opposed and persecuted, Safiya. May Allah forgive those who choose to stay blind and ignorant.' Muhammad smiled. 'Now that you have seen me, do you find me handsome?'

'I chose God and His messenger very willingly, Prophet,' Safiya confessed. 'My imagination was poor! You are more handsome than I thought.'

'Beware of the jealousy of my wives, Safiya,' Muhammad laughed. 'I hope you will find me more handsome when I return from Zainab's dinner. I promised her, but my heart is against it. It feels like some sort of warning I can't explain.'

'Beware, Prophet.' Safiya's heart was thundering. 'Zainab is not known to offer hospitality to anyone, and I am surprised that she did. She is known to be cruel.'

'It is not good to speak ill of anyone behind their back, my Safiya.' Muhammad got to his feet. 'You have much to learn. Trust in Allah is the first step towards learning and understanding. We should pray for those who are unkind and unforgiving, so that Allah's love may reach their hearts. Pray that Allah may guide and protect me. You will be in my thoughts and prayers too, while I dine, and we will return to Medina with joy and peace in our hearts.' He left hurriedly.

An opulent chamber in Zainab's house hosted Ali, Bishr, Abu Bakr, Umar ibn Khattab and the Prophet as honoured guests. Dates, barley cakes, and fresh goats' milk in silver tumblers were served, as hot, steaming dishes were brought in by the servants. Platters of chicken garnished with almonds, and several bowls of curds and vegetables, were just a few of the delectable dishes. Roast lamb on a large platter, wafting the aromas of rare spices, was the first choice of the guests, so Muhammad himself carved it. He had barely tasted a morsel before he spat it out.

'Hold off, my friends! Don't eat – this lamb is poisoned!' Muhammad warned desperately.

But his warning was too late, for Bishr had already swallowed a mouthful, and was writhing in agony. Muhammad stuck his fingers down Bishr's throat to induce vomiting, but he went limp in his arms, emitting only green bile and one last, heart-rending groan. Muhammad tenderly laid Bishr down, and then stood facing the Jewess.

'Why have you done this, Zainab?' An agonised cry escaped Muhammad's lips.

'You have inflicted grievous injuries on my people, Prophet,' Zainab spat. 'You have slain my uncle, my father, my brother, my husband. Therefore, I said to myself, if this man is a Prophet, he will know that the meat is poisoned, and he will not eat it. And if he is an impostor, he will die, and it will be better for the world.'

'May Allah guide you on the path to love, Zainab.' Muhammad's voice was choked with grief. 'Next time you doubt the word of Allah and His mercy, just remember: God saith, *verily My compassion overcometh My wrath*.' He shifted his attention to his companions. 'Let us bury Bishr, and then go back to Medina before Allah's mercy turns to anger. If the seeds of forgiveness turn dry and brittle, no buds of love or hope will ever sprout, making this world ugly and barren.' He closed his eyes, tears flooding down his cheeks in pearls of sorrow.

Chapter 16
Pilgrims at Mecca
Year 629 AD

The Great Soul of Mecca, this particular morning, offered the joy of hope and peace to the pilgrims from Medina, as they performed the rites of pilgrimage. They had returned to Mecca exactly one year after the peace treaty of Hudaybiyah, and this was the third and last day allotted to them by the Meccans.

Muhammad's thoughts were on their own journey. Zainab was forgiven, and so were the plotters who had sought to kill the Muslims. On his return to Medina he was rewarded with the good news that Mary was pregnant. King Chrosoes had assassinated by his son the very night Muhammad had said that the king was dead. Abu Baseer had suddenly fallen ill and died in the middle of his journey towards Medina. Walid, who was accompanying him, had died too. His death was all the more tragic since earlier his camel had stumbled and hurled him against a rock, and he had only injured a single finger. He had written a letter to his brother, Khalid ibn Walid, urging him to accept Islam, and finishing his letter with a couplet:

What art thou but a finger shedding blood
With no wound else upon the path of God.

Here I am at your service, O God! Here I am!

The rite of running between the hills of As-Safa and Al-Marwah seven times was nearly complete, and Muhammad's gaze had turned towards the mountain of Abu Qubays, where the Meccan chiefs were posted, spellbound.

'We are here O Allah! We are here!' This song of ecstasy from the lips of the pilgrims was Muhammad's gift of bliss, as he stood kissing the Black Stone.

His heart had begun to throb with the agony of his longing to enter the Holy House, which was shut and locked by order of the Meccans. On his first day of pilgrimage, he had requested the Keepers of the Kaaba to unlock it, but they had denied him the privilege of entering.

La Illaha illah Allah
Mohammed Ar Rusul Allah.

Bilal had climbed onto the rooftop of the Kaaba, as he had done for the past two days, calling the faithful to prayer three times a day. Muhammad poised himself for prayer, the white ocean of pilgrims behind him following, their devotion and surrender to the will of God and His messenger in perfect harmony, heads turning in unison, bodies bowing together and prostrating.

God is most great, God is most great
I witness that there is no God but God
I witness that Muhammad is the Messenger of God
Come to pray, come to prayer
Come to good work
God is most great, God is most great.

Bilal's call to prayer had ended. Suddenly, a flock of pigeons unfurled their wings, taking flight, splintering the spell of awe and peace.

'Allah is with us, Prophet. I feel His Presence!' Umar ibn Khattab declared.

'Yes.' Muhammad smiled. 'Allah says: if my slave draws near Me by a span, I draw nearer unto him by a cubit. And if he draws nearer to Me by a cubit, I draw nearer to him by a fathom. And if he comes unto Me slowly, I come unto him speedily.' He paused, before reciting, 'It was revealed to this poor slave, Al-Mustafa: *O thou soul which are at peace, return unto thy Lord, with gladness that is thine in Him and His in thee. Enter thou among My slaves, enter thou My paradise* (89:27–30). *Enter into paradise, you and your wives with delight*' (43:70).

'You are the richest of prophets on earth, Prophet; rich in God!' Othman ibn Affan intoned reverently.

'*O mankind! Ye are the poor in relation to Allah. And Allah! He is the Absolute, the Owner of Praise*' (35:15), Muhammad recited in response.

'Everything perisheth but His Face!' Ali sang ecstatically.

'Ali, by Allah, sounds just like the Prophet!' Hassan the poet stood laughing.

'I am the city of knowledge, and Ali is its gate!' Muhammad sang joyfully.

'If Ali has become that gate by worshipping Allah, Prophet, then teach us that mode of worship, so that we too can have access to the city of your knowledge!' Abdallah ibn Ubbay could not help voicing his doubt and astonishment.

'You should worship Allah as if you see Him. And if you see Him not, He still sees you. That's the true mode of worship, Abdallah. Practise it, and you will gain knowledge beyond your imagination.' Muhammad smiled indulgently.

'Will you share the riches of your divine inspiration with us, Prophet, so that we can write them down for the benefit of generations to come?' Zaid asked.

'Won't you read all the divine inspirations in the Quran?' Muhammad recited. '*And if all the trees in the earth were pens, and the sea with seven more seas to help it, were ink, the words of Allah could not be exhausted. Lo! Allah is Mighty, Wise'* (31:27).

'Do we seek knowledge only from the Quran, Prophet?' Aisha broke her silence.

'Here speaks my scholar wife!' Muhammad laughed. 'Acquire knowledge from all quarters of the world, and travel if you have to, as far as China, to obtain such treasures. Acquisition of knowledge is obligatory for every Muslim, male and female.'

'What need have women to seek knowledge, Prophet, when we can teach them all they need to know?' Abu Huraira declared fervently. 'Aren't they our garments, which we need to protect by keeping them at home?'

'Do not distort the words of Allah, nor cut short the message of revelations!' Muhammad flashed him a quick reproof. '*They are a garment to you, and you are a garment to them* (2:187). *The best garment is the garment of God-consciousness'* (7:26).

'How does one attain God-consciousness?' Anas asked, baffled.

'Ponder upon this revelation, my son, and you might get the answer.' Muhammad smiled wistfully. '*I cast the garment of love over thee from Me, and this in order that thou mayest be reared under Mine eyes'* (20:39).

From this revelation wafted the scent of peace. Time was suspended. Hassan began to sway back and forth, his eyes radiant and his face glowing.

'Allah, Allah, Allah!' Hassan's voice rippled with music and ecstasy.

'Are you bewitched, Hassan?' Othman ibn Affan's expression was incredulous; he didn't notice that the Prophet himself had begun to sway right and left.

'I am intoxicated by the love of Allah!' Hassan sang. 'I have received two stores of knowledge from the Messenger of God. The meaning of one, which I can disclose, is embodied in this revelation: *And lower thy wing in kindness unto those believers who follow thee* (26:215). The other I dare not divulge, for you would cut my throat.'

'How has he received this knowledge from you, Prophet? Is he…' Othman ibn Affan could not continue when he saw the rapturous look of the Prophet.

'He has received this knowledge, Othman, through the fire of love inside his own spiritual heart.' Muhammad pressed his hand to his breast. 'I can't explain either, for it can't be comprehended with reason, only with love. Just remember that remembrance of Allah is the key to the heart of knowledge in all of us, which unlocks the door to love. If we repeat Allah's name often enough, perhaps one day He will choose to repeat His Name through us. Remembrance of Allah is called *Dhikr,* and it can transport a person from being the namer to being the named. Dhikr leads you to *Khidr,* the invisible knight of knowledge, who holds out green wisdom to those who confess their ignorance with humility, and strive towards union with the beloved. To truth-seekers, Khidr might even reveal the two cities of divine wisdom where the lover is united with the beloved, and the seeker is dissolved into the sought.'

'Is this a parable or a revelation, Prophet? I confess, I don't understand.' Othman ibn Affan was flustered. 'Yet my heart longs for Allah. In what form will I ever see Him? Will the whole of creation come face to face with Allah after death?'

'Die before dying, and you will see Allah now. Here and everywhere.' Muhammad's eyes were shining. 'On the day of resurrection, everyone will see Allah. He will manifest Himself to creatures in the forms they themselves have left, announcing, "I am your Lord." In the face of this unfamiliar apparition, they will seek refuge in their own representation of God. Then God will appear in that representation, and they will believe that indeed it is Him. Seek the comforts of your tents till the time for evening prayer. And hold this revelation close to your hearts: *Whoso doeth which is right, and believes, male or female, him or her will We quicken to happy life*' (16:97).

Muhammad stood watching the white sea of pilgrims. He turned to Ali.

'If I am the gate to your knowledge, Prophet, then guide me towards it so that I don't go astray?' Ali lowered his gaze from the profundity in the Prophet's eyes.

'*O My servants, all of you are astray except for those I have guided, so seek guidance of Me and I shall guide you,*' Muhammad began urgently. '*O My servants, all of you are hungry except for those I have fed, so seek food of Me and I shall feed you. O My servants, all of you are naked except for those I have clothed, so seek clothing of Me and I shall clothe you. O My servants, you sin by night and by day, and I forgive all sins, so seek forgiveness of Me and I shall forgive you. O My servants, it is but your deeds that I reckon up for you and then recompense you for, so let him who finds good praise Allah, and let him who finds other than that, blame no one but himself.*' His inspiration was splintered as he caught sight of his uncle Al Abbas.

'I have come, my nephew, with an offer of alliance with the Quraysh. Not that they have sent me, mind you.' Al Abbas hobbled closer. 'My sister-in-law Maymuna; her husband died recently. If you marry her, the chiefs of the Quraysh might not oppose you as strongly as they do now, since you would become their ally through marriage ties.'

'I would be honoured to marry her. I'll even invite the Qurayshi chiefs to the wedding to gain their friendship!' Muhammad was quick to embrace his uncle. 'Are you going to accept Islam as your own wedding gift to Maymuna?' he teased.

'A grand wedding feast, that's the only gift I can afford,' Al Abbas chortled with glee, shifting his gaze to Ali. 'And I will make it doubly rich, if Ali is willing to marry Omara, the beautiful daughter of my late brother Hamza?'

'I, yes, I would be happy—' Ali could not harness his confusion and bewilderment against the sudden flood of torment in the eyes of the Prophet.

'Ali is not at liberty to marry anyone, unless he is willing to divorce Fatima!' Muhammad declared most firmly. 'Fatima is a part of my body and soul, and what hurts her, hurts me. Fatima is my soul and spirit, and Ali is the soul of my soul. We are linked together in a chain of love, which must not be broken by hatred and jealousy, which would be sure to follow if Ali thinks of marrying.'

Ali bowed his head, shamed and contrite. Al Abbas stood glaring at Muhammad.

'Forgive me, I need to be alone. Grant me this little favour, so that I may commune with Allah, and seek forgiveness for my own sins.' Muhammad ignored his uncle and son-in-law as they left him alone.

The desert evening, robed in ochre and vermillion, arrived too soon, invading even the Prophet's tent. He was seated with a few of his companions, snatching snippets of conversations outside his tent. He had discovered bliss within himself, inside the sanctuary of his own inner Kaaba, even though access to the real Kaaba was denied him by order of the Meccans. The voices from outside his tent strayed into his thoughts.

'The streets of Mecca are quiet as a graveyard.' Saad ibn Waqqas' voice was muffled compared to a louder one, unmistakably Zaid's.

'Every door and window is locked. Even if I were allowed into the streets, I would see no one: no music in the shops, no gossip in the bazaars. Why do they have to stay indoors just because we are here? They didn't have to close the shops. I don't understand.' Zaid's voice floated inside the tent, clear and crisp.

'No mules, horses, or donkeys are in sight either. Have they trained their beasts to stay away from the streets too?' Talha ibn Ubaidullah was heard laughing.

'At least Abu Sofyan has kept to his part of the pledge, and granted us freedom to perform this pilgrimage without any hurdles,' Abu Bakr was saying.

Muhammad and his companions inside the tent heard a sudden noise. Before Muhammad could speak, Huweidib and Suhail ibn Amr had stormed in.

'Your time is up, Muhammad, exactly three days since you came. After sunset, you must leave Mecca,' Suhail ibn Amr announced with the arrogance of a mighty lord.

'I am getting married,' Muhammad responded with utmost calm and kindness. 'My uncle is inviting you all to a grand feast. After the wedding, we will leave.'

'We don't want any grand feasts, Muhammad!' Huweidib sneered. 'You were granted permission to stay in Mecca for three days, and now you must pack and leave, unless you want to break the peace treaty!' he challenged.

'How dare you speak to our Prophet so rudely?' Al Harith leapt to his feet.

'Sit down, Al Harith,' Muhammad commanded. 'No ill words to those who come into our tent.' He returned his attention to Huweidib. 'Abu Rafi will go with you to fetch my bride-to-be. After that, it will take us only a couple of hours to leave.'

Muhammad left Mecca within two hours as promised. This particular morning, astride Qaswa, his thoughts cherished his memories of the past few days with gratitude. Maymuna had arrived, escorted by Abu Rafi, chaperoned by Salma and Omara, who were Hamza's widow and their daughter. His marriage to her was celebrated in the small town of Sarif. Suddenly, he became aware of loud voices.

'Omara is my uncle's daughter!' Ali was saying, probably provoked by Zaid and Jafar. 'She and Fatima have become great friends during this short journey. And Fatima treats her like a sister, so she should stay with us.'

'What logic is that, Ali? We're brothers – he's my uncle too!' Jafar was adamant. 'Her aunt Asma is my wife, so it is only right that she stays with us.'

'I have the right to claim Omara as an exclusive guest in my house, since she is my brother's daughter,' Zaid declared happily. 'And don't you two start arguments about it, because the Prophet adopted me as his son and after we came to Medina he made a pact between me and Hamza, proclaiming us brothers.'

'You three are vying with each other for the privilege of having Omara as your guest, as if suing for her hand in marriage,' Muhammad observed absently.

'Not me, Prophet, since you forbade me to marry any,' Ali mockingly lamented.

'She wouldn't accept me, Prophet, so I dare not even propose,' Zaid chirped.

'I'd like to marry her, Prophet, if she'd accept me,' Jafar breathed low.

'Then propose to her, Jafar. And if she is willing, marry her.' Muhammad laughed. 'You look most like me, and no woman so far has rejected me!'

In a flash, Jafar jumped down from his horse and began dancing in circles around Qaswa, as if enacting some rite of a pilgrimage. This bizarre act attracted the attention of all the pilgrims, including the ladies of the harem. They urged their mounts to fly to the scene, which was marked by cheers and great applause.

'What is this, Jafar?' Muhammad could not stop laughing.

'It is what I saw the Abyssinians do in honour of their king.' Jafar pranced and whirled. 'If ever King Negus gave any man a good reason to rejoice, that man would rise and dance about him.'

'And why are you rejoicing?' Muhammad teased.

'Perhaps another bride for you, Prophet?' Aisha asked.

'No more brides for the Prophet, Aisha, I assure you.' The laughter faded from Muhammad's eyes. 'Maymuna is the last one. Had I been wise, I would have married only one. Besides, this new revelation puts an end to further marriages. For no man, not even a prophet, is able to treat each wife with equal justice.'

If you fear that you will not be able
To deal justly with the orphans
Marry the women of your choice
Two, three or four
But if you fear you will not be able
To deal justly with them, then only one. (4:3)

'I wish, Prophet, you had received this revelation after I got married to you!' Aisha's eyes were bright with relief.

'Be kind to Maymuna, Aisha,' Muhammad replied. 'She is not only a dear relative of my uncle, but the widow of a chief from the clan of Najd. Her heart is a seat of love and compassion; she is even mourning the deaths of our seventy men, who were murdered by members of her clan.'

'I remember that, Father!' Fatima reminisced aloud. 'And have you embraced the clan of Najd into your fold of forgiveness too, Father?'

'How can I not, my child?' Muhammad was looking at a cat in the distance, guarding her litters. 'Isn't it revealed: *Whosoever cuts you off, draw him to yourself. Whosoever deprives you, give to him. Whosoever do you wrong, pardon him*' (3:135, 45:14). He brought Qaswa to an abrupt halt. 'This is a good place to rest before we resume our journey. Do not disturb this cat and her litter. If she is still here when we are ready to move, go around her with the utmost caution, so as not to frighten her.'

The pilgrims fell asleep on the rocky ground. The sunshine was no more though, replaced by a heliotropic, awe-inspiring sunset. Muhammad had chosen a secluded spot to rest. He hung his sword on a palm branch overhead and drifted into sleep. In his dream, he was praying at the grave of his daughter, Zainab. His eyes opened, and a sword floated in front of his eyes. This was no dream. An Arab Bedouin, holding Muhammad's own sword, was leaning over him.

'Who is going to save you from my hands now, *Prophet*?' the Arab Bedouin hissed triumphantly. 'You claim to be a prophet, don't you?'

'Allah, the Lord of the Worlds, will save me, His servant,' Muhammad responded with utmost calm.

The sword fell from the Bedouin's hand, as he stood there aghast. Muhammad picked up his sword, which had landed at his feet, his eyes glowing with compassion.

'Who will save you from me now?' Muhammad asked.

'You, Messenger of God,' the Bedouin murmured, shuddering with awe.

'Why would I save your life, when you tried to take mine?' Muhammad held him captive in his gaze, which glinted no threat, only kindness.

'Because you don't repay evil with evil, I have heard...' The Bedouin's voice was choked by the sudden arrival of two men, murder flashing in their eyes.

'Put away your sword, Anas,' Muhammad commanded. 'And step back, Bilal; you are draining the life out of this man with your gaze alone. He is the victim of his own folly and ignorance, and may yet learn to do good. We must be on the road to Medina, wearing only the robes of forgiveness.' He strode away.

Six long months, muddied at times with sorrows, had passed since Muhammad's return to Medina. This particular afternoon he was seated in the courtyard between his quarters and the mosque. His eyes were closed and his thoughts straying. Zainab was no more, the spark of life snuffed out of her within two weeks of his return to Medina. Mary's time was drawing near. An astonishing sense of magic and mystery pervaded his senses, with two faces emerging forth from the mists: Suhail ibn Amr and Khalid ibn Walid.

Suhail ibn Amr and Khalid ibn Walid had been Muhammad's staunchest enemies, and had fought against him at the battles of Badr and Ohud. Shortly after his return to Medina, both these men had appeared suddenly, seeking to embrace Islam. At the same time, two more men had joined the fold; one was Jubayr, the son of Mutim, and the other was the dearest of his nephews, Aqil, the brother of Ali and Jafar. Muhammad, at this precise moment, recalled the words of his greeting. 'I love you with two loves, Aqil. One, for your near kinship to me, and the other for the love which I ever saw in you in my uncle.'

He opened his eyes.

'Suhail! Khalid! How long have you been sitting here for?' Muhammad gasped for breath.

'Not for long, Prophet,' Suhail ibn Amr smiled in response.

'We have come to seek your advice, Prophet, concerning the raids on Medina.' Khalid ibn Walid was quick to voice his fears. 'One of our envoys, as you know, was killed in the town of Muta in Palestine. The chief from the clan of Ghassan sanctioned the murder; he boasted that no harm can ever come to him since he is under the protection of the Emperor of Rome, Heraclius.'

'My advice would be to march to the very gates of Rome, to seek justice,' Muhammad decided. 'I wish to appoint you as my generals. But before I do that, I want to know what made you come to Medina to accept the message of Islam?'

'Your message of love and peace, Prophet. No one can resist for long!' Khalid ibn Walid declared. 'True, my father died at Badr, but we Meccans were the aggressors, and you didn't even take part in the fighting. We Meccans were so inhospitable when you came to perform the pilgrimage, not even permitting you to enter the Holy House of the Kaaba! That broke my heart, and I started for Medina. I hadn't gone too far when I found my friend Uthman. We talked about old times, and he told me about his father, two of his uncles, and his four brothers who had died at the battle of Ohud. After that we journeyed for hours in silence. As we approached Medina, I said, "Our plight is no better than that of a fox in a ditch: dump a pail of water over him, and he must come out." He understood what I meant, and both of us shared our thoughts of becoming Muslims. Approaching Haddah we spotted Suhail, and the rest you know, Prophet. But how Suhail got there is for him to tell.'

'My story of how and why leads me back to my own state of ignorance,' Suhail ibn Amr began urgently. 'The very idea of Islam was abhorrent to me, and I was possessed by this urge to stop Muslims from migrating. I thought I could change the mind of King Negus through gifts, so I decided to go to Abyssinia. King Negus received me graciously and I presented him gifts fashioned out of the finest leather. But when I started talking against Muslims, he stopped me, saying, "Your talk and your gifts of leather will earn you no favour in my court. It will be better for you if you follow Muhammad." I was stunned, and asked if he believed in your message. He said, "I bear witness to it before God. Muhammad is the Truth by God, and he will triumph over every mountain of persecution which may stretch itself against him, even as Moses triumphed over Pharaoh and his hosts." Something snapped inside me then. I can't explain it; it was the agony of grief and longing which whipped me on the road to Medina.'

'Be comforted, Suhail, and Khalid. Allah has forgiven you both for the purity of your faith and belief. And Allah is merciful,' Muhammad intoned kindly. 'Never despair of the infinite mercy of Allah, which is forever a source of love and light to us all. Allah says: *O sons of Adam, so long as you call upon Me and ask of Me, I shall forgive you for what you have done, and I shall not mind. O sons of Adam, were your sins to reach the clouds of the sky and were you then to ask forgiveness of Me, I would forgive you. O sons of Adam, were you to come to me with sins nearly as great as the earth and were you then to face Me, I would bring you forgiveness as great as the earth.*'

'With a God like that, so loving and forgiving, we should have no fear of the Romans or of the Meccans. They might be able to kill us, but never our faith!' Khalid ibn Walid sang ecstatically.

'You are of more service to God alive than dead,' Muhammad laughed. 'We have to defend ourselves when oppressed, but we should not be the ones oppressing. Yet we must not sit idle when confronted with oppression. And yet we must at all times sue for peace even against the forces of opposition, fighting only in self-defence, and to cease fighting when peace is offered. Allah says: *O my servants, I have forbidden oppression for Myself, and have made it forbidden amongst you, so do not oppress one another.*'

'How do we distinguish between the oppressor and the oppressed, Prophet? Or between truth and falsehood?' Suhail ibn Amr murmured.

'Cast aside anything which makes you suspicious, Suhail, and take only that which does not involve you in suspicion. Truth brings peace, and falsehood brings suspicion.' Muhammad's look was kind and profound.

'Do faith and prayer bring us peace and true knowledge, Prophet?' Suhail ibn Amr's eyes were glinting doubts, his look troubled.

'Yes,' Muhammad intoned warmly. 'But after you say your prayers, do not go off to sleep, neglecting your duty to seek your livelihood. Do you remember this revelation? *And forget not thy portion of the present world* (28:77). The imminent threat of the Romans is much too dangerous to be ignored. They are gloating over their might and power, and their raids over the tribes of Medina are on the rise. People are losing their lives and properties, and we need to mobilise our forces against the Roman legions to safeguard the lives and homes of all the tribes of Medina.'

'Is this jihad, Prophet?' Khalid ibn Walid's voice was charged with fervour.

'Jihad is not what you think, Khalid,' Muhammad was quick to answer. 'Do not distort the meaning of jihad with your own whip of fervour and judgement; that leads to fanaticism – a great error, which might become the bane of Islam, I fear. Jihad is, remember, to bring peace and harmony into the world by virtuous deeds, and by setting the example of goodwill against evil deeds and barbaric laws. It is to accomplish all that without raising a sword, unless to save one's own life and the lives of others. Jihad is acquiring knowledge. Helping mankind is Jihad. Feeding the poor and orphans is—' His prophetic injunctions were silenced by the stormy approach of Anas.

'Prophet, you are blessed with a son! A beautiful boy!' Anas sang joyfully.

Muhammad sprang to his feet, running towards his humble quarters, oblivious to the cries of congratulations from Suhail and Khalid. He was carried on the wings of the wind, sailing right into Mary's room. He lifted his son into his arms, gazing into his wife's eyes. A ripple of laughter from his wives behind him broke the spell, and he turned to them.

'We will call him Ibrahim, after the name of the Great Patriarch.' Muhammad stood facing Aisha. 'Look at him, Aisha – isn't he beautiful?'

'What are you making so much fuss about, Prophet?' Aisha snapped.

'Are you unhappy, my Aisha?' Muhammad's joy was replaced by concern.

'No, Prophet,' Aisha murmured contritely. 'It's just that I have no child of my own to boast about. If you let me adopt one, I will soar to the heavens with joy.' She floated on her toes, sweeping her arms in a mock curtsy.

'Why, then, Aisha, adopt your nephew Addallah, whom you love!' Muhammad laughed. 'But dare not leave this earthly heaven before I do.'

'Just because she is jealous she gets a gift?' Safiya protested. 'That's not fair, Prophet. She calls me a Jewess, and tells me I am inferior to her.'

'You have to learn to deal with Aisha with as much cleverness as can be mustered, Safiya,' Muhammad advised. 'Next time she says that to you, tell her that Aaron is your brother, Moses your uncle, and Muhammad your husband. So how could you possibly be inferior to her?' He fled all protests. 'I have to show my son to the world!' He raced beyond the courtyard towards the mosque.

The world which had witnessed the birth of Ibrahim had already mounted the rungs of six months as Muhammad sought relief from the afternoon sun. They had waited four months since the Muslim army had marched against the Roman legions to check their spree of raids, and today was the first day that Khalid ibn Walid had brought back the defeated army to Medina. Muhammad groped his way towards Jafar's house, but the dust of grief inside him was hovering above the waters of tragedies.

The Muslim army of three thousand against the Roman legion of one hundred thousand had met at the borders of Muta. Zaid was the first to receive a mortal wound. Jafar was the next to be killed. While Muslim soldiers were seeking refuge down the valley of Belka, Abdallah ibn Masud too had fallen victim. The Romans were vigilant, so Khalid ibn Walid had only succeeded in recovering the body of Jafar, before commanding a hasty retreat.

Muhammad was approaching Jafar's house. He could see Jafar's wife Asma standing at the doorstep, and his thoughts churned in pain and disconsolation.

'Where are your sons, O Asma? Bring them to me...' Muhammad became aware of the boys racing towards him, as was their wont whenever he visited.

All three of Jafar's sons clung to Muhammad, demanding attention. But Muhammad could not speak as he gathered them into his arms, his eyes blinded by tears.

'O Messenger of God, dearer than my father and mother, why are you weeping thus?' Asma implored. 'Have you received any news from Jafar and his companions?'

'O Asma, yes. Many were killed, and dear Jafar too,' Muhammad could barely murmur, his arms tightening around the boys in a crushing embrace.

The afternoon haze was at Muhammad's heels on his way home. Asma had uttered a heart-rending cry and fainted after hearing about the death of her husband, cradled in the comforting arms of the wives of her neighbours. A few words of prayer had shuddered upon Muhammad's lips before he had drifted away. He was plodding past the mosque when he stumbled against a little flower of a girl, Salima, the daughter of Zaid. He scooped her into his arms, his body racked by sobs. Saeed bin Udadah stood not far away, watching without being noticed by the Prophet.

'What is this, O Messenger of God?' Saeed bin Udadah cried suddenly.

'This is not the Messenger of God, O Saeed, but a man who loves hopelessly, begging for crumbs of peace and comfort. Imploring guidance from Allah, and bathing His feet with tears.' Muhammad lowered Salima to the ground most gently, and drifted away.

'*It is He Who has made you His representatives on earth. He has raised you in ranks, some above others, that He may test you with the gifts He has given. For your Sustainer is swift with stringency. Yet ever ready to Forgive, Infinitely Merciful*' (6:166). Muhammad's feet carried him towards Aisha's room. '*Again and again, Allah Most High turns mercifully towards human beings, flooding every mind and heart in His Creation with Living Presence and Divine Light*' (110:1–3).

The congregation at the mosque in Medina during noon prayers was caught in a flood of mirth, as Ibrahim climbed on Muhammad's back. Ibrahim was now a year old. Muhammad's head was pressed to the ground, laughter bubbling inside his heart. He could not raise his head, lest he deprive Ibrahim of his joy-ride.

Hasan, five years old, and Hussain, almost three, climbed up in front of Ibrahim. Muhammad surrendered himself to the will of the children, playing with them, yet his thoughts were in the past.

Two months after the tragedy at Muta, peace in Medina was once again threatened by the tribes of Bali and Qudaah. So Muhammad had dispatched an army of five hundred men under the command of Suhail ibn Amr to check their advance. A battle was fought on the Syrian border, both tribes were defeated, and peace was restored between the borders of Syria and Yemen.

In Mecca, the clan of Khuzaah, because it had accepted the message of Islam, was attacked by the clan of Banu Bakr. A night raid was planned and executed within the sacred territory of Mecca, and the leaders of the Quraysh had actively taken part in killing and looting. The families of the Khuzaah clan were heart-broken, sending their leader Kaab to Medina to plead with the Prophet to come to their assistance. Muhammad, in return, had sent his envoy to the leaders of the Quraysh with a message that the peace treaty of Hudaybiyah would be rendered void, unless the Quraysh were willing to break their alliance with the Banu Bakr, and to compensate the victims with blood money and assist them in rebuilding their homes. The Quraysh were quick to send a haughty response that they were the first to acknowledge the peace treaty null and void. So great was Muhammad's distress after receiving this response that Aisha could not endure the flood of torment in his eyes, and asked what was wrong.

'May I not be helped if I help not the sons of Kaab?' Muhammad had exclaimed.

This comment was in Aisha's thoughts at this precise moment, watching Ibrahim bouncing on the lap of the Prophet.

'Ibrahim has made you his slave, Prophet! And one of these days he is going to break your back.' Aisha sought her husband's attention, her thoughts still troubled.

'No one can break my back, Aisha, but pious fools!' Muhammad laughed. 'Since I am the servant of Allah, I must serve His creation, and the best way to serve Him is to be the slave of children.'

'What about serving your wives, Prophet?' Mary rejoindered.

'Don't I serve you all with utmost devotion?' Muhammad began passionately. 'Cleaning the house, cooking, buying provisions, patching my clothes, and mending my shoes. I have done my morning rounds of serving, sweeping the courtyard, fetching oil and barley from the bazaar, and much more which I don't remember. Now, why don't you all go home, and fix me something to eat?'

'Can't we stay, Prophet?' Maymuna appealed wistfully. 'Mosque is the place where I learn the most about Islam.'

'If that's what you wish, Maymuna,' Muhammad smiled. 'But whose turn is it to cook today?'

'Safiya's, Prophet,' Maymuna murmured happily.

'I switched it with Hafsa two days ago,' Safiya declared quickly.

'While Juwairya, Umm Salmah, Umm Habiba and I were busy drawing lots, Swadah generously offered to cook for a whole week,' Hafsa confessed.

'None of us gets a chance to put in a word, Prophet, when your wives are here!' Ali could not help intervening. 'They have plenty of time to talk with you at home.'

'If I am ever home these days, that is,' Muhammad chided.

'Who is the best amongst us men, Prophet?' Usama asked.

'The best amongst you is the one who is best to his wife,' Muhammad intoned. 'The one who can provide for his wives and make room for them to grow spiritually.'

'Your wives are guarding a secret in their spiritual hearts, Prophet.' Abu Bakr stole a look at Aisha. 'Don't be surprised if Abu Sofyan walks into your house, begging for a favour that the peace treaty be ratified.'

'Abu Sofyan in Medina?' Muhammad gasped. 'How do you know?'

'Because, Prophet, he came to my house.' Abu Bakr was too happy to share his own astonishing experience with the Prophet. 'The Meccans, somehow, have found out about our resolve to redress the wrongs done to the clan of Khuzaah. Now they are afraid, and want to ratify the peace treaty, and have chosen Abu Sofyan as their envoy. He came to me last night, pleading with me to convince you, Prophet, to consider the peace treaty valid like before. I told him I can't intercede on his behalf, since the Messenger of God has decided already what action to take.'

'They are the ones who broke the peace treaty, Abu Bakr, and they know it,' Muhammad murmured. 'Didn't I offer them another chance to negotiate peace, and what was their answer? They have betrayed us again and again, and they have slaughtered our men once again, and brazenly allied with the clan of Banu Bakr. They're not even willing to compensate the surviving victims for their losses.'

'Abu Sofyan visited me too, Prophet,' was Ali's flustered confession. 'I meant to tell you about it after the prayers. He asked me, too, to intercede on his behalf, and my answer was the same as Abu Bakr's.'

'Have I not consulted with you all about this already?' Muhammad murmured. 'You know my answer, which is contained in this revelation. *Consult them about affairs, and when thou art resolved, then trust in Allah* (3:159). I have made my decision, and my trust rests in Allah.'

'A day of unfolding secrets, Prophet,' Umm Habiba began bashfully. 'My father paid me a visit too. I was praying in my room when he came, and I quickly folded the prayer rug up before greeting him. He was angry and he scolded me, saying, "O little daughter, is the Prophet's rug of more value to you than the love of your father?" I was taken aback, so I said, "I wonder why you haven't accepted Islam?" To this, he replied harshly, "Wonder of wonder, am I to forsake my religion to accept Muhammad's?" And then he left without another word.'

'Your father, Umm Habiba, was your guest,' Muhammad chided. 'You have been unkind to your guest and to your father. Seek his forgiveness as soon as possible. Islam, my Habiba, means devotion and peace-making surrender to the will of Allah. It is forbidden in Islam to taunt, force, or coerce anyone into accepting its message. There has never been a time on the face of this earth when people didn't receive a divine messenger of their own. Since the creation of this world, Allah has sent down one hundred and twenty-four thousand prophets, the most remembered amongst them being Adam, Noah, Abraham, Moses, and Jesus, the pure and sinless. Jesus was the Word of God, the Spirit of God, the Worker of Miracles. He himself was a divine miracle, since he was conceived in the virgin womb of his mother, Mary.'

'In the Talmudic traditions of the Jews, Prophet, severe punishments are meted out to adulteresses. How should such a sin be dealt with in Islam?' Abdallah ibn Ubbay concealed his guile behind a charming smile.

'There would be no adulteress, if there were no adulterer.' Muhammad smiled. 'If you were to judge such a case, Abdallah, use this revelation as a guidepost. *If two persons among you are guilty of adultery, punish them both. If they repent and amend themselves, leave them alone. For Allah is oft-returning, Most Merciful*' (4:16). He could see Abu Sofyan approaching.

'O daughter of Muhammad,' Abu Sofyan sought Fatima's attention. 'Intercede on my behalf with your father to honour the peace treaty, which has been rendered void by some unfortunate events beyond our control. For the love of your sons, Fatima, do it.'

'Why don't you speak with my father, Abu Sofyan? He might grant you what you wish,' was Fatima's kind and candid response.

'Won't you suggest a course of action, Ali? A pact between man and man?' Abu Sofyan stood there deflated, still not meeting Muhammad's gaze.

'You are the Lord of Kinanah, Abu Sofyan, yet nothing will avail you at all today, for your promise of peace is false.' Ali indicated him a seat.

'By God, I don't think Muhammad will fail to uphold me, though I haven't appealed to him so far!' Abu Sofyan's eyes turned to Muhammad.

'Islam is a religion of peace, Abu Sofyan, and we offer love to everyone who sues for peace.' Muhammad held him captive in his gaze. 'Peace, my friend, is a field of friendship. It nurtures love, and kills the roots of hatred. It cultivates the flower of understanding, and shares the fruits of justice and equality. And yet, the offer of peace which you bring, Abu Sofyan, is hollow, and you know it. It was handed to you by the leaders of the Quraysh to be filled with our promises, while they still continue to oppress and to persecute. What justice is in this, tell me, when the Quraysh are still allied with the clan of Banu Bakr, and refuse to compensate the widows and the orphans they have left behind, and still wield daggers of murder and destruction?'

'It is true, then, Muhammad, that you have decided to march to Mecca, armed with swords of vengeance, though you will not admit it to yourself?' was Abu Sofyan's bitter response, as he turned on his heel.

'Vengeance is the weapon of unbelievers. The faithful wear only the armour of love and compassion, even when defending the oppressed and persecuted,' Muhammad intoned sadly. 'We will come, yes, but as pilgrims of peace. Our hearts will be as pure as the dawn of hope, cradling the breath of life, renewal, and forgiveness.'

'The light of victory is in your eyes, Prophet! Am I worthy to behold the promise of such glory?' was Umar ibn Khattab's awed exclamation after Abu Sofyan had left.

'Every servant of Allah is worthy of beholding the glory of love and forgiveness in peace and prosperity. Victory, too, will come to us, without the corruption of bloodshed and suffering,' Muhammad breathed prophetically, his gaze alighting upon the Bedouin who was threading his way straight towards him.

'Prophet, I am very poor,' the Bedouin began feverishly. 'Could you give me a goat, so that I can nourish my body with milk, and be able to cultivate the small patch of my land to live from?'

'Do I have a goat?' Muhammad asked his companions.

'This morning, Prophet, Judd ibn Qays sent you a gift of ten goats. They are for Ibrahim, he said,' Talha ibn Ubaidullah recounted with great delight.

'Give all those goats to this poor man, Talha.' Muhammad stole a glance at Ibrahim sleeping peacefully in his mother's lap. He shifted his attention to the Bedouin. 'Go with Talha, my friend, and take home all the goats. May Allah help you in your desire to work hard.' He eased himself up, smiling into the eyes of the Bedouin.

'You are so kind, Prophet. How can I ever…' The Bedouin was overwhelmed.

'I know, Prophet, that whatever gifts you get during the day are all gone by evening. But you could have kept one goat at least for Ibrahim,' was Umar ibn Khattab's resentful protest, knowing that Muhammad would not pay heed.

'To the poor, milk is gold; riches beyond imagination, Umar.' Muhammad drifted towards Mary, lifting Ibrahim into his arms. 'And yet, if the mountain of Ohud were turned to gold and given to me, I would not keep one little piece of its wealth to disturb my peace at night.' He laughed, urging his wives to their feet. 'Till evening, my friends.' He was leaving the mosque, accompanied by his wives. 'If anyone else brings me a gift today, be sure to tell me, for it must be shared. How else will I receive any gift from Allah's bounty the next morning, if I live yet another day?'

Chapter 17

Glorious Peace

Year 630 AD

The Meccan desert was hosting ten thousand pilgrims, with Muhammad riding ahead on Qaswa. Some sort of a whirlwind had entered Muhammad's head, of memories long forgotten: of six Muslim men being murdered most brutally. These men were sent to Mecca at the request of the Khuzaah clan to teach them the precepts of Islam. But the Quraysh had intercepted them near a watering place called Raji. Allied with the Lihyante tribe, with a man called Hudhayl at its head, the Quraysh had launched a night attack. Three Muslims were killed; Asim, Zayd and Khubayb were made captive. While they were being dragged towards Mecca, Asim was murdered by one of his captors, and then the other two were sold into slavery. After the festival of Safar, the two slaves were taken to Tanim to be publicly tortured. Zayd's master was Safwan bin Khalaf, and Khubayb's was Ikrimah. Both were vying with each other in their acts of cruelty. Ikrimah, after torturing Khubayb for a whole hour, had tried to be kind.

'I will let you go free, Khubayb, if you abandon Islam. If you renounce Islam, you can have everything you want, and enjoy the comforts of home and wealth.'

'I would not that the Prophet should be pierced by a single thorn that I might thereby be sitting at home,' was Khubayb's response before his head was severed.

Safwan bin Khalaf was quick to offer the same choice to Zayd, but he too had refused. 'My being slain for Allah is but a trifle, if I die in Him.' Zayd had requested that he be allowed to pray before being killed. Safwan bin Khalaf was incensed, and had kicked him in the ribs when he tried to turn towards Mecca. But before Safwan bin Khalaf could kill him, Zayd had cried out, '*Wheresoever you turn, there is the Face of Allah!*' (11:115).

Muhammad's gaze halted at the constellation of the Pleiades, and then shifted to the sickle moon above.

'O crescent of good and guidance, my faith is in Him who created thee.' Muhammad muttered a prayer.

The sea of pilgrims came to an abrupt halt at Muhammad's command. He had spotted a dog with its litter, and ordered his cavalcade to go around it so as not to disturb the mother and the newly born pups. The pilgrims cheered; some were protesting, but all were in good spirits. The cheers and protests were all silenced though as one bold rider appeared on the scene: none other than Al Abbas.

'Why are you on a march towards Mecca, Muhammad, with ten thousand warriors, and under the cover of darkness?' Al Abbas demanded boisterously.

'These are not warriors, Uncle, but pilgrims of peace, as prophesied by Moses in the old Scriptures,' Muhammad laughed. '*He came with ten thousands of holy ones* (Deut 33:2). Be assured, Uncle, my men have instructions not to engage in any kind of fighting, except for the sake of their lives, if attacked. They are forbidden to kill any child or woman, even when forced to fight in self-defence. Now, tell me, my wise Uncle, how did you know we were coming? What prompted you to challenge fate?'

'The same reason which prompted Hatib to warn the Meccans,' Al Abbas jeered. 'The woman whom you captured, Muhammad; the one who was carrying the letter? And have you already forgotten about Hatib? Have you forgiven them both?'

'That woman was not captured, Uncle, but brought back to Medina, and forgiven of course,' Muhammad remembered. 'Hatib too was forgiven, since his motive was not one of betrayal; he feared only for the safety of his relatives in Mecca, and that's why he attempted to warn them. Hatib, it is obvious, has contacted you. But would you be so kind as to tell us why you have come to see us in the middle of the night?'

'I have decided to become a Muslim, Prophet of Islam! Does that surprise you?' Al Abbas grinned.

'If I were to tell you, Uncle, that I had knowledge of this even before you came, would you believe me? Muhammad smiled. 'Even if the Meccans handed me the keys of the Kaaba tonight, it would not surprise me. You will be the last of the immigrants, Uncle. And you are the first to hear my confession that I am the last of the prophets.'

'My Prophet, till my last breath, and beyond that!' Al Abbas declared. 'The valley of Man Azzahran is not far from Mecca, Prophet, and I myself will guide you there. A propitious site for your camp! Let your campfires roar and blaze to let the Meccans know that you are here to fight and conquer.'

'Once again, Uncle – we have come as pilgrims of peace.' Muhammad's eyes shone with love. 'We are returning home to reclaim the sanctity of the Kaaba for Allah. Allah has promised us peace, and victory. The holiness of the Kaaba is not to be desecrated with enmity and bloodshed. The servants of Allah have come, it is true, not to fight with the mighty Meccans, but to befriend them with the warmth of love and forgiveness.' He paused, noticing the deflated expression of his uncle. 'And yet the red flames of our campfires will reach over the hills northwards, to let the Meccans know that the lowly slaves of Allah have come to proclaim their message of love, peace and unity.'

'By Allah, you have the manliness of Moses!' Al Abbas exclaimed. 'The tender-heartedness of Aaron, the generalship of

Joshua, the patience of Job, the daring of David, the grandeur of Solomon, the simplicity of John, and the humility of Jesus!'

'You yourself have proclaimed me as a prophet of the world, Uncle, before I myself could claim this burden too heavy for my weak shoulders.' Muhammad's features were transfigured with joy. 'There is not a nation on the face of this earth, but it has had a messenger of its own. From time to time, various reformers have appeared to strengthen the faith based on one principle alone – Allah's love for mankind, embracing His creation as one family, and deriding no one regardless of their race, colour or station in life. *Revile not those unto whom they pray beside Allah lest they wrongfully revile Allah through ignorance. Thus unto every nation have We made their deed seem fair. Then unto their Lord is their return, and He will tell them what they used to do* (6:109). *Come to an equitable proposition between us and you: that is the law of the Quran*' (3:64). He paused. 'I can recite revelations all night, but we must be on our way to the valley of Man Azzahran.' He gave a signal to resume their journey. 'Ride gently, my friends. Make sure you don't disturb the gentle pups, nor frighten their mother.'

The camp at the valley of Man Azzahran was stirred into activity after the dawn prayer. Muhammad had returned to his tent, accompanied by a few of his friends and family, including three of his wives, Zainab, Umm Salmah and Maymuna. Fatima was seated beside him, privileged to be a part of the pilgrimage. Privileged in health, too, since she had given birth to another daughter, who was only four months old and whom she had named after her sister Khultum.

After the morning prayers, Al Abbas had vanished behind the dusty hills, under a cloud of haste and mystery. Probably to warn the Meccans to surrender peacefully, Muhammad thought. He could almost see him talking with the leaders of the Quraysh.

'It feels like home, Father.' Fatima's dark eyes were shining. 'Coming back to Mecca is like entering Paradise. I wonder if heavenly Paradise will fill us with the same kind of feeling after we die?'

'A piece of Paradise the size of a bow is better than everything under the sun, whatever it rises and sets on, my child,' Muhammad murmured. 'If a woman of Paradise appeared to the people of the earth, she would fill the space between heaven and here below with light and fragrance.'

'Will the Meccans heed your message, Prophet, now that you are here with a large force to proclaim the Oneness of Allah?' Maymuna was voicing her own fears.

'*And they will not heed until Allah wills it. He is the fount of fear. He is the fount of mercy*' (74:56), Muhammad recited in response.

'How will you treat them, Prophet, if they don't heed?' Umm Salmah asked.

'In conformity with the Law of Creation, Umm Salmah.' Muhammad smiled. 'This creation is one family of Allah; its sustenance comes from Him. Therefore Allah's most beloved is the person who does good to God's family.'

'What are our duties towards Allah's creation, Prophet?' Zainab asked.

'To do unto all as you would wish to have done to you,' Muhammad intoned patiently. 'Yes, my scholar wife, that alone is our supreme duty towards Allah and His creation. And to reject for others that which you would reject for yourself. To feed the hungry and to visit the sick. To free the captive, if unjustly confined. To assist anyone oppressed, whether Muslim or non-Muslim.'

'Whoever does justice, Prophet, is that person a perfect believer, and one of us?' Abu Bakr sought Muhammad's attention, his look thoughtful.

'A perfect believer is one who wishes for others what he wishes for himself, Abu Bakr; one should never tire of stressing this point, and practising it at all times,' Muhammad intoned. 'That person is not one of us who invites others to aid him in oppression. And he is not one of us who fights for his tribe in injustice. And he is not one of us who dies in assisting any tribe in tyranny. *Say: O my servants who have transgressed against your own selves! Do not despair of Allah's compassion, for Allah forgives all mistakes. For, He is forgiving. Infinitely merciful* (39:53). *Turn to Him and—*' His thoughts were disrupted as Al Abbas stormed into the tent, flustered.

'I have talked with the leaders of the Quraysh, Prophet, to tell them that they have no chance of winning, and that they should surrender peacefully,' Al Abbas began passionately. 'They are frightened, saying amongst themselves that they will surely be killed for their past acts of cruelty and oppression against Muslims. They have sent Abu Sofyan as their spokesman. He is waiting outside your tent, craving your audience. He wants to talk with you before you march to Mecca, to plead for the safety of the Meccans. Should I grant him permission to speak with you, Prophet?'

'Yes, Uncle, invite him to the tent next to mine, where most of my worthy generals are lodged.' Muhammad got to his feet. 'They will bear witness to what we say to each other.' He stepped outside, coming face to face with Abu Sofyan.

'I have come, Muhammad, not to plead for my life, but to profess my faith in Islam, and in Allah,' Abu Sofyan blurted out.

'I have come, Abu Sofyan, as the Messenger of Peace, not of punishment.' Muhammad's gaze was piercing. 'Are you willing to profess your faith in Islam only because you fear for your life?' he asked kindly.

'I don't know, Muhammad.' Abu Sofyan lowered his eyes.

'Then don't hurry, till your heart is open to the grace of Allah,' Muhammad intoned softly. 'And have no fear for your life, or for the lives of others who have persecuted us in the past, as long as they don't oppose us when we enter Mecca to claim the Kaaba as the house of one God, Allah.'

'But I wish to profess my faith!' A cry of shame ripped from the lips of Abu Sofyan. 'There is no God, but Allah…' But his pride wouldn't let him accept Muhammad as Allah's messenger. 'What surety is there, Muhammad, that your men will not wreak vengeance upon us, who have tortured and persecuted Muslims for years?'

'Allah is all mercy and forgiveness, Abu Sofyan; have faith,' Muhammad consoled. 'Nobody will be harmed today when we enter Mecca and the Holy House of the Kaaba. Go in peace, Abu Sofyan, and proclaim to the Meccans that whosoever stays in the house of Abu Sofyan is safe. And whosoever stays in his house behind closed doors is safe. We have come to claim the Kaaba for Allah, not to claim the lives of its people. Our hearts are pure with love and it leaves no room for the cankers of hatred or vengeance.'

Abu Sofyan fled, pressed by his need to protect his family. Muhammad's last instruction to his followers was that they were not to engage in any kind of fighting. Astride Qaswa, Muhammad led the middle contingent, south of him, to his right, Khalid ibn Walid guided his own ranks of three hundred men. To Muhammad's left was another contingent of soldiers under the command of Saeed bin Udadah.

'Today is the day for fighting. It is not a safe day for the Meccans!' Saeed bin Udadah raised a wild cry, brandishing his sword in the air.

'This is how you distort the message of the Prophet, O Saeed? Pilgrims of Peace are forbidden to fight, as I said before, unless compelled to do so in self-defence.' Muhammad snatched the sword from Saeed's hand, and held it out to his son. 'You, Abu Qays, are entrusted with this sword, under an oath not to raise it in boast, and never to use it as a weapon of vengeance. This contingent of men is under your command now. You will lead them into Mecca in a manner worthy of a true Muslim.'

The north and south ranks were swallowed into silence after the humbling of Saeed bin Udadah, and Abu Qays' northern contingent vanished behind the hills. Not far to the south Khalid ibn Walid's troops were still in view, advancing towards the looming hills.

Muhammad's heart was exploring the familiar paths expanding before his sight. The house of his uncle, Abu Talib. The dearest of his homes, his haven of bliss with Khadija. The streets of Mecca were deserted, but as Qaswa padded towards the Kaaba, a window in Abu Sofyan's house was thrown open.

'O friends of the Quraysh and brave Meccans, kill this fat greasy bladder of a lord, my husband! He has surrendered your city to the—' Hind's cry of rage was silenced, as Abu Sofyan pushed her behind him.

'Woe betide you, my friends!' Abu Sofyan's voice boomed out from behind the window, slammed shut. 'Do not listen to this madwoman! Make sure you are not deceived against your better judgement, for there has come before you that which you cannot resist.'

The town of Dhu Tuwa came into view, beyond which could be seen the face of the Kaaba. A sudden noise, the sound of clashing swords, could not be missed by Muhammad, his gaze fluttering down to the pass of Adnakhir where Khalid ibn Walid's troops were crossing the lower entrance.

'Didn't I forbid fighting?' Muhammad turned to Abu Bakr. 'Make haste, Abu Bakr. Go, unarm Khalid, before he stains the hearth of peace with blood.'

Abu Bakr, carrying only the weapon of a command from the Prophet, succeeded in extinguishing the flame of contention, which had ensued from a little skirmish between the Quraysh and Khalid ibn Walid's men. All was silent once again, as Muhammad entered the holy grounds of the Kaaba.

Here I am, O Lord, at Thy service, the pilgrims had begun to chant.

Muhammad appeared to be in a trance, kissing the Black Stone. He drifted back to Qaswa and caressing her hump before seating himself with utmost grace. He could see the Meccans appearing down the slopes of Abu Qubays.

'*Praise be to God, the Lord of the Worlds. The infinitely Good, the All-Merciful. Master of the Day of Judgement. Thee we worship, and in Thee we seek help. Guide us on the straight path of those upon whom Thy Grace is. Not those on whom Thy anger is. Nor those who go astray*' (1:1–7).

Men and women, their eyes glittering with curiosity, were abandoning their safe havens and drifting towards this ocean of silence and surrender.

'Now that you have conquered Mecca, Muhammad, what will be the measure of your vengeance?' Othman ibn Talha, the custodian of the keys of the Kaaba, asked.

'Vengeance is for God alone,' Muhammad intoned kindly. 'I have not been sent as a curse to mankind, but as an inviter to good and mercy. And my prayer to Allah this blessed day is: My Perfect All, grant guidance to my people, for surely they know not. O people of Mecca, you, who have tortured, murdered and persecuted my friends, what kind of treatment do you expect from me?' He asked no one in particular.

'You have the right to wreak vengeance, Muhammad.' Muayiya ventured forth. 'But you are our noble brother, and the son of a noble brother, and we have always known you to be good and generous. So we expect no harsh treatment from you, only mercy and forgiveness.' His appeal was snatched up by others, chanting *Noble Brother*.

'O Allah, Thou art forgiving indeed, so pardon me.' Muhammad bowed his head. 'If Allah forgives us, who are we to refuse forgiveness to our fellow beings? Today there is no reproof against you. You are all forgiven. Go home in peace, for you are all free. Open your heart to Allah's mercy in this revelation. *No reproof be against you this day. Allah may forgive you, and He is the most merciful of those who show mercy* (12:92). *Allah commands justice, the doing of good, and liberality of kith and kin, and He forbids all wrong and shameful deeds, and injustice and rebellion. He instructs you that ye may take heed. For Allah loves those who are fair and just*' (16:90).

'Are you truly the Prophet of Allah?' Safwan bin Khalaf asked capriciously.

'I was Prophet when Adam was between water and clay,' Muhammad replied.

'Our hearts are filled with fear, Muhammad.' Safwan bin Khalaf could not contain his guilt. 'What is this new religion that you can't stop preaching? Are your followers really commanded to pray five times a day and fast for a whole month?'

'This is no new religion, my friend, but a continuation of the old one. It extends the gift of love to all who are willing to receive the grace of Allah and His message of unity,' Muhammad began profoundly. 'Do you not know the Sabaeans amongst you? For centuries they have believed in all the prophets before me, have prayed five times a day, and have fasted for thirty days each year. The revelation which I received confirms all that. *Those who believe in the Quran. Those who follow the Jewish Scriptures. And the Sabaeans and the Christians. And those who believe in Allah and the Last Day. And work righteousness. On them shall be no fear. Nor shall they grieve*' (5:69).

'Is there any revelation, Muhammad, in which our gods find favour with Allah?' Ikrimah asked caustically.

'*Noah said: O my Lord! They have disobeyed me. But they follow men. Whose wealth and children give them no increase, but only loss. And they have devised a tremendous plot. And they have said to each other. Abandon not your gods. Abandon neither Wadd, nor Suwa, neither Yaguth. Nor Yauq, nor Nasr. They have already misled many*' (71:21–24). Muhammad looked on kindly. 'Those gods, my friends, were mortal men like me and you, in the time of King Jared. They were pious men, and when they died their relatives grieved to such an extent that one of Cain's descendants took pity, and carved five idols in their likenesses. Those idols were fashioned to console the relatives, but later people started worshipping them as personal deities. They brought those idols to the Kaaba, to the House of Abraham, forgetting the covenant of Allah, and inviting more gods from other tribes to this First House in Becca, which is now known to us as Mecca. That covenant, forgotten by the Meccans for so long, is still alive and throbbing inside the hearts of a few. *Thou shalt not have other gods before me. Thou shalt not make unto thee a graven image, nor any manner of likeness, of anything that is in heaven above, or that is in the earth beneath, or that is in the water under the earth. Thou shalt not bow down unto them, nor serve them*' (Exodus 20:2–5).

'We can't see Allah, Muhammad! How can He help us change our hearts, or stop all these blood feuds amongst us?' Huweidib asked.

'*Unto Allah belongs the East and the West, and whithersoever ye turn, there is Allah's Countenance. Lo! Allah is All-Embracing, All-Knowing*' (2:115), Muhammad responded, more revelations shimmering in his eyes. '*Verily never will Allah change the condition of a people, until they change it themselves, with their own souls*' (13:11).

'You say the Kaaba is the House of Allah alone, Muhammad, yet there are gods and idols all over the world, the pilgrims and the merchants tell us. Has Allah commanded you to abolish the holy rituals of all the other nations? To challenge their beliefs, and urge them to forget the names of their gods and idols, and worship Allah alone?' Muayiya, encouraged by Muhammad's tenderness, threw out his own challenge.

'*Unto each nation We have given sacred rites, which they are to perform. So let them not dispute with thee of the matter. But summon thou unto thy Lord. Lo! thou indeed followest right guidance. And if they wrangle with thee. Say: Allah is best aware of what ye do.*

Allah will judge between you on the day of Resurrection concerning that wherein ye used to differ' (22:67–69). Muhammad continued profoundly, 'There are temples on this earth where gods of stone are revered, not vilified! And why they are revered is beyond the imagination of any Arab, because the devotees of those idols see the Creator behind the created, whom they fashion out of their Holy Scriptures. Why the Kaaba needs to be purified of all idols is that the Kaaba is the First House of God, consecrated in the name of Allah, free from the limitations of forms or names in order to reveal the Face of Allah. This is the centre of divine light, and its radiance reaches out to every nation inside their temples, churches, mosques or synagogues, wherever the name of the Lord is praised in any tongue, in any manner. This radiance of the one in the many returns to its original source, which is the Kaaba. Show me the Holy Scriptures where the names of your gods and goddesses are mentioned, and I will plead with Allah to bestow His grace and guidance on you, so that the eyes of your hearts and souls are opened to see the Kaaba in all its purity of Oneness, as the altar and throne of one God, Allah.'

'So you will break our idols, Muhammad, and break our hearts too! Is that not what you have intended all along?' Habbar challenged fearfully.

'Perception comes through the fire of love in your spiritual heart. Then, you cannot help but love the concept of unity and Oneness, loving Allah and His creation with your heart and soul!' Muhammad began wistfully. 'To break the idols means to pound your ego to dust, to recognise the idols of greed within your own self, and the idols of cruelty and injustice, and to dissolve those idols into nothingness, even if you need to break every bone in your body for the sake of a new birth in living and loving. Fill your heart with so much love that there is no room left for hatred. Die before dying, and live for love alone. Such purity of love can only be attained when you are able to approach the throne of Allah with your soul bare and your body naked, purged clean of all the idols of vile and corrupt passions. Breaking your idols does not mean desecrating your gods, but venerating the sparks of divinity in your own soul, guiding you towards Allah Whose face the material forms have concealed from you for so long.'

'To live without idols is hard enough, but how will we live if we break every bone in our body?' Washi lamented.

'Breaking your body doesn't mean to tear it limb from limb, but to grind away at the mountain of ego inside it, till nothing can be seen of its form, colour or stature, only the dust of humility.' Muhammad smiled. 'In order to get to the pearl of truth, one needs to break its shell. The mortar of our pride and prejudices must be chiselled away before we can see the vision of divinity inside us – the precious within. And breaking the idols means throwing open the gates of light to see the light of God within the mirror of divinity, which reflects no form, colour or shape; just light upon light. You have carved these idols for personal gain, making a mockery of your spiritual needs, slaves to your own greed. Are your hearts the seats of idols? Look deeper and you will behold the altar of silence where dwells Allah's grace, His love and beauty and formlessness. The Kaaba is the House of one God. Allah is the God of Abraham, Moses, Jesus, and of all the peoples, and of all the nations; he laments the presence of your stone gods here, who are fashioned and replaced according to your wont, depending on whether your prayers are accepted or repulsed. Adam built this House of Allah for the peoples of all nations to come and worship One God, to keep it pure and undefiled of all forms, to desist from filling it with the emblems of mockery, to learn not to deride the gods of others, wherever they may be worshipped.'

'We have our idols, Muhammad, and you have Allah. How would the Muslims treat idolaters if they were to witness the banishment of our idols from the Kaaba?' Abd Manaf lamented hopelessly.

'God's mercy is upon those who know their limitations,' was Muhammad's mystical response. '*He revealed to His servant that which He revealed* (3:3). If a Muslim truly loves Allah, he will love Allah's creatures foremost, believer or non-believer. And if he tries to know the essence of an idol, he will know religion in idolatry. And if an idolater wishes to discover the meaning of religion, he will know where he has gone astray. To come to such an understanding, one must scrape away all the layers of falsehood. That's the only way to find and nurture the flower of unity, the fragrance of which carries itself from north to south, from east to west, longing to gather us all into its love-beauty of brotherhood and sisterhood. No one is superior to anyone else. Arabs have no precedence over non-Arabs, nor whites over blacks. He is superior who is in possession of great love and piety. Such are the teachings of Islam, if you are wondering why I am saying all these things. In Islam, no one is a slave, and no one claims to be a master. Both rich and poor, depending on their own trials and struggles, have the privilege of contributing towards one whole, seeking to know our Sustainer who created us. That is the prime goal of our existence. Pain and pleasure are a part of this goal too: to know the difference between good and evil, to enjoy when we can and to endure grief with patience. We are all together on this earth, journeying towards our end, and to make this journey easy and peace-loving we must learn to obey the commands of Allah, enjoying what is permitted, and shunning what is forbidden. Love is the key to the gates of joy and peace. If we can learn to love everyone, the treasures of Paradise will come down to us, making this whole world a Garden of Eden.'

'Does Allah command us to break all our ties to our ancient beliefs? There are some Christians amongst us who would rather break their necks than abandon their faith in the Godhead. Do the Meccans have to become Muslims to enjoy the treasures of Paradise?' Addas cried, under a spell of fever and delirium.

'There is no compulsion in religion. The right direction is henceforth distinct from error. And he who rejecteth false deities and believeth in Allah has grasped a firm handhold which will never break. Allah is Hearer, Knower,' (2:256) Muhammad recited wistfully. 'We all invoke Allah's help, it matters not by what name, nor under what circumstances. We come from Allah, and to Him we return. Change is the pulse of time; every generation feels the pangs of birth and renewal; to exchange old beliefs and customs with better ones is not annihilation, but unification, by witnessing the glory of one in many. A man of limited intellect is incapable of understanding two things; those are truth and God. Yet, one can know God by the power of love in one's heart, knowing in essence the grace of divine love for all. By this act of love alone, one attains the wisdom to know truth, which is God. God is love, truth, beauty. If one were to break apart the Holy Trinity, one would see the Divinity of Christ, not only in the miracle of the Virgin Birth, but in the immortality of His life after death, in the miracle of Resurrection. He was not crucified, but lifted to the throne of God by the hands of Gabriel. Breaking up, or breaking away, means to slough off the burden of pride, and to be light enough in spirit to receive the gift of humility like Christ, who washed the feet of His disciples. When you are able to pluck out the thorn from your own self, then you can see the rosy glory of bliss with your inner eye, blessed by the sweet radiance of Allah's love, mercy and compassion. Such radiance nurtures in your heart the lotus of unity, without form, creed or colour, wafting forth the scent of joy, and this joy will penetrate every heart, even a heart of thorns. We are creatures of habit, ignorant of the wealth of eternal will concealed inside us. Upon awakening, one discovers this wealth, and sees the face of God in each and every thing. And God is love. The self is our veil and blindness – if we could only break ourself to pieces, and become like the dust from which we were moulded, we could rise to the heavens, carried by the wind of mercy, and become vessels of love in this world

and the hereafter. Love *is*; it gives, forgives; it cultivates the seeds of good deeds, and nourishes each little sapling with the water of wisdom from the font of profound holiness within all of us.' He took a deep breath, coaxing Qaswa to kneel. 'After we purify the Kaaba of all its idols, we will proclaim to all the Meccans that anyone wishing to join the Islamic fold of his or her own free will is welcome to see me at the foot of Mount As-Safa.' He dismounted slowly.

'These keys now belong to the Prophet of Islam!' Ali snatched the keys of the Kaaba from the hands of Othman ibn Talha, his eyes smouldering with zeal.

'Ali! Be kind and loving, and return those keys to Othman,' Muhammad commanded. 'Have I failed in my message of equal love, and equal respect for all? He is not one of us who inclines to zeal and disrespect. And he is not one of us who incites bigotry, or fights for bigotry, or dies in its pursuit. Othman, you have been the Keeper of the Kaaba for as long as I can remember, and you will remain its guardian whether you become Muslim or not. Now open the gate, and if you don't want to watch your idols removed, stay outside. After the Kaaba is purified of them all, you may do as you will.' He plodded towards the Sacred House, carrying the weight of grief on his shoulders.

Allah-hu Akbar, Allah-hu Akbar!

Muhammad's senses absorbed this chorus of joy and praise as he stood in a corner of the Kaaba, praying silently while the faithful removed the idols and hauled them outside the Sacred House. His gaze turned to the mural of the Virgin Mary and the Child Jesus, below which Abraham was painted as an old man, holding out his arms as a gesture of blessing. He noticed Othman beside him.

'Look, Othman, some unknown painter has wrought a miracle through his brushstrokes, revealing mysteries which only a few fortunate ones can see!' Muhammad exclaimed. 'The birth of the Word to the Virgin Mary is like the birth of the Word to the unlettered Prophet. The miracle of Islam is the Quran, like the miracle of Christianity is Christ. Make sure that this painting of the Virgin Mary, the Child Jesus and Abraham stay intact, while the rest are to be effaced.'

'Yes, Prophet,' Othman ibn Talha murmured in awe.

'Praise be to Allah, Who hath fulfilled His promise and has helped His slave to victory.' Muhammad closed his eyes. '*The truth has come, and falsehood has vanished away; surely, falsehood is certain to vanish*' (17:81). He opened his eyes, and his gaze fell on Bilal. 'Climb to the top of the Kaaba, Bilal, and call the faithful to prayer. After that we will rest in the shade of Mount As-Safa.' He drifted out of the Sanctuary. '*Verily I say as my brother Joseph said: This day there will be no upbraiding of you, nor reproach. God forgiveth you, and He is the most Merciful of the merciful*' (12:92). Muhammad faced the stunned crowd. 'There is no God but God. No one shares in His Power. He has fulfilled His promise. He helped His servant Muhammad, O people of Mecca. God has done away with the evil of ignorance. Blind loyalty to the tribe is gone forever. All human beings are united in brotherhood and sisterhood. They are the children of Adam, and Adam was made from dust. From now on, no one should take revenge. People must learn to live in peace.' He began circling the Kaaba, reciting, '*O humanity! We have created you from a male and female and made you into tribes and nations so that you can come to know each other. The best among you is the one who has the most piety*' (49:13).

Muhammad approached his red tent. Abu Bakr was jolted to awareness by loud arguments issuing forth from the tent, blocking the Prophet's way, though Muhammad himself had stopped. The voice of Umm Hani was drowning beneath the arguments from Fatima, Maymuna and Umm Salmah. Hudayfah's expressions were heard in between. Muhammad could hear another voice, but it was muffled under the protests of Maymuna.

'Didn't your uncle Abu Jahl persecute us, and not even repent on his death bed? Didn't you yourself fight against Khalid—'

Maymuna's vehemence was swallowed by another protest from Umm Salmah. 'Think twice, Umm Hani! You are seeking protection for your husband, who is an idolater—'

'The Prophet has forgiven everyone, has he not?' Fatima's voice was loud and clear.

'We are seeking protection to ensure the safety of every Meccan, lest we become the victims of zeal after the Prophet leaves Mecca,' Hudayfah was saying.

'By Allah, I will kill the pair of you, if you dare accuse me of zeal!' Ali's mad challenge was crisp and clear.

'By God, you will slay me first—' Umm Hani's cry was silenced by the abrupt appearance of the Prophet.

Muhammad stood aghast. Ali, with his back towards the Prophet, was standing there with his sword drawn, towering over Hudayfah. In a flash, Umm Hani had snatched her cloak off her shoulders and tossed it over the shoulders of her husband. Then she drifted towards Muhammad and was received into his arms in a warm embrace.

'I seek protection for my husband and for the kin of Abu Jahl,' Umm Hani could barely murmur, weeping and sobbing.

'Whom *you* make safe, dear Umm Hani, *we* make safe. Whom *you* protect, *we* protect.' Muhammad's gaze held Ali captive. 'Put your sword down, Ali. Have you not been reprimanded for your zeal already? If you entertain it one more time, you will not only be punished severely, but forbidden to carry any weapon.'

'Sorry, Prophet. Forgive…' Ali's voice was choked in a flood of shame.

'We have come to Mecca, not to persecute, but to protect and educate.' Muhammad held Umm Hani close to him. 'This whole earth is a sacred mosque; it pours love into the holy temples of our hearts, and does not distinguish between the idolater and the believer. *Say: O My servants who transgress against their souls.*

Despair not of the Mercy of Allah. For Allah forgives all sins. For He is oft Forgiving, Most Merciful (39:53). Forgiveness is the highest of virtues, and a divine gift from a divine hand. Allah's mercy and forgiveness are boundless. We are exhorted to turn to Allah in repentance now, for on Judgement Day it will be too late. But no soul need despair because of its sins…' His thoughts were disrupted by another din of arguments outside his tent. 'I might snatch a few moments of peace on the top of Mount Arafat, where Adam and Eve were united after their expulsion from the Garden of Eden.' He released Umm Hani, and stepped out into the glare of sunshine.

But he staggered into a pool of discord. Abu Bakr was pleading with Abu Rafi, Jubayr and Khalid ibn Walid, who were raging about Abdullah.

'I desire only peace on this earth, and inside the hearts of all, yet the face of zeal mocks me wherever I turn!' Muhammad exclaimed. 'Why are your tongues holding daggers and stabbing poor Abdullah?'

'He is an apostate and an idolater, Prophet!' Khalid ibn Walid declared. 'He should be killed for his apostasy, if not for his audacity in seeking forgiveness from you!'

'Allah forgive me, for my teachings are leading my own men astray!' Muhammad murmured a prayer. 'Do not distort the word of God, lest you be doomed for the sin of false piety, ruled by the evil of cruelty and injustice. Who has appointed you judge over matters of apostasy, with the authority of killing anyone for deserting Islam? *O you who believe: should anyone turn back from his religion, then he dies while an unbeliever, then Allah will bring a people, whom He loves and who love Him* (5:54). *And whosoever turns back from his religion, then he dies while an unbeliever, such are they whose works have fallen both in the world and the Hereafter* (2:217). *Our Lord! Cause not our hearts to stray after Thou hast guided us, and bestow upon us mercy from Thy Presence. Lo! Thou, only Thou art the Bestower. Our Lord! Lo! it is Thou Who gatherest mankind together to a Day of which there is no doubt. Lo! Allah faileth not to keep the tryst* (3:8–9). Is there any mention of killing any man for apostasy in these revelations? Abdullah, you are forgiven, my son. Go home in peace.'

'Forgive me, Prophet, I erred in my ignorance,' Abdullah murmured. 'Let me join the fold of Islam once again and I will remain forever the slave of Allah.'

'In your heart, you never swerved from your faith, Abdullah,' Muhammad consoled. 'Keep faith, Abdullah, and keep the mirror of your spiritual heart clean and bright, and you will never swerve from the path to glory. Now, do me a favour. Go, tell those men you see coming towards us that they need no further proof of my forgiveness, for Allah has already favoured them with the bounty of His mercy and forgiveness.'

'May I go with him, Prophet?' Abu Bakr shot a quick appeal.

'Yes, my friend.' Muhammad smiled. 'You would be doing me a great favour if you could lead them towards Mount Arafat, the Mountain of Mercy, while I contemplate here at As-Safa in perfect solitude. In the evening, they may return if they wish.' He returned his gaze to the trio of men. 'Khalid, you must burn your zeal to cinders before it moulds you into a tyrant. Zeal and bigotry are the fires of evil which will disfigure the face of Islam, I fear. Didn't I forbid fighting before we started from Medina? And yet I heard the clashing of swords in your ranks.'

'Not my fault, Prophet,' Khalid ibn Walid protested. 'A large battalion of the Qurayshi led by Ikrimah, Safwan bin Khalaf and Huweidib attacked us. I had no choice but to fight in self-defence.' He lowered his head.

'Walk gently on earth, Khalid, and provocation will be averted.' Muhammad turned on his heel, his thoughts hovering over the Meccans.

The hill of As-Safa appeared to be throbbing with awe as Muhammad sat down on a spur amongst his followers. He listened more to the voice in his psyche than to the questions of his companions.

'Will you forgive Washi also, Prophet, who killed your uncle Hamza?' Umar ibn Khattab was asking. 'Can you forgive Hind, who desecrated Hamza's body? Forgiveness all! Will you forgive Habbar too, who hurt your daughter Zainab?'

'Patience and forgiveness are gifts from God, bestowed upon those who have learnt to love.' Muhammad smiled. *'And you will certainly hear from those who have been given the Book before you and from those who are polytheists, much abuse, and if you are patient and keep your duty, surely this is an affair of great resolution* (3:184–185). Ponder upon this, Umar, and you might receive the gift of understanding.'

'What I don't understand, Prophet, is that the idolaters have done so much harm to us, and yet they have your forgiveness. Are we obliged to offer them protection too?' Umar ibn Khattab could not help but voice his bitterness and confusion.

'Do I have to recite all the revelations this blessed day, hoping and praying that the hearts of my companions be filled with the blessings of love and forgiveness?' Muhammad exclaimed. *'And Allah's is the sovereignty of the heavens and the earth. He forgiveth whom He will, and punisheth whom He will. And Allah is ever Forgiving, Merciful* (64:1–2). *And if any one of the idolaters seeketh thy protection, O Muhammad, so protect him that he may hear the word of Allah, and afterward convey him to his place of safety. This is because they are a folk who know not'* (9:6).

'Since the idols didn't protest against the command of Allah, Prophet, I have decided to profess my faith in Islam.' Quhafah hobbled closer, panting and sighing.

'Oh, Abu Bakr, why did you bring your aged father here?' Muhammad sprang to his feet. 'I would have gone to his house myself to offer him the message of Islam, and seek his blessings.' He embraced the old man gently, his face glowing with joy.

'Your gentle manners alone would have convinced me of your prophethood earlier than this, Muhammad, if I were wise enough to notice them before.' Quhafah's wrinkled features blossomed into a beatific smile.

'Father wouldn't rest, Prophet; he goaded us into bringing him here.' Queraybah laughed. 'I too was longing to come to be accepted into the fold.'

'The heart of the believer is held between two fingers of the Merciful. He turns it about as He wills.' Muhammad turned towards her. 'Say softly to yourself, *La Illaha illah Allah, Mohammed Ar Rusul Allah,* and you will become a bird of Paradise.'

'Yes, Prophet.' Qurayboh recited the Kalima.

'A noble daughter any father would love to have!' Muhammad complimented before turning his attention to the old man. 'Come, sit by me, Quhafah.'

'La Illaha illah Allah, Mohammed Ar Rusul Allah,' Quhafah recited fervently, declining the offer to be seated. 'Now I can rest in peace. I must go home now. Come and see me, Prophet, before you return to Medina.' He linked his arm into his daughter's. Abu Bakr claimed the other to assist his father.

'I will, for the honour of your blessings, Quhafah,' Muhammad promised. 'Be a dutiful son, Abu Bakr, but do come back after you break your fast of silence,' he teased.

'I am overwhelmed, Prophet, that's all,' Abu Bakr murmured.

Muhammad returned to his seat, spotting more visitors clambering up the ridge. Foremost amongst them were Hind and Abu Sofyan. 'O Messenger of God, praise be to Him Who has made triumph the religion which I choose for myself,' he said under his breath. Hind sailed closer, unveiling her face and smiling.

'Welcome, O daughter of Utbah, and receive the gift of Allah's grace.' Muhammad indicated a seat, his gaze turning to Abu Sofyan searchingly.

'She knows the Kalima by heart, Prophet, and she insisted that I accompany her here,' Abu Sofyan murmured rather apologetically.

'You are welcome, Abu Sofyan, and always welcome to join our circle of brotherhood and sisterhood.' Muhammad smiled, inviting him to sit close to his wife.

Mount As-Safa was turned into an ocean of love, as Muhammad sat receiving the Meccans. Washi and Habbar were the next to seek forgiveness, and the next to be forgiven. Huweidib and Safwan bin Khalaf followed suit, choosing not to become Muslims, but seeking forgiveness, and they too were forgiven. The Prophet's heart unfolded the prayer-rug of a song which he had sung during the rites of circumambulations.

'*Our Lord! We have heard the Call of One calling to Faith, "Believe ye in the Lord." And we have believed. Our Lord, forgive us our sins, blot out from us our iniquities, and take to Thyself our souls in the company of the righteous. Our Lord, grant us what Thou didst promise unto us through Thy apostles, and save us from shame on the Day of Judgement. O Lord, in Thee we put our complete Faith, to Thee we devote ourselves, and to Thee we return to ask Mercy. O Lord, forgive us and our brethren, who came before us into the Faith, and leave not in our hearts rancour or sense of injury against those who believed. Our Lord! Thou art indeed full of kindness, Most Merciful*' (59:10).

Then Muhammad welcomed the mother of Ikrimah.

'Prophet, I have come to plead forgiveness for my son. He has shut himself up in his house, and is afraid.' Umm Hakim stood wringing her hands.

'Welcome, Umm Hakim, a woman of the faithful,' Muhammad greeted kindly. 'Do not grieve that your son is not inclined to belief. Your own faith in Islam bestows upon him the gift of blessings. Tell him to have no fear; I have forgiven him.' His gaze fell on Usama. 'You seem proud of your turban of Yemeni cloth, Usama. Lend it to Umm Hakim, so that she can take it to her son as a token of my forgiveness.'

'Yes, Prophet.' Usama leapt to his feet, peeling the turban off his head.

Umm Hakim fled, hugging the length of turban to her breast, almost colliding with Al Abbas on the way. He was cantering ahead of his nephews, who had divorced the Prophet's daughters when Muhammad had first heard the Divine Call.

'I have brought our nephews, Prophet: do you recognise them?' Al Abbas announced. 'Despite their longing to join the fold of Islam, they were afraid to come.'

'Come close to me, my sons.' Muhammad smiled, his gaze returning to his uncle. 'I prayed to Allah for the boon of sons, Uncle, and he has granted me this favour.'

Allah's favour gilded Mount As-Safa in the light of love, as Meccans surged forth in droves to profess their faith in Islam.

La Illaha illah Allah
Mohammed Ar Rusul Allah.

Amidst the symphony of this Divine Creed, Umm Hakim was threading her way towards the Prophet. Ikrimah was at her heels, as if crushed under the weight of grief.

'First, I was afraid, Prophet, since my father persecuted you all his life, and I—' Ikrimah couldn't speak when he saw the flood of love and anguish in the Prophet's eyes.

'Ikrimah! Do not speak ill of your dead father, for it gives offence to the living,' Muhammad chided. 'Anything you ask of me today, I shall give to you.'

'I ask you, Prophet, that you pray to Allah that He may forgive me for all my enmity against you, which kept me blind to the truth,' Ikrimah murmured.

'Allah has forgiven you, my son,' Muhammad consoled. 'Remember to recite this revelation when you are in doubt. *Say: O my slaves who have been prodigal to their own hurt. Despair not of the mercy of Allah, Who forgiveth all sins. Lo! He is the Forgiving, the Merciful* (39:53). O God! Truly we ask Thee, O most forgiving and most merciful, to open for our prayers the doors of acceptance. O Thou Who respondeth to the petitions of the afflicted, O Thou Who sayest to a thing be and suddenly it is! O God! Truly we come in our multitude to Thee, to appeal for Thy forgiveness for our sins, and that we not be made to return in despair. And bestow upon us the best of that which Thou hast bestowed upon Thy virtuous servants, and make us not to return from this great and sacred place, except with success and happiness, without regrets and without further need to be penitent, and not as those who have gone astray, or who have been led into temptation. O most Merciful of those who show mercy! O God! Make us to be guided, and protect us from the cause of ignorance and destruction, and save us from the misfortunes of the sickness of the soul, for these are the worst of enemies. And make us to live in this world in faithfulness, and make us to die as Muslims! And make us to be of those who take the Book with their right hand, and make us to be of those who are secure on the Day of Great Fears, and bless us, O God, with the sight of Thy Exalted Countenance, by Thy Mercy, O Most Merciful of those who show mercy!'

A great hush had fallen upon everyone, as if the angels themselves had descended amongst them, listening, blessing. Muhammad's lips parted in a beatific smile.

'Now go to your homes, friends, and enjoy the comforts of rest and repast. Our bodies need as much nourishment as our souls in remembrance of God.'

The Meccans trooped down the hill of Mount As-Safa. Muhammad's lips unfolded the wistful song his soul had sung before he had migrated to Medina.

'O Mecca, you are the choicest of places on earth to me, and the most delectable. If your people had not cast me forth, I would never have forsaken you.'

'Now that you are the king of Mecca, Prophet, would you rather stay here and forsake us, and Medina?' Nasiba cried suddenly, more protests following.

'A king without a crown, and wearing only the cloak of faith!' Muhammad silenced all protest with a gentle wave of his arm. 'No, my friends, no! I will not stay in Mecca. When you pledged me your allegiance, I swore to live and die with you. I would not be acting as the servant of God, or His messenger, were I to leave you. Where you live, there will I live, and there too shall I die.'

'Though the Meccans have submitted to you, Prophet, some tribes are staging rebellion.' Othman ibn Affan approached hastily. 'The great tribe of Hawazin, allied with the clan of Banu Saad, is gathering its forces in the city of Taif with the intention of attacking us. They have been planning this siege since before we came to Mecca, Prophet. Abu Sofyan is the one who has told me about it. He says his spies returned this morning, and confirmed the danger of the assault.'

'We have come as pilgrims of peace, Othman, and we can offer them nothing but the gift of peace,' Muhammad intoned calmly.

'But they intend to fight, Prophet! And they are a rebellious lot,' Othman ibn Affan declared, in despair and urgency.

'As a last resort then, we might have to fight in self-defence. In self-defence only: remember that, Othman.' Muhammad's look was thoughtful and piercing.

'If they don't kill me, this heat will!' Othman ibn Affan lamented.

'Hell is hotter!' Muhammad turned on his heel. 'Yet I would like to be a bridge over the fires of hell, so that the creatures could pass over me and not be harmed.'

The victory of Mecca rolled on into a month of warfare. When peace had returned, Muhammad sat with his companions on a small hill, close to the sandy graveyard. Muhammad had chosen the site so that he could be near the graves of Abu Talib and Khadija, wishing to offer his prayers before returning to Medina.

Othman ibn Affan's fears had come true: Malik ibn Auf, after rejecting all offers of peace, had marched out of Taif towards the valley of Hunain. Employing women and children as human shields, he was sure of his success, since he knew that the Muslims would not attack any child or woman. This ploy worked to his advantage at the beginning, but then the Muslim soldiers managed to separate the combatants from behind the wall of women and children. Malik ibn Auf was defeated. Into the hands of the Muslims had fallen six thousand prisoners, besides four thousand ounces of silver, forty thousand sheep, and twenty-four thousand camels.

These Muslims won't be fully defeated until they are drowned in the sea.

Muhammad's thoughts remembered Abdallah ibn Ubbay's comment at the battle of Hunain. More comments were surfacing in his head.

This is my revenge against Muhammad. Muhammad didn't know who'd said that.

By God, it is better to be ruled by a man from the Quraysh, than by a man from Hawazin!

This comment by Abu Sofyan during the battle of Hunain was knocking at the gates of Muhammad's thoughts. All six thousand of the idolaters taken prisoner were released, though they had shown no inclination to accept Islam. In addition, they were given vast quantities of goods with which to barter, to be divided amongst themselves for the sustenance of their families. Amongst the captured was Shayma, the daughter of Halima.

By God, I am the foster-sister of your Prophet. Shayma's protest to one guard after the battle rose afresh in Muhammad's head. *Don't you remember me, Prophet? I am your foster-sister. Look, this scar on my arm; you bit me really hard one day when I was carrying you to the valley of Sarar—*

Muhammad had taken off his cloak, spreading it on the ground for her to be seated. Before she left, he had given her silver, goats and camels.

Another scene was fluttering open its wings inside his head. He could see his uncle, Al Abbas, rallying the Muslims when they thought they were going to lose the battle. *O hosts of Helpers! O companions of the Tree!*

Suddenly, Muhammad's thoughts awoke to the arguments around him.

'The Quraysh get rich gifts, and we get only a poor share of the booty!'

'Abu Sofyan got one hundred camels, and when he asked for gifts for his sons, both his sons received one hundred camels each! That means Abu Sofyan actually got three hundred camels!'

'What about Hakim, Khadija's nephew? Not even satisfied with the gift of one hundred camels, he asked for more, and got another two hundred!'

'Even the idolaters received more than we did!'

'Safwan ibn Khalaf received one hundred camels too! And on our return from victory, he happened to like the valley of Iranah, so he got that as well!'

'At least Safwan ibn Khalaf decided to become a Muslim after all. Huweidib only sought forgiveness, and even he received one hundred camels.'

'And Hisham! And the half-brother of Khalid, what's his name? And Zuhayar ibn Amr, the son of the Prophet's aunt Atika …'

'The booty is great, and we are poor. Why is it that we received only four camels each, and the rich Meccans are enriched more?'

'Why, I ask? Why is it that the Quraysh and their kinsmen received more than we did? And why is it that we are complaining, and wondering, as if the Prophet is not with us? Why don't we ask him?'

'Tell us, Prophet' – Saeed bin Udadah lowered his voice, as the Prophet opened his eyes – 'why in the time of the battle we were those who fought and defended the most, but when it came time to divide the spoils, the Quraysh received the biggest share.'

'The alms are for the poor and the needy, and for those who collect them, and for those whose hearts are to be reconciled, and to set free slaves and captives, and for the relief of the debtors, and for the cause of God and for the wayfarer – an obligation enjoined by God' (9:60), Muhammad recited in response. 'A fifth of the spoils is for alms, not booty, for the poor and the aggrieved. Did you not notice how poorly clad the captives were? Did I not send our own men to Mecca to buy clothes for them in exchange for the silver which came into our hands? Did your hearts not rejoice when you witnessed their joy and relief after they were released and well clad and amply provided for? Our duty and commitment to religion is difficult to understand right now perhaps, but time and experience will lend you understanding much later, for sure. Let it suffice for the present that the richest gifts were bestowed upon those whose hearts needed the balm of assurance to dissolve their doubts and bitternesses before they could be ready to wear the mantle of unity. The Quraysh and kinsmen, you say; but didn't the Bedouins of Mecca receive more riches than them? Ummayah of Ghatafan and Arqat of Tanim received more than our own companions – Juayl and others, though exceedingly poor, received only four camels each, that is true. And yet I tell you this, by Him in Whose hands my soul is: Juayl is worth more than a worldful of men like Arqat and Ummayah, but their souls need the fuel of hope and reconciliation, while Juayl's soul does not lack riches in faith and devotion. The nephew of my beloved Khadija, Hakim, received a hundred camels and asked for more; that too is true. But does anyone remember what I said when I gave him a hundred more? "Whoso taketh it in munificence of soul shall be blessed therein, but whoso taketh it for the pride of his soul shall not be blessed therein, and he shall be as one that eateth

and is not filled. The upper hand is better than the lower hand, and begin thy giving with such of thy family who are dependent upon thee." If you didn't hear me say that, did anyone of you hear what Hakim said?'

'I was there, Prophet,' Umar-al Khattar began meekly. 'He returned his second gift of a hundred camels and said, "By Him Who sent thee with the truth, I will not receive aught from any man after thee. And in future, my hand shall never be the lower."'

'You were riding with me, O Saeed, when I bestowed gifts upon Safwan. Do you remember what he said?' Muhammad's gaze was sad and profound.

'Yes, Prophet,' Saeed bin Udadah murmured, not meeting the Prophet's gaze. 'He said, "I bear witness that no soul could have such goodness as this, if it were not the soul of a Prophet." Then he recited the Kalima, as if his heart was breaking.'

'I came among you marked as a liar, and you believed in me. I was persecuted, and you protected me. I was helpless, and you helped me in my plight,' Muhammad began passionately. 'Think you I did not feel all that? Think you I can be ungrateful? You complain that I bestow gifts upon these people, and give none to you. It is true, I give them worldly gear, but it is to win their worldly hearts. To you, who have been true, I give *myself*. They return home with sheep and camels; you return with the Messenger of Allah amongst you. For, by Him in whose hand is the soul of Muhammad, even if the whole world goes one way and you go another, I will remain with you. Which of you, then, have I most rewarded, tell me?'

'Messenger of Allah! Messenger of Allah…' A flurry of protests from his followers was silenced by the sudden appearance of Abu Bakr.

'An unfortunate incident happened not far from the Kaaba, Prophet,' Abu Bakr announced hastily. 'A group of Bedouin Muslims from the clan of Khuzaah have killed an idolater from a rival tribe. They didn't want him to enter the Sacred City.'

'Lo! those who disbelieve and bar men from the way of Allah and from the Inviolable Place of worship which We have appointed for mankind together, the dweller therein and the nomad: whosoever seeketh wrongful partiality therein, him we shall cause to taste a painful doom' (22:25). Muhammad got to his feet. 'O my people, Allah made Mecca a holy place on the day when the heavens and the earth were created. Mecca is holy till the end of time. No one who believes in God and the Day of Judgement is allowed to shed blood, or destroy even a tree inside the limits of this city. Mecca has never been despoiled by anyone before me, and it will never be despoiled by anyone after me. Only for that brief hour of conquest, and because God's wrath was upon its people, did He permit us to enter armed, as both soldiers and pilgrims of peace. Now Mecca is restored to its previous holiness. Whoever is here, let him inform those who are absent that whoever argues that the Prophet of God fought in Mecca, say to him that God temporarily suspended its sanctity for His Prophet, but not for anyone else, and surely not for the Khuzaah men. All the killing must stop, for it is an evil crime that brings no advantage. A man has been killed, and now I must pay blood money to his people. From this day forward, the relatives of any murder victim will have the choice between executing the murderer or receiving compensation.' He turned on his heel. 'I want to be with Khadija this evening. We start for Medina tomorrow.' He plodded towards the grave of his beloved.

He sat next to Khadija's grave, feeling her nearness. Khadija was holding out her arms, her eyes absorbing him entirely.

I never did tell you, dear Muhammad, that I knew you to be a Prophet even before you received your Divine Call. Khadija's eyes and lips poured sweet melodies.

Remember my maid Maisra, dear Muhammad? The one who accompanied you on a trading trip to Bostra in southern Syria? Upon her return she was all flustered and befuddled, and she shared with me one of the incidents which had made her envious of my love for you, since a love like mine could not be concealed; you were the only one not to notice it. But listen to this, and try to remember. You were sitting under the shade of a tree in Bostra. Opposite that tree was the cell of a monk by the name of Nestor. He came out of his cell and asked Maisra who you were. She told him that you were a Qurayshi man from the clan of Banu Hashim. But the monk kept looking at you, and exclaiming, 'None other than a Prophet is sitting beneath that tree!' Now don't think, dear Muhammad, I married you for that. I was too much in love already; I was hoping that you would propose, but you never did, so I had to—

Khadija was embracing him.

Beloved. My All. My Sweetness. My Ever and Forever. Muhammad's soul was transformed into the shape of a divine harp, its silvery strings teasing songs from the sound of the falling of the leaves in the Garden of Eden.

Chapter 18

The Light of Medina
Year 631 AD

Dressed in pilgrim white with a turban of Yemeni cloth, Muhammad was seated amongst his companions in his mosque, but his thoughts were on a pilgrimage through the year that had passed since his return to Medina. Ibrahim was almost two years old. Fatima's daughter Zainab was nearly six. Hasan had turned seven, Hussain was almost five, and the youngest brother, Mushin, was only a year older than Ibrahim. But less than a year after his return to Medina, Fatima's youngest daughter Khultum had died. When the time came for the yearly pilgrimage, he had not the strength to journey to Mecca, so he had sent Abu Bakr with a few of his followers to perform the rites of Hajj.

Muhammad's thoughts were performing their own Hajj, as he sat listening to his followers and checking their zeal.

O God, I condemn what Khalid ibn Walid has done.

Such a lament had singed Muhammad's lips twice. Khalid ibn Walid had been sent to the Nakhlah Valley to remove the idol of al-Uzzah, but when a few of the members of the Jadhimah clan tried to prevent him, he had killed them on charges of provocation. After that, Muhammad thought that Khalid's zeal had been drained by penance, and he had allowed him the privilege of journeying with him on an expedition against the Romans. Since no war was fought on this expedition, Muhammad had returned to Medina, leaving Khalid behind to carry the message of Islam to the neighbouring tribes. The Christians of Duma were averse to his message, so, pressed by zeal, he killed a few of them and took their prince, Ukaidir ibn Malik, captive. Muhammad was aggrieved; he treated the prince of Duma courteously and granted him freedom. Then he commanded Khalid never to carry a sword until he had stabbed his zealotry with the knives of penance!

Muhammad's thoughts moved towards the present. Urwah was on the road to Mecca, compelled by his own impulse to acquaint the people of Thaqif with the precepts of Islam. Ali was dispatched to the north-east of Medina where the tribe of Tayy had risen in rebellion. King Negus had died soon after the victory of Mecca.

A few months after his death, Medina was astir with news that the Emperor Heraclius had mustered large forces to crush the power of Islam. So Muhammad had marched with a contingent of thirty thousand men towards the borders of Tebuk, midway between Medina and Damascus. The Roman legion was nowhere to be seen, so Muhammad commanded his men to halt to rest and to soothe their tired limbs in the cool waters.

'You have done well, for verily a Prophet does not die until he has been led in prayer by a pious man of his people,' Muhammad had said when he overslept on the first morning in Tebuk, and Abdul Rahman had led the morning prayers.

The Muslim troops camped in Tebuk for twenty days. On their journey back to Medina, tribe after tribe had sent their deputations to join the Islamic fold.

Ali was not included in the expedition to Tebuk, since Muhammad wished him to stay in Medina to take care of his wife and children. But Abdallah ibn Ubbay spread a rumour that the Prophet wanted to get rid of Ali. Ali, in return, riding with the speed of lightning, had caught up with the cavalcade and plied Muhammad with questions.

'O Ali, you will be unto me as Aaron was to Moses!' Muhammad had exclaimed before appeasing his fears, adding that Ali was hugging only a fabric of lies.

Muhammad's thoughts now turned to Abdallah ibn Ubbay, who had fallen ill after the expedition of Tebuk, and been called a barrage of names by the Medinese.

Chief of the Hypocrites was one, he remembered—

He became aware of Abdul Rahman suddenly.

'Prophet, this man here got into a fight with his neighbour, and struck him in the face,' Abdul Rahman began hastily. 'Now, what kind of punishment does he deserve, that will teach him to be kind to his neighbours and to cultivate good manners?'

'He should apologise to his neighbour most humbly, and ask his forgiveness. Then he should give alms to the poor as part of his penance,' Muhammad advised.

'I have neither food nor goods to give away, Prophet!' the poor man cried.

'Prophet, my father has sent you this gift.' Bishr offered a basket of dates.

'Allah's blessings!' Muhammad received the basket with a burst of joy, returning his attention to the poor man. 'Here you are, my impenitent friend! Take this basket, and distribute these dates amongst the poor.' He held out the basket to him.

'Honestly, Prophet, I do not know anyone who is poorer than me,' the poor man murmured, claiming the basket reluctantly.

'Then eat as many as you can; that might be your act of penance!' Muhammad laughed. 'And if you don't get the gripes, be assured that your penance is accepted.'

'What is the difference between almsgiving as an act of penance, and almsgiving as charity like we pay with the poor rate, Prophet?' Juayl asked after the man had fled, hugging his basket.

'They are both acts of virtue to help one's community; they feed the poor, the sick, the orphans and the widows.'

Muhammad smiled. 'When you consciously share a fifth of your wealth by paying your poor rate, you discipline yourself in the virtues of generosity, making sure that no one goes hungry in your community or in the whole wide world. And as an act of penance, almsgiving brings you close to God and closer to God-consciousness.'

'Why are the Jews and Christians in Medina exempt from paying the poor rate, Prophet?' Khira was quick to voice his doubts.

'They welcomed us into Medina, didn't they?' Muhammad began passionately. 'They helped us when we were poor, and fed us when we were hungry. Almsgiving like theirs should last us for generations, I should think.'

'What is *jizya*, Prophet?' was Musailamah's puzzled enquiry. 'Is the poor rate different from jizya? What I don't understand is why should I as a Christian have to pay jizya, while the others who live in Medina are exempt?'

'The poor rate is incumbent upon Muslims, while jizya is the payment for the services agreed upon between the Muslims and the other tribes, regardless of their faith or belief. And that payment is for the expenditure which is required to ensure the safety of the lives and properties of those exposed to violence or oppression from other tribes pressed by ambition or conquest. All those tribes outside Medina who have agreed to pay jizya are under our protection, and so far we remain successful in safeguarding their interests. Any fraction of negligence on our part – if we fail to protect their lives and properties – the pact of jizya fails too; it is rendered null and void.' Muhammad's gaze held Anas captive. 'For the benefit of the Christians present here, Anas, read the agreement we signed with the bishop. We should all benefit from it, since it highlights our duties towards furthering the interests of the clans and the tribes.'

'Yes, Prophet. I will test my memory with this one,' Anas began eagerly. 'In the Name of God, the Merciful, the Compassionate.

This is a secure pact from God and Muhammad, the Messenger of God, to Yohanna, the son of Ruba and the people of Iliya. Their ships and transport vessels, whether on sea or land, are under the protection of God and Muhammad, as are those of anyone who travels with them to Syria or Yemen. Any of them who suffer losses due to aggression shall not try to regain their goods from the usurpers, but will go to Muhammad, who will get their belongings back for them. They shall not be prevented from enjoying any oasis they wish to visit, nor from travelling on any roads they wish, whether upon sea or land.'

'A great tragedy, Prophet!' Ibn Kami appeared. 'Urwah is no more. In Taif, he invited people to join Islam, but they laughed at him. Then he climbed onto the roof of a house, calling the faithful to prayer. The crowds, joined by the tribes of Thaqif and Hawazin, pelted him with stones and he died.'

'May his soul rest in peace,' Muhammad murmured.

'Lay a curse on the tribes of Thaqif and Hawazin, Prophet!' Al Abbas proposed.

'Oh Allah, guide the tribes of Thaqif and Hawazin towards the path of love and understanding.' Muhammad joined his hands in an act of prayer.

'Why are you praying for these people, Prophet, who have become our enemies?' Al Abbas waved his arms desperately.

'Have I not been sent as a mercy to mankind, Uncle?' Muhammad intoned profoundly. 'Have I not said "love thy enemy"? Have I not preached equal love for all, equal respect for all, equal faith in all? They know not what they did.'

'This tragedy, Prophet, after much violence, has resulted in peace,' Ibn Kami observed. 'After the death of Urwah, his mother incited both the tribes against each other. Fist fights flared between the clans, but, realising their error, they decided to profess Islam as a pact of peace between them.'

'Alone unto God. Not to al-Lat, nor to al-Uzzah can be thine escape – if escape thou canst, on a day when escape there is none. No fleeing from men save for him whose heart is pure in submission to God—' Jubayr's exclamation was swallowed by the stormy appearance of Ali, leading a beautiful woman into the midst of the congregation.

'I was compelled to fight with the Tayy tribe, Prophet, but they finally submitted,' Ali explained. 'I have brought several prisoners with me. And this young lady Safarah here is the sister of their leader, Adi, who has fled to Syria. She insists on speaking with you, Prophet, on behalf of all the prisoners, and for herself.'

'My late father, Hatim Tai, was a generous man, Prophet!' Safarah cried suddenly. 'He was a benefactor of the poor and the needy. No one left empty handed from his palace. Its doors were always open to the hungry, whom he fed and clothed. He comforted the distressed whenever they sought his assistance, and helped free captives by paying ransoms out of his own treasury. No one has the right to make me – his daughter – a prisoner, whether I believe in Islam or not!' she challenged.

'*There is no compulsion in religion*' (2:257), Muhammad recited kindly. 'Islam forbids us to force our religion on anyone, my daughter; Ali knows that. And I hope he didn't take anyone captive on religious grounds. You cannot be held prisoner, that's true, by virtue of being the daughter of such a noble and generous man. I have heard about your father through one of my wives. Go in peace, my daughter; you are free.'

'How can I accept freedom, O Prophet, if my friends remain captive here?' Safarah murmured, awe and disbelief shining in her eyes.

'For your sake, my daughter, they are free to go home too, and are forgiven by the grace of Allah's mercy,' Muhammad murmured back. 'A young woman like you, endowed with the virtue of courage, can never be held captive, but should be treated like a queen whose purity of heart is a blessing for the kindred of all nations.'

'Thank you, Prophet,' Safarah bent low, touching his knees reverently. 'I will go to Syria to fetch my brother, so that he can be blessed with the honour of meeting a true Prophet.' She fled on the wings of her own devotion.

'Men are asleep, and they awaken when they die,' Muhammad murmured. 'Come, Ali; sit by me and try to see the beauty of religion, beyond words. Learn to love no matter what you do. Islam is in its infancy, a stranger in this world, and it will remain a stranger if it is not nourished with a passion for love, justice and kindness.'

'How should I comport myself, Prophet?' Ali asked 'Tell me; I do not know.'

'Live in the world, Ali, as if you are both a part of it and not.' Muhammad smiled. 'Do for this world as if you are to live forever, and for the next as if you are to die tomorrow.'

'I try to do right, Prophet, but I go about my faith blindfolded, it seems,' Ali lamented, averting his gaze.

'*Not blind are the eyes, but blind are the hearts within the breasts* (22:46). Don't you remember this revelation, Ali?' Muhammad's look was warm and piercing.

'How do I lend sight to my heart, Prophet, if it stays blind?' Ali appealed.

'Remembrance of Allah is the way to unlock the gates of one's spiritual heart and look into its eyes,' Muhammad breathed tenderly. 'There is polish for everything which takes away the rust, and the polish of the heart, to purify it, is the remembrance of God.'

'And how does one know one's heart is purified?' Ali's look was feverish.

'*My slave ceaseth not to draw near unto Me with devotions of his free will, until I love him. And when I love him I Am the hearing with which he heareth, and the sight with which he seeth, and the hand with which he graspeth, and the foot on which he walketh.*' Muhammad's eyes were shining with the light of inspiration.

'One would think one had died and gone to heaven, then,' Usama murmured.

'*God hath promised the believers, the men and the women, gardens that are watered by flowing rivers, wherein they shall dwell immortal, abodes of excellence in the Garden of Eden. And Ridwan from God is greater. That is the Infinite Beatitude* (9:72) …' Muhammad broke off as he noticed the slow approach of Abdullah.

'My father is no more, Prophet,' Abdullah announced, holding his grief at bay. 'But before he died he asked two favours from you. He wanted you to give him your cloak as a burial shroud, and to pray for him at his funeral, for forgiveness from Allah.'

'I would be doing myself a favour to fulfil the wishes of your late father, my son.' Muhammad got to his feet, with a sad and comforting expression.

'Abdallah ibn Ubbay! That Chief of the Hypocrites, Prophet?' Othman ibn Affan exclaimed. 'How could you even think of praying for him, after this was revealed to you? *Ask forgiveness for them, O Muhammad, or ask not forgiveness for them; though thou ask forgiveness for them seventy times, Allah will not forgive them*' (9:80).

'I'll have to pray more than seventy times, then, won't I?' Muhammad's eyes were blinded by tears, as he turned on his heel, Abdullah following in stunned silence.

Muhammad sat by the little grave along with his wives and a few friends. It had been four months since the death of Abdallah ibn Ubbay, and now his own son Ibrahim had died, suffering no ailment, his laughter still ringing in his ears.

'O Ibrahim. My son, my son!' Muhammad lamented. 'The eyes rain tears, the heart is broken, but we can only say what pleases Allah. I mourn for you, my son, but to Allah we belong, and to Him we return.'

'O Messenger of Islam, what bereavement is this?' was Abdul Rahman's abrupt plea. 'Did you not say that we are forbidden to weep or lament? Would we not also weep and lament when afflicted with grief, and the generation after us when they—' His voice was choked by dread, as a total eclipse of the sun engulfed everyone in darkness.

'When did I forbid this?' Muhammad sobbed. 'Tears are God's mercy. There is no harm in weeping. Tears are the channels of God's love; they make room to receive the balm of healing from Allah. O Ibrahim, if it were not that the promise of reunion is sure, and that this is a path that everyone must tread, and that the last of us shall overtake the first, verily we should grieve for thee with a greater sorrow.'

'The heaven itself is grieving for the death of Ibrahim, Prophet!' Bilal exclaimed. 'It is an omen and a warning, this eclipse.'

'Keep your heart pure of all superstition!' Muhammad chided. 'The sun and the moon are two of God's signs. Their light is not dimmed for the birth or death of anyone. When you see an eclipse, hasten to remember God through prayer.' He struggled to his feet, holding out his hands to assist Mary. '*Blessed is He Who hath placed in the heavens the constellations of the Zodiac, and hath placed therein a lamp and a light-giving moon. And He it is Who hath made the night and the day to succeed one over the other, as a sign for him who would reflect or give thanks* (25:61–62). *He it is Who sendeth down clear revelations unto His slave, that He may bring you forth from darkness unto light. And lo! for you, Allah is full of Pity, Merciful*' (57:9).

More than half a year had elapsed since Ibrahim's death, and the time for the annual Hajj had already arrived. Excited about the journey, his wives had developed their own ritual of detaining the Prophet after the midday meal, wanting to learn more about Islam, and this particular afternoon was no exception.

'What does *Alif-Lam-Mim* mean, Prophet? I have been reciting it like a parrot without knowing,' Swadah asked suddenly.

'In your parrot-like refrain, my Swadah, forget not to recite: *Verily we are for God, and verily unto Him we are returning*' (2:156). Muhammad smiled. 'Remembrance of God is knowledge. He alone has perfect knowledge, and is the bestower of knowledge upon whom He wills. The first letter, Alif, stands for Allah, of infinite beauty and goodness, signifying the flow of mercy, which creates and reveals revelations and messengers. The letter Lam is for Rusul or Messenger, meaning Allah's Prophet. The third letter, Mim, connotes my earthly name, Muhammad.'

'What other names has Allah given you, Prophet?' Aisha mocked.

'Al-Mustafa, my little rebel.' Muhammad laughed. 'And that means, the Elect, the Chosen One – an intimate friend of Allah, if you must know. Just like Moses who was clothed entirely in wool – in the garment of purity – when he spoke with Allah.'

'Is the Quran like the commandments of Moses, Prophet?' Hafsa asked.

'As pure and sacred as the Ten Commandments, my Hafsa,' Muhammad answered. 'When one recites its verses, it causes the skin of those who fear their Lord to glow and tingle, making their hearts grow pliant unto the remembrance of God.'

'Are our hearts purified, Prophet, when we recite Kalima?' Umm Salmah murmured to herself, her gold eyes sparkling all of a sudden.

'If the seven heavens and the seven earths were put in one scale, Salmah, they would be outweighed by *La Illaha illah Allah, Mohammed Ar Rusul Allah*.'

'Can the hearts of men and women be free of jealousy, Prophet, and of other passions equally harmful?' Zainab could not help voicing her own troubling thoughts.

'Our spiritual heart, Zainab, not the physical heart, can be purified by the will and grace of Allah, in return purifying the heart of blood and flesh,' Muhammad responded.

'Can our spiritual hearts feel the presence of Allah?' Juwairya asked suddenly.

'If our hearts are filled with the light of love, we can feel Allah's presence.' Muhammad reminisced aloud. 'God says: *I was a hidden treasure and loved to be known. And therefore I created the world that I might be known. God is all power; there is no power but God's. There is no thing whose treasuries are not with us*' (15:21).

'Some of your followers, Prophet, do they not dispute about the rights of women, parading their own ideas and arguments? And when talking about loving their wives, they seem to be expecting some sort of reward from Allah, or fearing punishment', said Umm Habiba with a toss of her head, as if thinking to herself.

'If you find them disputing, Habiba, remind them of this revelation. *And women have rights over men similar to those of men over women*' (2:228), Muhammad recited. 'Allah sets it down as a virtue for a man to walk with his wife hand in hand. And if he puts his arms around her shoulders in love, his virtue is increased tenfold.'

'Is the Kaaba really the First House of God, Prophet?' Safiya asked. 'And does Allah command all nations to come to the Kaaba for the annual pilgrimage?'

'Did Hafsa not copy this revelation for you, Safiya? It was on a piece of cloth, I remember,' Muhammad intoned warmly. '*The First House of worship appointed for men was that at Becca which is full of Blessings and Guidance for all creatures! In this are signs manifest. Wherein are plain memorials of Allah's Guidance, the place where Abraham stood up to pray; and whoso entereth is safe. And pilgrimage to the House is a duty unto Allah for mankind, for him who can find a way thither. As for him who disbelieveth, let him know that lo! Allah is independent of all creatures*' (3:96–97).

'It is so difficult to understand God, who doesn't need us,' Mary sighed to herself.

'God doesn't need us, but we need Him, so greater is our need to understand Him, sweet Mary,' Muhammad consoled. 'And yet God is all mercy; the light of His mercy flows towards us all at all times. Our limited intelligence can't comprehend the All-Merciful. And yet again, to understand God, one must believe that He is the one and only source of mercy. One must have faith that He is eternal, infinitely compassionate. He is absolute, not limited by time or place; His love is boundless and unconditional. All-Perfect. He is Allah, the creator of unity, and the source of mercy.'

'I have been meaning to ask you, Prophet.' Maymuna sought Muhammad's attention. 'Yesterday, a woman came to speak with you at the mosque, but you were not there. She looked sad and confused. Her husband wants to divorce her and take her son away. She told me she wanted you to intercede on her behalf to her husband, so that she can keep her son, whom she loves dearly.'

'She has the right to keep her son! A greater right than her husband, since she carried him in her womb for nine months, and nurtured him with her own milk, besides loving him,' Muhammad intoned sadly. 'I hope she comes back to the mosque today. If you see her, Maymuna, bring her to me.' He paused. 'Once again, you have succeeded in detaining me, and I must return to the mosque.' He left the room amidst a volley of protests.

Another volley of protests was rising within Muhammad from the treasure-trove of his psyche, as he emerged into sunshine. The mirror of his perception was reflecting the familiar faces, the intent of murder in their hearts stark and savage. The faces were those of Amir and Arbad. Muhammad, approaching the mosque, was astonished to see the wraiths of his imagination materialising before his sight.

'You look handsome in your turban of striped Yemeni cloth, Prophet! And your red cloak adds colour to your pale cheeks.' Amir planted himself in Muhammad's way.

'Peace be upon you, Amir.' Muhammad's look was piercing. 'What brings you to Medina? You are not here just to compliment me on my outfit, I am sure.'

'To be sure, Prophet, I want to learn about Islam, if you would be so kind as to teach me?' Amir elicited a broad smile. 'What are the duties of a good Muslim?'

'To feed the hungry and to visit the sick,' Muhammad murmured, noticing the discomfited expression of both men. 'The duties of a good Muslim are simple and varied. To free captives if they be unjustly confined. To assist any person oppressed, whether Muslim or non-Muslim.'

'Surely, Prophet, there must be religious duties a Muslim must perform?' Amir began hastily, all flustered. 'Who is the best Muslim in Allah's sight?'

'The best person in Allah's sight is the best amongst his friends,' Muhammad intoned patiently. 'Islam is the religion of love, and one cannot love Allah unless one learns to love one's fellow beings first.'

'Is Islam a religion of the heart then?' Amir asked, craftily.

'The Islam of the heart is its purity, and the Islam of the tongue withholds it from fruitless words.' Muhammad smiled, his gaze laying bare the evil in Amir's soul.

'Would you grant me a private audience, Prophet? I want to learn more about Islam,' Amir appealed, becoming aware of the approach of Abu Bakr.

'No,' Muhammad declined with a mingling of sadness and compassion. 'You may come another day when your heart is not burdened by deception.'

'Another day, Prophet? That will be the day when I meet you with an overwhelming force of opposition!' Amir stalked away, his companion following.

'O Allah, help me against Amir.' Muhammad was foretelling Amir's death in the hot sands of the desert in his mind's eye.

'That man must be taken captive, Prophet; he has designs of launching a massive attack on Medina,' Abu Bakr was quick to warn, his gaze following the evil plotters.

'Don't worry, Abu Bakr,' Muhammad consoled. 'Allah in His great mercy has saved Amir from the indignity of captivity. Death is waiting for him on his way back, eager to claim him as a victim of the plague. A tragedy vast and unfathomable.'

The purity of golden sunshine was bathing the friend and the Prophet in an aura of love and peace as they drifted towards the mosque. Abu Bakr was thinking about his young bride, Esma, who was now heavy with child. Muhammad's thoughts had turned to his daughter Fatima; he had shared a secret with her which he dared not share with his wives. His heart was bursting with hope as he seated himself in the middle of a semicircle, joining the delegations of men from Yemen and Najran.

'You have brought such love and friendship amongst us, O Messenger of Islam!' Abal Mish complimented. 'Please share with us more wisdom from the Quran, before we return to Najran.'

'*And We caused Jesus, Son of Mary, to follow in their Scriptures, confirming that which was revealed before him, and We bestowed on him the gospel wherein is the guidance and a light, confirming that which was revealed before it in the Torah – a guidance and an admonition unto those who ward off evil*' (5:46), Muhammad recited.

'So many revelations, O Messenger of Islam, and so many interpretations which cause rifts and arguments!' Al Harith began thoughtfully. 'Who are those best suited to interpret these revelations for us?'

'The best suited are the men and women whose hearts are filled with love, and who are endowed with great understanding.' Muhammad smiled. '*He it is Who hath revealed unto thee, Muhammad, the Scripture wherein are clear revelations. They are the substance of the Book, and others which are allegorical. But those in whose hearts hides doubt pursue, forsooth, that which is allegorical; seeking to cause dissension by seeking to explain it. None knoweth its explanation save Allah. And those who are of sound instruction say: We believe therein; the whole is from our Lord, but only men of understanding really heed*' (3:7).

'Isn't Allah also the Lord of the Jews and the Christians, O Messenger of Islam?' Musailamah's eyes were full of doubt and challenge.

'*Lo! those who believe in that which is revealed unto thee, Muhammad, and those who are Jews, and Christians, and Sabaeans – whoever believeth in Allah and the Last Day and doth right – surely, their reward is with their Lord, and there shall no fear come upon them, neither shall they grieve*' (2:62), was Muhammad's fervent response.

'Are some not better than others in love and faith, O Prophet, earning respect, if not envy?' Abu Rafi asked with a mingling of caprice and curiosity.

'Islam teaches equal love for all, equal respect for all, and equal faith in all,' Muhammad intoned patiently. '*And covet not the things in which Allah hath made some of you excel over others. Unto men a fortune from that which they have earned, and unto women a fortune from that which they have earned. Envy not one another, but ask Allah of His Bounty. Lo! Allah is ever knower of all things*' (4:32).

'Are our ill deeds forgiven, if we repent?' Khalid ibn Walid asked.

'The most merciful Allah forgives all who turn to Him in love and repentance,' answered Muhammad. '*Establish worship at the two ends of the day, and in some watches of the night. Lo, good deeds annul ill deeds. This is a reminder for the mindful*' (11:114).

'Yesterday, my sister got married, Prophet!' Juayl exclaimed suddenly. 'Her in-laws wanted me to recite a prayer of blessing. I couldn't think of anything, so I recited this revelation. *In the name of Allah, the Beneficent, the Merciful. Praise be to Allah, the Lord of the Worlds. The Beneficent, the Merciful. Owner of the Day of Judgement. Thee alone we worship. Thee alone we ask for help. Show us the straight path. The path of those whom Thou hast favoured. Not the path of those who can earn Thine anger. Nor of those who go astray* (1:1–7). I hope I did the right thing?'

'You did a noble thing, Juayl. Allah's love and blessings are with us all when this revelation is recited,' Muhammad complimented. 'Next time there is a wedding, say, "May Allah bless you, and may His blessings be upon you and your coming together be auspicious." Then recite the same revelation which you did, but add: *And among His signs is this that He created for you mates from among yourselves, that you may dwell in tranquility with them. And He has put Love and Mercy between your hearts. Verily in that are signs for those who reflect*' (30:21).

'Since we are going to Mecca for the pilgrimage, Prophet, what prayer should be dearest to our hearts during the journey?' Al Abbas asked fervently.

'Prayer and gratitude to the Lord of the Worlds, Who has granted us the favour of this pilgrimage. We will pray as Abraham prayed,' Muhammad said, and he demonstrated. *'Accept this from us, our Lord, because You are receptive and knowing. Help us to surrender to Your will and guide our descendants. Teach us to serve only You, and forgive us our sins, because You are forgiving, the source of all mercy. Bless our descendants with messengers of their own to guide them. Teach them the Scripture, give them wisdom, and correct their faults, because You are indeed mighty and wise'* (2:127–129).

'Though I myself am far away, yet take my words to my people at the Holy House. I dwell amidst the place God hath hallowed. Set then aside the sorrows ye have grieved. Weary not camels, scouring the earth for me. For I, praise be to God, am in the best of noble families, great in all its line.' Bilal sang a poem Zaid had taught him.

'How sweetly you have brought back the memory of Zaid, Bilal,' Muhammad breathed tenderly. 'Zaid, my son, my friend! He would have danced with joy at the mere thought of making such a pilgrimage. His father was from the tribe of Kalb, and his mother from the tribe of Tayy. Zaid was little when their town was raided by the men of Beni Kainuka, and he was carried off and sold into slavery. I adopted him. When his father came to get him, he didn't want to leave me and Khadija.'

'I could be his brother, Prophet, if you were to adopt me!' Kaab ibn Salma kept singing.

The Messenger of light is a source of Light
An Indian blade, a drawn sword of God's sword
Amid Qurayshi companions, when they chose
Islam in Mecca's vale, men said: 'Be gone!'
They went, not weaklings, not as men that flee
Swaying upon their mounts and poorly armed
But heroes, proud and noble of mien, bright-clad
In mail of David's weave for the encounter.

'God has a treasury beneath His throne, and the keys to it are the tongues of the poets.' Muhammad applauded, tossing his cloak to Kaab as a mark of honour. 'Put it on, Kaab, my Yemeni cloak, and be blessed with divine inspiration. And remember that the Prophet has been averse to war always, and will remain so till the end of his life. His sword and armour are not made of the earth's base metal, but of Allah's grace in mercy and forgiveness. David, too, was the slave of Allah's grace, inspired to fashion chain armour, yet guarding his heart against violence. *And assuredly We gave David grace from Us, saying: O ye hills and birds, echo the psalms of praise! And We made the iron supple unto him, saying: Make thou long coats of mail and measure the links thereof. And do ye right. Lo! I am seer of what ye do'* (34:10–11).

'Do alms, prayers and fasting bestow upon Muslims the reward of virtue and strength?' a stranger asked suddenly. All eyes turned to him.

'I shall inform you of a better act than alms, prayers and fasting,' Muhammad intoned profoundly. 'It is making peace between one another. Enmity and malice tear up heavenly rewards by the roots.'

'O Muhammad, what is the meaning of surrender to Allah?' the stranger asked.

'Does everything not belong to Allah?' Muhammad held the stranger captive in the intensity of his gaze. 'Yet, to surrender is to testify that there is no God but God, and that Muhammad is God's Messenger. To pray is to surrender, as is giving alms, fasting during Ramadan, and making a pilgrimage to the Holy House at least once if you can afford it.'

'Thou hast spoken truly, Muhammad.' The stranger's voice was casting a spell over everyone, as they listened in awe. 'What is faith?'

'To believe in God, His Angels and His books and His Messengers and in the Last Day.' Muhammad's eyes were oceans of light, his look radiant. 'And to believe that good or evil only comes by His Providence.'

'You speak only but truth, Muhammad!' The stranger got to his feet, his eyes locked into Muhammad's. 'What is excellence?'

'To worship God as if you see Him, and if you don't, God still sees the worshipper.' Muhammad too got to his feet, his eyes speaking volumes.

'Tell me of the Hour, O Muhammad?' The stranger was leaving. Only Muhammad was cognizant; the others were at pause, enveloped in a dream-state.

'The answer will be known when the Seeker and the Sought are One,' Muhammad murmured after the stranger. 'Yet, the Hour might come when the slave-girl shall give birth to her mistress and those who were but barefoot, naked, needy herdsmen shall build buildings higher and higher.'

'Where is he gone? That stranger, where is he? The one who was asking all those questions? Where is he?' Several voices hummed in astonishment.

'Know you this: he was Gabriel in the guise of a mortal man, and he came amongst you to teach you your religion.' Muhammad's tone was spilling tenderness.

'Where did he go, Prophet? Will he come back?' men were chanting.

'By Allah, I really do not know, even though I am God's Messenger,' Muhammad laughed. 'What will become of me, and what will become of you? That is the question I must ponder upon.' He turned on his heel. 'Come, Ali, leave everyone to their sweet contemplations, and talk to me about the imponderables. By the time we embark on our pilgrimage, we might know the answers to many of your questions.'

'I have much to learn, Prophet. Teach me wisdom.' Ali followed.

'Love is wisdom, Ali. You must love your fellow beings first before you can say that you love Allah,' Muhammad murmured over his shoulder. 'And purify your heart that you might get to know God. Pray most fervently: "O Lord, grant me the love of Thee, grant that I love those who love Thee. Grant that I may do the deeds that win Thy love."'

'It is so difficult to love everyone, Prophet. Especially those who injure or oppress us,' Ali ruminated, keeping pace with Muhammad.

'Strive towards spiritual purity, Ali, where the self becomes free of the limitations of injury or oppression,' Muhammad advised. 'Do not say that if people do good to us, we will do good to them; and if people oppress us, we will oppress them. But determine that if people do you good, you will do good to them, and if they oppress you, you will not oppress them. Abuse nobody, and if a man abuses you and lays open a vice which he finds in you, then do not disclose the one which you find in him. He is not strong who throws people down, but he is strong who withholds himself from anger. No person has drunk a better draught than that of anger, which he has swallowed for God's sake. The best acts of piety are humility and courtesy: remember that, Ali, always remember.'

'I never forget any word which escapes your blessed lips, Prophet,' Ali confessed tremulously. 'I want to be a perfect Muslim. Who is the perfect Muslim, Prophet, tell me, before you go home?' he pleaded.

'Go to Fatima, Ali, and you will find out,' Muhammad intoned tenderly. 'The most perfect of Muslims is the one whose disposition is most liked by his own family.' His thoughts were already hovering over Mecca: in his mind he was kissing the Black Stone.

Chapter 19

Farewell to the World

Year 632 AD

The Great Soul of Mecca was throbbing with the pulse of peace, as the pilgrims ran back and forth between the hills of As-Safa and Al-Marwah, performing the Hajj. They had circled around the Kaaba seven times, and now were making seven circuits between the hills, tracing the footsteps of Hagar. It was here that divine Providence had released Hagar from the valley of Bewilderment, folding her into the sanctuary of bliss. A great spring had bubbled forth from the spot where her infant son Ishmael had kicked the earth with his little heel, thirsty and wailing. After witnessing this great miracle, Hagar had cried under some spell of exaltation, 'Zumi Ya Mumaraka,' meaning 'Come together, O waters of divine Providence!' She had named the spring Zamzam, and since then its holy waters had become the sweetness of life for pilgrims.

Muhammad, astride Qaswa, was leading his followers through the rites. He was at the head of one hundred and twenty-four thousand pilgrims, donned in seamless white, and chanting praises to God.

I am here, O Lord! I am here! There is no other God but Thee! I am here! Praise, blessing, and dominion be to Thee! I am here! No one therein may share with Thee! I am here, O Lord! I am here!

Muhammad's senses caught this symphony of praises from the lips of the pilgrims while he watched Esma, the young bride of Abu Bakr. Esma had given birth to a son during their journey from Medina to Mecca, and Abu Bakr had wished to send her back to Medina, thinking that she wouldn't have the strength to perform the pilgrimage. But Muhammad had advised against it, infusing courage into Abu Bakr's heart that Esma's youth would grant her the strength to perform the Hajj. Muhammad's attention moved to Fatima. Before journeying forth from Medina, he had told Fatima that Gabriel, who was wont to recite to him the whole Quran every year, had recited it twice this year, preparing him in his journey to be united with his Lord.

This recollection alone invited a vision. Gabriel materialised, clothed in mists of light and splendour.

'*This year I have made the pilgrimage twice, Muhammad! I recited the Quran to you twice. Soon you will be meeting your Beloved,*' Gabriel warned, then left.

A furnace of longing opened up in Muhammad's soul and psyche, its flames soaring above the hills of As-Safa and Al-Marwah.

'*Glorified is He, and High Exalted above what they say! The seven heavens and the earth and all that is therein praise Him. And there is not a thing but hymneth His praise, but ye understand not their praise. Lo! He is ever Clement, Forgiving*' (17:43–44). Muhammad guided Qaswa in his last circuit towards As-Safa.

'*Glory to Him Who has subjected these to our use, for we could never have accomplished this by ourselves. And to our Lord, surely, must we turn back*' (57:1,5).

'*O Lord! Let my entry be by the Gate of Truth and Honour and likewise my exit be by the Gate of Truth and Honour, and grant me from Thy presence an Authority to aid me*' (17:80). Muhammad's lips snatched the songs of praises sung by the pilgrims.

'Our Lord, grant us good in this world, and good in the Hereafter, and save us from the torments of fire. And allow us to enter Paradise in the company of the pious. O Mighty, O all forgiving, O Lord of all creatures! O God! Thou art peace, from Thee is peace, and to Thee returneth peace! O God, open the doors of Thy mercy and forgiveness, and let us enter through the portals of Thy Paradise. In God's name! And praise be unto God! And blessings and peace to the Messenger of God!' Muhammad's thoughts tasted the dust of humility, and exploded forth in prayer.

'O God! Thou hast many claims on me for what is between Thee and me, and there are many claims against me, in my relation to the world of Thy creation. Make me content with what Thou hast made lawful, instead of that which is forbidden by Thee; knowing Thy bounty above all others, O most forgiving! O God! Verily Thy house is glorious, Thy countenance benign, and Thou art clement and bounteous. Great and oft-forgiving, therefore, forgive me.' Muhammad dismounted from Qaswa.

'God is most great! God is most great! God is most great! And unto God is due all praise.' Muhammad drank from Zamzam with his cupped hands.

'Allah hath appointed the Kaaba, the Sacred House, a standard for mankind, and the Sacred Month and the offerings and the garlands. That is so that ye may know that Allah knoweth whatsoever is in the heavens and whatsoever is on the earth, and that Allah is knower of all things' (5:97). Muhammad could hear Bilal's call to prayer.

The pilgrims were turning their heads from right to left, murmuring the greetings of peace. Muhammad's gaze was spilling its own light of love and compassion, the pomegranate red upon his lips polishing more praises: rubies to glorify God.

'I stand here before you today, not as the founder of a new religion, but as a servant of God, restoring a religion of mankind, to mankind, for all peoples, for all nations. This religion has been proclaimed through generations by a line of Prophets in succession in all parts of the world. To keep your faith pure from the rust of zealotry or despair, recite this revelation.' Muhammad paused. '*Faith isn't turning towards east or west. Faith is believing in God, the Last Day, the Angels, the Scriptures, and the Prophets. Faith is conquering your greed and giving generously to relatives, orphans, travellers, and those in need. It is freeing slaves, establishing prayer, giving in charity, fulfilling your promises, and being patient in danger, hardship, and adversity. Such people affirm the truth and are truly pious* (2:177). We will rest in our encampment tonight, then go to Mina in the morning and finish our rites.'

The Arabian sky was lowering a canopy of stars over the camp as Muhammad sat outside his tent, with his family and companions. The peace and quiet of the night sky penetrated Muhammad's awareness; his gaze contemplated the stars. Suddenly, a mighty wail from the fifteen-day-old infant of Esma and Abu Bakr shattered the silence.

'He would have been comfortable, Prophet, if we had accepted Umm Hani's offer to stay in her house,' Esma teased, laughing to herself. 'She invited us all, you know; but since you declined, I couldn't possibly accept.'

'Do you regret your decision, Esma?' Muhammad teased in return.

'How can I, Prophet, when you bestowed upon me the joy of this pilgrimage! All the comfort and sweetness I have longed for,' Esma confessed.

'Did you know, Prophet, that we named our son Muhammad?' Abu Bakr murmured.

'A beautiful name, Abu Bakr. I am honoured,' Muhammad laughed. 'The name alone can infuse universal love into the hearts of all peoples.'

'Does your name work wonders, Prophet?' Aisha challenged. 'Do you think it will make a person look virtuous, even if he does wrong, or commits evil?'

'*Men shall come forward in throngs to behold their works. And whosoever shall have wrought an atom's weight of good shall behold it. And whosoever shall have wrought an atom's worth of evil shall behold it. For, unto God belongeth the sovereignty of the heavens and of the earth and of all that they contain, and He hath the power over all things'* (99:6–8), Muhammad recited in response, laughter in his eyes.

'So men will be judged so?' Hafsa protested, her eyes flashing. 'What about the women, Prophet, hoping to enter Paradise?'

'*God hath promised to Believers, men and women, Gardens under which rivers flow, to dwell therein. And beautiful mansions in gardens of everlasting bliss. But the greatest of bliss is the good pleasure of God. That is the supreme felicity'* (9:72). Muhammad's eyes were portals of revelation.

'Does fasting earn the good pleasure of God, Prophet?' Umar ibn Khattab appeared to be challenging his own doubts, rather than exploring Islamic precepts.

'Fasting, just to give up food and drink, earns not much merit if one abstains not from evil thoughts, evil actions, or even forged speech,' Muhammad murmured.

'If a stranger asks me what Islam is, what do I tell him in the simplest terms so that he understands? I have been thinking about this, Prophet, during our whole journey from Medina to Mecca,' Al Abbas asked thoughtfully.

'Islam is belief in Allah, the one God of all peoples, all nations. That is simple enough, Uncle,' Muhammad breathed tenderly. 'And if anyone asks about Allah, tell them that Allah is not male or female. Allah does not resemble anything in all of creation, and Allah is beyond contemplation. Allah is beyond description: our finite, limited senses can't perceive the infinite; but we get to know the infinitely merciful through the light in our spiritual hearts. Islam teaches us to believe in angels, Scriptures and prophets. Prophets are people who are sent by God as guides towards righteousness, and righteousness means mercy and compassion towards Allah's creatures. Many prophets have come to this earth in different parts of the world, proclaiming love and peace, a belief in the afterlife and in the Day of Judgement, and a belief in destiny.'

'Does that mean, Prophet, that we can't change anything, and must let things happen as they come?' Usama asked, confused and flustered.

'Far from it, my son.' Muhammad smiled indulgently. 'Each individual must act within their ability within the eternal framework of God's mercy. A man cannot live without constant effort towards goodwill and improvement. Not even a prophet. The effort is from me, its fulfilment comes from Allah.'

'Do we change this world to be a better place if we kill those who corrupt it with evil?' Khalid ibn Walid was goaded by his zeal, which he could not silence.

'Killing is forbidden in Islam, unless one is compelled to kill in self-defence,' Muhammad warned. 'O Khalid, be gentle with everyone. Even if Mount Ohud turned to gold for you, and you spent it according to Allah's wishes, you would gain nothing if you were not kind to Allah's creatures! Have I not been sent as a mercy to all nations?' His gaze shifted towards his wives. 'Belief and non-belief are but two parallel streams, running their course towards the shore of understanding. Non-belief turns to belief when one believes that one has no belief: this affirmation itself becomes one's belief.' He drifted towards his tent. 'We must get some sleep before our journey to Mina.'

The sun-tortured valley of Arafat was coming into view as Muhammad rode ahead on Qaswa, followed by a white ocean of pilgrims. They had spent three days in the valley of Muzdalifah, celebrating Eid-ul-Adha. The ceremonial camels had been sacrificed, the meat distributed amongst the poor and the pilgrims.

As Qaswa padded through the narrow, sand-swept valley, Muhammad's attention was shifting to Swadah beside him. Swadah had asked to be allowed to leave the valley of Muzdalifah a day early so that she would have ample time to perform the rites of stoning the Devil's Pillars. His thoughts returned to them in the valley of Mina, where they were half buried in mounds of pebbles.

'Could we skip the stoning, Prophet, on our next pilgrimage?' Abbas ibn Mirdas had protested, revolted by the phallus-like shape of the Pillar, called Jamrat-al-Ula.

'Then how will believers fight the temptation from Satan in their own lives?' Muhammad's thoughts were echoing his own comments. 'Stoning the Devil's Pillars is a yearly reminder to the pilgrims of how Ishmael spurned Satan three times when he urged him to disobey his father, Abraham. Satan told him that he should not be led as a sacrificial lamb to be killed at the command of God. But Ishmael had faith in his father and in God, and rose above his fear of death, and above temptation. He proved to the world that surrender is freedom from evil, and that evil can be conquered by faith alone.'

'It is all a part of piety, Prophet, as I understand it: even the sacrifice.' Muhammad was recalling the comments of Swadah.

'You are right, Swadah.' Muhammad had recited this revelation. *'It is not their meat, nor their blood that reaches God: but it is your piety that reaches Him! He has thus made them subject to you, that ye may glorify God for His guidance to you! And O Prophet, proclaim the Good News to all who do right'* (22:37).

Returning to the present, Muhammad broke into praise. 'I am here, O Lord! I am here! There is none other God but Thee! I am here! Praise, blessing, and dominion be to Thee! I am here! No one therein may share with Thee. I am here, O Lord! I am here!'

The white ocean of pilgrims was surging up the slope and gathering around the Prophet, the symphony of his praise dancing on the sunbeams.

'O God, to Thee I turn, praying to approach Thy bounteous countenance. Make my sins forgiven and my Hajj acceptable, and have mercy on me, for Thou hast power over all things. O

God forgive me and assist me in my repentance and grant me all that I beseech of Thee. And wherever I turn, let me meet goodness. God be praised! Praise unto God! There is no deity except God! And God is most great.'

Muhammad's voice was lulling everyone into blissful comfort. He had begun to speak as if moved by some divine will; his eyes reflected awe and light.

'My beloved friends, listen to my words, because I don't know if I will be with you here again. Listen to what I am saying carefully, and take these words to those who could not be here today. My friends and family: your lives, property and honour are sacred to you until you appear before your Lord, just as you consider this month, this day and this city sacred. Return the things that are entrusted to you to their rightful owners. You will meet your Lord, and He will hold you answerable for your actions.

'You have rights over your wives, and your wives have rights over you. Treat your wives with love and kindness. Verily, you have taken them on the security of God, and their persons are made lawful unto you by the words of God.

'Free your slaves, following my example, and tell others to do the same. But if they wish to stay with you, see that you feed them with such food as you eat yourselves, and clothe them with the stuff you wear. And if they commit a fault which you are not inclined to forgive, then part from them, for they are servants of God like you and me, and are not to be treated harshly.

'Know that we are all equal in the sight of Allah, and we journey together in this world as a family: a brotherhood and sisterhood. All of us descend from Adam, and Adam was created from dust. This is the gift of knowledge for all who cultivate wisdom and humility. An Arab is no better than a non-Arab, nor is a white better than a black, or a black better than a white, except in piety. Nothing is allowed to a Muslim if it belongs to another, unless it is given freely and willingly; so do not oppress each other.

'I am leaving behind me two things: the Book of God and my example. If you follow these two, you will never go astray. Spend freely of what is given to you, whether in prosperity or in adversity. Restrain your anger and pardon everyone, for Allah loves those who do good, as it has been revealed. This Hajj is only acceptable to Allah if we have love in our hearts for each and every one of God's creatures. *Kill not your children for fear of want. We shall provide sustenance for them, as well as for you. Verily, the killing of them is a great sin*' (17:31). He paused, his gaze enveloping everyone in an ocean of love.

'*Today I have perfected your religion for you and completed my favour unto you, and have chosen for you as religion Al-Islam. Whoso is forced by hunger, not by will, to sin; for him, lo! Allah is Forgiving, Merciful*' (5:3), he recited, his eyes shining with mirth. 'Do you know what month it is? What territory it is? What day?'

'The sacred month! The sacred territory! The great day of pilgrimage!' Several voices spluttered forth, filling the Mount of Mercy with the music of joy.

'Even thus sacred and inviolable God made His life and the property of each of you unto the other, until you meet your Lord.' Muhammad's voice rippled above all, his arms held out. 'O Lord! I have delivered my message and accomplished my work!'

'Yes, you have, Prophet. Yes, you have!' the pilgrims cheered.

'O God, I beseech Thee, bear Thou witness,' Muhammad prayed. 'This is the day of true brotherhood and sisterhood, of devotion and repentance. This is the day when Allah is revealed to His servants, extending His Hands with generosity and immense blessing! We are promised that during these hours near Arafat, Allah will send down His mercy and forgiveness to those who deserve it and they will feel His presence!' Qaswa was carrying him down the slope, straight for Mecca, as if led by some invisible power.

That same power transported Muhammad to the grave of his beloved. Khadija was with him; her eyes offered him a feast of love, virtue and truthfulness. She was welcoming him home.

O Mankind, be careful of your duty to your Lord who created you from a single soul, and from it created the spouse thereof, and from their twain hath spread abroad a multitude of men and women (4:1). Khadija was holding dear the symphony of praise.

Muhammad saw his beloved clothed in light. Worlds upon worlds were unrolled before Muhammad's sight, pure and changeless. Yet hatred and affliction struggled forth from profounder deeps in tides upon tides. A storm was brewing; the cries of the oppressed were loud and heart-rending.

Seek refuge from the curses of the oppressed, to whatever community they may belong, for the portals of God are always open for the oppressed.

Muhammad was thrown into Khadija's loving arms; they melted in a fire of bliss. A supreme presence was cradling him to sleep: the song of unity. His lullaby!

Say: He is Allah, the One! Allah, the eternally besought of all. He begetteth not, nor was begotten. And there is none comparable to Him (112:1–4).

The harp of time itself carried the pilgrims from Mecca to Medina, but within three short months of their homecoming, Muhammad had fallen ill. He had become a victim of violent headaches, so intense at times that he could barely walk.

Muhammad lay breathing peacefully. He was dreaming, beholding the new bride of Abu Bakr soon after his return to Medina: Habibah, Kharijah's daughter. Usama kept appearing in his dreams. He had recently been sent on a campaign against Syria, where large forces were gathering on the borders of Byzantium with the intention of attacking Medina.

Fatima had stopped mending Ali's robe. She was gazing at the light which hovered above the Prophet as he lay dreaming.

Fatima was a part of his dream, although she didn't know it. Gabriel was there too, offering Muhammad the choice between two worlds: eternal life on earth, or life everlasting in the hereafter. Muhammad chose the hereafter, his heart thundering with joy.

'*With the supreme communion in Paradise, with those upon whom God hath showered His favour, the saints and the prophets and the righteous, most excellent for communion are they. Such is the bounty of Allah, and Allah sufficeth as Knower*' (4:69–70), Muhammad recited. His eyes shot open.

'How are you feeling, Father?' Fatima leapt to her feet, awed and frightened.

'Full of joy and health, my love.' Muhammad's voice was a tender caress. 'Come close, Fatima. I want to share two secrets with you.'

'Are they secrets which I may share with Ali, Father?' Fatima was at his side in a flash, settling herself in a heap beside him.

'Certainly. I have been given a choice! To continue living longer now, with the promise of Paradise to come, or to meet my Lord at once. I have chosen to meet my Lord,' Muhammad murmured wistfully.

'You are leaving us here to suffer loss and intolerable grief, Father?' Fatima began to weep silently.

'Why weep, dear Fatima?' Muhammad sat up and dried her tears with the edge of his cloak. 'You will be the first to join me,' he whispered.

'Allah be praised!' Fatima laughed, her tear-filled eyes sparkling with joy.

'Why are you crying and laughing at the same time, Fatima?' Aisha drifted into the room.

'I was hoping you would ask about my health first, Aisha,' Muhammad teased.

'Oh, Prophet, I have been praying! My prayers are answered.' Aisha tossed her curly head. 'What were you saying to Fatima, which made her…' Her attention had turned to Fatima. 'What did the Prophet say, Fatima, which made you laugh and cry? The Prophet is not going to tell me, I can see that in his eyes, so will you?'

'He told me two secrets, Aisha, but I can only share the one with you which made me laugh.' Fatima's eyes were filling with more tears. 'He told me I would be the first to follow him to Paradise.' She smiled through the mist of tears in her eyes.

'And which of your wives will be the first to follow you, Prophet?' Aisha appealed, sadly.

'And you don't care, Aisha, if I die first?' Muhammad laughed, heaving himself up slowly. 'But to comfort your pretty little head, Aisha, I can tell you that she of the longest reach will be the soonest of all of you to join me.'

'You mean, Prophet, the one with the longest arms?' Aisha murmured thoughtfully. 'I love you, Prophet, and I care. You don't even know how humbly and profoundly I pray to Allah for your—' Her sad confessions were swallowed by a chorus of cheers, as the other wives surged into the room in a billowing tide.

'We heard your voice, Prophet! Allah has granted you health! You look so well. What would you like to eat?' A flurry of comments fluttered aloft.

'Now that my health is restored, I want to go to the mosque to see how my faithful pray.' Muhammad's features quivered with delight. 'I am not hungry – I must go.' He made no move to leave though. His pallor was polished by a beatific smile.

'Abu Bakr is happy to lead the faithful to prayer, Prophet; you need not worry,' Maymuna pleaded softly. 'You need to eat something to get your strength back. And get plenty of rest! You can go to the mosque in the evening.'

'My case is like that of a mounted wayfarer who pauses at noon under the shade of a tree, just to rest for a while, and then proceeds on his way,' Muhammad murmured, as he remembered the threats of war. 'Has Usama left for Syria?'

A curtain of silence as thick as ice drew over the wives, but Muhammad's eyes cut holes in it with a piercing intensity.

'He marched as far as Al Jurf, Prophet, but didn't go any further after you became ill.' Swadah gasped for breath.

'Your followers say, Prophet, that he is not fit for this campaign,' Hafsa murmured.

'Your choice is not favoured by your men,' Umm Salmah confessed.

'Many argue that he is too young to lead this campaign, Prophet,' Zainab murmured to herself.

'And quite a few of them protest, Prophet, that he is inexperienced in warfare.' Juwairya unleashed her own quiver of information.

'Khalid keeps stressing that the Romans are very powerful, and that he should have been the one leading this campaign,' Umm Habiba thought aloud.

'Half of your followers are saying, Prophet, that you didn't consult any of the generals before nominating Usama for this campaign,' Safiya intoned, quietly.

'You, my wives, are the mothers of the faithful. So you must advise them after I am gone.' Muhammad plodded out of the room, hugging his cloak to himself.

The mosque was hosting a large congregation as Muhammad stole in from behind, soundlessly. Abu Bakr was leading the prayers. Noticing ripples of restlessness, he spotted Muhammad at the back of the congregation and stepped aside so that the Prophet himself could lead the prayers. Muhammad indicated with a gesture of his arm that he should continue, and kneeled, touching his forehead to the ground. Abu Bakr, in return, happy and flustered, hurried through the ritual and invited the Prophet to the pulpit amidst cheers of welcome.

'He is not one of us who does not treat our young with compassion, or acknowledge the dignity of our elders,' Muhammad began. 'Whoever has no compassion for people, God has no compassion for him.' He took a deep breath. 'The fire is stoked, and temptation comes like the darkness of the night. I have not made anything permissible unless the Quran permitted it, and I have not made anything forbidden unless the Quran forbade it. After me there will be many differences. Anything that complies with the Quran is from me, and anything that differs from the Quran is not from me. It has not been long since we returned from Hajj, and remember, Hajj attains its final stature only when there is love, sympathy and compassion amongst you all.' He paused again, pain ripping through his head like fire. 'My friends, I have heard that some of you oppose my appointment of Usama to command the Syrian expedition? Now if you blame my appointment of Usama, you should have blamed my appointment of his late father, Zaid. And I swear by the Lord that Zaid was fitted to command, and his son now is well fitted for this campaign. Usama is a man most dearly loved by me, even as his father was. Treat him well, for he is one of the best amongst you.' He espied Bani Afrida plodding towards him.

'I have brought these dates to be distributed amongst the poor, Prophet.' Bani Afrida lowered the basket at the feet of the Prophet, sighing with relief.

'Thank you, my friend, you have earned the weight of gold in virtue and goodness.' Muhammad took a date out of the basket and chewed on it thoughtfully. 'No one is poorer than the Prophet.' He smiled, fighting the fresh assault of pain inside his head. 'Feed the hungry and visit the sick: Islam demands that of every Muslim. Bani Afrida has started a good custom of bringing a generous gift to the mosque to share with the poor. Whoever introduces a good custom in Islam will have their reward, as well as the reward of those who act on it after his example. And whoever introduces a bad custom in Islam is responsible for its burdens, as well as the burdens of those who act on it after him, without that reducing their burden of responsibility at all.' He closed his eyes. 'Whoever calls for guidance has a reward equal to the rewards of those who follow him, without diminishing their guilt in any way. Remember, religion is goodwill.'

'Towards whom should our goodwill be directed, Prophet?' Ali asked abruptly.

'Towards God and His creation, and towards the Book of God.' Muhammad opened his eyes. 'In fact, the Lord has offered one of His servants a choice between this life and one which is nearer to Him, and the servant has chosen the one which is near to the Lord.'

'So you will be leaving us soon, Prophet?' Abu Bakr began to weep.

'Why weep for the Prophet, Abu Bakr, when he is going to meet his Divine Beloved? Don't we all yearn for such a meeting as this? Our souls are lost and restless in this world, remembering the agony of separation.' Muhammad laid his hands upon his friend's shoulders. 'Death is a bridge that unites friend with friend. Those who have a true, pure, merciful heart will enter the garden of bliss.'

'And yet my heart is saying, Prophet, that you should have chosen this world.' Abu Bakr wiped his tears on the back of his sleeve.

'The chiefest amongst you all, for love and devotion, is Abu Bakr,' Muhammad intoned. 'What have I to do with the world? I am like a rider and this world is like the tree beneath which he takes shelter. The next day, he goes on his way and leaves it behind him.'

'Please don't leave us yet, Prophet!' Anas cried suddenly. 'Tell us how to become perfect Muslims, and to understand our duties towards God and His creation.'

'He is the most perfect of Muslims, whose disposition is most liked by his own family.' Muhammad's face was pallid. 'He is not the perfect performer of relationship duties who only does good to his relatives when they do good to him. He is perfect who does good to his relatives even when they do not do good to him. God has not created anything better than reason or anything more perfect or more beautiful than reason; the benefits which God gives are on its account. And understanding comes with reason.' He closed his eyes. 'Now, anyone, who will assist me home? I am feeling weak.'

Bilal was the first to leap to the Prophet's side, before Abu Bakr stirred himself to action. Ali was next. All three men assisted the Prophet towards his quarters, though his gait was steady. The congregation was left behind, silent and mournful.

'My headache is gone.' Muhammad squeezed Bilal's hand with great affection. 'Now that I am feeling better, Abu Bakr, you must visit your wife Habibah, who is staying with her parents.'

'Yes, Prophet,' Abu Bakr murmured in response, his heart thundering.

'And Ali, tell Fatima, before I forget, that she is the highest of the women of the people of Paradise. Paradise longs for you and awaits you, Ali. Now, leave me here; I am feeling much better.' Muhammad stopped in the middle of the courtyard. 'But remember to tell the others this: I am the city of knowledge, and you, Ali, are its gate. And all my companions are like the stars; whichever of them you follow, you will be rightly guided.' He left the courtyard swiftly and thoughtfully.

Muhammad drifted towards Hafsa's room. His feet came to an abrupt halt at the door, a strange scene like he had never beheld before confronting his eyes. Divided into pairs, his wives were comparing their arms, talking and laughing.

'What novel game have you contrived in the absence of the Prophet?' Muhammad's note of astonishment enveloped them all in a mist of shame.

'We are comparing the lengths of our arms, Prophet, since you told Aisha that the one with the longest reach would join you first,' Mary offered in explanation.

'The one with the longest reach!' Pain flared in Muhammad's head. 'How dull-witted you have all become! I meant the one who is most generous!'

'Oh, my head,' Aisha moaned, afflicted by a sudden assault of headache.

'Nay, Aisha: oh *my* head.' Muhammad pressed his temples.

'Won't you pray for me, Prophet?' Aisha cried.

'O Lord of the people!' Muhammad drifted towards Aisha, blinded by his own pain, his right hand resting on her head. '*O Lord of the people, remove the difficulty and bring about healing as You are the Healer. There is no healing but Your Healing, a healing that will leave no ailment. We send down in the Quran that which is a healing and a mercy*' (17:82). A convulsion of pain ripped through his head. 'Pour water over my head, dear wives. A fire is raging in there. Water, seven skins of water—'

All the wives had been caught in such shock that they couldn't speak, but in a flash they were jolted out of it, and assisted the Prophet into the tub, since Hafsa's room was equipped with this luxury. Muhammad closed his eyes, shivering, while they doused his head with cold water. He could feel the fever coursing through his veins, his senses reeling against the assault of delirium.

'Oh Lord, assist me in my hard condition,' Muhammad murmured, gasping for breath. 'There are seven coins under my mat, Aisha. Give them to the poor. I can't meet my Lord until I am stripped bare of all my earthly possessions.'

'Yes, Prophet,' Aisha murmured back, her gaze pleading with the others for help.

'Let it be known that if I owe anything to anybody, it may be claimed. If I have offended anybody, he may have his revenge.' Muhammad's voice was hoarse and distant. 'Whose turn is it to be with me tonight?'

'Hafsa's, Prophet,' Maymuna murmured in response.

'And the day after?' Urgency choked Muhammad's thoughts.

'Umm Salmah's, Prophet,' Umm Habiba was quick to inform him.

A great sigh escaped Muhammad's lips, followed by a great shudder, his eyes still closed. All eyes had turned to Aisha, pledging mutely to her that they would forgo their turns so that she could be with the Prophet, though none dared speak.

Mary returned to this pool of silence, followed by Fatima, who was holding a jar of honey. The familiar fragrance from the Prophet's body was holding them all in thrall. Ali entered the hushed scene to apply some unguent to the Prophet's brow, which he had brought with him in an earthenware saucer. Suddenly Muhammad groaned.

'Prophet!' Ali cried, kissing his brow fervently and sorrowfully.

'Grieve not, Ali; I go but to meet my Lord,' Muhammad appealed. 'Has any prophet before me lived forever? Everything happens according to the will of Allah, and has its appointed time, which is not to be hastened or avoided. I return to Him Who sent me, and my last command to you is that you remain united: that you love, honour and uphold one another.'

'Father … Prophet! You are suffering!' Fatima stood sobbing and weeping.

'Do not weep, my daughter,' Muhammad tenderly appealed through his pain. 'Your father will not suffer the limitations of life on this earth any more.' His eyes were closing. A question escaped his delirium. 'Whose turn is it to be with me tonight?'

'All of us have decided to forgo our turns in favour of Aisha, Prophet, till your health is restored,' Safiya could barely murmur. 'I wish your suffering could be given to me, Prophet.'

'You are blessed, Safiya; most blessed.' Muhammad's features attained the glow of joy and peace. 'Blessed be this day, and blessed be this night.' He opened his eyes, slowly and painfully. 'Assist me, Ali, to Aisha's room. I will rest there.'

'Yes, Prophet.' Ali snatched the Prophet's hands into his own trembling ones.

'Tell my followers, Ali, their tryst with me is at the pool.' Muhammad's voice was clear as he was assisted out of the tub. 'The pool fed by Kawthaur, the celestial river given to the Prophet. This pool is a lake where believers quench their thirst on their entry into Paradise. And yet I fear for them, lest they rival one another in worldly gains.' He sighed in relief as Ali assisted him into Aisha's room.

The news of the Prophet's illness had spread like bolts of lightning. Another dawn in Medina, unlike any other, was yawning awake. While Bilal stood alone in the mosque, the Prophet slept, cradled by the white clouds of his own dreams, Aisha beside him lulled to sleep by the sheer weight of her grief and exhaustion. She had rubbed oil and vinegar on the Prophet's brow for half the night, splashing water over his face whenever he requested between long hours of wakefulness and slumbering.

'O Lord, I beseech Thee, assist me in the agonies of death,' Muhammad murmured in sleep. 'O Lord, grant me pardon and bring me into your companionship on high. O Allah, be it so among all the glorious associates in Paradise.' His eyes opened, holding Aisha captive in their sights. She jolted awake.

'Is your head still hurting, Prophet?' Aisha's eyes glinted with fear and sadness.

'No, Aisha, no. The pain is gone.' Muhammad closed his eyes. 'Fetch me my miswak, Aisha; I want to brush my teeth.'

Aisha rose to her feet, hurrying out of the room to fetch the miswak. Muhammad sat still, holding his breath, fearing lest the pain return. She returned with the miswak and was relieved to find him still sitting, his features glowing healthily. Muhammad claimed the miswak from her, and commenced the process of softening it with his teeth.

'Oh, Aisha, I can't do it, my mouth is too dry.' Muhammad held out the stick of miswak to her. 'Could you make it soft and sweet with your own teeth?'

'It will turn sour, Prophet, if you don't stop frightening us with your headaches,' Aisha laughed, before crushing it between her teeth furiously.

'And fetch me some water, while you are killing my miswak, rather than making it pliant. I'll have to revive it.' Muhammad's eyes were wrinkled with mirth. 'Do you know, my Aisha, that sleep is the brother of death, and the grave is the first stage of the journey into eternity?' he added profoundly.

'Why talk of death, Prophet, when the water of life is bubbling fresh in your eyes and upon your lips?' Aisha continued chewing on the miswak.

'Have I ever told you the story, Aisha, of the woman who went to the well to quench her dog's thirst, and earned Paradise?' Muhammad drank thirstily from the tumbler beside his mat, feeling a familiar stab of pain.

'No, Prophet, but I would love to hear it,' Aisha prompted eagerly.

'My miswak, Aisha?' A feeble smile curled around Muhammad's lips.

'Here, Prophet.' Aisha balanced it between his lips till his own hands held it firmly.

Muhammad chewed on it briefly and then laid it aside, his pallor returning.

'I'm just feeling weak, Aisha.' Muhammad's look was glazed, his voice strange and distant. 'Let me lay my head in your lap for a while. I want to rest.'

Aisha sat stunned, cradling the Prophet's head in her lap, unable to move or speak. Her heart was heavy, yet the Prophet's head was getting heavier in her lap, as her fingers brushed his hair absently. Something inside her was torn and bleeding. She could feel spasms of grief and despair, as if the whole world had grown dark and desolate, but then the Prophet's voice was wrenching her out of her ocean of grief and darkness.

'O thou soul which art at peace, return unto thy Lord with gladness that is thine in Him, and His in thine. Enter thou amongst my slaves. Enter thou my Paradise' (89:27–30).

Muhammad's soul had taken flight.

Aisha became aware of the stillness of the Prophet's body, his head cold in her lap. Trance-like, in a bewildered moment of disbelief, she laid the Prophet's head on the pillow. And then, suddenly, the reality of his death began to carve deep wounds into her shock. An agonised wail ripped from her soul as her body slumped beside the Prophet's in a shuddering heap.

Great sorrow and hopelessness had descended upon the house of the Prophet. Ali stood holding Fatima close to his heart, rivers of tears flooding down her cheeks. The Prophet's wives were huddled together in a woeful cluster, weeping tears of grief. Ali's were spluttering forth afresh, and he was drifting towards the Prophet.

'You were dearer to me than my father and mother, O Prophet…' Ali's voice choked as he kneeled beside him, kissing his brow feverishly.

The chamber of death was filled with an ocean of that subtle fragrance which was a part of the Prophet's being while he lived and loved. Abu Bakr waded through it, his eyes moist with tears and glistening. He was almost staggering towards his friend and prophet, dazed and bewildered.

'You were sweet in life, and you are sweet in death.' Abu Bakr knelt opposite Ali, combing the Prophet's hair with his fingers. 'Your life was blessed, Prophet, and you will be blessed in Paradise. May God's peace and blessings remain with us, though you cannot.' He kissed his brow gently.

A crescendo of laments from the heart of the mosque was filtering into the peaceful chamber, followed by angry voices.

Abu Bakr heaved himself up slowly, his eyes glittering with the pain of loss and grief. He stood gazing, his eyes offering the libations of prayer, but more voices, louder than before, were disrupting his peace and concentration. In a flash he was gone, as if commanded by a silent voice from the very soul of the Prophet. Ali followed at his heels, forlorn and stricken.

The scene which confronted them at the mosque was of utter confusion. Umar ibn Khattab was at the pulpit, towering tall and imperious over an ocean of mourners. His sword was poised before him, his features convulsed with anger.

'I don't believe that the Prophet is dead! And anyone who says he is will taste the violence of this naked blade, which already thirsts for the blood of liars and blasphemers!' Umar ibn Khattab brandished his sword, blinded by zeal and grief.

'Put that sword down, Umar!' Abu Bakr thundered. 'Has it not been revealed to the beloved Messenger of Allah? Verily, thou shalt die, and they shall die.' He gasped for breath. '*For that cause We decreed for the children of Israel, that whosoever killeth a human being for other than manslaughter or corruption on earth, it shall be as if he had killed all mankind, and whoso saveth the life of one, it shall be as if he had saved the life of all mankind. Our messengers came unto them of old with clear proofs of Allah's sovereignty, but afterwards, lo! many of them became prodigals in the earth!*' (5:32). He sailed closer to the pulpit where Umar stood shamefaced, his sword slung at his waist.

'My friends, and friends of the Prophet!' Abu Bakr stood by Umar. 'If anyone worships Muhammad, know that Muhammad has died. But if anyone worships God, then know that He is alive and cannot die.' He paused, blinking back his tears. '*Muhammad is no more than a Messenger. There were many messengers who passed away before him. If he dies, or is killed, would you then turn around and run? If anyone ran away, it wouldn't do any harm to God. But God would reward quickly those who serve Him thankfully*' (3:144). Abu Bakr stood, listening to Bilal's call to prayer.

'God is most great, God is most great. I witness that there is no God but God. I witness that Muhammad…' Bilal could not finish, his voice choked by grief.

An ocean of tears broke loose, it seemed; the entire congregation of men, women and children was weeping and their lips were humming prayers. Medina in its entirety appeared to be mourning. Even the palm fronds were waving a sad farewell. Their friend the noble prophet was gone, but his spirit was hovering above in the whispering wind, dancing the dance of love and peace on the golden strings of the sunlight.

Bibliography

Adil, Dr. Hafiz M. *Introduction to Qur'an*. Adam Publishers, 1987.

Al Hariri-Wendel, Tanja *Symbols of Islam*. Sterling Publishing Co., 2002.

Ali, Maulana Muhammad *Muhammad The Prophet*. Ahmadiyya Anjuman Isha'at Islam, 1993.

Ali, Maulana Muhammad *Muhammad The Prophet*. Moaref Press, Lahore, 1972.

Ali, Maulana Muhammad (trans.) *Teachings of Islam*. Ahmadiyya Anjuman Isha'at Islam, 1983.

Ali, Maulvi Sher (trans.) *The Holy Quran*. The Nusrat Jehan Project, 1971.

Ibn Arabi *Journey to the Lord of Power*. Inner Traditions International, 1981.

Armstrong, Karen *A History of God*. Ballantine Books, 1993.

Armstrong, Karen *Muhammad: A Biography of the Prophet*. HarperSanFrancisco, 1992.

Arnold, Sir Thomas W. and Guillaume, Alfred (eds.) *The Legacy of Islam*. Kitab Bhavan, 1997.

Azimabadi, Badr *Authenticated Miracles of Muhammad*. Adam Publishers, 1993.

Bakhtiar, Laleh *Sufi: Expressions of the Mystic Quest*. Thames and Hudson, 1976.

Bakr, Abu *The Book of Certainty*. The Islamic Texts Society, 1992.

Bashumail, Mohammad Ahmed *The Great battle of Badr*. Islamic Book Service, 1992.

Bayat, Mojdeh & Jamnia, Mohammad Ali *Tales from the Lands of the Sufis*. Shambhala, 1994.

Bodley, R.V.C. *The Messenger*. Doubleday & Company, 1946.

Burrell, David B. and Daher, Nazih (trans.) *Al-Ghazali on the Ninety-Nine Beautiful Names of God*. The Islamic Text Society, Cambridge, 1992.

Chebel, Malek *Symbols of Islam*. Assouline Publishing, 2000.

Chittick, William C. *Sufism*. Oneworld, 2000.

Cleary, Thomas *The Wisdom of the Prophet: The Sayings of Muhammad*. Shambhala Publications, 2001.

Craig, H.A.L. *Bilal*. Anchor Press Limited, 1977.

Dawood, N.J. (trans.) *The Koran*. Penguin Books, 1984.

Doi, Abdur Rahman I. *Woman in Shariah*. Islamic Book Center, 1996.

Edersheim, Alfred *The Temple*. Fleming H. Revell Company, 1950.

Emerick, Yahiya *Muhammad*. Alpha, 2002.

Ernst, Carl W. *The Shambhala Guide to Sufism*. Shambhala, 1997.

Ernst, Carl W. *Teachings of Sufism*. Shambhala, 1999.

Fadiman, James & Frager, Robert *Essential Sufism*. Castle Books, 1997.

Faruqui, N.A. *Ahmadiyyat in the Service of Islam*. Ahmadiyya Anjuman Isha'at Islam, 1983.

Frager, Robert *Heart, Self & Soul: The Sufi Psychology of Growth, Balance and Harmony*. Quest Books, 1999.

Friedlander, Shems *When You Hear Hoofbeats Think of a Zebra*. Perennial Library, 1987.

Ghazi, Abid'ullah & Ghazi, Tasneema K. *Stories of the Sirah Part VII*. Da'wah Academy, 1989.

Glubb, Sir John *Life and Times of Muhammad*. Cooper Square Press, 2001.

Green, Joey (ed.) *Jesus and Muhammad*. Seastone Press, 2003.

Harvey, Andrew *Teachings of Rumi*. Shambhala, 1999.

Helminski, Camille Adams *The Light of Dawn*. Threshold Books, 1998.

Helminski, Kabir *The Knowing Heart: A Sufi Path of Transformation*. Shambhala, 1999.

Hixon, Lex *Heart of the Koran*. Goodword Books, 1998.

Hussain, Riaz *Abdullah: The Father of the Holy Prophet*. International Islamic Publishers, 1988.

Hussain, S.A. *A Guide to Hajj*. Kitab Bhavan, 1992.

Ibrahim, Ezzeddin & Johnson-Davies, Denys *Forty Hadith Qudsi*. Islamic Book Service, 1980.

ibn Ismail, Muhammad & Khan, Muhammad Mushin *Sahih Al Bukhari*. Al-Saadawi Publications, 1996.

Khan, Hazrat Inayat *The Art of Being and Becoming*. Omega Publication Inc., 1989.

Khan, Maulana Wahiduddin *Muhammad: A Prophet for all Humanity*. Goodword Books, 1998.

Khan, Maulana Wahiduddin *Women between Islam and Western Society*. Al-Risala Books, 1997.

Khan, Pir Vilayat Inayat *Awakening*. Penguin Putnam Inc., 2000.

Khan, Pir Vilayat Inayat *In Search of the Hidden Treasure*. Penguin Putnam Inc., 2003.

Khan, Saniyasnain *Muhammad*. Goodword Books, 2002.

Khawaja, Ahmad Ali *Maulana Ashraf Ali Thanvi*. Kitab Bahavan, 1999.

Kritzeck, James *Anthology of Islamic Literature*. New American Library, 1964.

Kritzeck, James *Modern Islamic Literature*. New American Library, 1970.

Lewis, Bernard (ed.) *The World of Islam: Faith, People, Culture.* Thames and Hudson, 1997.

Lings, Martin *Muhammad.* Inner Traditions International, 1983.

Lings, Martin, *What is Sufism?* University of California Press, 1977.

Lunde, Paul *Islam*. DK Publishing Inc., 2002.

Markham, Ian S. (ed.) *A World of Religions*. Blackwell Publishers, 1996.

Miftahi, Mufti Zafeer Uddin *Mosque in Islam*. Qazi Publishers, 1996.

Nadvi, Shah Moinuddin *Hazrat Abu Bakr Siddique*. Bilal Books, 2000.

Nasir, Khalil Ahmad *Biblical Background of Islam*. Northwestern University, 1973.

Natiq, Abdul Qayyum *Sirat-E- Mustaqeem*. Al-Amin Publications, 1992.

Novak, Philip *The World's Wisdom*. HarperSanFrancisco, 1995.

Nurbakhsh, Dr. Javad *In the Tavern of Ruin*. Khaniqahi-Nimatullahi Publications, 1963.

Nurbakhsh, Dr. Javad *Traditions of the Prophet Vol. 2*. Khaniqahi-Nimatullahi Publications, 1982.

Payne, Robert *The History of Islam*. Dorset Press, 1990.

Picktall, Marmaduke (trans.) *The Koran*. Alfred A. Knopf, 1992.

Schwartz, Stephen *The Two Faces of Islam*. Doubleday, 2002.

Shah, Idries *Caravan of Dreams*. The Octagon Press, 1968.

Shah, Idries *The Sufis*. Anchor Books Doubleday, 1964.

Shah, Idries *The Way of the Sufi*. Penguin Books, 1968.

Shaikh, Fazlur Rehman *Footprints of Muhammad*. Adam Publishers, 1996.

Suhrawardi, Sir Abdullah *Sayings of Muhammad*. Goodword Books, 1997.

Tobias, Michael, Morrison, Jane and Gray, Bettina (eds.) *A Parliament of Souls*. KQED Books, 1995.

Vaughan-Lee, Llewellyn *The Circle of Love*. The Golden Sufi Center, 1999.

Vidyarthi, A.H. and Ali, U. *Muhammad in Parsi, Hindoo and Buddhist Scriptures*. Arora Offset Press, 1993.

Wadud, Amina *Quran and Woman*. Oxford University Press, 1999.

Wallace, Lew *The Prince of India*. Harper and Brothers Publishers, 1893.

Watt, W. Montgomery (trans.) *The Faith and Practice of Al Ghazali*. Oneworld, 1994.

Williams, John A. (ed.) *Islam*. George Braziller, 1962.